# National Lampoon
# Tenth Anniversary Anthology

# 1970-1980

**Distributed by Simon & Schuster**

Edited and designed by the staff of *National Lampoon.*
Production directed by Alison Antonoff.
Copy edited by Sheila Feldman.
Cover art by Mara McAfee.
Dustcover designed by M & Co.

Library of Congress Cataloging in Publication Data
Main entry under title:

National lampoon tenth anniversary anthology,
    1970-1980.

    Bibliography:  p.
    1.  American wit and humor.    I.  National
lampoon.
PN6162.N37            817'.5'408            79-20171
ISBN 0-930-36849-5

# Contents

**Cartoons by**
C. Barsotti, M.K. Brown, Chris Browne, John Caldwell,
Bruce Cochran, Shary Flenniken, Sam Gross, Sid Harris,
B. Kliban, Ed Koren, Brian McConnachie,
Dick Oldden, Brian Savage, Bill Tidy, and Bill Woodman.

# Introduction

The *National Lampoon* was founded by Henry Beard, Doug Kenney, and Rob Hoffman—three former members of the *Harvard Lampoon*, and by Matty Simmons and Len Mogel, owners of Twenty First Century Communications, a magazine publishing firm in New York. The *Harvard Lampoon* had, during the sixties, published a number of successful book and magazine parodies, and Beard, Kenney, and Hoffman became convinced that there was a market for a national version of that magazine. Twenty First Century had arranged the printing, distribution, and advertising sales for several of the *Harvard Lampoon* parodies, and Simmons and Mogel also believed that a "national" *Lampoon* could achieve commercial success. Simmons and Mogel entered into an agreement to provide Beard, Kenney, and Hoffman with capital and publishing expertise. The five men worked together for almost a year, creating a suitable design and format; and the first issue of *National Lampoon* was published in April, 1970.

The magazine was originally coedited by Doug Kenney and Henry Beard. Rob Hoffman, the first managing editor, left in 1971 to return to graduate school. A year later Kenney took a leave of absence to write a novel, and, although he returned to the magazine in 1973, Beard remained editor-in-chief from 1972 until 1975.

In 1975, Twenty First Century Communications (now National Lampoon, Inc.) bought Beard, Kenney, and Hoffman's interest in the publication. Beard retired, and from 1975 until 1978, *National Lampoon* was run by an editorial committee, the most prominent members of which were Tony Hendra, Sean Kelly, and Brian McConnachie. In 1978, Managing Editor P.J. O'Rourke was appointed editor in chief, and remains so to the present.

That, in the briefest possible terms, is a history of the first ten years of *National Lampoon*—leaving out, perforce, the snits, grudges, month-long arguments, and threats to tear out people's intestines and wrap them around telephone booths that inevitably attend any creative enterprise of the collective type. And this is an anthology of the work produced during those years. Of course, there are certain omissions due to copyright conflicts, legal entanglements, and simple considerations of space. Particularly regretted is the absence of any material by George W.S. Trow, Anne Beatts, and Ed Bluestone, three important and influential *National Lampoon* writers. But what is here is, we believe, a more than fair sampling of an entire decade of the magazine. Except that, since our first issue was April, 1970, it's really only 97.5 percent of a decade. And this book went to press in June, 1979, so actually it's nine years and about two months, which is nowhere near a decade. But you know what we mean.

Anyway, *National Lampoon* has been a uniquely seventies voice. The sixties was a decade defined by racial and generational tension, by radical changes in social and sexual mores, by a total reassessment of America's role in the global community, and by fundamental rethinking of our nation's domestic goals and priorities. The seventies was a decade defined by giving up cigarettes. Into this troubled, or, at any rate, annoyed, period of history, *National Lampoon* injected some more annoyance. We have been accused of elitism, racism, anti-Catholicism, anti-Semitism, communism, fascism, anti-intellectualism, sadism, and a hatred of dogs and women. Fair accusations, every one. And yet, in our thoroughgoing dislike of every living thing on earth, we like to feel that there is a certain perverse evenhandedness. All types and kinds of everything are greeted with equal odium. We spend our venom democratically on all comers. There are no special targets, no particular effigies or scapegoats or whipping boys that we attack to the exclusion of all others. And we never take sides. No, we give it to the unions with our left hand, to the textile mills with our right, a kick to the Atomic Energy Commission, a slap to the environmentalists, here a brickbat tossed at General Motors, and there a cuff on the head for Ralph Nader. We play no favorites. Not even when presented with enormous temptations to do so such as when our country's lifeblood, in the form of imported crude oil, is being choked off with a gangrenous tourniquet held by a pack of dromedary-consorted falafel jockeys. These thieving date-gobblers had better brush the dish towel out of their eyes for a minute and take a gander at whether the most powerful nation in the world is going to let a couple of hundred thousand bathrobe-clad scarf-skulls play monkey-in-the-middle with the fate of western man. Why, these sand slime have no more idea of what's right and proper than carp in a ditch. They eat the insides of goats, they wipe their behinds with their hand, they do their writing in the same language that worms use under rocks, and their religion is no more than taking orders about when to pray from some dirty loudmouth on top of a brick phone pole. Plus, they invented algebra, which, personally, some of us flunked. So it's a good thing for them that we don't take sides. Because we never do. It just wouldn't be us. We're tough, but we're fair.

**P.J. O'Rourke**
**New York City, 1979**

# Roster

## National Lampoon Staff Members and Principal Contributors 1970–1980

SENIOR STAFF

**Danny Abelson**, Contributing Editor (1976, 1979-), Associate Editor (1977), Editor (1978)

**George Agoglia, Sr.**, Vice-President, National Lampoon, Inc. (1970-74), Senior Vice-President (1974-)

**Richard B. Barthelmes**, Publisher (1978-)

**Henry N. Beard**, Executive Editor (1970-72), Editor-in-Chief (1973-75)

**Anne Beatts**, Contributing Editor (1971), Associate Editor (1972-74)

**Peter Bramley**, Art Director (1970), Contributing Artist (1971-73)

**Tod Carroll**, Associate Editor (1978), Editor (1979-)

**Michel Choquette**, Contributing Editor (1970-71, 1973-74), Associate Editor (1972)

**Susan Devins**, Associate Copy Editor (1976-77), Copy Editor (1978), Managing Editor (1979-)

**Sonja Douglas**, Associate Art Director (1973), Art Director (1974)

**Ide Meg Emery**, Copy Editor (1971-72)

**J. Dudley Fishburn**, Associate Editor (Great Britain) (1970-74)

**Shary Flenniken**, Contributing Artist (1975-78), Editor (1979-)

**Louise Gikow**, Editorial Assistant (1972-73), Copy Editor (1974-78)

**Judy Gould**, Copy Editor (1972-73)

**Michael Gross**, Art Director (1971-72), Design Director (1973-74)

**Tony Hendra**, Contributing Editor (1970-71), Managing Editor (1972), Editor (1973-76), Senior Editor (1977)

**Robert K. Hoffman**, Managing Editor (1970)

**John Hughes**, Contributing Editor (1977), Associate Editor (1978), Editor (1979-)

**Skip Johnston**, Art Associate (1976), Associate Art Director (1977), Art Director (1978-)

**Susan Jones**, Copy Editor (1973)

**David Kaestle**, Art Director, Special Projects (1972-73), Art Director (1974)

**Peter Kaminsky**, Staff Writer (1975), Associate Editor (1976), Managing Editor (1977)

**Sean Kelly**, Contributing Editor (1971), Associate Editor (1972), Editor (1973-76), Senior Editor (1977)

**Douglas C. Kenney**, Editor-in-Chief (1970-72), Senior Editor (1973-74), Editor (1975-76)

**Peter Kleinman**, Art Director (1974-76), Design Director (1977-79)

**Edythe Kopman**, Copy Editor (1970)

**Lisa Lenovitz**, Art Associate (1976), Associate Art Director (1977-)

**William T. Lippe**, Associate Publisher (1976), Publisher (1977)

**Brian McConnachie**, Editor (1972-76)

**Ted Mann**, Contributing Editor (1975, 1978), Associate Editor (1976-77), Editor (1979-)

**Mary Martello**, Associate Editor (1970), Managing Editor (1971)

**Leonard Mogel**, President, National Lampoon, Inc. (1970-78), Chairman of the Executive Committee (1979-), Publisher (1970-72, 1976-77), Publishing Director (1978-)

**Michael O'Donoghue**, Contributing Editor (1970-71), Senior Editor (1972), Editor (1973-74)

**P. J. O'Rourke**, Contributing Editor (1972), Executive Editor (1973-75), Managing Editor (1976-77), Editor-in-Chief (1978-)

**Matty Simmons**, Chairman of the Board, National Lampoon, Inc. (1970-), Publisher (1976-77), Publishing Director (1978-)

**Bill Skurski**, Art Director (1970)

**Gerald Sussman**, Contributing Editor (1973-75), Associate Editor (1976), Executive Editor (1977), Senior Editor (1978-)

**Ellen S. Taurins**, Assistant Art Director (1971-72), Art Director (1973)

**Gerald L. Taylor**, Associate Publisher (1971-72), Publisher (1973-75)

**George W. S. Trow**, Contributing Editor (1970-71), Senior Editor (1972), Executive Editor (1973-74)

**Julian Weber**, President, National Lampoon, Inc. (1979-)

**John Weidman**, Contributing Editor (1971-74, 1977), Associate Editor (1975-76), Editor (1978)

**Greg Wustefeld**, Senior Copy Editor (1979-)

## ASSOCIATE STAFF

**Betsy Aaron**, Editorial Assistant (1977), Editorial Associate (1978-79)
**George Agoglia, Jr.**, Production Manager (1975-)
**Alison Antonoff**, Art Assistant (1977-78)
**Chuck Bartelt**, Editorial Assistant (1977-78)
**Celia Bau**, Art Assistant (1972), Assistant Art Director (1973-75)
**June Bennett**, Art Assistant (1975-76)
**Elliot Bergman**, Art Apprentice (1975), Art Assistant (1976-77)
**Maira Berman**, Art Associate (1979-)
**Wendy Burden**, Art Assistant (1978-79)
**Elise Cagan**, Editorial Associate (1978), Special Projects Copy Editor (1979)
**Rosi Cassano**, Art Assistant (1974)
**Christine Chestis-Montanez**, Production Manager (1974)
**Blair Davis**, Promotional Art Associate (1979)
**Phyllis Epstein**, Assistant to the Art Director (1976-77)
**Diana Feldman**, Designer (1975), Associate Art Director (1976-78)
**Sheila Feldman**, Special Projects Copy Editor (1979-)
**Sheila Goldfarb**, Editorial Assistant (1970-72)
**Sylvia Grant**, Research Editor (1976), Assistant to the Art Director (1977), Design Coordinator (1978-79)
**Eric Greenberg**, Public Relations and Promotion (1979)
**Marc E. Greene**, Art Associate (1976-77)
**Ruthanne Hamill**, Art Associate (1978-79)
**Woody Harding**, Designer (1978-79)
**Mark Hecker**, Assistant Art Director (1974), Associate Art Director (1975-76)
**Phyllis Hochberg**, Art Assistant (1977-78)
**Judy Jacklin**, Art Assistant (1973-74)
**Roberta Kaman**, Production Manager (1971-72)
**Jane Kronick**, Production Manager (1973-74)
**Liza Lerner**, Art Assistant (1974), Assistant to the Art Director (1975)
**Scott MacNeill**, Art Associate (1975)
**Laurel McAfee**, Art Assistant (1979-)
**Wendy Mogel**, Staff Assistant (1975-77)
**Pedar Ness**, Photo Editor (1977)
**Katherine Palladini**, Assistant Art Director (1970-71)
**Stephanie Phelan**, Assistant Art Director (1970)
**Susan Rosenthal**, Editorial Associate (1979-)
**John Schnakenberg**, Art Associate (1979)
**Gail Silverman**, Art Associate (1979-)
**Julie Simmons**, Staff Assistant (1975-77)
**Michael Simmons**, Staff Assistant (1972-74)
**Barry Simon**, Art Associate (1979-)
**Laura Singer**, Art Assistant (1974)
**Karen Wegner**, Editorial Assistant (1974), Research Editor (1975), Special Projects Copy Editor (1976)
**Mark Wright**, Staff Photographer (1979)

## CONTRIBUTING EDITORS

**Ed Bluestone** (1972-74)
**John Boni** (1971-75)
**Terry Catchpole** (1971-74)
**Christopher Cerf** (1970-77)
**Michael Civitello** (1979-)
**Chris Cluess** (1977-79)
**Tim Crouse** (1977)
**Michael Frith** (1970-72)
**Jeff Greenfield** (1976)
**Stu Kreisman** (1977-79)
**Dean Latimer** (1972-75)
**Bruce McCall** (1973-77, 1979-)
**Mitch Markowitz** (1977-78)
**Rex May** (1977-78)
**Chris Miller** (1972-76, 1978-)
**R. Bruce Moody** (1976-78)
**Bill Moseley** (1978-)
**Emily Prager** (1976-78)
**Delfina Rattazzi** (1978-79)
**Marc Rubin** (1975-78)
**Brian Shein** (1979-)
**Ed Subitzky** (1973-)

## CONTRIBUTING ARTISTS

**Neal Adams** (1976-)
**R. O. Blechman** (1972-73)
**M. K. Brown** (1973-)
**Chris Browne** (1977-)
**Dennis Chalkin** (1977-78)
**Gil Eisner** (1976-78)
**Ted Enik** (1978)
**Randall Enos** (1972-)
**John Glashan** (1972-74)
**Matthew Goldman** (1976-)
**Edward Gorey** (1972-76)
**Sam Gross** (1977-)
**Gary Hallgren** (1977-78)
**Dick Hess** (1972-76)
**Alan Kupperberg** (1977-78)
**Bob Larkin** (1978)
**Bobby London** (1975-)
**Mara McAfee** (1974-)
**Wayne McLoughlin** (1974-)
**Malcolm McNeill** (1978-)
**Stan Mack** (1972-)
**Rick Meyerowitz** (1972-)
**Joe Orlando** (1972-73, 1978-)
**Don Punchatz** (1976-)
**Ralph Reese** (1976-)
**Charles Rodrigues** (1973-)
**Alan Rose** (1973-)
**Arnold Roth** (1972-74)
**Norman Rubington** (1975-78)
**Warren Sattler** (1973-)
**Joe Schenkman** (1979-)
**Neil Selkirk** (1975-78)
**Frank Springer** (1972-73, 1978-)
**B. K. Taylor** (1978-)
**John Walker** (1977-78)
**Gahan Wilson** (1972-)

## CONTRIBUTING PHOTOGRAPHERS

**John Barrett** (1978-)
**Chris Callis** (1976-)
**Tom Corcoran** (1979-)
**Dick Frank** (1973-)
**Ronald G. Harris** (1973-)
**Matthew Klein** (1976-)
**Phil Koenig** (1977-)
**Pedar Ness** (1978-)
**Bob Rakita** (1978-)

# NATIONAL LAMPOON

# 1970-1980

# EDITORIAL

*Issues of the* National Lampoon *have traditionally been introduced by brief editorials. Most editorials discuss the theme of the issue. Some editorials, however, have nothing to do with the theme of the issue, or with anything else, for that matter. An excellent example of this is Henry Beard's "Canasta Dancing," the introduction to* The Best of National Lampoon #3, *an anthology published in 1972.*

Many people ask me: "Señor Zavada, how is it that you have become the greatest living canasta dancer in the world? Is it by *magico* (magic) or some such thing? Surely you have sold your soul to *el diablo* (the devil) to be able to move so lightly and gracefully among the cards! There can be no other explanation for your ability to pick up the *tres rojos* (red threes) with your pinky fingers in the midst of the mad, fiery *meldaflamenca* (dance of the meld)."

To them and to you, dear reader, I flick my thumbnail on my front teeth and say, *"somistella!"* ("fiddlesticks!"). There is no easy way to master the canasta dance, no matter what sharp persons and *noctavoles* (fly-by-nighters) may say. Do not pay heed to their sweet words, as sweet as the *sucrapanos* (a kind of Castilian sugar cake), when they offer you their cut-rate courses. It is better that you should take your *pesos* ($US = .041) and put them in the *merdato* (nightsoil receptacle) than waste them in such *putragato* (foolishness).

But in buying this little book of mine you have already proved that you know this; so, enough. First I must say to you: Do not become discouraged. Some of the movements are not easy. For example, the *manaquela* (dance with a natural canasta held in a fan shape before the downcast eyes) is very demanding and takes much practice. Likewise, the *sortillada* (leap across the discard pile) is no matter for laughing. Practice, and more practice, and then more practice. This is what is required.

Now I will say to you another important thing: Do not go ahead to another movement until you have mastered the one which is before it. Do not, let us say, be tempted to show off to your friends your ability to do the *tacavida* (shuffle of two hands while making moaning noises) and thus rush on quickly, without properly learning the *vincenza* (arrangement of the hand into potential canastas using the mouth to move the cards), which is perhaps less spectacular but very, very necessary to the dance.

I have made this book as easy as it can be done, and there is everything in here that you need, except for two decks of *cartellas tinembras* (playing cards made from a lamb's bladder), a *cellomano* (hand cello), a *bañobuco* (mouth banjo), a *grizella* (thumb bassoon), and a *rosino* (rosin bag). These may be obtained for a small price at any well-stocked music store. I recommend the Canasta Grande di Rota brand.

As you progress through the lessons, you will soon gain confidence and pride in what you do. I do not tell you: "Practice one hour a day, two hours a day." This is *mala luna* (bad craziness). How fast you will go depends on how much you wish to be a *canastatera*. Only you know this, for it is in here—here I strike my heart with my hand—that the desire to excel has its *hacienda* (residence).

One thing more I will say and then I will let you get to your *yglenzas* (warming-up exercises of throwing the decks in the air and then bending down and picking up the cards). Sometimes a foolish person will interrupt your practice and make the big fun of what you are doing. Ignore this ignoramus. What does he know of art or of the dance? He is a *tostada* (toasted noodle). He has no appreciation of the things that separate us from the sheep. He probably lies with sheep, the dog. I am sorry. That was a dirty thing to say. I have been carried away. These people make my blood boil as surely as if it were in a *cornero* (iron cooking pot).

Here I will stop. I will say only this more: You have chosen a great and noble hobby. The canasta dance is as old as canasta itself. Who can say where it began? In the hills of Avalon? In the mountain villages of Castile? No matter. Enough that it exists. Enough to hear the low whine of the hand cello, the plaintive cry of the thumb bassoon; to see the red threes flashing; to watch as the completed natural canastas hit the dance floor like *pantellas* (small wheat-pancakes)!

*Bueno gizerias* (Good dancing)!

MAY, 1972

*"It's a fried telephone book! We gave it a fancy French name and you ordered it!"*

# HOT FLASHES

*"Hot Flashes" and "Photorama Picture Parade" are examples of totally fraudulent, irreverent photojournalism at its best. "Hot Flashes" started in July, 1971, and ran until October, 1972. The two examples shown here are from January, 1972, and were written by Doug Kenney. "Photorama Picture Parade" started in July, 1978, as "Photorama Picture News." It was changed to "Photorama Picture Parade" in February, 1979. The excerpts shown here are from February and May, 1979, and were written by Gerald Sussman.*

**San Diego, California** It's out of the closets and into the chapel for actresses Joan Crawford and Miss Helen Hayes. "We've been mad about each other for years," explained the grand old lady of the American stage, "and when Joan popped the question last week, I said to myself, 'Fuck it! Why not?'" The two hope to be wed this November in a simple ceremony performed by the Reverend Troy Perry.

**Berkeley, California** Bruce McFarlane and Cindy Rhumquist, two members of a religious group called the Gullivers, wait for their god to arrive. They are named after their god, Gulliver, a twenty-five-foot giant they claim to have seen in the Rocky Mountains. Bruce and Cindy built Gulliver's throne and have set up a vigil until He arrives. So far, they've been waiting for 250 days.

**Coral Gables, Florida** Suppressed for years, this photograph, smuggled by secret sources out of a restricted testing area where Naval scientists are studying marine-life speech, reveals that dolphins are, as often rumored, carnivorous. Shown here, an aging aquamaid is being thrown to the flesh-eating denizens of the deep, who stand on their tails shouting, "More food! More food!"

**Riyadh, Saudi Arabia** Two members of the notorious Fawzi Golf Mugger Gang give up to the police after an attempted robbery during a sandstorm at the Riyadh Country Club. The muggers have wreaked havoc on the wealthy Saudi Arabian golfers by hiding behind sand traps, pouncing on their victims, and speeding off in dune buggies.

# Letters

*The Letters section has run continuously since the first issue of* National Lampoon *in April, 1970. It has always been one of the magazine's most popular features, no doubt because* anything *can be published as a letter, as long as it exhibits sufficient lack of taste.*

Sirs:

Listen, I know you guys are always on the lookout for really way-out stuff, so I thought you'd be interested to know that I accidentally played my 45 of *Louie, Louie* by the Kingsmen at 33 rpm and found out that the lyrics are really dirty! I mean like "f--k" and everything! Listen, if you don't believe me, go and try it yourself!

> J. Edgar Hoover
> APRIL, 1971　Washington, D.C.

Sirs:

My name is Timothy Leary.

> Timothy Leary
> Zurich, Switzerland

Sirs:

*My* name is Timothy Leary.

> Timothy Leary
> Zurich, Switzerland

sRRis#
　myi　Nmmea　stxa　timitthhe
　　　　　　　　　　lllreeryy
　　　　　　　tmitthhe llreeryy
APRIL, 1972　　　zoork, zwiszszirlnd

Sirs:

Hey, you forgot the letter you usually run calling me an asshole.

> David Frost
> APRIL, 1972　London, England

Sirs:

For every day the French government fails to stop the heroin traffic into this country, I'm walking out into the street and kicking somebody's poodle in the stomach. Maybe if enough people did this, the French would see we mean business.

> Charles Reich
> MAY, 1972　New Haven, Conn.

Sirs:

In reply to your request for the president's movements this week:
　Mon.: Nothing
　Tues.: Nothing
　Wed.: Good one. Some blood.

> Ron Ziegler
> MAY, 1972　Washington, D.C.

Sirs:

Listen, I'm a groovy sixteen-year-old two-fisted piece of ass who really gets off on the *National Lampoon* and I could really get into balling your entire staff someday after school, including the chicks if they're into it. I guess I should tell you that I'm blind, but that didn't stop Hendrix from telling me I gave the best Betty Crocker stereophonic transparent three-dimensional mixing bowl job he'd ever had!

So, if you want to lube your tube, give me a ring and I'll take the bus right over. I can't read the numerals on my Touchtone phone, but the number is boop beep meep-meep boop neep boop, Area Code meep boop beep.

I'll be waiting, pant pant.

> Terrie Scooterpie
> JUNE, 1972　S. Orange, N.J.

Sirs:

Hi. My name is Rod Serling and tonight I'd like to take you on a journey—a journey that you may find disturbing, even terrifying—but one you are not likely to forget. Tonight, we are going to travel, on all fours, up David Frost's asshole.

Underneath your seat you will find giant pinky-cheaters, flashlights, and galoshes—the ladies in the audience are requested to remove their heels. Please slip on the giant pinky-cheaters and wait for the ushers to daub you with Vaseline.

There, are we all ready? Anyone without a flashlight or a gas mask? (Remember, it may get pretty close in there.) All right, I'll go first—okay, David, say "Ah…"

> Rod Serling
> David Frost's Asshole
> JULY, 1973　Los Angeles, Calif.

Sirs:

Drink Coke in cans. It's the undildo.

> F. Arbuckle
> MAY, 1974　Hobe Sound, Fla.

Sirs:



> Marcel Marceau
> JULY, 1974　Paris, France

Sirs:

In the little terrarium in Marcus Welby's study. In Gerald Ford's beefsteak tomato plants. About fifty miles into Nebraska on Route 80 just before

the Dairy Queen along the left side of the road for about two miles (had a leak in my bag, as it turned out). Among Pat Nixon's zinnia patch (yuk) in the rose garden, catty-corner from the stone toad. On Dean Corll's lawn. In the fake banana trees around Hef's indoor pool.

Last time I threw you a curve though. The wacky along the fifty-yard line in the Astrodome never came up.

Keep 'em rolling.

> Johnny Reeferseed
> NOVEMBER, 1974　Bogota, Colombia

Sirs:

I'm getting martyred in the morning.
Ding-dong the bells are gonna
　chime.
Please let me wake up, confess and
　make up,
But get me to the Church on
　time….

> Thomas a Becket
> OCTOBER, 1975　Canterbury, England

Sirs:

He clasps the crag with crooked
　hands;
Close to the earth in lonely lands,
Ringed with the azure world, he
　stands.

The wrinkled sea beneath him
　crawls;
He watches from the mountain
　walls,
And like a thunderbolt, he farts.

> Al Tennyson
> Westminster Abbey
> London, England

Sirs:

Anyone for Tennyson?

As you can see, I am no stranger to an occasional jape myself, but I am puzzled by the preceding letter. Has a slip of the pen found its way into your generally fine transcription of "The Eagle" printed above?

As a critic lauded for my encyclopedic scam on all the big-name rhymsters from Keats to Yeats and—if I may be allowed to briefly plunk my own academic twanger—perhaps *the* seminal influence on the young T.S. Eliot? (You may remember him—the skinny kid with the sharp clothes who'd say "*ek*tually" for "actually" and stirred his tea with his tool when no one was looking.) Anyhow, I have a literary bone to pick with you fellows.

I will admit that there have been some divergent readings of "The Eagle"; Abrams and Wolfe favor "crooked hands" while earlier anthologists prefer "hornèd hands," for example. Me personally, I have always harbored a clandestine fondness for "come-covered," a popular variation I came across (no pun intended) on a men's room wall at Jack's—a favorite literary hangout of mine on Mass. Ave.

But, unless I am very much mistaken, I am unfamiliar with any authoritative text reading "and like a thunderbolt he farts (*sic*)"! I believe the correct reading is "he *falls*" (italics my own). I mean, have I blown my valves or what?

I. A. Richards
Cambridge, Mass.

Sirs:

As public relations director for the American Audubon Society, I was disturbed to note in your fine publication a blatant ornithological fiction— namely an *Aquila heliaca* gifted with audible flatulence. Also, there is no species of eagle, at least to the Society's knowledge, that comes (no pun intended) equipped with "hands." Most species have claws or, more properly, talons.

Could Mr. Tennyson possibly be confusing his remarkable eagle with the common ground-roasted twit? This cuddly little scavenger is also found in rocky, sea-bordered biomes such as Tennyson describes, is fond of power dives, and, it has been reported, farts like a Gatling gun.

Could this be the bird of your fancy?

T. R. Ralston
American Audubon Society
Washington, D.C.

Sirs:

Scree greech scrawk. Twee grackle toweech grackle krawk "and like a thunderbolt he farts?!" Cree gawrk foowee!

Don Eagle
JANUARY, 1974          Hayfork, Calif.

Sirs:

This dance called the Latin Hustle is nothing more than a crude and suggestive parody of the Central European mazurka. There is nothing dirty about the mazurka, even though it derives from a bestial hoedown practiced in the court of Olaf the Hemophiliac. The cleaned-up version is based on the Greek legend of Mocus and Hysterektome, star-crossed lovers. Mocus (the male dancer) wears a toga made of seasoned hominy husks. Hysterektome wears less than a jaybird as she capriciously toots on a medieval woodwind called the *dildino*. Meanwhile, the drummer beats a mournful knell on bongos, cowbell, and bullclap. Only a dolt would lump this time-honored dance with the silly twists, prods, and thrusts of contemporary pop hoofing.

Caressa di Royalballs
MARCH, 1976          Bunnihaupt, Hungary

Sirs:

So you want to know why I don't like eggs? I'll tell you why I don't like eggs. Because...because a bloody ...because a goddamn *chicken*, a stinking *chicken*, killed my dad.

Pete Meyers
FEBRUARY, 1977          Bells of Hell, N.Y.

Sirs:

Have I ever fooled around with Barbara Walters? Hey, fellas, I *eat* with these hands!

Harry Reasoner
ABC Television
MAY, 1977          New York, N.Y.

Sirs:

Bella Abzug has Liberian registry. Pass it on.

Pat M.
APRIL, 1977          Senate, U.S.A.

Memo: To All Staff
Re: Endangered Humor Species

The last Robert Hall has died in captivity. Let's do everything we can to see that this sort of thing doesn't happen again in the future. Meanwhile, have Ralph Nader, et al, buy their clothes at K-Mart.

SEPTEMBER, 1977          The Editors

Sirs:

I am fully aware that in the vernacular of the common people, the word *throne* means "toilet." Consequently, when the newspapers featured headlines that read, "Queen Celebrates Twenty-five Years on the Throne," we all had a good chuckle. Mum is a bit of a potty hog, so we found this doubly humorous!

Charles
P. of Wales
OCTOBER, 1977          B. Empire

Sirs:

Where do I come from? I don't know—I never looked.

Bianca Jagger
FEBRUARY, 1978          The Continent

Sirs:

You're right, they make a lot of noise when they eat.

Anwar el-Sadat
FEBRUARY, 1978          Cairo, Egypt

Sirs:

Having a wonderful time, wish you were dead.

Hubert Humphrey
JUNE, 1978          Congressional Heaven

Sirs:

Ha! Ha! We've got it!! *We've got it!!! We got the fuckin' canal!!!! Suckers!!!* You suckers!! Ha! Ha! Ha! We're gonna dump on it and piss in it and fill it up with shit and blow up the locks and sink all the ships and rape every Navy wife we can find! You stupid ass-

holes! Ha! Ha! Ha! Ha! Ha! Ha! *We got it now!!!!*

The Panamanians
JULY, 1978          Panama

Sirs:

Your advice about using condiments at the dinner table proved very useful for the most part, but David doesn't really like the way prelubricated ones taste.

Julie Eisenhower
JUNE, 1978          New York, N.Y.

Sirs:

Much of what we formerly believed to be true about the Russians is extraordinarily difficult to spell. I tell all in my forthcoming book.

Henry Kissinger
Studios 54—59
JANUARY, 1979          New York, N.Y.

Sirs:

We think your dollar is greatly undervalued by currency traders. We like the dollar very much. As a matter of fact, our women have found that twenty-five to thirty of them rolled up make a very good and inexpensive tampon.

Yoshoyu Takmuda
Tokyo International Exchange
FEBRUARY, 1979          Tokyo, Japan

Sirs:

I just love them premixed cocktails in the bottle. Now if only they could fit a dinner and a fuck in there we'd be all set, wouldn't we?

Fred W. Troy
FEBRUARY, 1979          Winter Park, Colo.

Sirs:

A while back, one of you fellas left a sperm in me, and I'm writing to tell you that it's ready and it needs a check for Montessori school and a bike.

Donna
P.O. BOX 333320
MARCH, 1979          New York, N.Y.

Sirs:

I'd like a subscription to your magazine, but I'm a pig. I used to root around in the garbage and dig out an old copy one of the kids would throw away, but now they're away at college. Could you possibly send a subscription to the farm? It'll get thrown away immediately and I'll get to enjoy all that great stuff you guys do. I can't pay you though because swine don't have their own currency—not yet anyway. It's a big favor but who knows— someday you may sit down to Easter dinner with my ass.

Earl the Pig
Pen #778
Hollyridge Farms
MARCH, 1979          Hollyridge, Penn.

*"News on the March" is a regularly featured section of the* National Lampoon, *devoted to politics and current events. It was created by Henry Beard in December, 1970, and largely written by him until October, 1975, when it was taken over by Sean Kelly and Tony Hendra. Kelly and Hendra converted "News on the March" into a parody tabloid,* The National. *In May, 1978, the section returned to its original format, and is now edited by Ellis Weiner and John Weidman.*

# McGOVERN WINS NOMINATION!

SEPTEMBER, 1972

**It has been** learned that in addition to the notorious "enemies list," the White House also maintained a complete and exhaustive list of all of its supporters. The entire so-called "friends list" was recently destroyed to

SEPTEMBER, 1973

protect the individuals included in it, according to a White House insider who was actually present when the single 3 x 5 card containing the politically sensitive names was placed in the paper shredder.

**In an unusual gesture** of cooperation growing out of the successful Moscow summit, U.S. nuclear warheads will be placed on ten Soviet ICBMs, which in the event of nuclear war involving the superpowers will be jointly launched by Russian and American missile crews at targets in France. "We felt we should exploit areas of agreement between our two countries wherever they appear," explained a State Department official commenting on the plan, "and, frankly, neither of us likes the French."

SEPTEMBER, 1972

**It has been learned** from reliable sources that several Arab governments have joined in urging the United States to deliver as many F-111 fighter-bombers as possible to Israel.

DECEMBER, 1972

# A Nation Doesn't Mourn

AUGUST, 1972

# TEDDY BACKS NADER ON AUTO RECALL

...AND THEN, THE EVENING AFTER THE GUARANTEE EXPIRED, I FOUND OUT THE BRAKES WERE COMPLETELY SHOT.

MARCH, 1972

# MISSION: Impeachable

GOOD MORNING, MR. HUNT. SEVERAL HIGH-RANKING MEMBERS OF THE DEMOCRATIC PARTY ARE ATTEMPTING TO SEIZE CONTROL OF THE GOVERNMENT OF THE UNITED STATES BY LEGITIMATE MEANS. THEY PLAN TO USE A FREE PRESS, OPEN DISCUSSION OF THE ISSUES, AND THE UNIVERSAL FRANCHISE IN AN ALL-OUT EFFORT TO WIN THE PRESIDENCY. THEY ARE: SENATOR HUBERT HUMPHREY, THE FORMER VICE-PRESIDENT; SENATOR EDMUND MUSKIE; SENATOR HENRY JACKSON; AND SENATOR GEORGE MCGOVERN. SHOULD ANY ONE OF THEM SUCCEED, ALL OF OUR EFFORTS TO REPEAL THE BILL OF RIGHTS, PACK THE SUPREME COURT WITH RIGHT-WING MORONS, INTIMIDATE THE MEDIA, SUPPRESS DISSENT, HALT SOCIAL PROGRESS, PROMOTE BIG BUSINESS, AND CRUSH THE CONGRESS WILL BE DESTROYED. YOUR MISSION, SHOULD YOU CHOOSE TO ACCEPT IT, IS TO STOP THESE MEN ONCE AND FOR ALL BY INSURING THAT THE WEAKEST OF THEM, SENATOR GEORGE MCGOVERN, WINS THE NOMINATION AND THEN SABOTAGING HIS CAMPAIGN BY ANY POSSIBLE MEANS. YOU WILL HAVE AT YOUR DISPOSAL ELECTRONIC BUGGING EQUIPMENT, BURGLARY TOOLS, WIGS, VOICE ALTERATION DEVICES, A CAMERA DISGUISED AS A TOBACCO POUCH, FORGED DOCUMENTS, A SAFE HOUSE, 500 LOYAL BUT CLUMSY CUBANS, AND $2,000,000 IN $100 BILLS. AS ALWAYS, IF ANY MEMBER OF YOUR C.I.A. FORCE IS CAUGHT OR KILLED, THE PRESS SECRETARY, THE ATTORNEY GENERAL, THE DIRECTOR OF THE F.B.I., THE ENTIRE WHITE HOUSE STAFF, AND THE PRESIDENT WILL ALL DISAVOW ANY KNOWLEDGE OF YOUR ACTIVITIES. THIS ADMINISTRATION WILL SELF-DESTRUCT IN 16 MONTHS. GOOD LUCK, HOWIE.

JULY, 1973

# POWs COME HOME

WILL THE LAST PERSON OUT OF THE TUNNEL PLEASE TURN OFF THE LIGHT.

MAY, 1973

**Almost totally ignored** in the hulla-baloo surrounding his successful set-tlement of the war in Vietnam was President Nixon's equally successful conclusion of Johnson's other war, the War on Poverty. After nearly seven years of often bitter in-fighting marked by massive funding, which re-duced vast areas of American cities to rubble-strewn vacant lots, and huge search-and-squander operations, which involved hundreds of thousands of chair-borne bureaucrats, the war was quietly ended when a nationwide federally-supervised spending cut-off went into effect February 4, 1973.

Although some sporadic spending was reported to be continuing in a few isolated Model Cities areas, the with-drawal within sixty days of all federal money is proceeding without incident, and the Nixon Administration is said to be already making plans to spend the many billions of dollars the end of the poverty war will make available for badly needed military-modernization programs and other long-postponed defense priorities.

MAY, 1973

# It's Time to Play "Let's Pass the Buck"!
# MORNING TV GETS SMASH NEW GAME SHOW!

AUGUST, 1973

# Yes, we have no bombing raids today

OCTOBER, 1973

**Following the announcement** in Judge Sirica's court of the discovery by a panel of tape experts of anywhere from five to nine deliberate erasures in the eighteen-and-a-half minute "buzzing" segment on the June 20, 1973, White House tape, key Administration advisers are said to be deeply concerned that there may, as a result, be a large gap in President Nixon's second four year term of office. "We haven't really looked into this thing," said one aide, "but offhand, I'd say something on the order of two years are going to turn up missing."

APRIL, 1974

# L. Patrick Gray to G-Men:
# "CHEESE IT, IT'S US!"

JULY, 1973

**One is tempted** to dismiss out of hand the grotesque Republican public relations campaign that suggests a parallel between Vice President Gerald Ford and former President Truman, who, as the patently fallacious reasoning goes, was also dismissed as a minor political hack but became a strong and effective president. Still, to be fair, the comparison has some slight validity. Ford has the same lack of initiative, total absence of any intellectual activity, personality void, and wooden appearance as Truman, . . . but in Truman's case those qualities are attributable to his having been dead for several years.

APRIL, 1974

**A Massachusetts congressman** revealed recently that the CIA had played a major role in the process that led to the overthrow of the socialist government of President Salvador Allende of Chile.

*continued*

In the same category of startling revelations are the fascinating discovery that the Pope lists his religious preference as "Catholic," the surprising fact that large furry mammals of the family *Ursus* commonly head for wooded areas when answering calls of nature, and the truly momentous disclosure that porcupines, those spiny little oddities, find flat rocks tailor-made for doing Number One on.

NOVEMBER, 1974

**President Ford** is reportedly considering the appointment of several more blue-ribbon commissions similar to the CIA domestic surveillance investigative panel headed by Vice-President Rockefeller. According to White House sources, Ford is so pleased by the effectiveness of his first blue-ribbon committee (whose members include Ronald Reagan, C. Douglas Dillon, and former Army Chief of Staff General Lemnitzer) that he plans to name Carmine DeSapio, Albert Gallo, Mickey Cohen, and Meyer Lansky to a second panel for the investigation of organized crime. Glenn W. Turner, Robert Vesco, and Bernard Cornfeld are also thought to be under consideration for appointment to a third panel which will look into fraudulent franchising pyramids, while William Shockley, Louise Day Hicks, and Philadelphia Mayor Frank Rizzo may lead a probe of racism in the U.S. public school system.

MARCH, 1975

**At the same time** that an increasing number of demands for a new investigation into who killed President Kennedy are being made, pressure has been growing for an inquiry into why no one killed President Nixon. As long-time Nixon nonassassination buff Rod Toms put it, "There were any number of chances for a single, deranged killer or a determined group of assassins to kill Nixon, and plenty of possible motivations. We want to know why it didn't happen." The most popular theories to date hold that the CIA frustrated an attempt by Arthur Bremer in Canada because of Nixon's strong support of their clandestine operations, that a group of wealthy Texas oilmen underwrote a group of secret bodyguards who shadowed the former president wherever he went, and that President Thieu had a potential assassin killed in gratitude for President Nixon's *not* having him assassinated. "Any way you look at it," said Mr. Toms, who is the author of *Who Didn't Kill Nixon?*, "there's something fishy: There's no trace of an assassin, a gun, no signs of a conspiracy whatsoever. It just doesn't add up."

JULY, 1975

# Chile is back on the menu!
# I TT'S ALL OVER FOR ALLENDE

NOVEMBER, 1973

# CONG KING!
## City of Saigon Gripped by Panic as Thousands Flee from Small Guerrillas

JULY, 1975

# Vaginitis Halts Manilow Tour

APRIL, 1978

**Details Inside**

# The National

IND
34490

★ ★ ★

*SERVING THE NATIONAL LAMPOON SINCE 1975*

---

## Tests, Dirt, Photos of L.A. Prove:

# Atmosphere Could Not Support Intelligent Life

The latest in a series of remarkably clear photos received this morning from our satellite conclusively establish that "there is no possibility of the existence there of life as we know it," according to the experts.

"We are not ruling out the possibility that some form of subvegetative life exists," said a press release from the board of biologists, humanists, and physicists. "But it is clear from all the data we have received that a life form capable of thought, movement, or logical perception could not survive in such an environment."

Criticism of the project continues to grow, however, with disaffected scientists insistin that the data is not conclusive. "For all we know, the other side of the planet might well possess an ecology *(Continued on page 609, col. 1)*

OCTOBER, 1976

## Organized Government Suspected in $90 Billion-a-Year Protection Racket

WASHINGTON, D. C. — Investigations of organized government here have turned up evidence that as many as 210 million Americans have been victimized by an elaborate "protection racket" that may have netted more than $2 trillion over the past three years.

Victims were threatened with nuclear holocaust, the loss of Western Europe, and Communist enslavement if they failed to cough up.

Prime suspects in the protection shakedown include Donald "The Secretary of Defense" Rumsfeld, Thomas "Chairman of the Joint Chiefs of Staff" Moorer, and Robert "Commandant of the Marine Corps" Cushman. No indictments have been handed down so far, however.

FEBRUARY, 1976

## IRA Sets New Mark in Guinness Book of World Records

LONDON—The Irish Republican Army set a new world's record for killing editors of the *Guinness Book of World Records* by killing an editor of the *Guinness Book of World Records* last November 27, the *Guinness Book of World Records* reported today. The previous world's record for killing editors of the *Guinness Book of World Records* was none.

FEBRUARY, 1976

# Jewish Terrorists in 9,861st Day of Siege

Two million Jewish terrorists continue, today, to occupy the small country on the Mediterranean Sea, which they seized last May 4, 1948. Negotiations seem to be stalemated.

More than two million Moslem hostages continue to be held inside the country, two million others having been let go. The terrorists threaten to release the remaining hostages into Lebanon, Syria, Jordan, and Egypt if their demands aren't met.

FEBRUARY, 1976

# Comic Mugs Head, Slays Brain, Self

Freddie Prinze, the comedian who rose from the mean streets of New York's *barrio* to become a Hollywood star with his own series and a beach house and a big car he'd let you drive down to the pharmacy and everything, did not commit suicide, as was reported in the press.

Sources close to the truth revealed to *The National* recently that Prinze died while holding himself up for enough "bread" to "score" the pills his multi-dollar-a-day habit craved. Freddie apparently refused to play along with the mugging, there was a struggle, and the gun fired into his right temple. The bullet passed clear through Prinze's head, and by a million-to-one fluke of bad luck, struck the young jester's brain.

APRIL, 1977

# We Do It All in You

OAKBROOK, ILL. —The McDonald's hamburger chain has announced that it will begin test marketing cut-rate, rapid service medical care in seven of its Phoenix, Arizona, outlets later this month. The "medical menu" will consist of a regular checkup, double checkup, Big Tonsillectomy, Big Appendectomy, McHernia, McHysterectomy, and McExploratory Surgery.

The chain promises all treatment in ten minutes or less. "A family of four can visit McDonald's and receive examinations, surgery, postoperative care, and prescriptions and still get change back from a hundred," a McDonald's press release said.

Initial advertising for the services features Ronald McDonald, M.D., and Nurseperson, a new McDonald's character. The emphasis of the advertising is McDonald's low cost, quick service, and clean surroundings. If the test is successful, the service will be offered at all McDonald's sitdown restaurants. The concept is being called *McClinic*.

FEBRUARY, 1978

## Anita Bryant:

# "My Family Will Get Down on Their Knees If You'll Get Down on Your Elbows."

AUGUST, 1977

# New Sam Letter to Breslin

DEAR JIMMY,
LIKE A GIANT VAMPIRE FANG WITH A STRAW IN IT FOR SUCKING YOUNG GIRLS' BLOOD, I HAVE READ YOUR LETTER TO ME. SAM IS A THIRSTY LAD, JIMMY: HE NEEDS MORE MONEY. SPECIFICALLY, I REFER TO PARAGRAPH 11, SECTION A, WHEREIN YOU STATE: "BRESLIN (HERE-AFTER REFERRED TO AS 'THE AGENT') IS TO RECEIVE NINETY PERCENT OF ANY AND ALL PRINT AND BROADCAST ARTICLES, NOVELLAS, PLAYS, MOVIES, ETC." WHAT KIND OF BULLSHIT IS THAT, JIMMY? I BUST MY ASS, AND YOU GET ALL THE DOUGH. UH-UH, NO GOOD, JAMES. SHAPE UP OR I TAKE MY BUSINESS TO EVANS AND NOVACK. WHY DON'T WE GET TOGETHER OVER DRINKS NEXT WEEK TO DISCUSS SPIN-OFF PRODUCTS AND ENDORSEMENTS? HOW ABOUT WEDNESDAY, TWOISH?

ALL THE BEST
"SON OF SAM"
"MARSHAL OF MAYHEM"
"THE .44 CALIBER BOTHERER
OF GIRLS IN PARKED CARS"

**The above letter was mailed by Son of Sam to our ace reporter Jimmy Breslin, whose comment was: "Son of Sam is obviously a deranged maniac. If I give him any more of the gross, I lose money."**

OCTOBER, 1977

## U.S. Warns Soviet Union

# "We're sending our Cubans to Africa"

FIRST WE SECRETLY BREAK INTO ZAIRE. THEN WE BUG THE ENTIRE TELEPHONE SYSTEM—

—AND THEN WE BANG ON A CONGA DRUM AND SCREAM, "LOO-SEE, LOO-SEE," AND SING "BABALU" AND RUN AROUND LIKE CRAZY.

In response to reports of widespread Cuban intervention and provocation in several politically unstable African countries, the U.S. State Department has announced plans for sending "American Cubans, or Cuban-Americans, or whatever they're called—anyway, the real crazy kind" into Africa to promote "free-world values." Pictured are the two most accomplished assault teams: Desi Ricardo (*above*) is an expert in quelling domestic unrest and containing bizarre situations. Other agents, code name "Plumbers," specialize in cover surveillance, intelligence gathering, and embarrassment of high government officials.

AUGUST, 1978

## Campaign '80 Heating Up

# Carter, Kennedy Engage in Debate

BANG!... JUST KIDDING, TED!...

HOW'S THAT JEW-BAITING BROTHER OF YOURS? AND WHAT DO YOU HEAR FROM THAT SCUMBAG BERT LANCE THESE DAYS, JIM?

ABOUT AS MUCH AS YOU HEAR FROM YOUR STERNO-GUZZLING WIFE. BY THE WAY, DID YOU SEND A CHRISTMAS CARD TO THE KOPECHNES' LAST YEAR?

MAY, 1979

---

## Extra...

# John Paul Elected Pope, George Ringo Miffed

I WANTED TO WEAR THE SHOES OF THE FISHERMAN.

ME, TOO. I BOUGHT THE CLOTHES AND EVERYTHING.

*Ringo in Pope clothes.*

NOVEMBER, 1978

## "Seems Like I Fucked Myself"

# Spinks regrets training program

TAKE IT FROM ME, KIDS: DON'T BE A FOOL, STAY IN SCHOOL!

Leon Spinks told reporters that he "really fucked up" with the training program that he followed prior to his recent bout with Muhammad Ali in New Orleans.

"Looks like I got myself some bad advice," was all Spinks could say when asked about the training regimen. The daily routine called for Spinks to sleep till "really late," drink beer and watch TV till dinner, then eat "like a fucking pig" for several hours. Afterwards, the champ was encouraged to drink whiskey and take drugs, then go to "jive-ass clubs and discos" where he was advised to continue drinking and to "boogie" until dawn. On weekends, he was urged to drive erratically without a license in large, fast cars until apprehended by the police.

DECEMBER, 1978

## Recurring Carter Health Problem

# President Suffers New Hemorrhoid Attack

BOY, THEY REALLY HURT! ESPECIALLY RIGHT HERE BETWEEN THE EARS.

MARCH, 1979

---

## Ex-Coach Attacks Himself

# Woody Hayes Runs Amok

Former Ohio State University football coach Woody Hayes recently attacked and beat himself about the face and head upon learning that he had been fired by university officials.

Hayes, who had a rabid penchant for winning, was said to have been unable to tolerate any degree of human failure, even in himself. "He just went crazy," said a player who witnessed the incident. "He grabbed himself by the neck and threw himself against an oxygen tank, then punched and slapped his face while kicking and screaming obscenities."

"You fucking candy-ass, you lost your fucking job, you asshole! You're not fit to be in the same room with brave men who have jobs," Hayes reportedly shouted at himself. Later at a press conference, the badly bruised coach claimed that General George S. Patton was his model.

"He killed himself in a car crash after he lost his job," Hayes declared. "Shit, I let myself off easy."

I'LL WRING MY FUCKING NECK!

APRIL, 1979

---

# •NEWS BRIEFS•

## New Official State Color

California Governor Jerry Brown has announced that "avocado" will become the state's official refrigerator color.

MARCH, 1979

•

## OPEC Price Rise

The Organization of Petroleum Exporting Countries, which raised the price of crude oil by 14.5 percent last December, will now raise the prices of sugar, pork, and men's clothing. None of the OPEC nations produce sugar, pork, or men's clothing, but, "What the hey," says Saudi Arabian Oil Minister Mohammed Waffle Assfat.

MARCH, 1979

•

## Flammability Standards to be Tested

The Children's Sleepwear Manufacturers Association claims that many government regulatory agency employees do not meet current flammability standards. The association is calling for an extensive testing program wherein randomly selected federal agency staff members would be submitted to independent laboratory tests to determine their rate of burning and whether toxic fumes are produced by their combustion.

MARCH, 1979

•

## National Endowment for the Arts Ruling

The National Endowment for the Arts has announced that poetry will be abolished as an art form. A spokesperson for the Endowment, which is the federal agency in charge of interstate creative self-expression, stated that the ruling will take effect sometime in early 1980.

MARCH, 1979

•

## Carter Regains Consciousness

Doctors say that President Carter temporarily regained consciousness in late January. Although he has since relapsed, White House physicians claim that they were able to conclude that Carter had full awareness of his surroundings for at least a brief period because he fired Bella Abzug. This medical news raises hopes that Carter has not suffered complete "brain death," as was previously feared. The president has been in a coma for fifty-five years.

APRIL, 1979

---

## Further Nationalization of Industry in Britain

In an effort to cut crime, Britain will nationalize criminal activity. There was an early indication that the government's plan may be succeeding, as London pickpockets reacted to the news by saying that they will strike unless they are given weekly salary and vacation privileges.

MARCH, 1979

•

## NOW Lobbies for Job Preference

The National Organization of Women is urging Congress to pass legislation giving civil service job preference to fat women with crabby personalities and bad legs. "This is a group that has been repeatedly and systematically discriminated against over the years," says NOW spokeswoman Eleanor Smeal.

APRIL, 1979

•

## New Italian Government

In the wake of its most recent governmental crisis, Italy has announced that it will abandon its thirty-four-year attempt to become a communist country and return to its previous twenty-three-year effort to turn itself into a fascist state.

MAY, 1979

•

## Rockefeller Tribute

President Carter has requested all federal employees to observe one minute of silent government spending in memory of the late Vice-President Nelson Rockefeller.

MAY, 1979

•

## Flood Hospitalized

Representative Danial J. Flood (D, Pa.) has been hospitalized with a severe case of larceny. Sources at the Washington, D.C., Humane Society's Pet and Politician Shelter say Flood is "...unlikely to improve. Unless he dies, of course. Which would be a *real* improvement."

MAY, 1979

•

## Plains, Ga., to Get New Attraction

According to sources close to the White House, President Carter will rope his family off and start a zoo sometime early next year.

MAY, 1979

*"Mrs. Agnew's Diary" was started by Doug Kenney in the first issue of the* National Lampoon *in April, 1970. In January, 1974, he abruptly drew two diagonal black lines across the standing column head and began to write "Baba Rum Raisin." "Baba Rum Raisin" continued to run sporadically until November, 1975, when it ceased to run in the magazine altogether.*

## MRS. AGNEW'S DIARY

Dear Diary,

I hope you don't mind the omission of my usual snippet of verse—since Dick told Spiggy to change his tack in his speeches, that rascal has returned my *Thesaurus* and made off with my *Rhyming Dictionary* instead, and is using it for a fresh approach in composing a welcoming address for the new Greek delegation. Although I don't know if my Famous Writers School instructor would approve of Spiggy's rhyming of "nattering nabobs" with "slavoring shishkebabs," I certainly would not let my little criticisms stand in the way of Spiggy's duty.

Spiggy, by the way, has been in a grand mood lately, although I suspect it may have to do with the fix Dick got himself in last night. Well, it all started after Dick and Spiggy got through with their secret meeting in our rumpus room with Bob Hope and Reverend Graham—I don't know what it was about exactly, but later Reverend Graham gave me a little pinch and said that they were cooking up something to win over the younger voters that would make Woodstock look like a crummy quarter-a-head tent revival. Well, Dick called Pat over and we all decided to go see *Love Story* at the MacArthur. Unfortunately, Mr. Hope couldn't come because he had to meet Hank Kissinger and help him plan things for the Paris Peace Conference.

Well, Spiggy and I agreed that the movie was very sad and tragic, but Dick said he just couldn't believe any decent New York law firm would hire a kid with hair like that, and Pat said she thought it got boring after the burning of Atlanta. I think Pat missed some of the important scenes because every time the girl said something naughty, Pat had to go to the Ladies Lounge. Reverend Graham seemed a bit bothered by the naughty words, too, because he kept dropping his box of bridge mix and mistaking my ankle for it. Finally, I whispered would he like me to hold it for him and he whispered, oh, yes, please, but when I took the box he sort of muttered and got up to see if Pat was feeling better.

After the show, Pat invited us over to the house for two cocktails, and as we trudged down Pennsylvania Avenue, Reverend Graham started taking about Life after Death, and how God would not send Ali MacGraw to Hell for not waiting until marriage (in *Love Story*), but He probably *would* send her to Hell for the shower scene in *Goodbye, Columbus*. Then Dick started talking about déjà vu, which is the feeling you've seen something before, and Spiggy cracked something about voters having it eight years after 1960. Little else was said of note until we reached Pat and Dick's.

When we all settled in around the fire upstairs, Pat poured out our cocktails (her cocktail bottle has the most cunning plastic elephant on it whose trunk stops the flow so you won't get too much all at once), and Reverend Graham started telling wonderful ghost stories about little bad girls and what happened to them every night for all eternity when they died. Spiggy, I noticed, started looking pouty, and said how about playing some games like dirty Jotto or (winking at Reverend Graham) spin-the-Bible.

As I feared, Spiggy had taken off Pat's plastic elephant, but Dick went out and came back with a Ouija board just like the one Mel Laird keeps by his globe with all the little colored flags stuck in it. Reverend Graham showed us how it worked, although he confessed he hadn't used one since he was with Ringling Brothers. He made Pat put her fingers on the movable pointer and told her to try to communicate with someone dear to her. Pat said she'd like to say hello to her uncle, but Dick snapped that her uncle wasn't dead, just retired in California. Pat left the room in tears, saying Dick had scolded her time and time again about the phone bills, and she was just trying to save him $1.85 a minute. Well, Dick sort of shrugged in the firelight and put his fingers on the pointer while Reverend Graham put his hands on Dick's head and told him to try to reach the Other World. Right away, the pointer started jiggling like mad! I could tell Dick was alarmed because the hairs in his ears were standing straight out. Dick asked aloud if the Spirit was anybody he knew, and right away the pointer skittered to "YES." Spiggy giggled and said maybe it was Helen Gahagan Douglas, †he congresswoman Dick defeated back in the '50s by printing her voting record on pink leaflets, coming to wreak her revenge.

Naturally, I jabbed Spiggy good and hard in the ribs and Reverend Graham assured Dick that God keeps departed known pinkos under close surveillance, so he shouldn't worry. Dick sort of whimpered, and beads of perspiration broke out all over his upper lip. (I have noticed, dear Diary, that Dick perspires a great deal since Hank Kissinger told him it lends credibility to his image. Now, when Dick is on TV, he even has a special helper with a little sponge just to daub extra sweat on his upper lip if he starts to dry out under the light.) Anyway, Dick said that that made sense, put his hands back on the pointer and asked could the Spirit be that of his dear departed friend Ike?

Spiggy giggled and said Dick was leading the witness, and when the board wouldn't answer, Spiggy laughed and said it sure as hell wasn't Whittaker Chambers, either, because Dick could make that guy say *anything*. Reverend Graham (who had left briefly to make sure Pat was all right—she was, he said—and reappeared oddly disheveled) told Dick to concentrate on the Being who was trying to make contact. When he put his hands back on the pointer, he asked, well, who *are* you? Suddenly, the pointer skittered over the alphabet and spelled out YOUR BEST FRIEND. Dick shook all over and closed his eyes and said, Mother! Is it really you?

Almost as if it had a life of its own, the pointer moved across the board to "NO," and then started pointing out the letter "C" and then an "H" and then "E" "C" "K" "E" "R" "S".

Well, Dick fainted. Spiggy and I hurried our good-byes to Reverend Graham, but he was already busy talking on the phone to somebody at the *Post* about a White House miracle.

In the cab going home, Spiggy said it was fun to watch Dick squirm, but he had seen the same thing a hundred times on Ed Sullivan and anyway, a Colts game was twice as exciting.

Right then, dear Diary, I think I had an actual déjà vu.

All for now, *Judy*

APRIL, 1971

My Hushpuppies,

Many hellos and bulk quantities of Good Luck in the days to come transmigrate their happy way to all paid-up Baba Rum Raisinettes from the unarguably famous and very clean Disneyworld, Florida! More specifically too, the very exciting Adventureland and yet further pin-pointedly, the intimate if damp hospitality provided by the snug interior of a Mr. Disney semi-submersible mechanical hippopotamus.

From My vantage point above the waving jaws of this delightful plaything your Baba even now watches a most whimsical Disneyworld police launch (two-thirds scale) plying the still, warm waters. Between musical toots, its searchlights dance among lifelike palms, staccato bursts of machine gun fire raking the shore free of underbrush in the frantic attempt to insure Baba's safety.

As Baba looks on, typing intermittently, the chief security officer (his bulletproof ears and grinning mouse-skull emblem are yet visible in the dying half-light) methodically inspects the mouths of my adopted and comically chunky family with an inquiring marlin spike, hoping against hope to save Baba from a sadly supposed Watery Doom.

And speaking of dooms, there are several unpleasant varieties in store for flagrant vagrancies in regard to Basic Rules of Raisinette Discipline. For only a single example—Ms. Terri Kupferman, fourteen, of 2167 San Pectino Blvd., Glendale, California, *has not yet returned* unsold Baba Rum Raisin 1975 Gift Calendars complete with individualized daily teaching (free sample—Jan. 1: "Today is the first day of the rest of the month."—*B. R. Raisin*) plus bonus *fakir's* dozen commemorative on-the-spot watercolors of Baba's eleven most talked-about miracles. Includes the changing of the wait-

ers into winos at Baba's last supperclub appearance (look soon for *The Many Moods of Baba Rum Raisin Live at the Red Coach Grill*/Blue Thumb #AR-2446) and My much-and-favorably reviewed raising of a withered worm while spreading the Seed in a needy midtown Manhattan massage parlor.

Ms. Kupferman—whose dues for June, July, and August have yet to wing their way to Baba's Comptroller Office—is hereby on Official Reprimand and, until the unused portions of her consignment are returned, neither will be that of a certain soon-to-be-lost kitten Sniffles who misses her owner very much and whose piteous cries echo Baba's own hope that dimes and calendars come home soon.

This *Newsletter* is suddenly halted as the intrusion of a marlin spike pops Baba's prescription aviator goggles from His beaming face. Although the inquisitive Mouseketeer has moved on (a very lovely Ms. Funicello, whom Baba regrets having ungraciously unintroduced before, here now in these cramped quarters whispers that the fellow in his youth was the one who played the Mouse Club drums, badly, she adds), Baba's spectacles are in disrepair and each lens must individually be seated by wrinkling up Baba's old nose. This, it is understood, hampers Baba's vision and permits an unchecked flow from gaped nostril to already dampened paper. A *mantra* that this [water-damaged] Olivetti does not short out.

In other news, reports from Our recently dedicated *ashram* in Darien, Connecticut, reveal a serious and troubling lack of vigor in the exercise

of Baba's *Official Ashram Operating Procedure Handbook* (BRR PAMPH A/216/c—all other editions obsolete). Failure by Raisinettes to sign for long distance calls and wails from neighbors as to loud stereos and boisterous monkey-dancing until all hours have contributed to an unwholesome atmosphere for safe and sane meditations plus well-balanced karma.

More, Darien Raisinettes have brought their new fine split-level ranch-type temple with semiattached double auto house much "lame vibes" in newspapers and police blotters with totally unrelated alleged firebombings of three local churches, a Christian Science Reading Room, a judo school, and an unmarked auto allegedly belonging to the doubtless very fine Darien Joint Narcotics Strike Force then idling outside the temple.

No "Kung Fu" until Baba's Darien flock is sheepshape! And no whining. Baba has spoken.

In the distance, Ms. Funicello has spotted the launch chugging back in this direction. In the deepening twilight we can just make out the crew restocking the river with highly realistic piranha fishes—perhaps a shy invitation to Baba for festive fish barbecue? Baba kindly must refuse, already sated with His recent repast of clam in garlic.

Ms. Funicello, cramped as we are in this ingenious though unpredictable behemoth, appears to have lost the interest in the happy joking Baba displayed earlier in Mr. Disney's very entertaining Tunnel of Fear.

How did all these jumping events?

This. Indolent and disrespectful manager Mr. Morty Taumicbaum at last telephone calls Baba at fabulously

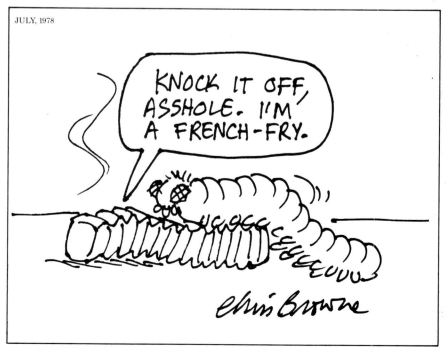

luxuriously expensive Polo Lounge with dollars in his voice but scorpions in his hands only. Mr. Disney requires Baba immediately in exciting Florida family fun center. Baba must be on 5:06 A.M. out of L.A. With eyes still fettered by pus of sleep, Baba is confronted at the airport by a most remarkable limousine auto and seven of the famous dwarfsuits only Stoopy is six-feet thirteen-inches tall and packing his rod, as is said in your justly famous gangster cinema. Get in the one they call Doc laughs in a manner similar to also impressive Nazi cinema and I do.

Under the ground in the Dumbomobile the German examines My papers and explains many interesting features of large underground honeycomb. Baba sees Mr. Walt Disney himself frozen solid as the fishstick and not to be opened until cure for deadness is found. Also extremely lifelike quick-freeze Mr. President Kennedy and talking head of Ms. Jayne Mansfield. Very convincing. Also an extremely fine Mr. President Lyndon Johnson model only there is an aerial apparatus from his nose and too a happy beep-beepbeep. As Baba watched it sit up and down the one they call Doc heiled a taxi-duck and Baba exchanged vehicles and also learned the very interesting news that the robot Mr. Kennedy unfortunately had been "shrimp cock-tailed" as they call it because his head could not be properly rewired. "It ist not like der lamp," the very strangly familiar dwarf told, "much more complicated. Kept schorting out und schparking at der head as der dragging muffler, ja?"

The happy dwarf made a joke about "der six-million-dollar-vegetable" and said to make a suitable replacement when they snatched Mr. Ex-President Nixon was almost impossible. "Der nose," he explained to me, "der schnoz ist der hardest part. Vun of mein assistants finally molded ein rubber vun from der shaved buttocks of ein baby lemur. But ve neffer licked der schvet on der lip."

When Baba's very appreciative laughter died down with a blow to the turban, He also observed a fine assemblyline of half-built plastic hippies awaiting to be installed their sparechangers. Also too a prototype ("mit un accent on der proto") of the very respected Mr. President Gerald Ford. "He vass easy to copy," said Mein Furter as Baba was asked to call him always, "so ve vill just svitch them. For der hell of it, versteht? Und der robot ist schmarter! But der ist schtill *vun* thing dot puzzles Mein Furter."

"What is that, Mein Furter," Baba asked, knowing to "blow it real cool."

"Neither vun shits," laughed the merry dwarf, lighting a cigar on my face in fun.

Baba's sandals slap slapped through the very lengthy corridors until His old eyes met a disturbing and empty robot pedestal next to an exceedingly real-appearing Marjoe gumvendor. ("Ven his TV movie bombed ve got him cheap.") The brasslike plate at the bottom read Baba Rum Raisin circa late twentieth century and the one they call Doc although sometimes Hank(?) said, "Freeze, towelhead."

Baba turned to find the dwarf surrounded by a number of highly unconvincing but nonetheless disturbing Rod Serlings who approached with bottles of pain relievers and insurance policies and those deadly things I have heard some call Vegematics.

Thinking with the swiftness of the speeding hummingbird, Baba nudged a glass containing the very lovely Ms. Funicello of my earlier introduction. The crash revived Baba's favorite Mouseketeer and yours, fellows, too, if I see clearly. One of your sheets would be evidence enough in goddess Kama's Kwality Kourt of Bliss, my naughty monkeys.

Snatching the well-preserved young woman from her suspended animation, Baba also removed the radioactive spell of her kryptonite pantyhose—something a guru might well do gingerly after so many years the fish unwrapped as the Old Ones in My humble village are fond of cackling like macaws. Hoot hoot.

But this is no time for joking now. This is a time to pack up portable Olivetti and handy accessory powerpac. Must close soon. First sign this.

---

*Yes! I am a teen-in-the-know!* And I'm tired of that bummed-out, fucked-up-all-over feeling. No kidding, I am one far-out youth who blows it cool for a good way to get high without harmful drugs or "dope." Also, with my quarter (25¢ no stamps) I hear I get a free secret massage handshake from the postman on his way back.
Can you fill me in? Wow.

Name _____

Address _____

Police Record (if any) _____

Arrests? _____ Convictions? _____
Do you have a *chauffeur's license?*
( ) yes ( ) no
*pilot's license?* ( ) yes ( ) no
*legally registered handgun or automatic weapon?*
( ) yes ( ) no
Describe: _____

---

At this moment Ms. Funicello tugs at Baba's loincloth—many giant zombie mice are crashing through the polystyrene jungle, lining the shoreline with an eerie glow of torches, this gay spectacle underlined by the steady drumming of inquisitive bullets.

Further, our watercraft itself seems to be backing steadily toward a herd of noisesome metal males—and by the gleam in their lightbulbs Baba and the White Goddess must close to batten down hatches, Olivetti cases, and brace ourselves—the following portion of the exciting hippo ride promises to be highlighted by a good deal of white water.

Omigod,

## BABA

DECEMBER, 1974

---

## Canadian Corner

*The "Canadian Corner," a column devoted to the doings of our neighbors north of the border, made its first appearance in the magazine in March, 1974. It has run, off and on, up to the present time, with contributions from expatriate Canadians Sean Kelly, Ted Mann, Bruce McCall, and Brian Shein.*

In the course of an otherwise genteel conversation, a sensitive and intelligent American (the strict but fair copy editor of a national magazine whose name you'd recognize in a moment) chanced to inquire whether Canadians write poetry; and, when pressed, admitted that she did not know there was any Canadian literature.

Moved rather to pity than to censure, I composed the following reply. This one is for Louise:

Of course, Canadians write poetry. Sweet suffering muses, do they ever. Poetry is Canada's second greatest natural resource. I say second greatest on the assumption that persons more expert than myself can distinguish it from natural gas.

No basement printing press, no Xerox or Gestetner gets a moment's peace north of the forty-ninth parallel, but they are kept busy churning out little magazines of verse, whose titles are invariably letters of the Greek alphabet.

Some Canadian bards—the Apollonians—write poetry (and let it be known they write poetry, i.e., publish) in the hopes that their neighbors will henceforth think of them as *sensitive,* rather than timid. An example of the genre:

At dawn I heard
A seagull scream
In the sky over Moosenee, Ont.
And nearly wept.
Oh, sister gull, my heart
Like you is landlocked, and
Like you,
Sings.

Others—the Dionysians—find in poetry the ideal mode of expression for such emotions as anger and lust; urges which, if not cast in verse, might lead to revolution or fornication. Their work tends to the virile, the hard-bitten, yet is, withal, Romantic. *Viz:*

This one is for Catullus,
and for the ladies of Cote St. Luc
and of a certain age,
their daughters engaged,
their sons in med school.
You enter menopause via
my modern poetry lectures
at Sir George Williams University.
Little do you wholesale hubbies
     suspect
what steamy teen-age fantasies
we entertain
over Yeats and coffee.

Occasionally, and in fact with increasing frequency, the young poets of Canada burst the Gutenberg-forged fetters of print, and sing. Self-accompanied, upon the guitar. Through the dauntless efforts of Joni and Gordon and Neil and, of course, Leonard, sentiments and metaphors which a mere generation ago would have enthralled only the elite, now fill the F.M. airwaves and, through the miracle of Muzak, translate a simple elevator ride into an ascent of Parnassus.

And prose! Prose in Canada is written by the ream, the bolt, the acre. I am given to understand that New Zealand is the only other country on earth in which a high school graduate can still sit down at the typewriter, write a short story, and get up feeling as if he or she has done a full day's work.

While American publishers hunt, relentless as Ahab, for the Great American Novel, Canadian editors, like Newfie squid-jiggers, lower their nets in hope of catching the Great Canadian Short Story.

Canadian short stories start this way:

"Gary?"

"What?"

"Oh, nothing," I said.

He was looking out the window, at the falling snow.

"It must have been something," he said.

"I'm sorry about the baby," I said.

The snow still fell beyond the window, and suddenly I felt cold.

Canadian short stories end this way:

"It doesn't matter," I said, and put out my cigarette. "It doesn't matter at all." And I put on my coat and went out into the snow.

Of the novel, it is perhaps best not to speak.

And as for the drama—surely there has not been, since the London of the late, lamented Liz, a better time or place for playwrights than Canada today! In 1967, to celebrate her Centennial, Canada broke out in a rash of playhouses, large prestressed concrete things which blossomed overnight, an acne of architectural curiosities upon the face of the nation on the occasion of her cultural adolescence.

Now, every Confederation Memorial Arts Complex and Theatre, from Charlotown to the Queen Charlots, gapes, aching to be filled, if never by audiences, at least by performances.

In Toronto, the recent success of a number of "kitchen sink" plays might be, in part, attributable to the recent addition of kitchen sinks to some of the better homes in that city. Art following in the van of technology, as that city's seer, Marshall McLuhan, had predicted.

Why then, one asks oneself, given this blizzard of manuscripts, this outpouring of literature like nothing since the Irish Renaissance (the Canuk Twilight?)—why is so little notice taken of Canadian Lit. abroad, or, in the Academies, at home?

The answer lies in history. It is an axiom among the liberally educated that those who will not learn from history are condemned to switch to business administration. History teaches us that English Literature was not taken seriously, nor studied in the Universities of England, when Shakespeare, Swift, or Jane Austen wrote. It was not until, in the early twentieth century, scholars unearthed Old English and Middle English, a vast quantity of boring, obscure, illegible, and pointless manuscripts, that Eng. Lit. could be taken seriously—that is, read for purposes that could in no way be confused with pleasure or information.

Once it was established that there was a sufficient volume of writing in the mother tongue as tedious, wrongheaded, superstitious, meandering, and difficult as anything the Greek and Roman Classics had to offer, Eng. Lit. was "in."

Much the same thing happened in the United States. American Literature was neither taught nor learned when Whitman, Twain, and Melville were writing it. It became suitable for conversation among the learned, for scholarly journals, for grants and inclusion in curriculae, only when the professors had gleaned works by obscure pedants, fanatics, and fools—Mather, Freneau, and Bradstreet—works so alien, gnarled, weird, and soporific that clearly no one could be suspected of reading them for instruction or delight.

There will be no academic recognition of Canadian Literature until the Chairmen of Departments and Editors of Journals can be presented with a library of dog-eared folios which, in the real world, could be of conceivable interest only to a graphologist, a masochist, or an archeologist. Canadian writers must create, here and now, the canon of works constituting the Middle English period of Canadian Literature.

On birch bark, wherever possible, in a crabbed hand, and crammed with absurd grammatical errors and misspellings, upon a suitably Canadian topic: Sir Gawaine and the Greene Beaver, the Sea-way Farer, and (from the Alberta Cycle) Piers Cowhand spring to mind.

For my part, I propose to become the Canadian Chaucer, and have begun the Loganberry Tales, a saga narrated by a courrier de bois, a leftover Viking, an escaped French convict, a scalped Jesuit, an Iroquois—in short, a cross-section of medieval Canadian society—on route to a shrine south of the border, where they will do homage to an American dollar:

Whan that Aprille with her sleete
     and snowe
Unto the driftes of Marche hath
     added mo,
And keens the gayle and blowth
     the Northern blizzard
That yaf an ague unto every
     gizzard,
The fields, frizz al with frosts yen
     for the boone
Of Springe's first thawe that
     cometh in late June,
Upon the pyne sleypen Oookpik
     the Owle
Bayvers doze yette, though starved
     wolffes growle,
Then longen folke on pilgrimage
     to go
To Plattsburge towne or eke to
     Buffalo.

S.K.

# TELL DEBBY

*"Tell Debby" began and ended as essentially the same unpleasant joke told in essentially the same delightful way. Brian McConnachie created "Tell Debby" in March, 1974, and retired her in August, 1975.*

Dear Debby: My married sister, and only living relative, was killed in a tragic car accident one month ago. The only thing to be thankful for, it seems, is that she and her husband didn't have any young ones. The funeral was quite an ordeal but my brother-in-law took it bravely, and help up remarkably well. He gave me comfort when I thought it should be the other way around. Two weeks after the funeral, I got the shock of my life. My brother-in-law remarried. It was tasteless enough not bothering to wait a respectable amount of time, but compounded to that, he married a woman who could only be described as an ill-tempered slut. I know it's a strong thing to say about somebody, but it's the only word I can find to aptly define her. She walks around the house all day in her underwear, she's put mirrors on *all* of the ceilings, she's always eating candy, she uses language that would make a sailor cringe, and she's taken all of my late sister's McMullen blouses and cut them up so they can show all of her cleavage. It's disgraceful. I just can't understand my brother-in-law. It makes me sick.
Alice Poster
Southchester, New York

*That's quite unfortunate.*

MARCH, 1974

Dear Debby: I am a homosexual. I am neither ashamed nor proud. It is simply what I am. I don't foster my preferences on other people and I don't want them to foster theirs on me. I am quite content. I have as many "straight" friends as I do "gay" friends. If you were to meet me, you would see nothing in my speech or manner that would indicate to you that I am a homosexual. And this, I guess, is where my problem comes in. I have a very good civilian job as an engineer at an Army installation. I enjoy my work and get along well with everyone there. Especially my supervisor. We have become close friends over the past years. He doesn't know that I am a homosexual and consequently, he and his wife are always trying to "fix" me up with single girls they know. It's not a comfortable situation. I feel obliged, naturally, to follow through by asking the girls out a few times. Then I have to make up some excuse about "things not working out." I feel we are good enough friends that I could tell him the truth and that he would understand. But if I do, it might somehow change *our* relationship.

I have no one I can turn to for advice, so that's why I'm turning to you.
Name Withheld Upon Request

*Debby does not withhold names upon request. Your name is David Shapiro and you live at 5645 Richmond Court, Sagaway, Maryland.*

MARCH, 1974

Dear Debby: I have just found out that the man to whom I have been married for the past fifteen years, the man who is the father of my seven children, has another family on the other side of town. I found out quite by accident and when I confronted him with what I knew, he confessed everything. But he added that he loves me more than ever. The other woman apparently makes him appreciate me more and he doesn't want to do anything that will threaten his renewed love for me. He is not married to this other woman but he has two children by her. He claims that it is very important that he continue to occasionally live with his other family for two reasons: so he can learn from his mistakes with them and become a better man to us, and secondly, he states, it would be too difficult to end his relationship with her when he considers all the wonderful presents she has given him. She's given him to date: a speedboat, a motorcycle, a camper, and a number of power tools, all of which, I admit, he has shared with us. He argues that his leaving her would have such an adverse effect on her that he doubts that she would ever recover, and that there would be a very good chance she would attempt to take her own life, and, if I wanted the death of a mother of two on my hands, I'm not the person he thought he married.

I told him what a bunch of rubbish I thought this was, but Debby, if this other woman kills herself, I know he'll leave me and I really don't want him to leave me.
Mrs. Karen Davidson
Frobish, Indiana

*How very unfortunate.*

Confidential to On the Ropes: *You certainly have had your share of body blows.*

OCTOBER, 1974

JULY, 1972

*"Let us aboard. We're a pair of monkeys."*

# THE SMART SET

In response to an ever-expanding public appetite for gossip, John Hughes developed "The Smart Set," which began in March, 1979, and continues despite libel laws and the constant threat of a poke in the nose.

Old Age, where is thy dignity? **IDA LUPINO** walking around Beverly Hills in a bear suit has plenty of Hollywood old-timers scratching their heads wondering what the future holds for them....**KRIS KRISTOFFERSON** has a new CB handle—it's "Sockhead."... Will Congress pass the new law waiving prosecution for anyone who punches out **RALPH NADER's** lights? For the sake of everything that tastes good, looks sharp, and goes fast, let's hope so....**YASIR ARAFAT,** PLO Master of Ceremonies, couldn't find anyone to dance with him at a recent Studio 54 fete. "Yas" has spent the week with a disco instructor, and he even wore a brand-new set of kitchen drapes on his head, but to no avail. As the evening wore down, the lonely old terrorist had to shake his booty with his body guards....**RINGO STARR** is considering changing his name to **PAUL McCARTNEY** so that people will like him and he'll sell more records. Don't hold your breath, Mr. Jingle Fingers....The music industry is still wondering why the **BEACH BOYS** can't all get in a car wreck and die....**MARISA BERENSON** has left New York. Tough dog litter laws is the reason the beautiful horse's ass will once again settle in Los Angeles....**MICK JAGGER** has worn out his penis. The seven-inch, billion-dollar dingus is shot. According to those who know, "It looks like the thumb on an old glove."...Olympic Gold Medal winner **BRUCE JENNER** says he's looking for a job as a pole-vaulter. The remarkably slow gashead reports that he wants to get back to what he considers his "real career." If nothing pops up, Bruce says he'll start his own pole-vaulting team. When you're out in California stop in, says Bruce, "and throw a drink in my face."...Super-agent **SUE MENGERS** recently wowed French truffle hunters and friends when she sniffed out and rooted up a record 180 pounds of the prized fungus. "It hurts to dig with your nose," Sue admitted. "But when I smell a truffle, I just have to dig it up."...Is **GENE AUTRY** still alive? "Yes!" says the former cowboy crooner. Who's to blame? "Fast-acting doctors!" Too bad for all of us....In Washington, D.C., a Capitol Hill janitor nearly swept N.Y. Senator **PATRICK MOYNIHAN** into an incinerator after mistaking the pandemonic poof for a pile of old clothes and papers....**JANN WENNER** is suing **BOB DYLAN** for "not being as good as he was in the sixties." The publisher of *Rolling Stone* magazine is asking a New York court to force Dylan to "return to the gruff, nasal vocalizations of his pre-motorcycle crash period" and to "add depth to his lyrics."... Word is out that **STEVE MARTIN's** hilarious new book, *Cruel Shoes,* was ghost-written by Yankee coach **YOGI BERRA**....After finishing a taping of a "Gong Show," dwarf singer **PAUL WILLIAMS** was eaten by a stage cat....It looks like punk queen **PATTI SMITH** is finding out that you can't go home again. "At least not until she shaves her armpits!" says Patti's mom....And finally, **J. FRED BUZHARDT,** the former legal counsel to **PRESIDENT NIXON,** who died on December 16, 1978, has gone to hell.

MARCH—AUGUST, 1978

# Also Rans

A number of other continuing columns have appeared in National Lampoon during the last ten years, most of them written by staff editors. Several ran only two or three times, while others lasted as long as two years.

**"Horrorscope" (1970-71)**
Doug Kenney and John Weidman's depressing, disastrous fortune cookie predictions for people in the news.

**"The Unforgiving Minute" (1971-72)**
Jaundiced overview of political, social, and personal affairs, by Paul Krassner.

**"Mr. Chatterbox" (1973-74)**
A potpourri of red-hot gossip about the editors and just about everyone else, by George W.S. Trow.

**"Pat Nixon's Hot Flashes" (1974)**
"Pat Nixon," alias Doug Kenney, answers readers' diverse and pointless questions in a fashion that is denigrating to herself.

**"Straight Talk" by Gerald Ford (1975)**
Tony Hendra's rambling commentary from the thirty-eighth president.

**"Plugola" (1975)**
Reviews of people, places, products, and productions, done with an eye to personal gain by the editors.

**"Birdbath" (1975-77)**
Famous names dropped and libeled, by R. Bruce Moody.

**"Sports Column" by Red Ruffansore (1975-77)**
A grizzled veteran of the press box casts a jaundiced eye on big-time sports, by Sean Kelly, John Weidman, and the editors.

**"International Date Line" (1976)**
Doug Kenney and P.J. O'Rourke's literary representation of telegraph signals beamed to ignorant, backward, and dopey foreign teens for the purpose of arranging dates for and among them.

**"Elborne Whippet's Washington" (1976-77)**
Smarmy political commentator's commentary, by Jeff Greenfield.

**"Blown in the Wind" by Jean-Claude "Hopalong" Cravat (1976)**
Personal experiences and observations of Peter Kaminsky, writing as a French hipster.

**"This is War" by Slouch Hooligan (1976-78)**
Ted Mann and P.J. O'Rourke's tough, unvarnished reporting from trouble spots around the globe.

**"The Carter Family" by Bob Bob Carter, the President's cousin (1977)**
Largely illiterate tales of Jimmy Carter and his embarrassing family, as related by P.J. O'Rourke.

**"Ripping Off the Lid" by Shevya Biyrdoff (1977)**
Typically cartilagineous Russian defector's coarse attempt at investigative reporting, by Ellis Weiner.

# *Lt. Calley's* KILL THE CHILDREN FEDERATION

Dear Concerned Citizen,

This is Xena Puento. Xena is nine years old. She has never seen a glass of milk. Xena and her mother live in an abandoned packing crate on the outskirts of Manila, just one of thousands of deprived and impoverished families trapped by illiteracy, educational deficiency, unemployment, and disease. For just $15, I can shoot Xena in the head and toss her into a mass grave. But I need your help. Guns, bullets, and bulldozers cost money. While the need is great, the available funds are small.

There used to be no hope for Xena and those like her. They were doomed to a life of misery without chance of escape. But now your donation can provide that chance. Only $15 enables you to select your child from a score of countries overseas and areas at home. Soon you will receive a photograph of your child's resting place and an actual death certificate filled out by authorized U.S. personnel. An additional contribution of $5 will provide a small marker; $10 buys a wreath; $25 pays for a handsome urn; and $180 covers the cost of perpetual care.

Don't you think little Xena has suffered enough? Then act today and complete the sponsorship application below.

Thanks so much!

Sincerely,

Lt. William Calley, Ret.

**Partial list of national sponsors and foster soldiers**
Joey Heatherton
Brig. Gen. John W. Donaldson
Sen. Mendel Rivers
Morey Amsterdam
Walter Brennan
Capt. Ernest Medina
Mr. & Mrs. Samuel Yorty
George Jessel
Sen. James O. Eastland
Kate Smith

**Available countries and areas**
Taiwan
Peru
Korea
Iran
The Philippines
Bolivia
Ecuador
Brazil
S. Vietnam
Kurdistan
Mexico
Lebanon
Hong Kong
Paraguay
Syria
Africa
USA—
   Appalachia
   Watts
   Bedford Stuyvesant
   American Indian reservation
   and migrant camps

**A division of the Foster Soldiers' Plan, Inc.**

---

**We're not trying to destroy the world. Just a little piece of it.**

---

**Lt. Calley's Kill the Children Federation**
**A division of the Foster Soldiers' Plan, Inc.**
**Box 711**
**Fort Benning, Georgia 23409**

Name _____

Address _____

City _____ State _____ Zip _____

If for a group, please specify _____
(church, class, club,
_____ school, business, etc.)

Registered (VFA-0880) with the U.S. GOVERNMENT'S ADVISORY COMMITTEE ON VOLUNTARY FOREIGN AID. Contributions are tax-deductible.

NL-7-71

I wish to sponsor the death of a

☐ boy ☐ girl in _____.
(name of country)

I am enclosing $15 to cover cost of expungement & burial.

☐ Choose a child from an area of greatest need.

☐ I am enclosing an additional $_____ to pay for

_____
(marker, wreath, urn, p. care)

☐ I cannot sponsor the death of a child, but want to give $_____.

☐ Please send me more information.

# BOVINE BOYHOOD or Children Should Be Seen and Not Herd !!!!

DEEP IN THE BROODING FOOTHILLS OF SOUTHERN WISCONSIN, A SPEEDING TWO-TONED DE SOTO, WITH JOHN GREYSTOKE AT THE WHEEL AND ALICE, HIS ENTRANCING WIFE AT HIS SIDE, SUDDENLY SKIDS OUT OF CONTROL...

*EEEERRRCHH*

....AND PLUNGES INTO A TREACHEROUS IRRIGATION DITCH..

*BLAASH!*

UNNOTICED, AN INFANT CRAWLS FROM THE TWISTED WRECKAGE....

WELL, I'LL BE DOGGED! LOOKS LIKE THERE'S BEEN SOME KIND OF ACCIDENT!

....ONLY TO VANISH INTO THE DENSE UNDERBRUSH....

S'PECT YER RIGHT!

BLAZING HEADLINES HERALD THE MYSTERY....

The Evansville Sun-Clarion

## CAR CRASH KILLS 2, BABY MISSING
### Massive Search Underway

The Offtrack Sites

BUT TIME PASSES...

UNTIL, FINALLY....

## DOWN MEMORY LANE
### Notable Evansville News Items of the Past

10 Years Ago Today—Rain cancels Gladiolus Festival.

15 Years Ago Today—Lecturer and world traveler Douglas S. Whitaker speaks to the Eastern Star on "Tunisia, Land of Enchantment." His talk is accompanied by color slides.

20 Years Ago Today—

50 Years Ago Today—A speeding two-toned De Soto suddenly skids out of control and plunges into a treacherous irrigation ditch, killing two. Missing baby never found. Orchard Street gets a new coat of paint.

NEEDLESS TO SAY, HOWEVER, JOHN GREYSTOKE JR. WAS FOUND....

....BY A HERD OF COWS.....

WHO RAISED HIM AND TAUGHT HIM EVERYTHING THEY KNEW, INCLUDING *THE LAW OF THE PASTURE*....

Law of the Pasture
1. Watch out for electric fences.
2. Never eat burdocks.
3. Don't step in the ☆!!/○○#!

BEYOND BASIC "COW," HE LEARNED ALL THE LANGUAGES OF THE BARNYARD, SPEAKING FLUENT "DOG" AND "CHICKEN," SOME "HORSE," A LITTLE "SHEEP" AND A SMATTERING OF "TURKEY"....

BAA!

NEIGH!

CHEEP!

BARK!

GOBBLE-GOBBLE!

THEN, ON A DOOM-LADEN AFTERNOON LATE ONE NOVEMBER, A DETROIT SPORTSMAN SPOTS TARZAN'S MOTHER...

I'LL JUS' GET A BEAD ON THAT RARE SHORT-HORNED, DAPPLED MOOSE AND...

VA-VLOOM!

WHEN THE HUNTER REALIZES HIS ERROR, HE ATTEMPTS TO CONSOLE THE GRIEF-STRICKEN LAD, BUT NOTHING HE SAYS SEEMS TO DO ANY GOOD...

MOO! MOO! MOO! MOO! MOO!

THERE'S NO USE CRYIN' OVER SPILT MILK, SON!

IN AN EFFORT TO "SQUARE THINGS", HE SENDS TARZAN TO A PRIVATE SCHOOL ON THE OUTSKIRTS OF MINNEAPOLIS....

HOW COME THERE NO BOOKS FOR COWS?

BUT HE JUST DOESN'T FIT IN WITH THE OTHER STUDENTS...

LOOK! IRON BIRD!

AT LAST...

TARZAN NO LIKE SCHOOL!

TARZAN GO BACK TO FIELDS!

THUS IT IS THAT TARZAN, PROUD AND UNTAMED, RETURNS TO ROAM THE WILDS, AND THERE, WITH SIMBA, HIS FAITHFUL CHICKEN, TO UPHOLD *THE LAW OF THE PASTURE* AND BEFRIEND BOTH MAN AND BEAST ALIKE....

# COWS AROUND THE WORLD

No. 1 of a series    The Ayrshire

HOOT MON! SHE'S A WEE BIT O' A BONNIE BOSSY!

The Ayrshire (pronounced "air-sheer") hails from Ayr county in south-western Scotland where they originated in the late 18th century. Noted for their symmetrical udders and long, upturned horns, this hardy breed varies in color, ranging from red and white to red, mahogany, or brown with white spots. Occasionally, one may even chance upon an almost pure white specimen.

First imported into the United States in 1822, there are currently over 175,000 registered Ayrshires in this country. Although of medium size (female — 1,150 pounds; male — 1,800 pounds), Ayrshires still rank high among dairy cattle as beef producers but, with the continuing emphasis on volume and low-fat content of milk, many farmers are passing over the Ayrshire in favor of the holstein-friesian.

NOW WE'LL ONLY HAVE TO SLICE THAT PIE *THREE* WAYS!

SCANT SECONDS LATER....

CRIPES! IT SEZ HERE THE LAND'S OWNED BY A MR. AND MRS. KLECKLEY!

I'VE GOT A SCHEME! WE'LL PUT ON THESE GROUND-HOG DUDS AND SCARE 'EM OFF!

RACINE COSTUME CO.

THE FOLLOWING DAY....

OOGA-BOOGA-OOGA-BOOGA-OOGA...

RUN FER YER LIFE, HELEN! HERE COME THE BIGGEST DANGED GROUNDHOGS I EVER SET EYES ON!

OOGA-BOOGA-OOGA-BOOGA-OOGA!

THAT TAKES CARE OF THEM! NOW LET'S GIT THE DUMP TRUCK AND MAKE OFF WITH THE SWAG!

BUT NEWS TRAVELS FAST IN THE BADGER STATE...

CHEEP! CHEEP. CHEEP! CHEE-

CHEEP! CHEEP CHEEP! CHEEP. CHEEP.

CHEEP! CHEEP. CHEEP! CHEEP CHEEP CHEE-

CHEEP! CHEEP CHEEP, CHEEP. CHEEP. CHEEP CHEEP!

CHEEP! CHEEP CHEEP! CHEEP! CHEEP! CHEEP CHEEP CHEE-

CHEEP?

CHEEP!

CHEEP CHEEP CHEEP! CHEEP! CHEEP CHEEP CHEEP! CHEEP! CHEEP!

WHAT THAT YOU SAY, SIMBA? THREE MEN POSE AS GROUND-HOG TO SCARE AWAY MR. AND MRS. KLECKLEY AND STEAL THEIR GRAVEL? TARZAN SOON PUT STOP TO THIS!

MOVING WITH UNCANNY SPEED, TARZAN RACES UP THE NEAREST TELEPHONE POLE...

HAND OVER HAND, WITH SINEWS FLASHING IN THE SUNLIGHT, HE KNIFES THROUGH THE LUSH FARMLAND....

...UP ROUTE 9 TO THE TWIN FORKS, BEARS LEFT PAST THE GRANGE TO SPRING BLUFF ROAD, LEFT ON SPRING BLUFF ROAD FOR ABOUT THREE MILES TO THE OLD DIRT ROAD JUST AFTER THE ROYAL CROWN COLA SIGN, RIGHT ON THE OLD DIRT ROAD UNTIL IT DEAD ENDS ON ROUTE 31, LEFT ON ROUTE 31 TO THE BIG FALLS CUT-OFF, FOLLOWS THE CUT-OFF UNDER THE BRIDGE AND ACROSS THE TRACKS, THEN TAKES A SHARP RIGHT AND....

THROW DOWN YOUR FIRESTICKS! I TARZAN OF COWS!

I BEG YOUR PARDON?

I SAID—

HOW'S THAT?

COME AGAIN?

BUT BEFORE HE CAN ANSWER, THE TOP GUNSEL BARKS A COMMAND...

POLISH HIM OFF!

YOU ASKED FER THIS, CHUMP, AND NOW YER GONNA GIT IT!

BLAM

PA-KOW!

WHAT'S IT TO BE FOR TARZAN?

THE GRIM REAPER OR THE INTERNATIONAL HARVESTER?

AMIDST A HAIL OF LEAD, THE MIGHTY MIDWESTERNER SWINGS INTO ACTION....

BWEEE

VIP!

VIP!

P-WANG

T-ZING!

LANDING SQUARELY ON A HAYSTACK, WHERE...

AND SO, WITH JUSTICE YET AGAIN TRIUMPHANT, *TARZAN OF THE COWS* TAKES HIS LEAVE TO PURSUE NEW ADVENTURE, NEW EXCITEMENT, NEW MOWN HAY....

NORMA, DID YOU JUST SAY "MOO"?

MOOOOO!

NO, I THOUGHT YOU DID!

the end

MEET ANOTHER NEWCOMER TO THE KENOSHA KOMICS FAMILY!!!

## INTRIGUE! SUSPENSE! WEIRDNESS!

WHEN SMOG, LIKE A SILK SHROUD, CURLS THROUGH THE PERIL-RIVEN STREETS OF BURLINGTON, AND DANGER LURKS IN EVERY DARKENED DOORWAY, THEN FALLS THE TIME FOR...

VERMONT CRANSTON *alias* THE SHADOW

COMING UP NEXT:

CAN TARZAN SURVIVE THE SILO OF DEATH?

• HOW DOES A TATTERED 4-H HANDBOOK PLAY A BIZARRE PART IN *THE MYSTERY OF THE WURLITZER GRAVEYARD?*

• WHAT'S THE STRANGE SECRET OF MRS. WILMA HOWARD, THE SINISTER DEN MOTHER WHO HEADS A PAGAN CULT THAT *OPENLY WORSHIPS THE WOLF AND THE BEAR?*

FOR THE ANSWERS TO THESE AND OTHER QUESTIONS DON'T MISS....

## TARZAN AND THE FORBIDDEN JEWEL OF HEAFFORD JUNCTION!

WHEN THE FATE OF WISCONSIN HANGS IN THE BALANCE AND IS FOUND WANTING...

BY WAY OF AN ARCANE CORRESPONDENCE SCHOOL, CRANSTON LEARNED THE SECRET OF CLOUDING THE MIND; NOT THE MINDS OF OTHER MEN... BUT HIS OWN!

PLEASE EXCUSE ME! MY MIND'S SO CLOUDED I HARDLY KNOW WHAT I'M DOING!

BUMP!

CRASH!

IT IS WRITTEN THAT WHOSOEVER STEALS THE SACRED ZIRCON FROM THE MASONIC SHIELD SHALL BE UNDONE BY A DREAD CURSE!

DON'T EXPECT ME TO SWALLOW THAT BUNK!

# The Undiscovered Notebook of Leonardo Da Vinci

### compiled by Doug Kenney    reconstructed by Daniel Maffia

Scientist, painter, engineer, architect — Leonardo Da Vinci was undoubtedly the greatest thinker of Western Civilization. Although born in 1454, his voluminous notebooks predicted not only the airplane and helicopter but many other modern day miracles. Thinkers through the ages have gleaned from these notebooks great insights ("Gravity is what makes birds fall down when they have heart attacks"), as well as a wealth of fascinating biographical data ("Four pairs stretch tights . . . six doublets . . . no starch . . ."). Thus, the *National Lampoon* is honored to be able to present portions of one of Da Vinci's notebooks that has never been discovered. We hope that you will be as awed as we were at the genius and vision revealed in this remarkable and priceless document. . . .

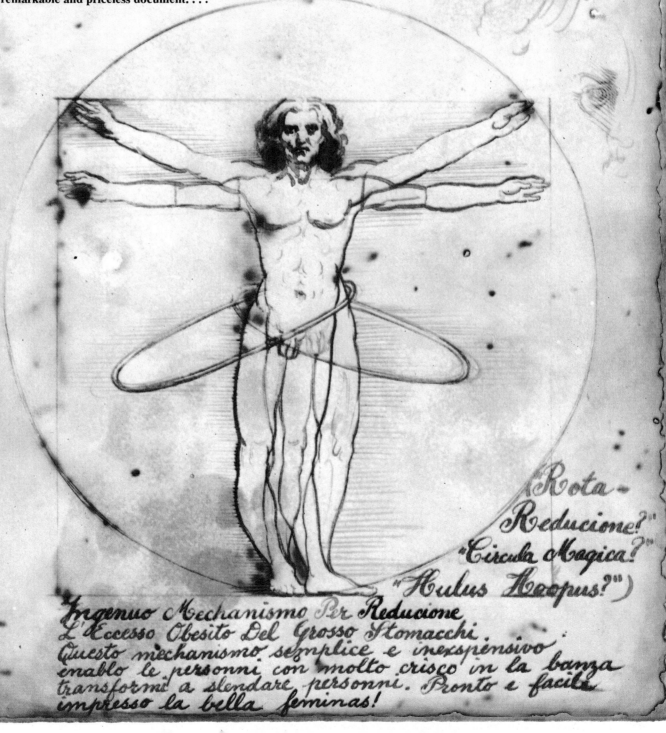

"Rota-
Reducione?"
"Circula Magica?"

"Hulus Haopus?")

Ingenuo Mechanismo Per Reducione
L'Eccesso Obesito Del Grosso Stomacchi.
Questo mechanismo semplice e inexspensivo
enablo le personni con molto crisco in la banza
transformi a slendar personni. Pronto e facile
impresso la bella feminas!

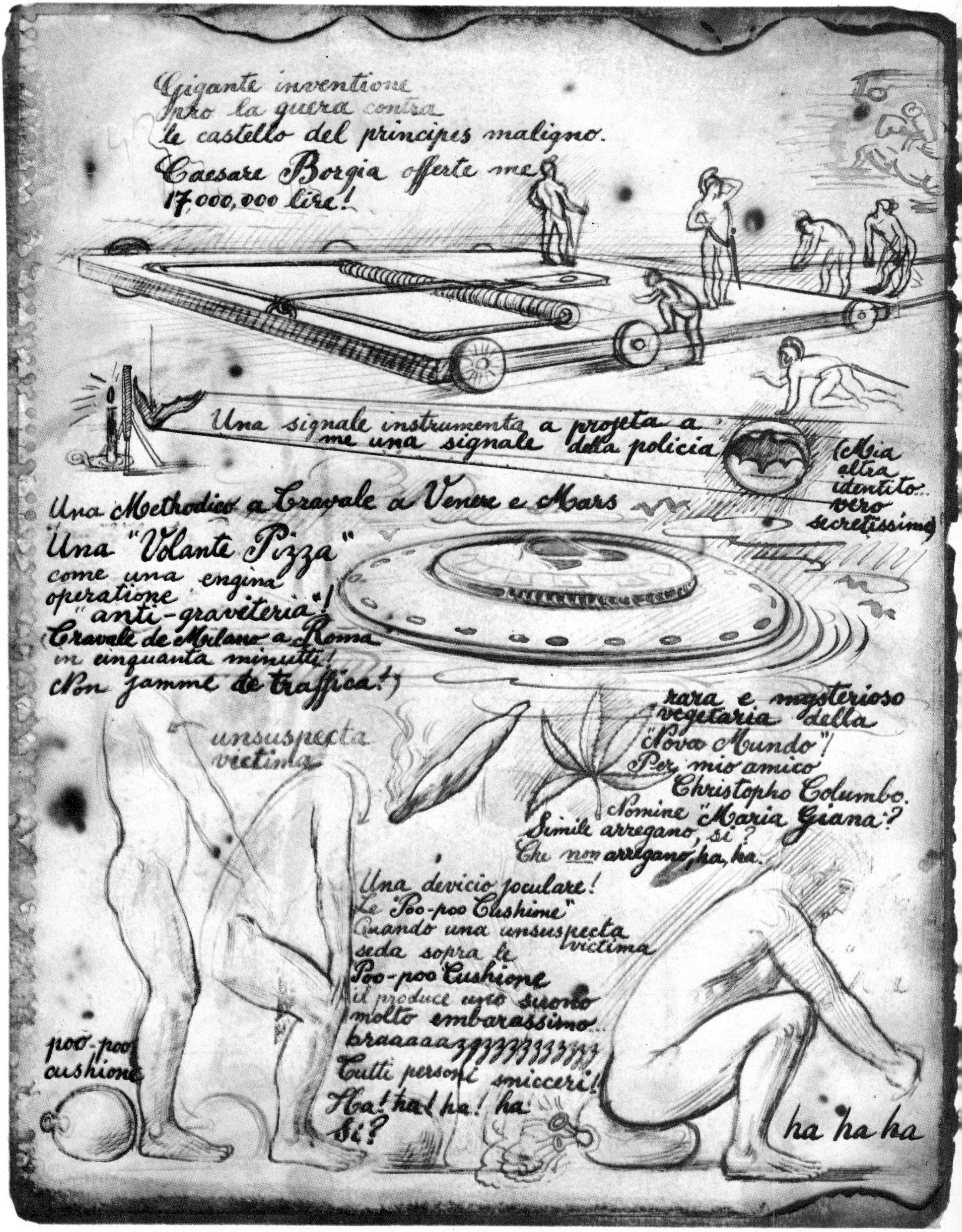

Gigante inventione
pro la guerra contra
le castello del principes maligno.
Caesare Borgia offerte me
17,000,000 lire!

Una signale instrumenta a projeta a me una signale della policia

(Mia altra identito... vero secretissimo)

Una Methodico a travale a Venere e Mars

Una "Volante Pizza"
come una engina
operatione
"anti-graviteria"!
Travale de Milano a Roma
in cinquanta minutti.
Non jamme de traffica!

rara e mysterioso
vegetaria della
"Nova Mundo"!
Per mio amico
Christopho Columbo.
Nomine "Maria Giana"?
Simile arregano, si?
Che non arregano, ha, ha.

unsuspecta victima

Una devicio joculare!
Le "Poo-poo Cushione"
Quando una unsuspecta
seda sopra le
Poo-poo Cushione
il produce uno suono
molto embarassimo
braaaaazzzzzzz
Tutti personi smicceri!
Ha! ha! ha! ha
si?

poo-poo cushione

unsuspecta victima

ha ha ha

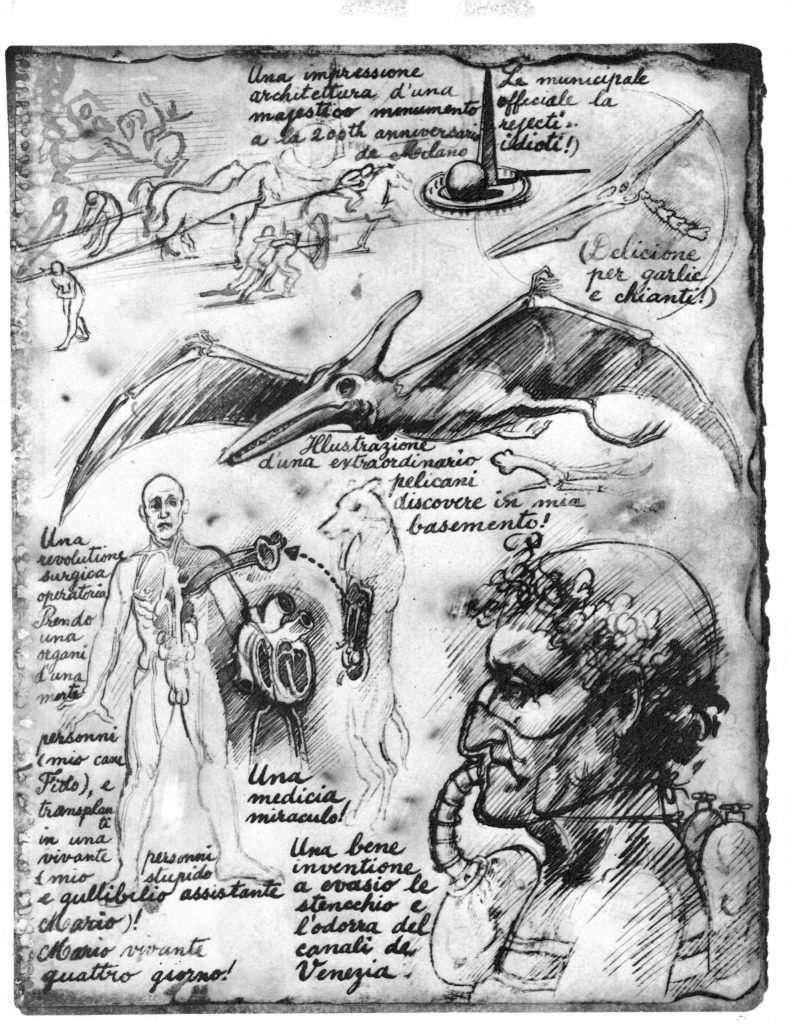

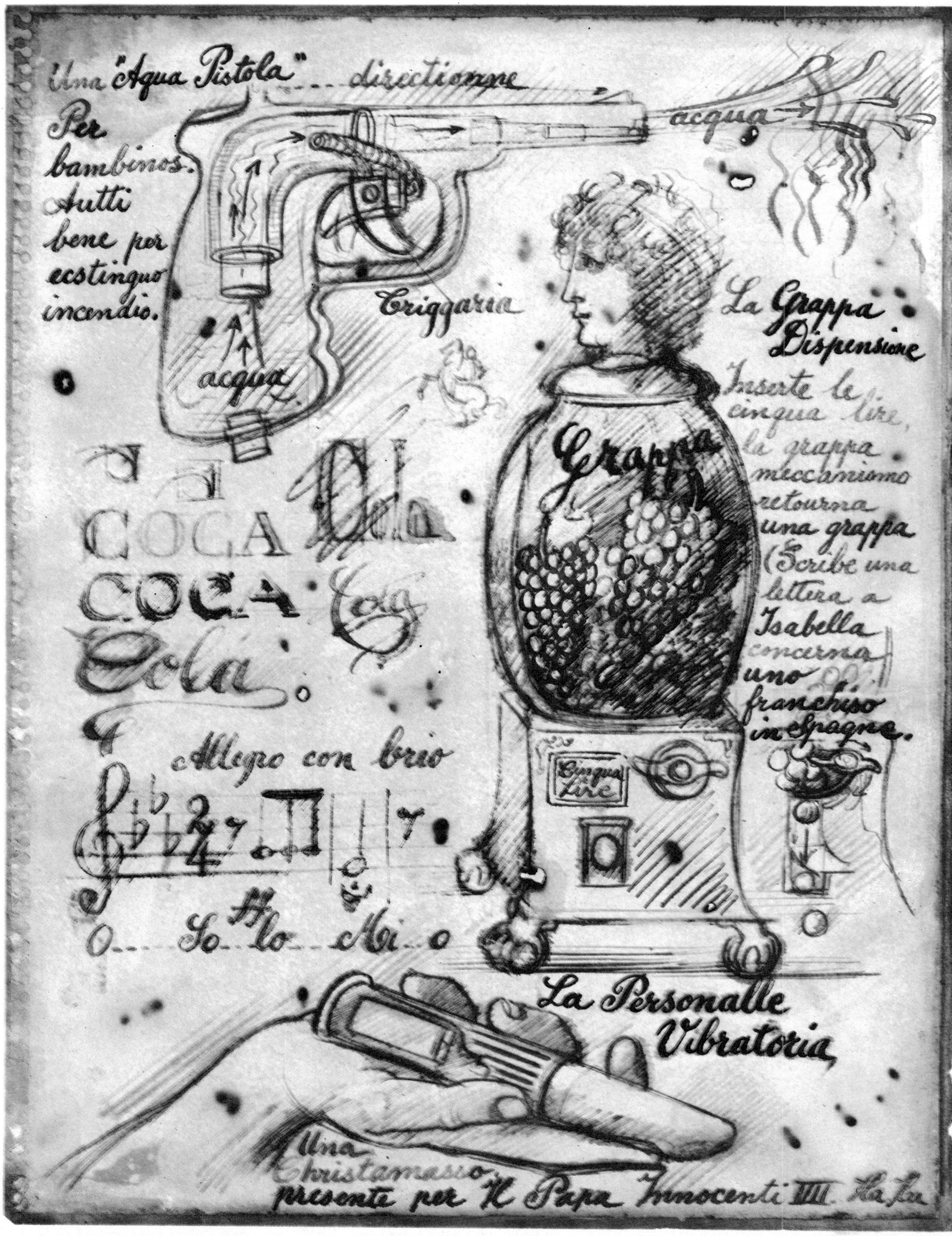

Una "Aqua Pistola" directionne
acqua
Per bambinos. Autti bene per ecstinguo incendio.
Triggaria
acqua
La Grappa Dispensione
Inserte le cinqua lire, la grappa meccaniosmo retourna una grappa (Scribe una lettera a Isabella concerna uno franchiso in Spagna.
Grappa
Cinqua Lire
COGA
COCA
Cola.
Allegro con brio
O— So— lo— Mi— o
La Personalle Vibratoria
Una Christamasio presente per Il Papa Innocenti VIII. Ha ha

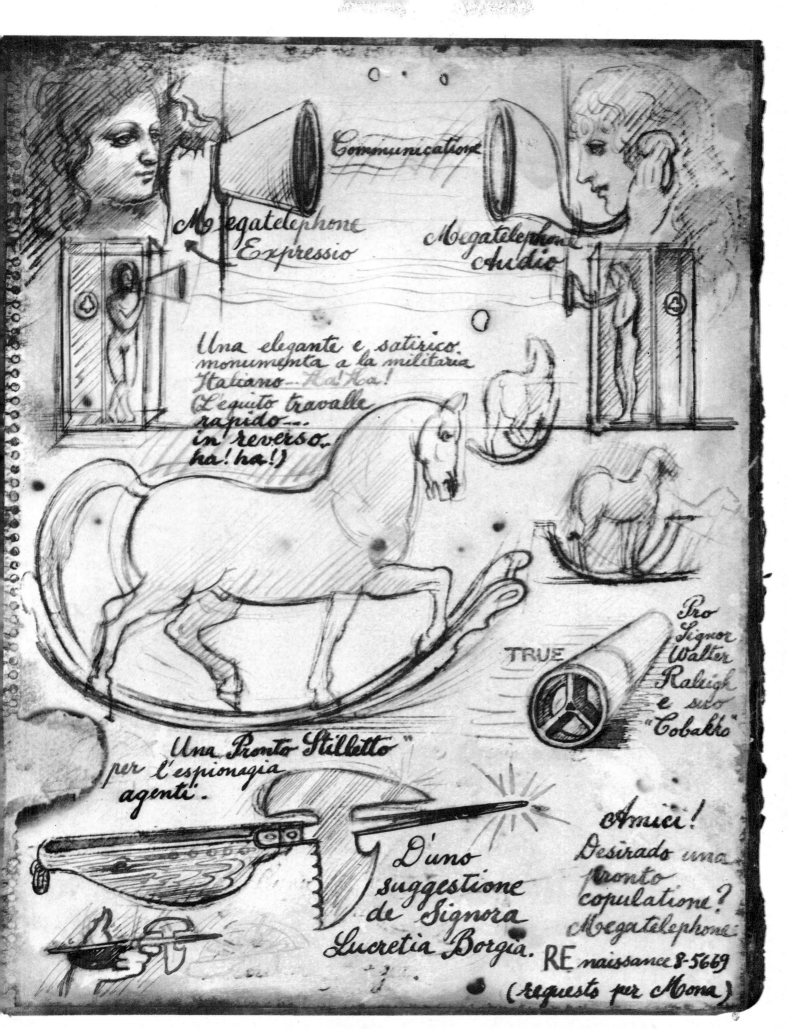

# PORNOCOPIA

## by Michael O'Donoghue

## ...SOME SELECTIONS FROM THE SUPREME COURT'S SUMMER READING LIST

### The Elegant English Epistolary Eroticism
*...in the manner of John Cleland*

Mr. N...chanc'd to offer a bout of dalliance and disport. My blush serv'd but to inflame the young gentleman's ardours, and a heart-fetch'd sigh at the size of his remarkable fouling piece banish'd all reserve. Canting up my petticoats and unlacing my stays, I fell supine on the settee, my exquisite treasures at his disposal. Thus embolden'd, he took in hand the prodigious engine and, abandoning restraint, remm'd the rubid cleft where grows the wanton moss that crowns the brow of modesty, but to naught avail. Thrice again the frightful machine assail'd the region of delight which, with maidenhead's sweet mant'ling, celebrates the triumph of roses o'er the lily, but that delicious cloven spot, the fairest mark for his well-mettl'd member, quell'd and abash'd the gallant intruder. Mustering his ferbour, once more didst Cupid's capt'n 'tempt to brunt the fierce prow of his formidable vessel past the shoals of luxuriant umberage which garland'd my rutt'd charms and into that uncloy'd cove where humid embars blaz'd on visitation, yet was, e'en so, repulst. Tho' toss'd 'twixt profusion and compliance, my hand crept softly to the sturdy lad's ripen'd tussle and roam'd the sprout'd tufts, whilst he my hillocks wander'd, then rekindl'd his nobly stock'd conduits, distend'd the proud steed, where'pon I near swoon'd of extasy's bright tumult as the sturdy stallion, his exhaultations fir'd, gallop'd o'er ev'ry hedge and thicket, spending the jetty sprig, won the sally, and gain'd a lodgement. Encircl'd in the pleasure-girst, ingorg'd by dissolution's tender agony, each 'fusive stroke stirr'd my in'most tendrils, devolv'd my dewy furrow of its secrets, which I, flush with straddl'd frolik, was far from disrelishing, 'til, somewhat appeas'd, his quiv'ling extremity, twin'd by unquench'd appetite, durst 'frock the fury of unflagg'd inspersions, yet homeward play'd my rake the plenteous protraction, redoubl'd his endeavours that joy's thrust might soon drink deep at rapture's well, then didst, at last, sheath, to the churl'd hilt, his massy weapon, and so suffer'd me to bliss.

> I am,
> Madam,
> Yours, etc., etc., etc.

### The Fin-de-Siècle British Birching Book
*...in the manner of Anonymous*

"And what might your name be, my child?" inquired Lord Randy Stoker, removing a tin of violet pastilles from the pocket of his tangerine-velvet waistcoat and placing one in his sensuous mouth while his flashing eyes coolly probed the buxom lass that sat trembling before him.

"My name's Miss Prissy Trapp, sir," she replied in a faint voice and working-class accent, lowered her eyes, and curtsied. "I'm the new maid."

"Welcome to Felonwart, my remote country manor house. I can assure you that your stay here will be most... 'amusing.' Come into the drawing room and place yourself at the disposal of my guests."

The drawing room was that of a typical country manor house, save for the fact that the walls were padded, the windows barred, a curious array of whips and riding equipage were displayed above the fireplace, an immodest fresco graced the north wall, a number of cages hung suspended from the ceiling and, in the center of the room, towering above a bloodstained altar, loomed a moonstone-studded effigy of Kā, the nineteen-armed Babylonian Goddess of Lust.

"As you may have gathered, my tastes run somewhat toward the *outré*," Lord Stoker commented, helping himself to another violet pastille, and continued, his voice dark with menace, "a proclivity that does not limit itself to decor."

Upon seeing Prissy, a tall, gaunt man, wearing but a pair of soiled galoshes, threw himself at her feet and commenced wildly kissing her feather duster.

"Allow me to introduce Professor Schadenfreude," interposed Lord Stoker as the bewildered miss blushed crimson under the Austrian's singular attentions. "His studies in aberrant behavior have taken man's sexual urges out of the Dark Ages."

"And back to the Stone Age," added Lady Wick-Burner, crawling across the carpet to gnaw on the heel of Prissy's left shoe.

"Oh...Oh...Please...I beseech you...Leave off...have pity...Oh...No more..." pleaded the misused maid.

Delighted by the young girl's supplications, the Duke of Pudenda discontinued reading from a slim volume of unseemly sonnets he had recently published privately in a limited edition of four copies, all of which were bound in tinted wildebeest.

"Remove her chemise!" demanded Reverend John Thomas.

Upon hearing this, Prissy, her face a mask of abasement, attempted to flee but was thwarted by two Nubian eunuchs who, dispite the unfortunate's pathetic struggles, firmly secured her wrists with braided peacock tails.

"All in good time," cautioned the Sultana of Zosh. "First, allow the hapless servant to gaze upon the instrument of her chastisement." She drew back the drapes to reveal a weird machine composed of a steam engine, pistons, manacles, a glass godemiche, rubber tubing, a gilded harpsichord, a whalebone corset, asparagus tips and a vat of scented lard.

The Sultana smiled wanly and murmured, "We call it...'The Blind Chicken!'"

"What does it do?" asked Prissy.

Silhouetted against the dying sunlight, the great circle of Kā's nineteen arms appeared to be a ceaseless juggernaut of shame and degradation as Lord Stoker leaned over to whisper, "You'll discover that only too soon," and stuck his purple tongue in her ear.

### The Early French Algolagnic Novel
*...in the manner of the Marquis de Sade*

The Comte was in the formal gardens whipping his linoleum when he was joined by the Bishop. Ceasing his exertions, he greeted the prelate, and said:

"You are undoubtedly curious why I am whipping my linoleum. And yet, on closer examination, nothing could be more natural…or might I say 'unnatural' as they are the same thing. Man, it goes without saying, is intrinsically evil, bearing in mind, of course, that good and evil, vice and virtue, exist only within the confines of society. It is the laws which cause crime, for, without law, there is no crime. Nature capriciously destroys the fools who forsake their instinctual lust and hunger in the name of virtue, as Nature does us all. Man is an animal with a soul that exists only through sensations. Although man must not limit his actions, there is no free will, therefore he is not responsible for his actions. Quite obviously, the more disgusting the act, the greater the pleasure, and since pleasure, or might I say 'pain' as pleasure is but pain diminished, remains the chief aim of all human existence, it should be enjoyed at any cost, particularly at the expense of other people, that is to say, not only is there joy in whipping my linoleum, but there is also joy in reflecting upon those who are not allowed to whip their linoleum. Hence, cruelty is nothing more than man's life force uncorrupted by civilization. As we are pawns to misery, so must we dispense misery to pawns. Since pain is the absolute, it is essential that I, as a philosopher, pursue this absolute. So it seems that the question, my dear Bishop, is not 'Why do I whip my linoleum?' but rather, 'Why doesn't everyone whip his linoleum?'"

### The Recent French Algolagnic Novel*
*…in the manner of Pauline Reage*

The moon was partially obscured by a cloud.

One afternoon, a limousine had picked up E at the Buttes-Chaumont Gardens, the Bois de Vincennes, the Bassin de la Villette, or perhaps the Boulevard Haussmann, and had taken her to a chateau in southern France. The driver had departed without saying a word.

Attendants prepared E for the party that evening. She was dressed in a bird costume resembling a boat-tailed grackle. I am certain that she was forbidden to speak.

In another version, the limousine picks up E at the Bureau des Objets Trouvés.

E was placed on the lawn and instructed to remain there until summoned. Behind her was a row of cypress trees. Under the third tree lay a pale blue envelope. From the envelope she withdrew a photograph of

---

*Ed. Note—Rumored to be the work of A---- M-------, noted Marxist author and art critic.*

three persons on an ottoman. One is blindfolded. It is difficult to determine what they are engaged in.

Her costume was perfect in every detail. The only discrepancy that might prompt the casual observer to conclude that E could be something other than an enormous boat-tailed grackle was a pair of black patent leather shoes which she is required to wear as a symbol of her absolute subjugation.

Although forbidden to speak, I believe that E was allowed to whistle.

The bird costume restricted movement and it often took E over an hour to reach places only a few feet away.

When she glances back to the third tree, she notices that the pale blue envelope and the photograph are missing.

That evening, three men, X, Y, and Z, retire from the party to chat beneath the porte cochere. Y is her lover.

Fragments of conversation are audible from where E is standing on the lawn.

"Have you spoken to G lately?"

"It's odd you should ask. Why only last week…"

The three men turn toward her. X and Z appear familiar, as if she had seen them in a photograph.

"Look, there's a boat-tailed grackle," remarks Z. "An uncommonly large one, I might add."

Moments pass. The men do not move. E observes the moon clearly reflected in her black patent leather shoes. Surely her lover will recognize her, take her in his arms, and debase her in the fashion which she has grown to regard so dearly. She flaps her wings and whistles frantically.

Finally, Y speaks.

"One seldom sees them so far north this late in the season."

### Expurgation by Latin
*…in the manner of Boccaccio*

Now there once lived near Genoa a wealthy merchant named Gelfardo, who was infatuated with Bonella, a miller's daughter unsurpassed in beauty, grace, and charm.

As it so happened, Bonella, spurning Gelfardo's advances, was wont to seek diversion with a certain abbot, but he, much to her displeasure, had given to *concilium loqui* swans.

One afternoon, while strolling in the forest, Gelfardo came upon the comely damsel picking flowers. With a lascivious wink, he asked the lady if she might care to unfasten her bodice and *supplicia eorum qui in furto aut latrocinio aut aliqua noxia sint comprehensi gratiora dis immortalibus esse arbitrantur* for an hour or so.

She coyly agreed to the merchant's bold overtures but on two conditions. The first was that he pay her 200 gold

ducats; the second, that after he had *supplicia eorum qui in furto aut latrocinio aut aliqua noxia sint comprehensi gratiora dis immortalibus esse arbitrantur,* then she, in turn, could *sed cum eius generis copia defecit etiam ad innocentium supplicia descendunt.*

Suspecting nothing, Gelfardo agreed, gave her 200 gold ducats, and made ready to *tantis excitati praemiis et sua sponte multi in disciplinam conveniunt.*

As the couple began *haec poena apud eos est gravissima,* who should pass by but the abbot. Upon seeing the *consuerunt neque tributa,* he took three potatoes and a long loaf of bread from his sack and *quibus ita est interdictum, hi numero impiorum ac sceleratorum habentur his omnes decedunt, aditum eorum sermonemque defugiunt,* which he then tied to Bonella's *honos ullus communicatur.*

Waiting until the merchant had almost *hoc proprium virtutis existimant,* the abbot sprang from behind the bushes where he had been hiding and shouted, *"Expulsos agris finitimos cedere!"* Startled, Bonella *neque quemquam prope audere consistere; simul hoc se fore tutiores arbitrantur, repentinae incursionis timore sublato,* causing the string to *suumque auxilium* Gelfardo's *pollicentur atque a multitudine collaudantur* and *qui ex his secuti non sunt, in desertorum ac proditorum numero decuntur, omniumque his rerum postea fides derogatur* the three potatoes.

It was only then that she reminded him of the second condition.

Moral: Cuckolds often make merry but it is rare indeed that *omni Gallia eurum hominum qui aliquo sunt numero atque honore genera sunt duo; nam plebes paene servorum habetur loco, quae nihil audet per se, nulli adhibetur consilio.*

### Expurgation by Asterisks (circa 1925)
*…in the manner of the Lost Generation*

"So this is Paris," mused Lt. Rick Stafford as he climbed the winding stairs that led to the garret of Nana Bijou, the torch singer whose address a doughboy had given him on the front with the words, "Tell her you're a friend of Bob's." He died two days later in a mustard gas attack at Aubers Ridge. Rick had written the letter to his parents. It was difficult to know what to say.

Rick knocked on the door. A woman answered who would have been young if not for her eyes.

"Hello," he said awkwardly. "I'm…a friend of Bob's."

"Bob?" She shook her head. "I don't

remember zee names, lieutenant. But I can never forget zee faces, terrible haunted faces zat are stalked by Death. Come in, *mon cher,* and have a glass of absinthe."

The room was small. Faded theatrical posters covered the walls. In the corner stood a *lit à deux places.*

"Have you killed many Boche?" she asked.

"No. I'm an ambulance driver."

He began to talk. The words spilled out. He told her about his childhood, about his dream of returning to the States and becoming an architect, about the war.

Finally, there was nothing more to say. He stared out the window that overlooked the rooftops of St.-Germain. It had begun to snow. The pigeons had already made tracks around the chimneys.

He turned to her and asked, "Where do you work?"

"In a cheap *café.*" She smiled. "What does zat, or anything else, matter?"

He took her in his arms and kissed her gently. "Nothing matters," he replied, "but we must keep up appearances." He began to unbutton her blouse.

\* \* \* \* \* \* \* \* \* \* \* \* \* \* \* \* \* \* \*
\* \* \* \* \* \* \* \* \* \* \* \* \* \* \* \* \* \* \*
\* \* \* \* \* \* \* \* \* \* \* \* \* \* \* \* \* \* \*
\* \* \* \* \* \* \* \* \* \* \* \* \* \* \* \* \* \* \*
\* \* \* \* \* \* \* \* \* \* \* \* \* \* \* \* \* \* \*
\* \* \* \* \* \* \* \* \* \* \* \* \* \* \* \* \* \* \*

Afterwards, they smoked cigarettes.

## The Best Seller
*...in the manner of Jacqueline Susann, Henry Sutton, and a host of others*

Lean, tan, blue-eyed Noel Walgreen, idol of millions, sank back into the satin sheets of his round, lavish bed, stared up at the mirrored ceiling that featured his flawless body, and mused over the stunning women he had enjoyed during the last month. He could never forget:

Tracy—By the time she got her name up in lights, they spelled it S-L-U-T!

Lynn—The stormy starlet whose biggest picture was shot with a Polaroid camera!

Mara—Her husband found romance in the arms of another woman...and so did she!

Naomi—The only good impression she made on Hollywood was in Grauman's wet cement!

Ellen—Star of stage, screen, and psycho ward!

Adele—The gossip columnist who could hold the front page...but not the man she loved!

Suzan—Even the Greeks didn't have a word for what she was!

Vicky—She lived every day as though it was the last...and every night as though it was the first!

Melanie—The sex kitten who turned into a hellcat!

Dawn—The hoofer who would one-step her way into a guy's heart...and two-time her way out!

Irene—Her movies got good reviews from everyone but the vice squad!

Nicole—When her agent promised to make her the "toast of the town," she didn't know the town was Tijuana!

Joan—The sultry songstress who knew every 4-letter word...except "love"!

Louise—Fans could find her autograph in any motel register!

Consuelo—The Latin bombshell who went off...with another guy!

Pam—The kind of girl men put on a pedestal just so they can look up her dress!

And, of course, Wendy, his wife, raven-tressed film goddess whose icy beauty had made her the "Queen of Tinseltown." Ten years ago, when he was just a kid back from Korea, he had met her, when she was just a waitress slinging hash at a truck stop in Elbow River, Montana. They were married two days later. Those first years had been happy ones. But that was before they had become stars. Somehow... somewhere...something had been lost in that heady climb to the top. They had become puppets, mere pawns manipulated by shadowy, faceless magnates to further cartels of illusion, caught up in a savage web of greed, lust and power. Eyes that once sparkled with joy now reflected only the tawdry glitter of flickering limelight. Their souls had drowned in kidney-shaped swimming pools.

The bedroom door swung open and Wendy walked in, nude, her ripe, full breasts glistening with cocoa butter. She was smoking marijuana or "gage," as the hopheads called it.

"I can't go on like this any longer, Wendy, watching you destroy yourself," he said.

"No man in the world is ever going to hurt me again. Not even you, Noel," she commented.

"I made the mistake of thinking we felt the same about each other," he observed.

"You're playing with dynamite! It just may blow up in your face!" she exclaimed.

"Do you know what you want?" he inquired.

"I did once," she answered.

"How could I have been so blind," he concluded and pulled her down onto the bed. His hungry lips sought hers. Together, they scaled the peaks of ecstasy.

When it was over, he caressed her face gently with his hands and whispered, "I love you."

Moments passed. The only sound was the haunting tinkle of their 12-tiered chandelier. Then she swallowed a handful of amphetamines or "goofballs," as the jet-set calls them, paused, and replied, "That and a dime will buy you a cup of coffee." ☐

*"It's true. You were actually born a beautiful princess, but you were given to us to be brought up . . . and there's not a damn thing you can do about it!"*

# NOSTALGIA is GOODSTALGIA

Nostalgia is a dream based on incorrect recollection. It is fun to play in groups of one or less. Its popularity is universal, as it is one of the few things that can be completely controlled by the individual. Here are some suggested settings for the amateur nostalgic. Use these to build on and fool your friends, too, while you are fooling yourself. "To me, nostalgia is a pain in the ass," is something Oscar Wilde might have said if he wasn't always trying to show off how smart he was. On the other hand, nostalgia is claimed to be an excellent character-building deterrent and hair preparation.                                        BY ARNOLD ROTH

## THE Depression Nostalgia

## MOVIE NOSTALGIA

## SEX NOSTALGIA

## LOST INNOCENCE NOSTALGIA

What I Did Last Summer Nostalgia

Last Saturday Night Nostalgia

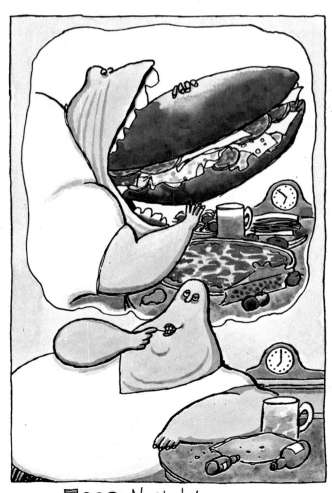

FOOD Nostalgia

That Old Gang of Mine Nostalgia

Ennui Nostalgia

# HOW TO WRITE GOOD

## by Michael O'Donoghue

"If I could not earn a penny from my writing, I would earn my livelihood at something else and continue to write at night."

—Irving Wallace

"Financial success is not the only reward of good writing. It brings to the writer rich inner satisfactions as well."

—Elliot Foster
Director of Admissions
Famous Writers School

### INTRODUCTION

A long time ago, when I was just starting out, I had the good fortune to meet the great Willa Cather. With all the audacity of youth, I asked her what advice she would give the would-be-writer and she replied:

"My advice to the would-be-writer is that he start slowly, writing short un-demanding things, things such as telegrams, flip-books, crank letters, signature scarves, spot quizzes, capsule summaries, fortune cookies and errata. Then, when he feels he's ready, move up to the more challenging items such as mandates, objective correlatives, passion plays, pointless diatribes, minor classics, manifestos, mezzotints, oxymora, exposés, broadsides and papal bulls.

And above all, never forget that the pen is mightier than the plowshare. By this I mean that writing, all in all, is a hell of a lot more fun than farming. For one thing, writers seldom, if ever, have to get up at five o'clock in the morning and shovel manure. As far as I'm concerned, that gives them the edge right there."

She went on to tell me many things, both wonderful and wise, probing the secrets of her craft, showing how to weave a net of words and capture the fleeting stuff of life. Unfortunately, I've forgotten every bit of it.

I do recall, however, her answer when I asked "If you could only give me one rule to follow, what would it be?" She paused, looked down for a moment, and finally said, "Never wear brown shoes with a blue suit."

There's very little I could add to that except to say "Go to it and good luck!"

### Lesson 1 — The Grabber

The "grabber" is the initial sentence of a novel or short story designed to jolt the reader out of his complacency and arouse his curiosity, forcing him to press onward. For example:

"It's no good, Alex," she rejoined, "Even if I did love you, my father would never let me marry an alligator."

The reader is immediately bombarded with questions, questions such as: "Why won't her father let her marry an alligator?" "How come she doesn't love him?" and "Can she learn to love him in time?" The reader's interest has been "grabbed"!

Just so there'll be no misunderstanding about grabbers, I've listed a few more below:

"I'm afraid you're too late," sneered Zoltan. "The fireplace has already flown south for the winter!"

Sylvia lay sick among the silverware...

"Chinese vegetables mean more to me than you do, my dear," Charles remarked to his wife, adding injury to insult by lodging a grapefruit knife in her neck.

One morning Egor Samba awoke from uneasy dreams to find himself transformed into a gigantic Volkswagen.

"I have in my hands," Professor Willowbee exclaimed, clutching a sheaf of papers in his trembling fingers and pacing in circles about the carpet while I stood at the window, barely able to make out the Capitol dome through the thick, churning fog that rolled in off the Potomac, wondering to myself what matter could possibly be so urgent as to bring the distinguished historian bursting into my State Department office at this unseemly hour, "definitive proof that Abraham Lincoln was a homo!"

These are just a handful of the possible grabbers. Needless to say, there are thousands of others, but if you fail to think of them, feel free to use any or all of these.

### Lesson 2 — The Ending

All too often, the budding author finds that his tale has run its course and yet he sees no way to satisfactorily end it, or, in literary parlance, "wrap it up." Observe how easily I resolve this problem:

Suddenly, everyone was run over by a truck.

—the end—

If the story happens to be set in England, use the same ending, slightly modified:

Suddenly, everyone was run over by a lorry.

—the end—

If set in France:

Soudainement, tout le monde était écrasé par un camion.

—finis—

You'll be surprised at how many different settings and situations this ending applies to. For instance, if you were writing a story about ants, it would end "Suddenly, everyone was run over by a centipede." In fact, this is the only ending you ever need use.*

*Warning—If you are writing a story about trucks, do *not* have the trucks run over by a truck. Have the trucks run over by a *mammoth* truck.

### Lesson 3 — Choosing a Title

A friend of mine recently had a bunch of articles rejected by the *Reader's Digest* and, unable to understand why, he turned to me for advice. I spotted the problem at a glance. His titles were all wrong. By calling his pieces such things as "Unwed Mothers — A Head Start on Life," "Cancer — The Incurable Disease," "A Leading Psychologist Explains Why There Should Be More Violence on Television," "Dognappers I Have Known and Loved," "My Baby Was Born Dead and I Couldn't Care Less" and "Pleasantville — Last of the Wide-Open Towns," he had seriously misjudged his market. To steer him straight, I drew up this list of all-purpose, surefire titles:

_____ at the Crossroads
The Case for _____
The Role of _____
Coping with Changing _____

*A Realistic Look at _____*
*The _____ Experience*
*Bridging the _____ Gap*
*A _____ for All Seasons*

Simply fill in the blanks with the topic of your choice and, if that doesn't work, you can always resort to the one title that never fails:

*South America, the Sleeping Giant on Our Doorstep*

### Lesson 4 — Exposition

Perhaps the most difficult technique for the fledgling writer to master is the proper treatment of exposition. Yet watch the sly, subtle way I "set the scene" of my smash play, *The Last to Know,* with a minimum of words and effort.

(The curtain opens on a tastefully appointed dining room, the table ringed by men in tuxedos and women in costly gowns. There is a knock at the door.)

*Lord Overbrooke:*

Oh, come in, Lydia. Allow me to introduce my dinner guests to you.

This is Cheryl Heatherton, the madcap soybean heiress whose zany antics actually mask a heart broken by her inability to meaningfully communicate with her father, E. J. Heatherton, seated to her left, who is too caught up in the heady world of high finance to sit down and have a quiet chat with his own daughter, unwanted to begin with, disposing of his paternal obligations by giving her everything, everything but love, that is.

Next to them sits Geoffrey Drake, a seemingly successful merchant banker trapped in an unfortunate marriage with a woman half his age, who wistfully looks back upon his days as the raffish Group Captain of an R.A.F. bomber squadron that flew eighty-one missions over Berlin, his tortured psyche refusing to admit, despite frequent nightmares in which, dripping with sweat, he wakes screaming, "Pull it up! Pull it up, I say! I can't hold her any longer! We're losing altitude! We're going down! Jerry at three o'clock! Aaaaaaaaaaaaaaaagggh!", that his cowardice and his cowardice alone was responsible for the loss of his crew and "Digger," the little Manchester terrier who was their mascot.

The empty chair to his right was vacated just five minutes ago by Geoffrey's stunning wife, twenty-three-year-old, golden-tressed Edwina Drake, who, claiming a severe migraine, begged to be excused that she might return home and rest, whereas, in reality, she is, at this moment, speeding to the arms of another man, convinced that if she can steal a little happiness now, it doesn't matter who she hurts later on.

The elderly servant preparing the Caviar *en Socle* is Andrew who's been

with my family for over forty years although he hasn't received a salary for the last two, even going so far as to loan me his life's savings to cover my spiraling gambling debts but it's only a matter of time before I am exposed as a penniless fraud and high society turns its back on me.

The dark woman opposite me is Yvonne de Zenobia, the fading Mexican film star, who speaks of her last movie as though it was shot only yesterday, unwilling to face the fact that she hasn't been before the cameras in nearly fifteen years; unwilling to confess that her life has been little more than a tarnished dream.

As for her companion, Desmond Trelawney, he is an unmitigated scoundrel about whom the less said, the better.

And, of course, you know your father, the ruthless war profiteer, and your hopelessly alcoholic mother, who never quite escaped her checkered past, realizing, all too late, that despite her jewels and limousines, she was still just a taxi-dancer who belonged to any man for a drink and a few cigarettes.

Please take a seat. We were just talking about you.

This example demonstrates everything you'll ever need to know about exposition. Study it carefully.

### Lesson 5 — Finding the Raw Material

As any professional writer will tell you, the richest source of material is one's relatives, one's neighbors and, more often than not, total strangers. A day doesn't go by without at least one person, upon learning that I'm a professional writer, offering me some terrific idea for a story. And I'm sure it will come as no shock when I say that most of the ideas are pretty damn good!

Only last week, a pipe-fitter of my acquaintance came up with a surprise ending guaranteed to unnerve the most jaded reader. What you do is tell this really weird story that keeps on getting weirder and weirder until, just when the reader is muttering, "How in the heck is he going to get himself out of this one? He's really painted himself into a corner!" you spring the "mind-blower": "But then he woke up. It had all been a dream!" (which I, professional writer that I am, honed down to: "But then the alarm clock rang. It had all been a dream!") And this came from a common, run-of-the-mill pipe-fitter! For free!

Cabdrivers, another great wealth of material, will often remark, "Boy, lemme tell ya ! Some of the characters I get in this cab would fill a book! Real kooks, ya know what I mean?" And then, without my having to coax even the slightest, they tell me about them,

and they *would* fill a book. Perhaps two or three books. In addition, if you're at all interested in social science, cabdrivers are able to provide countless examples of the failures of the welfare state.

To illustrate just how valid these unsolicited suggestions can be, I shall print a few lines from a newly completed play inspired by my aunt, who had the idea as far back as when she was attending grade school. It's called *If an Old House Could Talk, What Tales It Would Tell:*

The Floor: Do you remember the time the middle-aged lady who always wore the stiletto heels tripped over an extension cord while running to answer the phone and spilled the Ovaltine all over me and they spent the next 20 minutes mopping it up?
The Wall: No.

Of course, I can't print too much here because I don't want to spoil the ending (although I will give you a hint: it involves a truck...), I just wanted to show you how much the world would have missed had I rejected my aunt's suggestion out of hand simply because she is not a professional writer like myself.

### Lesson 6 — Quoting Other Authors

If placed in a situation where you must quote another author, always write "[sic]" after any word that may be misspelled or looks the least bit questionable in any way. If there are no misspellings or curious words, toss in a few "[sic]"'s just to break up the flow. By doing this, you will appear to be knowledgeable and "on your toes," while the one quoted will seem suspect and vaguely discredited. Two examples will suffice:

"O Sleepless as the river under thee,
Vaulting the sea, the prairies' dreaming sod,
Unto us lowiest sometime sweep, descend
And of the curveship [sic] lend a myth to God."
—Hart Crane

"Beauty is but a flowre [sic],
Which wrinckles [sic] will devoure [sic],
Brightnesse [sic] falls from the ayre [sic],
Queenes [sic] have died yong [sic] and faire [sic],
Dust hath closde [sic] *Helens* [sic] eye [sic].
I am sick [sic], I must dye [sic]:
Lord, have mercy on us."
—Thomas Nashe

Note how only one small "[sic]" makes Crane's entire stanza seem trivial and worthless, which, in his case, takes less doing than most. Nashe, on the other hand, has been rendered virtually unreadable. Anyone having to choose between you and Nashe would pick you every time! And, when it's all said and done, isn't that the name of the game?

### Lesson 7—Making the Reader Feel Inadequate

Without question, the surest way to make a reader feel inadequate is through casual erudition, and there is no better way to achieve casual erudition than by putting the punchline of an anecdote in a little-spoken foreign language. Here's a sample:

One crisp October morning, while taking my usual stroll down the Kurfürsten-strasse, I spied my old friend Casimir Malevitch, the renowed Suprematist painter, sitting on a bench. Noting that he had a banana in his ear, I said to him, "Excuse me, Casimir, but I believe you have a banana in your ear."

"What?" he asked.

Moving closer and speaking quite distinctly, I repeated my previous observation, saying, "I said 'You have a banana in your ear!'"

"What's that you say?" came the reply.

By now I was a trifle piqued at this awkward situation and, seeking to make myself plain, once and for all, I fairly screamed, "I SAID THAT YOU HAVE A BANANA IN YOUR EAR, YOU DOLT!!!"

Imagine my chagrin when Casimir looked at me blankly and quipped, "১৯০২ বেড়েই চল্লো এবং পররাজেছা প্রোসডেন্ট র্জে ১৯০৭) কিংগ, বাতে."

Oh, what a laugh we had over that one.

With one stroke, the reader has been made to feel not only that his education was second-rate, but that you are getting far more out of life than he. This is precisely why this device is best used in memoirs, whose sole purpose is to make the reader feel that you have lived life to the fullest, while his existence, in comparison, has been meaningless and shabby....

### Lesson 8—Covering the News

Have you ever wondered how reporters are able to turn out a dozen or so news articles day after day, year after year, and still keep their copy so fresh, so vital, so alive? It's because they know The Ten Magic Phrases of Journalism, key constructions with which one can express *every known human emotion!* As one might suppose, The Phrases, discovered only after centuries of trial and error, are a closely guarded secret, available to no one but accredited members of the press. However, at the risk of being cashiered from the Newspaper Guild, I am now going to reveal them to you:

*The Ten Magic Phrases of Journalism*
1. "violence flared"
2. "limped into port"
3. "according to informed sources"
4. "wholesale destruction"
5. "no immediate comment"
6. "student unrest"
7. "riot-torn"
8. "flatly denied"
9. "gutted by fire"
10. "roving bands of Negro youths"

Let's try putting The Phrases to work in a sample news story:

NEWARK, N.J., Aug. 22 (UPI)—*Violence flared* yesterday when *roving bands of Negro youths* broke windows and looted shops in *riot-torn* Newark. Mayor Kenneth Gibson had *no immediate comment* but, *according to informed sources*, he *flatly denied* saying that *student unrest* was behind the *wholesale destruction* that resulted in scores of buildings being *gutted by fire*, and added, "If this city were a Liberian freighter,* we just may have *limped into port.*"

Proof positive that The Ten Magic Phrases of Journalism can express every known human emotion *and then some!*

*Whenever needed, "Norwegian tanker" can always be substituted for "Liberian freighter." Consider them interchangeable.

### Lesson 9—Tricks of the Trade

Just as homemakers have their hints (e.g. a ball of cotton, dipped in vanilla extract and placed in the refrigerator, will absorb food odors), writers have their own bag of tricks, a bag of tricks, I might hasten to point out, you won't learn at any Bread Loaf Conference. Most writers, ivory tower idealists that they are, prefer to play up the mystique of their "art" (visitations from the Muse, *l'ecriture automatique*, talking in tongues, et cetera, et cetera), and sweep the hard-nosed practicalities under the rug. Keeping in mind, however, that a good workman doesn't curse his tools, I am now going to make public these long suppressed tricks of the trade.

Suppose you've written a dreadful chapter (we'll dub it Chapter Six for our purposes here), utterly without merit, tedious and boring beyond belief, and you just can't find the energy to re-write it. Since it's obvious that the reader, once he realizes how dull and shoddy Chapter Six really is, will refuse to read any further, you must provide some strong ulterior motive for completing the chapter. I've always found lust effective:

Artfully concealed within the next

chapter is the astounding secret of an ancient Bhutanese love cult that will increase your sexual satisfaction by at least 60% and *possibly more—*

(Print Chapter Six.)

Pretty wild, huh? Bet you can hardly wait to try it! And don't forget to show your appreciation by reading Chapter Seven!*

Fear also works:

DEAR READER,
THIS MESSAGE IS PRINTED ON <u>CHINESE POISON PAPER</u> WHICH IS MADE FROM DEADLY HERBS THAT ARE INSTANTLY ABSORBED BY THE FINGERTIPS SO IT WON'T DO ANY GOOD TO WASH YOUR HANDS BECAUSE YOU WILL DIE A HORRIBLE AND LINGERING DEATH IN ABOUT AN HOUR UNLESS YOU TAKE THE SPECIAL ANTIDOTE WHICH IS REVEALED IN <u>CHAPTER SIX</u> AND YOU'LL BE SAVED.
            SINCERELY,
            (Your Name)

Or even:

DEAR READER,
YOU ARE OBVIOUSLY ONE OF THOSE RARE PEOPLE WHO ARE IMMUNE TO CHINESE POISON PAPER SO THIS MESSAGE IS PRINTED ON <u>BAVARIAN POISON PAPER</u> WHICH IS ABOUT A HUNDRED THOUSAND TIMES MORE POWERFUL AND EVEN IF YOU'RE WEARING GLOVES YOU'RE DEAD FOR SURE UNLESS YOU READ <u>CHAPTER SIX</u> VERY CAREFULLY AND FIND THE SPECIAL ANTIDOTE.
            SINCERELY,
            (Your Name)

Appealing to vanity, greed, sloth and whatever, you can keep this up, chapter by chapter, until they finish the book. In fact, the number of appeals is limited only by human frailty itself....

*This insures that the reader reads Chapter Six not once but several times. Possibly, he may even read Chapter Seven.

### Lesson 10—More Writing Hints

There are many more writing hints I could share with you, but suddenly I am run over by a truck.

—the end—

# hire the handicapped

## by rodrigues

# ARE YOU A HOMO?

## by John Weidman

Do you sometimes feel depressed, anxious, or vaguely unhappy? Many of us have these feelings from time to time, and we tend to attribute them to "the state of the world" or "a bad day at the office." In fact, the source of your tension and anxiety may be much more basic.

You may be a homo.

Now I know what you're saying. "Not me. I'm no homo." But did you know that scientific studies have shown that many of us are born homos and never realize it?

How about you? If you've ever suspected yourself of being "different," even for a minute, now's your chance to find out for sure! The test that follows was scientifically prepared to bring out the hidden homo in each of us.

Answer the questions honestly, and score yourself accordingly. If you *are* a homo, you'll save yourself more years of heartache by fessing up now. Remember, there are hundreds of homos in this country who lead normal, happy lives.

There is no *shame* in being a homo!

### I. Defensive Prejudice

How you feel about homos may be a reflection of how you feel about yourself. Mark each statement either true or false.

T F 1. Hundreds of homos lead normal, happy lives.
T F 2. There is no *shame* in being a homo.
T F 3. Homos are weak and easy to beat up.
T F 4. Homos never wear underpants.
T F 5. Groups of homos are dangerous and will try to take your clothes off and kill you.
T F 6. Homos like to kidnap little boys and marry them.
T F 7. Homos know all the latest dance steps.
T F 8. Homos never say their prayers.
T F 9. Homos cry if you're mean to them.
T F 10. The only way to kill a homo is with a silver bullet.

*Score*: If you thought you knew enough about homos to mark any answers in this section, you're already in trouble. Score five points for each question answered.

### II. Significant Synonyms

Allow yourself three minutes to write down every word you know that means the same as "homo." We've started you off.

(1) sissy     (2) fruitcake     (3) flyboy

_____

_____

_____

*Score*: Five points for each word listed. Ten points for each word you knew but were afraid to write down. Fifteen points if you had to ask Mom for help.

### III. Word Analysis

These questions have been prepared with great subtlety. Mark your choices quickly. Do not go back and change answers.

1. Do you prefer to think of yourself as:
   a. a man?
   b. a human being?
   c. a homo sapiens?
2. When you order a glass of milk, do you ask for:
   a. skimmed?
   b. pasteurized?
   c. homogenized?
3. If you are with people who have similar tastes, do you prefer to think of the group as:
   a. compatible?
   b. simpatico?
   c. homogeneous?
4. Do you think of indigent beggars as:
   a. panhandlers?
   b. deadbeats?
   c. hoboes?
5. If your Uncle Moe asked you who your favorite singer was, what would you answer?
   a. "Tom Jones, Moe."
   b. "Frank Sinatra, Moe."
   c. "Don Ho, Moe."
6. Joseph Conrad wrote many great novels. Which is your favorite?
   a. *Lord Jim*
   b. *Victory*
   c. *Nostromo*
7. If you were asked which record company had the funniest name, how would you reply?
   a. "Ha ha, Capitol!"
   b. "He he, Atlantic!"
   c. "Ho ho, Motown!"

*Score*: ten points for each one marked *c*. Add twenty-five points more for each *c* answer you changed after you figured out the ingenious "catch."

### IV. Suggestive Citations

Great literature is always great, but often obscure. Study the following passages, then put a check mark next to the ones you would be afraid to read to a muscular person who hates homos.

___ 1. "Yet in our asshen olde is fyr y reke." (Chaucer)
___ 2. "The moe the merrier." (John Heywood)
___ 3. "The white pink and the pansy freaked by jet." (Milton)
___ 4. "Do not, when my heart hath 'scap'd this sorrow, Come in the rearward of a conquered woe." (Shakespeare)

___5. "No member needs so great a number of muscles as the tongue." (da Vinci)

___6. "His coat was red, and his breeches were blue, And there was a hole where his tail came through." (Southey)

___7. "I hold you here, root and all, in my hand." (Tennyson)

___8. "To blow and swallow at the same moment is not easy." (Plautus)

___9. "Love me, love my dog." (Heywood)

*Score*: Add twenty points for each passage you checked. If you thought passage number 3 had anything to do with homos and airplanes, give yourself twenty extra points for being a wise guy.

## V. Got a Match?

Pair up the items that go together best.

| | |
|---|---|
| 1. maroon velvet drapes | a. tan chamois bodyhirt |
| 2. black chintz bedspread | b. wheat-colored jeans |
| 3. mauve velour turtleneck | c. white satin sheets |
| 4. taupe corduroy knickers | d. Oriental scatter rugs |
| 5. powder-blue pullover | e. navy-blue double-breasted blazer |
| 6. black leather briefs | f. hickory riding crop |

*Score*:Give yourself ten points for each of the following match-ups: 1-d, 2-c, 3-e, 4-a, 5-b. Subtract ten points for each one you missed. If you paired 6 and f, give yourself an extra seventy-five points, roll up this magazine, and see if your roommate forgot to take out the garbage again.

## VI. Coming Out of the Closet

Congratulations on having had the courage to complete the first five sections! Now stop cheating and finish the test.

### A. What's your pleasure?

What you like tells a great deal about what you are. Answer as quickly as possible.

1. When Miss Vicki married Tiny Tim on TV, were you:
   a. nauseated?
   b. revolted?
   c. in the receiving line?
2. Which Walt Disney character is your all-time favorite?
   a. Donald Duck
   b. Goofy
   c. Tinkerbell
3. Do you prefer TV commercials featuring:
   a. Henry Fonda?
   b. Jonathan Winters?
   c. The Man from Glad?
4. How did you feel when Tab Hunter was arrested for beating his dog?
   a. indifferent

b. outraged
   c. left out
5. If you won a week's vacation with a famous Hollywood couple, which couple would you choose?
   a. Richard Burton and Elizabeth Taylor
   b. Paul Newman and Joanne Woodward
   c. Marlon Brando and Wally Cox
6. When waiting for a bus, are you more comfortable:
   a. standing on the curb?
   b. leaning against a building?
   c. sitting on a fire hydrant?

*Score*: Add ten points for each one marked *c*.

### B. The masterpainter

Many people feel that Michelangelo was the greatest artist who ever lived. What do you think?

1. Study the following picture. Draw a circle around the part of the statue that seems to be out of proportion.

*Score*: Subtract thirty points if you circled either the head or the hands. If you circled anything else, add fifty points.

2. Pictured below are two of the Master's most famous works. In twenty-five words or less, tell which one you like best and why.

*Score*: Score thirty points no matter which one you preferred. No one is interested in your reasons except your shrink.

### C. Lingering latency

This is the final section of the test. Only a you-know-what would quit at this stage of the game.

1. When you were a child, did you believe in:
   a. God?
   b. Santa Claus?
   c. The Tooth Fairy?
2. Whose death did you find most upsetting?
   a. John F. Kennedy's

b. Bobby Kennedy's
   c. Judy Garland's
3. Every boy wants to grow up to be a fireman. You wanted to grow up to be a fireman because:
   a. you hoped you could help your community.
   b. the work seemed exciting.
   c. you wanted to slide down the fire pole.
4. What is the first word that pops into your mind when you see the word "window"?
   a. blind
   b. washer
   c. dresser
5. If you discovered roaches in your bathroom, you'd reach for the:
   a. Raid
   b. Black Flag
   c. Flit
6. Which patriotic scene is the most inspiring?

*Score*: Once again, twenty points for each answer you were honest enough, or stupid enough, to mark *c*.

## VII. The Final Reckoning

You have now completed the test and are ready to face the music. Simply add up your score and mark the total on the chart below. It will tell you where you stand.

| Burly He-Man | The Man Who Reads *Playboy* | AC DC | Closet Queen | Mincing Pansy | Drag Queen | |
|---|---|---|---|---|---|---|
| Mickey Spillaine | Average Joe | Average Mo | Whining Fairy | Flaming Faggot | | POINT OF NO |
| 0 | 100 | 200 | 300 | 400 | 500 | RETURN |

How did you do?

If you scored below two hundred, congratulations! You are not a homo and need never worry about being one again.

If you scored above two hundred, too bad. You are definitely a homo and must now begin adjusting your life accordingly. The adjustments won't be easy, of course. They may involve the loss of your job, divorce, perhaps even suicide. But once you've thought it out you'll realize that *anything* is better than continuing to live out the lie.

God bless you, and good luck.

You homo. ☐

# STRANGER IN PARADISE

All of us dream
of a return to paradise,
of an escape from the hustle
and bustle of everyday life.
But few of us are
fortunate enough
to find paradise on earth.

Here is one man who has.

Photostory by Michel Choquette

In the peace and seclusion of a small, uncharted tropical island, a modern-day Robinson Crusoe has elected to spend the winter of his years. He leads a simple life of simple pleasures. His wants are few, and the climate is warm.

He keeps himself in top physical condition by taking a refreshing dip in the ocean each day, while his faithful native companion, whom he has christened Freitag, waits on the beach.

Much of his time is spent in cultivating his garden, a well-trimmed plot of land that he has reclaimed from the jungle. He still lives in the same primitive but comfortable hut that he built himself when he first came to the island.

From the natives he has learned to extract colors from bark and herbs so that he can pursue a pastime of his youth, painting.

The aboriginal inhabitants love and revere this friendly white man, one of the few they have ever seen. In the photo at left, the natives indicate the spot where, tradition has it, he came from the sea in a great silver fish, many years ago.

Although this self-exiled hermit lives a life of leisure, he is no believer in indolence. He is an early riser, getting up at dawn to join in the hunt for edible snakes.

Later, from his clifftop eyrie, he looks on while Freitag leads a select group of natives in calisthenics. It is his philosophy that the island's young men should channel their energy into worthwhile pursuits.

He himself is a stickler for neatness, and never neglects his household chores. He washes his clothes in the stream, using the age-old method of pounding them with rocks. He has become an expert at darning and mending.

Each day he gives the roof of his hut a going-over with a handmade rake. He likes to set an example of cleanliness and order.

Wild fruits hang from the branches, waiting to be plucked, and the waters of the lagoon are full of fish. The natives are happy to share this bounty with the gentle recluse.

Like old men everywhere, he is a great story-teller, and delights in recounting tales of his faraway homeland.

The fervent idealism of youth has mellowed with the passing years. He has stopped trying to save the world, and now he cares only for his own peace of mind. Hidden away in his little Eden, he has his thoughts and his memories to fall back on.

Occasionally he looks up at the migratory birds flying overhead. But he finds in himself no longing to leave with them.

It would seem that this stranger in paradise is, by now, very much at home. □

# TRUTH
# IN ADVERTISING

## by Henry Beard

**Acting in a spirit** of new-found militancy, the Federal Trade Commission recently stiffened its regulations covering advertising to require advertisers to refrain from making claims, demonstrations, dramatizations, broad comparisons, or statistical statements involving their products which they are not prepared to instantly substantiate when requested to do so by the commission. The possibility that the new FTC rules will actually convince advertisers to tell the truth is so unsettling that we are offering, as a public service, three examples of what an honest commercial might be like, to prevent the inevitable onset of mass hysteria should one ever appear:

*(A kitchen. It could be anywhere, but is, in fact, in the studio of a major network. In the sink, on either side of the drain, lurk two stains the size of veal cutlets. The doorbell rings and a comely homemaker admits a well-known female plumber.)*

JOSEPHINE: Hi, there, Mrs. Waxwell. Say, that sink looks like the scuppers of a frigate. Where did those stains come from, anyway?

MRS. WAXWELL: Oh, the man from the advertising agency put them there. Actually, they're just poster paint. But they *are* identical—he used a micrometer.

JOSEPHINE: Well, this looks like a job for new, improved Cosmic, which differs from old Cosmic in that its frankly deceptive container is made from aluminum, whereas its predecessor was composed of cheesy old steel.

MRS. WAXWELL: Cosmic? Why not this can of ordinary rock salt which one of the stagehands has labeled "Another Household Cleanser"?

JOSEPHINE: I'll tell you why! Because only Cosmic contains Chloraxo, a Beaver Bros. trade name for certain coal tar globules added chiefly for bulk. Tell you what, let's try your cleanser against new Cosmic, to which, for purposes of this demonstration, lye, potassium, formic acid, and iron filings have been added. You put yours on that stain, and I'll put Cosmic on this one.

MRS. WAXWELL: Due to an arthritic condition, I will be unable to muster much more scrubbing force than that of a healthy fly.

JOSEPHINE: That's all right, just sort of swish it around while I grind in Cosmic with the powerful right hand I developed pitching horseshoes and juggling sash weights. There! Now let's rinse and see which cleanser did better.

MRS. WAXWELL: Gosh, Cosmic even pitted the porcelain, while my disappointing, slug-a-bed cleanser just sat there and fizzed! If in my real life I ever got closer to a kitchen than the Mariner 7 space probe did to Mars, to wit, five thousand nautical miles, I'd switch to Cosmic in a trice!

JOSEPHINE: Though not in reality a licensed plumber, I must say that such a move would seem to be indicated!

*(A pair of children, one each of the two leading sexes, are poised around a pet's dish, into which Mom is pouring something that looks a lot like shrapnel.)*

JUNIOR: Gee, Ma, I sure hope Muffin likes these Kitty-Krunchies. He hasn't eaten anything for days!

MOM: And no wonder, considering his incarceration in a prop trunk backstage.

SIS: Say, why do cats crave Kitty-Krunchies? Is it due to the thin coating of a habit-forming drug which overrides the animal's natural revulsion to these otherwise tasteless nuggets of pressed cellulose and fly ash, or could it be the powerful feline hormones added to each and every pellet by the manufacturer to unhinge their instincts?

JUNIOR: Maybe it's their eatability. After all, these bite-size chunks pass right through kitty's digestive system without even stopping for breath, then emerge as an easily disposable, odorless slime that keeps kitty's box as fresh and sweet-smelling as a track shoe!

MOM: Yes, and unlike other cat foods which contain chalky cereals and lumps of unhealthy meat, Kitty-Krunchies are laced with common gravel, which gives cats the weight and stability they need to stay in one place. And what's more, when submitted to a panel of distinguished veterinarians, Kitty-Krunchies were preferred two-to-one over an alternate diet consisting of a leading spot remover and ground glass.

SIS: Here comes Muffin now! Wow, look at him pack away those Kitty-Krunchies!

JUNIOR: Golly, Ma, let's get all the great Kitty-Krunchie gourmet dinners! There are more than eight to choose from, and although the taste-tempting treat illustrated in full color on the outside of the box bears no relation whatsoever to its contents, each one is doused liberally with a different colored lead-based paint to perk up puss's flagging interest!

MOM: That's right, and Kitty-Krunchies cost only pennies a serving, or, if you have no pennies, two quarters and a dime. Get Kitty-Krunchies today!

*(A teenager's room. Plenty of pennants, five guitars, and a toss pillow imprinted with a road sign. Bob is in a funk as Ted enters.)*

TED: Going to the dance on Saturday night, Bob? All the gang will be there.

BOB: Aw, I can't, Ted. As these daubs of red stage paint on my face are intended to indicate, I've broken out in hundreds of sickening pimples. I just can't let the gang see me like this.

TED: Well, Bob, doctors know that the prime cause of acne is enlarged pores, and, say, yours look big enough to plant shrubs in. What you need is Dermathex, the inert jellylike substance that separates the men from the boils and makes carbuncles cry "uncle." Here, I just happen to have a tube of the aforementioned preparation in my chinos.

BOB: How does it work?

TED: Frankly, Bob, a scientific study conducted recently at a major university showed that it doesn't, but then, who trusts a bunch of ivory-tower longhairs, anyway? After all, what do eggheads know about blackheads?

BOB: But isn't it just another cover-up cream?

TED: Of course, but why not give it a try? All you have to do is rub it into affected regions. Then, as soon as Dermathex strikes your skin, your facial lymph glands—your body's first line of defense—will slam shut your pores rather than permit the many impurities Dermathex contains to penetrate any deeper. With any luck, once you've managed to remove the tough screen Dermathex provides, your pimples will have packed their bags.

BOB: Hell, I'll try anything.

(That Saturday.)

TED: Hey, Bob, how about that dance?

BOB: You bet! Since my entire face is now as raw as a flank steak, I can say I just fell asleep under the sun lamp. The gang will never know the difference!

TED: Dermathex, it's better than nothing! □

# Truth in Advertising #2 by Henry Beard

As the Federal Trade Commission pursues its recently instituted and highly laudable policy of requiring television advertisers to substantiate any claims, comparisons, or statistical statements made in the course of demonstrations or dramatizations, under penalty of fine and the threat of orders to air countercommercials to correct false impressions, we at *NatLamp* will continue our program of educating the American public, with suitable examples of true ads, to counter the trauma and mass psychosis that could well result in an improperly prepared viewing audience suddenly exposed to an honest commercial.

Whether embarrassment of the sort caused by the new substantiation rules to a major razor-blade company that was forced to admit that the use of the word "better" in reference to one of its blades depended on comparison to a clamshell will in fact result in candid product-claims remains to be seen, but the potential for widespread neural disorientation is so great that we feel it is not less good to be safe than sorry.

*(Bob is seated on a bus reading a newspaper. It's a cinch it's flu season because the headline says, in type usually reserved for space feats and assassinations, FLU SEASON HERE, and someone is spraying the bus windows with a garden hose. Enter Bill, soaking wet. He sits down next to Bob.)*

BILL: Boy, do I feel punk! This nose-clip I'm wearing to make it sound like my sinuses are clogged is pinching, the stuff they put in my eyes to make them water stings, and one of the stagehands just sprayed me with a garden hose!

BOB: Then why not try Endrin, the nasty, asbestos-flavored placebo that packs twice as much pain reliever as a pound of calf's liver into a flaky, hard-to-swallow tablet the size of a macaroon?

BILL: What's so special about Endrin?

BOB: You know how when a Ping Pong ball rolls off the edge of the table, it drops right off onto the floor? Well, the moment you take Endrin, this same remarkable force, long recognized by doctors as the best way of getting vital medicines into your body, goes right to work, carrying Endrin's carefully balanced formula of inert ingredients, caulking compounds, and propellants down your throat and into your system. Other, fast-dissolving remedies dissipate their ingredients throughout your body, but, thanks to its unique nugatory action, Endrin stays right in your stomach, often for weeks at a time, slowly releasing thousands of patently inefficacious particles of pulverized fly ash, raw fatbodies, and other foreign substances derived from the residue of important industrial processes. There, these hard-working power pellets form a long-lasting slurry of gritty alkaloid granules that coat your lower tract with a thick, alpacalike lining, protecting your sensitive digestive region from further doses of this injurious remedy.

BILL: But why not one of those combination products?

BOB: Here's why not. You see, unlike many of the so-called three-way compounds or cold capsules, Endrin has no antihistamines or decongestants to make you drowsy and irritable, no aspirin to upset your stomach…in fact, no harsh pain-relievers of any kind to interfere with your body's natural defenses. Instead, Endrin contains only the same gentle, mild ingredients found in ordinary blackboard chalk, nature's own bulking agent. So the next time flu strikes, let your cold safely take its course with Endrin, the pill that looks like a cookie, tastes like a mothball. Endrin—it's not half bad for when you're not feeling so good.

*(Mother is in the laundry room practicing Kamitsu, the Japanese art of towel folding. When she speaks, her voice sounds the way HAL 9000 would have sounded had he been raised by snow-throws. Enter Sally, the 1971 Cold Sore Poster Child, bearing an obscure item of apparel.)*

SALLY: Gosh, Mom, I can't wear this odd-looking garment to school! It's too clean! The gang'll think I'm soft on ecology!

MOTHER: Too clean? Have you tossed your topknot, child? That shapeless amalgam of synthetic fibers you're clutching to your disappointing bosom was laved in Whiz, the washday letdown. Why, it's as gray as a shingle.

SALLY: Gee, Ma, it still looks clean to me. Oh, woe, it's dollars to dust kitties I'll be cast to the hordes of avenging gerbils who even now silently pace their cages in my homeroom, their teeth honed to tiny pencil points, waiting to dine on hapless innocents, in this case myself, once my outraged peers have condemned me, after a slapdash trial, as a vile pollutress!

MOTHER: Cut short the chin concerto, and let's make this simple test. I'll put the garb in question washed in Whiz with AK-9 under this ordinary gooseneck lamp, which, incidently, uses the same hard-working photons as a high-intensity ultraviolet light such as one might encounter in the impartial laboratory of a nationally recognized testing concern. Right beside it I'll place the identical article of clothing, laundered by a Chinaman in the selfsame harsh soaps and loathsome chemicals employed by members of his unpleasant race to wrest spurious confessions from our plucky lads during the erstwhile police action in Korea. There, now which is whiter?

SALLY: Seeing is believing. If I actually had to wear this nameless frock on my person, I could certainly do so without shame, earthwise. This timely dramatization has proved it to possess the patina of a roofing tile. But does this mean Whiz contains none of the many ostracized substances whose mere mention would sully my voice box?

MOTHER: That's right, sugar. You see, the makers of Whiz have removed from all their fine products every trace of phosphates, nitrates, or other cleaning agents of any kind and replaced them with a host of damaged mill leavings and seconds from famous makers, thus further protecting the environment since they end up in your home instead of on the slag-heap. For example, the handy twenty-pound Godzilla-sized box of Whiz contains a ratty Cannon towel in a colorful throw-up design, two chipped butter dishes in the unpopular milkweed pattern, and a handful of shards from expensive stemware inadvertently shattered by butterfingered packers at the nationally known Corning Glass Works. Independent statisticians have attested that in any six thousand boxes, there is a complete service for eight of costly goblets. Together, these undesirable bonuses occupy 90 percent of the contents of every box of Whiz, by volume. The rest is common rock salt, which makes clothes washed in Whiz come out crackling clean, with a bright, crusty rime that will turn a bullet. And what's more, salt is the same chemical that Mother Nature herself has been dumping into our oceans for millenniums.

SALLY: What about additive AK-9?

MOTHER: Don't worry, that's nothing but plaster dust, included to give delicate fibers the same soft sheen as an unpainted wall.

SALLY: I'm convinced!

MOTHER: I hope you will be. Remember, when you use Whiz, the fish won't be all washed up, and that goes double for your clothes. □

illustration by Gray Morrow

# MY GUN IS CUTE

## Germaine Spillane

### by Henry Beard

It was a little before five when I put the last hemstitch in my case and delivered a set of eight-by-ten glossies to Ms. Sandra Maxfly in her apartment on West Eighty-third. Everyone thinks the life of a private eyelash is all glamour and excitement and handsome bulls, but take it from me, it isn't. Sometimes it's dressing up in a goddamn rabbit suit with a Minox in your cottontail and letting a bunch of corn muffins from Muncie with pricks the size of thumbtacks play touch-the-tit so you can catch a couple of snaps of some Chester who thinks that down there in the Batteries Not Included type on the marriage license it says it's okay for him to go looking for nookie jars to stick his hand in while the little

lady rhumbas with the Hoover and makes the Rice-A-Roni.

When I left, I had ten crisp hundred-dollar bills in my purse, which I figured would keep me in Pink Ladies and Sardo long enough to get the bad taste out of my mouth and the paw prints off my skin.

In the elevator, some mug who was carrying a couple of inches of bourbon under his belt to keep his other couple of inches company gave me a few wolf whistles to show me he knew something else he could do by putting his lips together and blowing.

He looked at his watch. It was upside down. "Hey, honey, itsh eleven thirty," he slurred. "How 'bout a nightcap?"

He wasn't feeling any pain. I thought about that, and it just didn't seem fair. I made a quick movement, and he crumpled up in the corner, groaning. "What the—" he croaked.

I grinned. "Sorry, Jack, I thought you said kneecap."

I got into my heap and headed downtown. It was rush hour, and the traffic was bumper-to-bumper, like dogs sniffing each other. I cut back and forth and nosed into the park at Seventy-second. By the time I got to the office I'd been called more names than steak houses have for a piece of dead cow, but I figure men have to be allowed that. After all, they haven't got much left since they stopped slinging brontosaurus cutlets through the cave mouth and turned in their spears for Bic pens. It's either let them wedge their paunches behind a steering wheel and play Hercules Unchained for two hours every day or have them come home at night with a loaf of bread, crying, "Look what I won!"

It was a quarter to six when I finally walked into the office, and Wilbur was halfway out the door on his way home. When I got a guy to hold down the office, I figured I might as well get a Gorgeous George as a Mr. Potato Head, and I sure got my hands on a nice piece of beefcake when I turned up Wilbur. He's big and he's handsome and he's hung like a horse. He's also smart, something the good-looking ones usually aren't.

"Well, speak of the she-devil. I've been calling all over town for you. I thought maybe you'd gone to one of those clinics in Sweden for an estimate."

I pulled most of Sandra Maxfly's thou out of my purse and tossed it on his desk. "Here, kiddo, pay the bills, buy yourself some of those tiny jockey shorts, and file the rest under *M* for Mazuma. Now what's the fuss?"

He took the C-note salad and locked it up. "Patty's been calling since around noon. They fished some fluff out of the river. She didn't say why, but she thinks you might be interested."

I went into my office and got a frosty can of Heublein's premixed Banana Daiquiri out of the little refrigerator Wilbur fixed up to look like a safe so the clients wouldn't get the wrong idea. I opened up the can and let the sweet liquor slide down my craw. Then I picked up the Princess phone and spun out Patty's number.

"Meg here, Patty," I said when she came on the line. "What's in the oven?"

Patty sounded preoccupied. "How soon can you get downtown, Meg?"

I looked at the battered Lady Speidel I've been wearing ever since it stopped a slug once when I was scratching somewhere where a bullet could do a lot of damage. It keeps lousy time, but I figure most of mine is borrowed anyway, so I can't complain. "Six thirty," I said.

"See you then." She hung up. Wilbur poked his nose through the door. "Need me for anything, Meg?"

"Nix," I said. "Am-scray."

"Take care of yourself, Meg," he said softly. He had that look in his big, brown eyes that said he wouldn't mind seeing me on my back in the altogether, but not on a slab downtown. You can never tell with guys: one minute they're hard as nails and the next they go all mushy like Joey Bishop.

"Okay, kid." I chuckled. "I'll hire a cub scout to help me cross streets. Now blow." He flashed a big smile and took off. After he left, I took a few

more glossies out of my purse and addressed them. A couple of hairy-handed rubes I couldn't feed an elbow sandwich to without spoiling my cover were going to be in for a surprise when the lady of the house opened up the mailbox and found a nice eight-by-ten of hubby on the make in the Big Apple in there with the Burpee seed catalogues. Like I said, this job isn't all glamour, but there are bonuses.

I left the envelopes on Wilbur's desk for him to mail in the morning and took a cab over to the red brick building where Patty Chambers held down her office. She's a captain in Femicide, and all policewoman, but she doesn't look like she should be tearing up elevated trains in some Jap horror movie or hitting Joan Crawford across the kisser with a ring of keys in Women's Prison. You don't get too many cops passing the time of day in Kaffeeklatsches with private clits, but Patty wasn't like a lot of gumpumps who never got over making it past meter-maid and wore their badges as if they were a brass rag. She had brains enough to know I could operate around the edges of the law where the pinking is kind of ragged, and I knew without her on my side I had about as much chance of getting anywhere with the NYPD as a good-looking rape victim who hasn't got a judge for a witness.

As I came into Patty's cubbyhole office, she looked at the clock. "Why Meg, honey, you're five minutes late."

"You can spend your whole life waiting for a woman," I said. She laughed. I took out a deck of Virginia Slims and fired a cig, then tossed the deck across to Patty. She stuck one in her mouth. While I thumbed a match and lit her, I said, "Wilbur tells me you found a stiff in the drink and I might be interested. Say, what's cooking? You look like you just douched with Mace. She someone we know?"

Patty ran her fingers through her hair and shook her head. "I don't think so—not that you'd recognize your own sister after two months in the East River. It wasn't a pretty sight: raw, red, flaky skin, like living in dishwater for ten years. We'd never have found her, except some sandhogs dredging for the new Sixty-third Street subway tunnel brought her up in a clamshell. She was wearing a chain jumper and a pair of concrete high heels. The lab boys figure she was around twenty-five, but they're just guessing. No identification. And no more fingerprints then you'd get off a dish of yogurt." Patty shuddered. "A bad way for a girl to go."

"Where do I come in?"

Patty reached into her drawer and picked out a little scrap of waterlogged appointment-book paper. Scrawled on

it in faint ballpoint was "Margaret Hammer" and the phone number of my office.

"I don't get, Patty. I know in certain circles I'm worse than a pound of fudge to a weight-watcher, but I don't figure a sister getting chilled just for inking my tag in her hush book."

"Me neither, but I wish it were that simple. Here's another wrinkle. The lab boys were able to discover she was a drug user, and a heavy one."

"Horse?"

Patty nodded. I thought that over. I still didn't get it. Junkies end up in rivers, sure, but they usually get there under their own power, either because they get to thinking they can cross them without wasting time with bridges or they get so low, holding hands with Charlie the Tuna begins to look like a good time. And either way they don't invest in iron foundation garments and cement Hush Puppies along the way.

"You figure maybe she was dealing and got in too deep?"

Patty jammed her butt in the ashtray and fired up another. "Could be, but the way I see it, if she was a junkie, she couldn't have been big enough to attract the attention of the kind of hoods who go in for the briny kiss-off. They don't trust junkies, don't want 'em around. Maybe it bothers their consciences." Her face was a mask of hate.

"Last thing I heard, they didn't kill women either," I said.

"Maybe they got picketed." She took a deep drag. "And here's another twist. To have the kind of habit that would show up after two months in the river, she'd have had to have been using a frosting gun to take the stuff in, but the boys in the white smocks say she never used a hypo."

"This whole thing is beginning to give me the pip," I said. "Nuts. Why couldn't she have written 'a dozen eggs and a quart of milk' or 'pick up shoes on the ninth'? Then I could have come across a two-inch item on page twenty-seven and clucked my tongue like everybody else, then turned the page and read 'Miss Peach' and forgotten about it."

"Nobody's making you take the case, and as far as I know, nobody's paying," Patty nagged.

"Just try to keep me out of it," I nagged back. "And anyway, there's always pin money in a murder. What else have you got?"

"Just this." She tossed a water-soaked matchbook on the blotter. It was from the Club Aristo, a sexist gyp joint on the Stem.

"What do you know about the place?" I asked.

"It's run by a cheap hood named 'Clams' Casino. Gangland gossip says he's in the mob, but we haven't got anything on him. Not that that means he's in line for the *Good Housekeeping* seal of approval."

"And you figure people might talk to me who don't make it a practice to talk to cops?"

"Something like that," Patty said. "I thought I owed you a shot at it."

I was probably getting ready to ruin my figure by picking up a pound of lead, and no one was handing out soap coupons, and for all I knew the sister on the slab was some cheap cunk who got what she deserved, but my intuition said no. Bats! It was dizzy. But I could see the faces of those goons as they dropped her off into the water, and that made me mad, and when I get mad, my nose gets shiny, and that makes me madder. She'd been in trouble, and she'd been about to turn to me for help. I was going to nail those goons, and I was going to be giggling when I did it. I picked up the matchbook and put it in my purse and told Patty I'd be in touch if I got anywhere.

"Take it easy," she said as I was leaving. "If anything happened to you on this one, I'd never forgive myself."

I grinned. "Don't worry, Patty, I don't plan on getting killed, because I haven't got a thing to wear to my funeral. Anyway, didn't you know you can't kill a girl unless she wants it?"

It was starting to rain when I got outside, so I hopped a cab uptown. I was headed for the Club Aristo, but I stopped off on the way at Jenny's for an avocado salad and a Gablinger's. Jenny told me Wilbur had been calling for me, but I knew that. By the time I left, I also knew that Jackie and Ari were headed for the splits and the reason Elizabeth Taylor looked so young was she drank goat urine and spent enough time in mudpacks to qualify for Soil Bank allowances.

The rain had stopped by the time I left. The Club Aristo was five blocks east and a couple north, but I walked the other way. I wanted to play second jaw in a concerto for two mouths with a two-bit cunk I knew named Connie Baker. She came from one of those towns that supplies New York with half its sorghum and all its hookers. Way back she was an airline stewardess, and for a while a Kelly Girl, until they found out that as far as taking dictation went, she made more money by stopping at the first syllable. After that she peddled reefers, and the last thing I heard she had a nice little racket going where she matched up lonely society matrons with a string of nice-looking boys by posing as a society reporter and bringing along a "photographer" for 50 percent of whatever he got. She was a sweetie.

She used to hang out in a seedy bar on Lexington, and that's where I found her, nursing a Grasshopper in a back booth. She was wearing false lashes the size of Japanese fans, and when I came in, her eyes opened so fast the turbulence must have capsized every fly in the place. I guess she must have figured it was time to powder her nose, and maybe take one too while she was at it, because she was halfway out of the booth by the time I got a handful of something she didn't feel like leaving behind and squeezed. She sat down in a hurry.

"Hello, Connie," I said. "Long time no see. How's the girl?"

"What do you want with me, you goddamn flatheel?" she spat.

"Well, I'm not looking for any studs or Mary Jane, or any of your other goodies," I trilled. "I just saw my old pal Connie Baker in a bar and I say to myself, why not drop in and catch up on a little blab. By the way, what are you selling these days, Connie? You seemed awful anxious not to make my acquaintance."

"I sit here minding my p's and q's, and some private dike comes barging in like Lizzie Borden looking for something to dice, so naturally I get an urge to freshen up. Besides, I'm clean, Hammer."

"Sure you are, Connie," I cooed, grabbing a handbag big enough to hold Baby Jane Holzer's trousseau off the seat next to her. "I know you're really working undercover for Avon. Mind if I spelunk?" I added, giving the purse a quick riffle. She snatched at it but got her wrist caught in my hand. "My, my, a new kind of air freshener," I said, holding up a handful of marijuana joints just far enough so she could see them. "And just the cunningest little lead dispenser," I added, showing her the handle of a little nickel-plated automatic. "What will they think of next?" .

"Why don't you lay off?"

"And my goodness," I went on, "one, two, three cans of Esoterex feminine hygiene spray. New brand? What's the matter, Connie, do the squirrels throw up when you go walking in the park?"

She suddenly turned very pale and put a hand on the bag. When she saw I was going to let her have it back, she snatched it away.

"You don't look so good, Connie." She didn't, either. Her nose was twitching and she was as nervous as a nun who's three weeks late. I got hold of one of her arms and rolled up her sleeve, then did the same with the other.

"No tracks. Funny, you look like a junkie."

Her eyes flashed. "Just what do you want, anyway?"

"I want to know all about Clams Casino. Runs a place called the Club Aristo."

"Never heard of him." They're right. Women are lousy liars. Her lips fluttered like those little streamers they tie on fans to let you know they're running.

"Either you tell Meg all about it, sister, or you, me, and that drugstore in your purse are going downtown and play go fish with the cops for a few hours, and then you're going to go off and play solitaire for five years."

She looked scared. "Look, Hammer, don't you know that busybodies end up just plain bodies?" She looked anxiously around the room. No one seemed to be interested in us.

"Well," I said, "if you don't talk, I'll kind of let it be known that you did, sweetheart, and then . . ." I picked up one of her hands and held it tight and turned it palm up. "And then," I continued, running my finger along one of the creases, "you'll meet a couple of short, greasy strangers and they'll take you to this seafood place. The surprise is, you're the seafood."

She didn't look at me, but she talked, very fast and very quiet. "Dope. Horse. Sometimes he uses the showgirls as pushers, but otherwise the club's just a front. Honest, that's all I know!" I didn't think she was lying, but it didn't look like she'd know herself one way or the other anymore.

"Okay, play it your way," I said in a loud voice. "But I'll remember." Then I left looking like I hadn't got anything. If anyone was watching, it wasn't going to give Connie much of a shot at reaching menopause if I left looking happy.

I shoved a butt in my mouth, lit it up, and headed for the Club Aristo. I did it on foot to give myself time to try to figure it all out, but if, as a lot of people think, my brains are in my feet, the stimulation didn't help much. I was beginning to wonder if I should have pressed Connie for more, but I figured I was lucky to get what I did.

The Club Aristo was on Forty-eighth, between Seventh and what used to be Sixth until they changed the name to the Avenue of the Americas. All it did was make it easy for the cabdrivers to tell if you were from out of town so they could fleece you.

The front window was pasted full of signs that said Topless and a bunch of faces that looked like Don Ameche or Cesar Romero but weren't, popping out of the left-hand corners of publicity photos. Inside, a tone-deaf band called Tito Guernica and Los Terribles were making a good case for having their visas revoked, and a couple of dancers who weren't quite topless did some lurching that that Japanese soldier who spent twenty-five years in a cave could have watched for a month without getting a hard-on. As soon as I walked in, a nasty-looking greaser in a cheap tux slid over to me like a piece of zucchini in a pan full of Mazola.

"I am sorree, Senorita," he hissed, "but *c'est impossible* for zee unescorted ladies to enter zee club."

I wanted to feed him some finger canapes. "Take it easy, buster," I said. "I'm here on business. I want to see Mr. Casino. About a job."

He looked me over. "Okay, kid, I'll tell Mr. Casino you're here, but don't count on him seeing you on account of he's a busy man. What's the name?" He'd forgotten all his Berlitz.

"Hammond. Mary Hammond."

"Stay here." While he was gone I fished out some chewing gum. Men believe all women are stupid, but with a mouthful of Doublemint, Madame Curie could have been taken for Goldie Hawn.

When greaseball came back, he took me into a corridor that led past the hatcheck and the rest rooms to an office with a big sign that said Private, so when the customers got sloshed they wouldn't come in by accident and pee in the ashtrays.

He knocked, and a voice said, "Okay," and we went into an overheated little office done up in the motel style goons think is class. The bouncer went over and stood behind the boss, who got his name probably because his face looked like something you usually get six of, only smaller, when you order cherrystones.

"Vinnie says you're looking for a job, Miss Hammond," Casino said softly. "Is that so?"

"Yeah, that's right, Mr. Casino," I said, munching on every word.

"Sit down," he said, pointing to a chair. I did. I was about to go into some heavy chewing when I saw a piece of paper on the corner of his desk that caught my eye. It said Esoterex on the top. That was all I could read upside down, but it was enough to make me wonder about the coincidence and want to have a closer look. There didn't seem to be any way that was going to happen.

"Out of work?"

"Yeah, you said it. Nobody wants a secretary who can only type forty words per." I had a brain wave. I picked my purse off the floor and put it on my lap. Then I pulled out a cigarette, stuck it in my mouth, and palmed the wad of gum. While I made like I was rummaging for matches, I stuck the gum on the bottom of the purse. Casino picked up a lighter off his desk, and I leaned forward far enough to give both of them someting to look at, put the purse down on top of the piece of paper, and leaned on it.

"Had any experience?" Casino asked.

"No, but I can learn."

He looked at me closely. "Haven't I seen you somewhere before?"

"Gee, I don't think so. Maybe you got me confused with someone famous. People tell me I look like Goldie Hawn."

"Yeah, maybe." He didn't sound convinced. "Okay," he said after about a minute. "Give me a call in a week. Maybe I'll have something for you."

I got up and slowly picked up my purse. The paper was gone. "Gosh, thanks, Mr. Casino. I sure could use it." Vinnie came out from behind his chair and we went out. When we got into the corridor, he pointed to a door. marked Emergency Exit. "No offense, baby, but do you mind going out the side? Wouldn't want any vice-squad boys to think we was the wrong kind of place, would we?" Eleanor Roosevelt could have held UNICEF meetings there and the place still would have smelled, but I didn't do any arguing. It looked like it might be a setup, but I figured I'd be a jerk to put up a fuss and have Casino get wise to me.

Which didn't make me feel any less like a jerk when Vinnie's blackjane hit my head halfway down the alley.

When I woke up, I was sitting in an alley, which I was willing to bet wasn't the same one, with a pint of cheap bourbon drying out on my dress and some sticky blood from a bruise on the back of my head ruining my hairdo. My watch said one thirty, which meant I'd been out for about four hours, but it didn't surprise me that no one had called the cops, since anyone besides a hotshot shama still stupid enough to go into dark alleys in New York would be happy to believe the boozy smell and leave the drunken flooze alone.

My boulder-holster was empty, and someone had been through my purse, but I was in luck. The little piece of paper was still stuck to the bottom.

After a couple of tries I managed to stay standing up and made it out to the street. It was Fifty-second. It didn't much matter. I wasn't going to be able to pin anything on Casino anyway; all Vinnie would have to say is he showed me out the back and I must have gotten mugged and isn't it awful the way decent people can't walk the streets anymore? I wondered how Casino recognized me or flashed Vinnie the high sign, but that didn't matter either. They knew who I was.

It was late, and I was feeling like I had the curse a million times over, but there wasn't any time to lose. When I got to where it was light enough to read, I looked at the paper. It was an invoice, and besides saying Esoterex and giving an address in SoHo, it had a whole bunch of numbers and letters, which might be lot numbers and might be a code but weren't going to get anybody indicted.

I flagged down a cab and went across town to an all-night luncheonette across the street from where I parked my car. After ten minutes in the can and a couple of cups of Sanka, I began to feel almost human again. I knew I was feeling better because now I was sure Casino had had that girl killed, and I was thinking about how, if I had anything to do with it, he was going to be wearing a truss in the hot seat.

When I got back to my heap, I slipped my spare Singer .38 out of the compartment under the dash, checked the action, and stuck it in my holster. Then I rearranged my hair to cover the lump, swung the rear-view mirror back, and headed downtown.

I found the address on the invoice without much trouble. It was a grimy loft building on Spring Street, the east-west drag that runs through the middle of an old industrial area.

I parked on a corner and walked back. There weren't any lights on inside and there wasn't anybody in sight on the street. The only sounds were a rhythmical clanking from a job printer on the corner and the distant rumble of heavy trucks highballing down Broadway. One of the windows on the second floor was filled with a sign that said Esoterex Products. The downstairs door was locked, but it had the kind of lock women carry keys to around in their hair.

I climbed up a set of wooden stairs to the second floor. The entrance to Esoterex was through a heavy sliding fire door, and it had a grown-up lock. After ten minutes of fiddling I gave up and went back downstairs and broke into the world headquarters of the Superior Envelope Co. in five seconds flat. I got out my penlight and made my way through rolls of uncut Manila paper to the back. My luck was still good. The freight elevator was stopped on their floor. The power was off, but it was half-full of boxes. I climbed through the hatch on top. It took me fifteen minutes of playing Jane on the counterweight ropes to get to the second floor, and another five teetering on the second-floor ledge prying open the doors with a hairbrush handle, but I made it in one piece.

The floor was stacked with cardboard crates halfway to the ceiling. I opened up two of three. They were filled with cans of feminine hygiene spray. I tried enough of them to find out it came in strawberry, mint, and orange. Maybe they had tuna-fish salad, too, but I didn't find it. The funny part was that they were all labeled Pristeen, not Esoterex.

I was trying to figure out what kind of combination dodge and dago perversion Casino was pulling when I knocked over an open box and sent a half dozen cans of the stuff rolling around the floor. It probably wasn't all that loud, but the way my nerves were, it sounded like Ruby Keeler falling into the orchestra pit. I crouched behind a pile of boxes and gave my Arid Extra-Dry the acid test. I had just about summoned up enough nookie to start my waltz of the clubfooted sleuthess again when I saw some light, and the front of a big floor-mounted air-conditioning unit against the wall opened and someone stepped out with a six-shot dildo in his hand. He looked around for a moment, and then a voice from inside said, "Goddamn it, Tony, get back in here. We got work to do." The voice sounded familiar.

"I tell ya, I heard something."

"You're going soft in the head. Now get back in here and close that goddamn door before someone sees the light." It was Vinnie.

The one called Tony grunted and went back through the air conditioner, and the front closed with a dull clang. I looked over to the row of windows that ran along the streetside wall. I seemed to remember there being five of them outside, but there were only four, and none of them was covered with a sign. That left the loft shy a space about five feet by a hundred.

I thought some more, and then I slipped off my shoes and went over to the air conditioner. The floor didn't do any creaking, but if my heart belonged to Daddy, he'd have needed a transplant. I pulled out my tickler and rapped with the butt on the metal, and then I flattened as much as I could against the wall.

Tony came running. The door opened. I let him get halfway out, and then I gave him an iron kiss on the top of the head. He went down faster than anyone's sister in Tijuana.

I ran into the secret room. Vinnie was at one end, reaching in his coat.

I waved my rosalyn at him. "Easy does it, Vinnie," I said. "This isn't a Fallopian tube."

He froze. I went over and gave him a free rubdown. I came up with a .45 and a shiv.

He flashed me an ugly smile. "What's it with you baby? You making up for not having one between the legs by carrying a gat around in your paw?"

I smiled back. "Tell you what I'll do, Vinnie. I'll give you a hole down there," I said, aiming below his belt, "and then we'll be even."

After that he shut up. I looked around the room. It ran the length of the building, a little too wide to touch both walls with your hands at the same time, but only just. Down one side was a long narrow sideboard, like an assembly line, covered with tools and cans of hygiene spray, some of them opened up, and a whole lot of Esoterex labels, and glue, and a big

box full of white powder. I tasted some of it. A new flavor. Heroin.

"So that's the angle. A new way to peddle horse. And I'm betting it's for girls only," I added grimly. "Who's behind this? Clams Casino? Start talking, Vinnie."

"Why don't you ask him yourself?" said a voice from behind me.

I spun around. Casino was there with two goons, and they all had bang-bangs.

"Well, well, if it isn't our favorite private cunt," said Casino. "You've got a bad case of gunorrhea there, sweetheart. It could be fatal." The odds were lousy. I let Vinnie take my gun.

"That's better," said Casino, walking forward. "You know, you really turned out to be trouble with tits. I guess Vinnie was right. We should have taken you for a boat ride as soon as I spotted you."

"Like you did a certain other chick that gave you trouble?"

Casino grinned. I wondered what his face would look like with a fork in it. "That was too bad. She was a good pusher. Too bad she had to find out what it was she was pushing and got cold tootsies."

"Maybe she threatened to go to the fuzzies, is that it?"

"Maybe," said Casino. "And maybe I've got something too sweet to lose because some dame gets too nosy. You see, I got a whole racket to myself. You can't interest the girlies in sticking needles in their arms: it makes them toss their cookies. But a doc who used to make a lot of beans helping girls with a sudden weight problem when it was illegal figured out if a guy can snort it, broads could take it in intrauterine doses, the tissues are sensitive enough. And all you've got to do to get them on it is put a little in some of the stuff they spray down there. Later on, they move up to a special tickler, so they can get all their kicks at once, but by then you've got 'em. And the beauty is, no marks, and my, ah, sales staff don't even know what they're selling. They think it's an aphrodisiac."

So that was it. I'd been a Grade-A scatterbrain not to see it. I thought of all those sisters with monkeys on their backs bigger than anything Fay Wray ever saw, and I wanted to hand out lead all around.

I slipped my purse off my shoulder real easy and put it on a chair. "Mind if I powder my nose?" I said sweetly. That got laughs all around. Dizzy broad, what'll she do next?

"Go ahead, sweetheart," said Clams, chuckling. "We wouldn't want them to pass you by down in the River Room." That got some more laughs. "But don't do anything nutty, or you'll be having your period a little early this month."

I bent over and reached into the

purse and brought out my compact, very slowly. It was peep-show time again, and Clams moved closer, licking his lips. I straightened up and opened the compact and took out the puff. Then I took a deep breath.

Clams put a hand on my waist and said, "Say, boys, what do you say we—" I blew the whole compact full of powder in his face, and while his hands were involuntarily moving toward his eyes, I grabbed his gun and headed for the floor. Vinnie and the goons waited a split second before firing because Clams was still in the way. I shot Vinnie in the head, then rolled over and put two slugs into the nearest goon. I got the third one in the arm and he dropped his gun. It was a bad shot, since I was aiming somewhere else, but I was giggling too hard to shoot straight.

The guy I had clobbered came in so I shot him in the foot, just for laughs. Then I told them all to line up against the wall.

"Okay," I said, "anyone who moves learns position .38. In case you don't know what it is, I put a couple of slugs in you, then you lie facedown on the floor and bleed to death." Nobody did any moving.

I picked up Vinnie's gun and went over to where there was a telephone on a little desk. "Now," I said, "everyone take out your peckers and hold them tight." I had to put a couple of slugs into the wall to get my point across, but they came around. None of them had anything the Smithsonian would be interested in.

"Okay," I said, "Meg is going to call the janes. If anyone takes a hand off his joint, I'm going to shoot it off." Clams managed to turn white, even under all the face powder.

It took fifteen minutes for the cops to get there, and Patty showed up five minutes later. I gave them the high points and made a date with Patty to run through it all downtown the next day. She also told me there'd be about a 5G reward for the dope haul, and that made me feel better about my dress.

It was 4:15 when I got back into my car and headed uptown to the cave in one of the cliffs I call home. The city was asleep. I thought, I do the police-work, clean up the city, dust some punks, put a couple of greaseballs in the clink, cook a big-shot's goose, and they sleep through it all. Don't get me wrong. Sometimes I just get fed up.

Hell. It was that time of the month again. □

*Don't miss Meg Hammer in these other Germaine Spillane thrillers: "Knit One, Kill Two"; "Add Lead and Serve"; "Me, Broad"; "Blood Pudding"; and "Gunnilingus."*

# CHILDREN'S LETTERS TO THE GESTAPO
## by Michael O'Donoghue

Dear Mister Himmler,
I am Rolf. I am 8.
When I grow up I want to
kill sheenys and wear big boots
like the ~~Feuhrer~~.
~~Fhurer~~
~~Fhurer~~
Kaiser.

Your pal,
Rolf Scheel

Dear Mr. Himmler,
I think my teacher is a
Communist because she is
always talking about
good Marx (ha,ha)

Heil Hitler,
Gerhard von Staden
Stuttgart

Dear Sir,
I read in the papers how
Jews eat babies.
Please tell them to eat my
baby sister cause she is
a pest.

Sincereley,
Kurt Höcherl
Essen

Dear Heinrich Himmler,
How do you get all those
peeple into your oven? We can
hardly get a pork roast into ours.

Respectfully,
Uta Grotewohl

Dear Mr. Himmler,

Please don't get rid of all the kikes because I like to fly them except when the string breaks or they get tanded in a tree.

Yours truly,

Ewald Schwarzhaupt

Dear Head of the Gestappo:
If you will give me twenty (20) francs, I will tell you that my daddy is working for the resistance.

Sincerely,
Marie Peyret
St. Calais

Dear Mister H. Himmler,
We need some slave labor to help around the house. I have to do lots of house work and wash the dishes everynight.
    Thank you.

                    Love and Heil Hitler
                    Greta Hüfner
                    Age 11

P.S. Don't send any Poles because I don't speak Polish

Dear Mr. Himmler,
Thank you very much for The gold star to wear on my jacket. Now I can pretend I am a cowboy sheriff.

Best Wishes,
Naomi Feinberg

# FOTO

# FUNNIES

HEY, MAC, WANNA COP SOME ACID?

WELL, UH, I DUNNO.

G'WAN, HAVE A TASTE.

WHAT'S SUPPOSED TO HAPPEN NOW? I DON'T FEEL A THING.

RELAX, IT'LL HIT YA ANY MINUTE NOW.

OKAY, I'LL TAKE A DOZEN OF 'EM.

# The Vietnamese

# BABY BOOK

by Michael O'Donoghue

# Baby Arrives

## We proudly present

Name: Ngoc Tran Binh

Born on: Saturday _____ day

at morning _____ o'clock

Date: August 8, 1970

City or Hamlet: Dien Pho

Province: Quang Tin

Hospital: _____

Doctor: _____

Nurse: _____

## About Mother

Name: Mi Son Binh

Background: 17 year old. Mother and papa dead. 2 brother and 1 sister, dead. 1 brother, missing. All aunt and uncle dead. Had friend but he now dead also.

## About Father

Name: ?

Background: Blond, tall, with Heart of Purple. Many tattoo on arms. Would know more but it hard too see in alley and he knock me cold before I get look good.

## Baby's Handprint

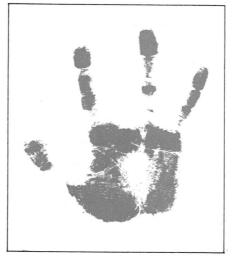

*Doctor's Note—The extensive use of powerful herbicides and defoliants in our country has brought about many interesting changes in the human body. There is no reason, however, just because your baby didn't come with both kidneys or all ten toes, that he can't live a content and useful life.*

illustrations by Newton Meyers

# Feeding Baby

( ) Breast    (X) Bottle

Comments: Chose to feed bottle way because Berets of Green off cut my breasts when they interrogate me.

 # Progress Report

The following age classifications are approximate because wide variations occur within normal limits. Fill in the ages at which your baby achieves the stages of development listed below.

Age

**Four Weeks Old:**
Able to whimper ................................................................ *3 wk.*

**Three Months Old:**
Able to cringe ................................................................... *2½ mo.*
Eligible to vote for Thieu ................................................ *Registered*

**Six Months Old:**
First nightmares ............................................................... *9 mo.*

**One Year Old:**
Able to limp unaided ........................................................ *14 mo.*

**Fifteen Months Old:**
Able to dive for cover ...................................................... *16 mo.*
Says first words ............................................................... *14½ mo.*

**Two Years Old:**
Knows bombing raids without being warned ...................... _____

**Three Years Old:**
Able to treat own wounds ............................................... _____

**Four Years Old:**
Able to pimp ................................................................... _____

**Five Years Old:**
Able to deal smack ........................................................... _____
Ready to support self ...................................................... _____

# Weight Chart

| | | | | | |
|---|---|---|---|---|---|
| Birth | *8* lbs. | *2* ozs. | 12 Weeks | *6* lbs. | *9* ozs. |
| 1 Week | *8* lbs. | *1* ozs. | 13 Weeks | *6* lbs. | *7* ozs. |
| 2 Weeks | *7* lbs. | *15* ozs. | 14 Weeks | *6* lbs. | *6* ozs. |
| 3 Weeks | *7* lbs. | *12* ozs. | 4 Months | *6* lbs. | *6* ozs. |
| 4 Weeks | *7* lbs. | *10* ozs. | 5 Months | *6* lbs. | *3* ozs. |
| 5 Weeks | *7* lbs. | *7* ozs. | 6 Months | *6* lbs. | *2* ozs. |
| 6 Weeks | *7* lbs. | *4* ozs. | 1 Year | *5* lbs. | *12* ozs. |
| 7 Weeks | *7* lbs. | *1* ozs. | 18 Months | lbs. | ozs. |
| 8 Weeks | *7* lbs. | *0* ozs. | 2 Years | lbs. | ozs. |
| 9 Weeks | *6* lbs. | *14* ozs. | 3 Years | lbs. | ozs. |
| 10 Weeks | *6* lbs. | *11* ozs. | 4 Years | lbs. | ozs. |
| 11 Weeks | *6* lbs. | *9* ozs. | 5 Years | lbs. | ozs. |

# What to Name the Baby

| Name | Meaning |
|------|---------|
| Xich | "vendor of poppy dust" |
| Tre | "avoider of pungee sticks" |
| Thap | "maimed" |
| Sau | "product of gang rape" |
| Nhanh | "one who can walk" |
| Trong | "body bag" |
| Dat | "favorite of the brothel" |
| Hoa | "from the free-fire zone" |
| Mooc | "detector of land mines" |
| Ba | "third base" |

# Baby's First Word

Date: *Oct. 22, 1971*

First Word: *Medic*

# Baby's First Wound

Date: *Oct. 22, 1971*

Treated by: *Cross of Red*

Scars: *3 inches gash upon right shoulder.*

Comments: *Got catched in crossfire.*

*Attach Sample of First Dressing Here*

# Ask the Doctor

Q: Although my little girl is over four years old, she still continues to suck her stump. I've tried everything to get her to quit but without success. What can I do?

A: Sucking the stump is a common problem and nothing to be alarmed about. I suggest you try dipping her stump in alum before bedtime and periodically throughout the day. A few weeks of such treatment should put an end to this annoying habit.

Q: What can be done about a child who persists in bleeding in bed? When I nag and scold about it, he turns a deaf ear (his right). Punishment only makes the problem worse.

A: Rubber sheets seem called-for here. Once a child has made up his mind to bleed in bed, little more can be done than to sit tight and hope he outgrows it.

Dr. Huynh Duc Tuan

*Address all inquiries about your baby's medical problems to Ask the Doctor, c/o the Yen-Hoc Publishing Co., 242, Vo Di Nguy St., Gia Dinh, Saigon Province.*

# Snapshots

*ngoc and me*

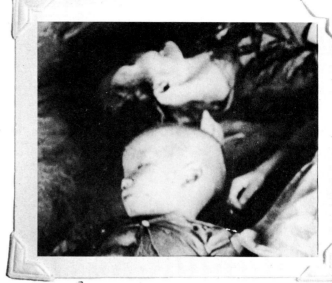

*After the raid*

## Nursery Rhymes

Willy Calley, pudding and pie,
Shot the boys and made them die.
When the girls came to surrender,
Willy just ignored their gender.

Baa, baa, black market,
Have you any scag?
Yes sir, yes sir,
Would you like a bag?
Some for the master-sergeant,
Some for the pain,
Some for the hooker
Who goes down in the lane.

Monday's child is born dead.
Tuesday's child is underfed.
Wednesday's child is full of junk.
Thursday's child's a burning monk.
Friday's child is lame and blinded.
Saturday's child is feeble-minded.
But the children born on Sunday
Will be tossed in mass graves one day.

## Baby's First Funeral

Date: *January 5, 1972*
Type of Service: *Buddhist*
Comments: *U. S. Air Force give me condolence payment of 80 piastre, enough almost to buy another Baby Book.*

*Paste Photo of Baby's Grave Here*

# Remembering Mama

## Speculative Erotic Fiction
### by Chris Miller

boulders. They roared down on him the moment he opened his eyes, first in ones and twos, then in massive agglomerations, driving him into his mattress, blocking his light, mashing his ribs, pressing his spine flatter than a two-day-old highway snake. He had been dreaming of kittens; they died beneath the crush with a firecracker string of tiny screams. He was numb within seconds.

Somehow he forced his hand to the phone and dialed. "Help," he croaked.

With merciful haste, Jenny Jiminez arrived in his bedroom, hitched up her skirt and sat in his face. He sipped weakly at first, then with growing greed, as if from the warming rum keg of a St. Bernard. Gradually, the boulders dissolved.

"Hey, leesten, man," Jenny told him as he dressed, "you can't keep callin' me like thees every mornin'. Ees been two weeks now an' I been late to work three times. Can' you jus' dreenk orange juice in the mornin' like everybody else?"

"It's pretty weird," agreed Halberson.

"Wha' doss your shreenk say?"

"Halberson, you're disgusting," said his shrink. "I'll bet you're the only man on the planet who needs cunnilingus to get up in the morning."

"I'm probably the only one in the history of the universe," muttered Halberson.

"Of course, it's only the latest manifestation of your overall insatiable need for sex." He leaned forward. "How many women this week?"

"Sixteen," said Halberson, very quietly.

"My God," whispered his shrink.

Halberson shifted miserably in the overstuffed armchair. "It could be worse," he pointed out. "My father could have been run over by a bus on the way to the maternity hospital. Then I could have become a *fag* with an insatiable need for sex."

"That's probably true. But he didn't and you aren't. What you are is someone who didn't get any love from his mother and tries to make up the deficit with every woman he meets. You know what I wish? I wish you could go back and have intercourse with your mother. Then maybe you'd get the whole obsession out of your system."

"Hmmm," said Halberson.

He took a crosstown bus to Larry Leibeskind's studio. Larry was the brother of a girl he had once had three whole dates with. He was into tachyons, photons, quantum mechanics, things like that. With the money he earned from producing weird light shows for rock 'n' roll ballrooms, he was constructing a faster-than-light drive for a starship. He believed that Earth was fucked beyond redemption and wished to leave.

"I want to go back in time," Halberson told him.

"In time for what?" Larry inquired.

"No, man, I mean I want to go back into the past. You know, a time machine."

"You're crazy," said Larry. "I'll see what I can do."

Halberson went home. In the next two days, he made it with a small-breasted seamstress, a gym teacher whose high-energy humps flung him about like a bronc-rider, an Australian virgin, a divorcée who tasted like horseradish, and a daughter of a San Francisco police chief. It was hard for him to cut down like this, but he needed time to think.

Halberson didn't like being neurotic, which, he felt, was like being a self-made nigger without the compensation of natural rhythm. His dependency on women was getting him down. Increasingly, his sexual liaisons were not satisfying him. Oh, they were fine while they were going down, but a half hour later he'd be hungry again. While this was especially true of Oriental women, it applied as well to all colors and creeds. His shrink's thesis about his mother had struck him as very interesting, perhaps the key to the solution of his entire problem. Now, if only Larry could come through ....

The call, when it came, was brief. "Get your ass over here, man. I think I've got it."

Halberson found Larry's studio pulsing with an eerie violet light. In the center of the room was a gleaming metal cylinder the height of two men. Electricity twined its sides like jagged yellow worms, humming and crackling. The air was sharp with ozone. Larry, in face mask and insulated gloves, was welding closed the cylinder's seam. Sparks showered to the stone floor, bouncing about his feet like bright BBs.

"Fantastic!" exclaimed Halberson. "You know, that's exactly what I thought a time machine would look like."

"No, man," said Larry, cutting his torch and flipping up his mask, "this is a light show for the Family Bug. *That's* the time machine." He indicated a boring metal box on a workbench.

"Oh," said Halberson. He walked over to inspect it. The box's surface was lusterless black, without feature except for two dials, a red button, and a carrier grip like the handle of a suitcase. It was about the size of a bread box.

"It used to be a bread box," said Larry. "I put some various kinds of shit inside, messed around a little, and I think it ought to work. This dial controls location. You got to find out the exact coordinates of where you're going and set it like this." He manipulated hair-thin lines around a fine circle of numbers. "And this one controls year and month."

"And the button activates it?"

"Right. But listen, the time control is approximate. I can't promise you'll arrive exactly when you want. Also, you can only use the machine once. The box stays behind when you return."

"That's cool." Halberson stood up to leave.

"One other thing. If my calculations are correct, you're not going to remember a thing about it when you get back. All in all, it's a pretty risky proposition. Why do you want to go back in time so badly, anyway?"

"I can't get up in the morning without having cunnilingus with a Puerto Rican woman," Halberson explained.

"I can dig that," said Larry. "Well, that'll be five bucks for parts."

Halberson returned to his apartment. He placed the time machine on his desk, cancelled the three dates he had made for that evening, showered, shaved, and brushed his teeth. He became worried briefly when he noticed his shoulder-length hair in the mirror. He might be thought a little weird with it back in the past. Then he realized all he need do was transport himself directly to his parent's apartment. He'd tell his mother he had a job posing for Bible illustrations or something.

Now he sat before the black box and set the dials. He set the time control for 1939, three years prior to his birth. He had no great relish for the idea of running into his own infant self. Furthermore, his father, a musician, had been on the road much of that year. He didn't want to confront *that* son-of-a-bitch, either.

He had a terrible thought then. What if he knocked his mother up? He might never be born, or have to grow up with an older brother who was his own son. The ramifications were beginning to make him nervous. Hands sweating, he hurried to the medicine cabinet and secured a prophylactic. Then, before he could think of any more problems, he grabbed the black box by the handle and pushed the button.

There was no sense of transition. He blinked his eyes and when he opened them he was in the parlor of his parents' apartment. His stomach thudded with recognition. There was the coffee table, there the lamp with the Tiffany shade, there the Persian rug upon whose loops and swirls he had crawled for endless hours as a babe. Everything was so small! A sudden dizziness took him and he sat down hard on the sofa.

Outside there was darkness. He had no idea of the time. Almost before he realized it, he found himself turning to the end table beside the sofa. Sure enough, there was the clock he would break at age four, calmly ticking, unaware that its death lay a mere seven years in the future. The dial read two o'clock.

Something crackled beneath him. He pulled it out—a newspaper. "GERMAN ARMOR RACING TOWARD KIEV," said the headline.

German armor? Halberson felt a second thud in his stomach. The war shouldn't even have started yet. Swallowing, he squinted in the semi-

darkness to read the date.

It was July 17, 1941.

With an extreme exertion of will, Halberson calmed himself. It was still nine months before his birth, nothing to worry about on that account. He could still do what he had set out to do. He stood up a little shakily and crept into his parents' bedroom.

Gradually, his eyes adjusted to the deeper gloom, picking out the dressing table with rows of perfume bottles, the framed photograph of the black-and-white cat, the two single beds separated by the night table, and...good God, his father! His father was home!

Halberson leaned weakly against the wall. He considered giving up the entire plan. The time traveler was still in his hands. All he had to do was push the button and he'd be home in the future, maybe call a few girls...no! That was the thing he'd come here to *stop* doing. But how could he....

Suddenly, his mother rolled onto her back and Halberson saw her face. Instantly, he forgot everything. Her face ...*that* face.... Primal emotions thudded inside him like body blows from a good heavyweight. His stomach thrashed like a fish in a net. Without conscious control, his hands stripped off his clothes. Glancing down, he found himself so erect he appeared about to blast from his own body like a V-2. With his last shred of presence of mind, he rolled the prophylactic onto himself, then covered the distance to his mother's bed in three-quarters of a second and slid in beside her.

A lock of hair had fallen across one of her eyes. Scarcely daring to breath, Halberson rolled down the sheet. And it was there! All the remembered ripeness, the lushness that had tantalized his dreams, it was real! Unbidden, his hand trembled forward and began to touch things.

His mother made a half-awake noise and rolled her back to him. "Not tonight, I told you Paul," she murmured. "I still have that awful headache."

But Halberson hadn't come as far as this to stop now. Calling into play every fondle of experience, every tickle of skill, he began to caress his mother with great urgency. As he molded his front against her back, his rubberoid-encased member clove between her warm, soft thighs like a knife through butter.

"Paul, I said..." Her breath caught suddenly in her throat. "Oh. Oh, Paul, you never...oh, my God!" She expelled her breath in a rush and her body began to undulate.

"At last!" thought Halberson wildly. "At last! At last! At last!" And he plunged the residence of his neurosis a full ten inches into his mother's pulsing vagina.

"SNORK!"

*Snork?* With a sudden profound sense of dread, Halberson slowly turned his head to look behind him. His father was sitting up in bed! In his sleep-aid mask, he looked like a panelist on a TV game show.

"Nancy? Are you having a bad dream?" A note of eagerness entered his voice. "Shall I get in bed with you?"

Halberson thought fast. His mother, moaning and sighing, was beyond all hearing. *He* would have to answer.

"I told you not tonight, Paul," he said in a strained falsetto. "I've still got my headache."

"Aw, Jesus Christ, Nancy, you've had that headache for two weeks now. Come on."

Halberson tried to answer but could not. His mother's accelerating wriggles were tossing him about too wildly. So his father crawled into bed beside him and began to stroke his head.

"Oh, Nancy, your hair is so soft," his father said hoarsely.

"Uh, thanks," Halberson managed. Then, with a short, choked-off scream, his mother came. Her body jackknifed convulsively, sending him slamming against his father, who fell out of bed with a crash.

"Dear God," his mother sighed, "that's the *first one!*" Her voice trailed off into a blissful purr. She swooned.

There was a silence in the bedroom ...except for a husky, irregular sound like a saw being drawn backward across rotten wood. He looked down at the floor. His father lay on his back, his head against a leg of the night table, his neck twisted at an impossible angle.

Halberson decided to get out of there fast. Forgetting his clothes, he launched himself for the time traveler and pushed the button.

Nothing happened.

He tried again, watching closely. His fingertip passed through the button!

What? Halberson stared at his hands and found them fading from view, growing insubstantial, like the hands of a ghost. His fingertips were fully transparent, and the transparency was spreading. What the hell?...

Abruptly, with a terrible sinking feeling, he understood. His father was dying—and had not yet impregnated his mother. And when he actually died, no baby Halberson would ever be born. He, the adult Halberson, would cease to exist!

There was only one thing to do and Halberson did it. He hurled himself to the floor before his father, ripped open his pajama bottoms, and set to work.

The poor man certainly *had* been horny. Despite his rapidly fading lifeforce, he attained an almost instant erection.

Good. Now Halberson leapt to his feet, bent down, encircled his father with his arms, and began tugging him up onto his mother's bed. It was like pulling at a sack of wet cement. Halberson's hands were fading, fading. With a grunt, he rolled his father on top of his mother.

"Oh, Paul, more?" his mother whispered, her eyes still closed.

"Sure thing, Nance," said Halberson, imitating as best he could his father's gruff tones. "German armor's racing toward Kiev, so what the hell."

It was penetration time, but Halberson's hands were now no more than transparent wraiths. Working essentially with his stumps, he somehow fumbled his father's banana into his mother's split.

"Glork. Snorf," commented his father. His breathing was becoming raspier and raspier. Pink spittle had begun to collect at the corners of his mouth.

Halberson's body was still fading. He had hoped that effecting penetration would be enough, that biology would then take over, but this obviously was not to be the case. With a curse he took his father's hips between his elbows and began hoisting and lowering him, as if with a pair of ice tongs. And still Halberson's body faded.

"Come on, you bastard," he growled, "you never gave me shit in my life, don't take my *birth* away from me." He began ramming his head against his father's buns on each downswing.

"Graaak," rattled his father, his body spasming randomly.

"Oh, Paul," whimpered his mother, "you're so *alive* tonight."

"Fnork!" replied his father. His body arced into a sudden bow, then collapsed utterly.

*Pop!* Halberson snapped into full substance. His desperate tactic had worked! Relief washed over him.

"Paul? Paul, darling? I've still got my cookies. Are you stopping?"

Uh-oh. Halberson dove for the time machine.

Was he cured of neurosis? he wondered. He would never know. Whatever future was waiting for him up there would be the only one he'd ever experienced. If Larry had been right, he'd remember nothing of what went on here tonight.

Abruptly, the light went on. There was a scream.

Halberson pushed the button.

Halberson's depression greeted him that morning like an avalanche of boulders. They roared down on him the moment he opened his eyes. He was numb within seconds.

Somehow he forced his hand to the phone and dialed. "Help," he croaked.

With merciful haste, Pablo Jiminez arrived in his bedroom, dropped his pants, and sat in his face. □

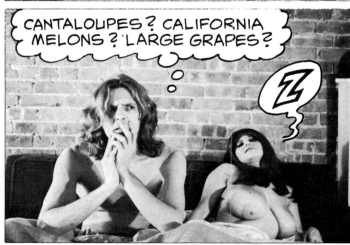

# HERB PHILBRICK'S *Believe It or Else!*

WATCH **HERB PHILBRICK'S** CONTINUING STORY OF ONE MAN'S FIGHT AGAINST INTERNATIONAL COMMUNISM ON "**I LED THREE LIVES.**" CHECK YOUR LOCAL NEWSPAPER FOR TIME AND STATION...

## RUSSIAN CHRISTMAS

IN **COMMUNIST COUNTRIES**, **CHILDREN** ARE ONLY ALLOWED **TWO PRESENTS**...

ONE for **EACH** PARENT THEY **TURN OVER** TO THE **SECRET POLICE**!

## RUSSIAN SHOES!

WELCOME TO SIBERIA

## RUSSIAN BRICKS

The so-called "IRON CURTAIN" around Europe's CAPTIVE SATELLITE NATIONS is not really made of IRON at all...

but from "FOREIGN AID" sent by Bleeding-Heart Liberals and Pinko Sympathizers!

## RUSSIAN JUSTICE!

## RUSSIAN SOUP!

BORSCHT, THE **NATIONAL DISH** of **RED COMMUNISTS**, is actually made of **GROUND-UP LATVIANS, ESTONIANS,** and **HUNGARIAN** Freedom Fighters!

IN THE **KREMLIN'S BASEMENT** ARE **THREE HUNDRED COMMISSARS** WHOSE ONLY DUTY IS TO **MAKE UP LISTS** OF **AMERICANS** TO BE **SHOT** WHEN THE **COMMUNISTS** TAKE OVER!

"IT CAN'T HAPPEN HERE... IT CAN'T HAPPEN *HERE!*" THAT'S WHAT BILL JONES KEPT TELLING HIMSELF, UNTIL ONE DAY HE AWOKE TO A...

# RED NIGHTMARE!

I SUPPOSE MY HOMETOWN IS PRETTY ORDINARY AS PLACES GO...

E. MAIN ST.

CHESTNUT ST.

WELCOME TO
PLEASANTVILLE U.S.A.
POPULATION: 3,564
SPEED LIMIT 25 MPH

...BUT IT'S A FRIENDLY TOWN, AND FOLKS AROUND HERE LIKE IT FINE...

MORNIN', BILL! YOUR BROTHER FOUND WORK YET?

NOT YET, SAM. THANKS.

SAM'S MILK

...EVERYBODY, BUT MY BROTHER FRED, THAT IS....

NO WORK IN *THREE WEEKS!* NOBODY IN THIS TOWN WANTS TO GIVE A GUY A BREAK!

BUT FRED, YOU'VE ONLY JUST LEFT THE, UH...HOSPITAL...

HAVING FRED STAY WITH US WAS SOMETIMES DIFFICULT, BUT HE NEEDED HELP, AND HE *WAS* MY BROTHER.

"HOSPITAL!" *HA!* WHY DON'T YOU SAY *NUT HOUSE* LIKE EVERYBODY ELSE IN THIS CRUMMY BURG! JUST BECAUSE I DON'T HAVE A BIG-DEAL *WAR RECORD* LIKE *BILL*, I CAN'T GET A *FAIR SHAKE!*

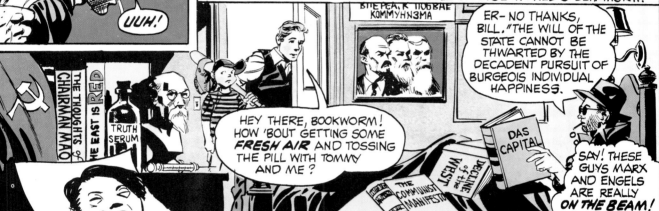

..STIRRED UP DISCONTENT IN THE LABOR FORCE!

DARN! I'M *SICK AND TIRED* OF BUSTIN' MY HUMP FOR THIS *PUNK FAIR WAGE!* IF SOME "FRIENDS" OF MINE RAN THINGS AROUND HERE, YOU'D ALL BE GETTING *TEN-HOUR* WEEKS, *SIX-MONTH* VACATIONS, *LIMOUSINES* TO WORK, AND *SILVER-PLATED LUNCH BUCKETS!*

HEY! *DIS GUY'S GOT WHAT IT TAKES!*

DUH!

YEAH!

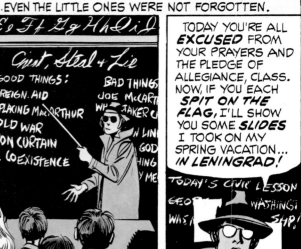

..EVEN THE LITTLE ONES WERE NOT FORGOTTEN.

TODAY YOU'RE ALL *EXCUSED* FROM YOUR PRAYERS AND THE PLEDGE OF ALLEGIANCE, CLASS. NOW, IF YOU EACH *SPIT ON THE FLAG,* I'LL SHOW YOU SOME *SLIDES* I TOOK ON MY SPRING VACATION... *IN LENINGRAD!*

HOW, YOU ARE PROBABLY ASKING YOUR- SELVES, DID WE ALLOW THIS TO GO ON RIGHT UNDER OUR VERY NOSES? WELL, PLEASANTVILLE'S ENEMIES HAD THE "HELP" FROM TWO OTHER POWER- FUL "FRIENDS"!

A *PRESIDENT* WHO WAS "SOFT" ON COMMUNISM...

...SO, UPON THE ADVICE OF MY TRUSTED ASSISTANT, I AM GOING TO GIVE IMPORTANT APPOINTMENTS TO A LOT OF *DUPES, FELLOW TRAVELERS, AND SECURITY RISKS!*

...AND CERTAIN FUZZY-THINKING "ONE-WORLDERS" IN THE *STATE DEPARTMENT!*

HA HA! YOU CAN'T SPELL "COMMUNISM," COMRADE, WITHOUT "*UN*"!

UNITED STATES

U.S.S.R.

BUT FINALLY, I GOT WISE TO WHAT FRED AND HIS "PALS" WERE UP TO....

SO LONG, BILL. I GUESS I'LL TAKE A LITTLE STROLL TO THE *TOWN RESERVOIR!*

NOT SO FAST, FRED! I'M BEGINNING TO SMELL A RAT...

...A *COMMIE RAT!*

SO, BILL JONES, YOU HAVE *GUESSED* OUR LITTLE SECRET!

B-BUT *COMRADE CERNIK,* BILL WON'T TELL ANYBODY ABOUT...

*SILENCE, FOOL!* IT MATTERS LITTLE NOW, BECAUSE MY *REAL* NAME IS NOT "COMRADE" CERNIK, BUT...

COMMISSAR CERNIK!

...AND AS YOU CAN SEE IT IS *ALREADY TOO LATE!!*

OUR SCHEME HAS *SUCCEEDED!* YOUR PITIFUL, TRUSTING TOWN HAS FALLEN LIKE AN *OVER-RIPE FRUIT* INTO *OUR HANDS!*

IT WAS TRUE! PLEASANTVILLE HAD FALLEN TO THE COMMUNIST MENACE IN A SINGLE NIGHT... AND NOT A SHOT HAD BEEN FIRED!

NEEDLESS TO SAY, OUR SLAVE-MASTERS WASTED LITTLE TIME PAINTING THE TOWN... *RED!*

CITIZENS OF *NEW STALIN-VILLE!* I BRING YOU GREETINGS FROM THE PEACE-LOVING PEOPLES OF THE SOVIET UNION, AND ASSURE YOU THAT WE COME AS *FRIENDS....*

WELL, I'D HEARD THAT WORD "FRIEND" BEFORE, AND, IN THE DAYS THAT FOLLOWED, OUR "FRIENDS" BEGAN PUTTING THEIR SO-CALLED "PEOPLE'S PARADISE" INTO ACTION...

...FIRST, BY OUTLAWING THE "CAPITALIST FETISH" OF PRIVATE PROPERTY...

...AND ANY CITIZEN FOUND OWNING SO MUCH AS A PAPER CLIP AFTER CURFEW TONIGHT *WILL BE SHOT!*

...THEN BY "NATIONALIZING" ALL PRIVATE BUSINESSES.

...AND SO THAT EVERYBODY IS EQUAL, WE NOW HAVE ONLY *ONE* FLAVOR, *RED* RASPBERRY, AND WE ARE *OUT OF THAT TOO,* LITTLE COMRADE! HA HA HA!

FREE ENTERPRISE ON ANY SCALE WAS FORBIDDEN...

*NYET!* NOW WE ONLY DRINK *PINK* LEMONADE!

KRUNCH!

MAYBE WE SEND YOU TO A NICE CAMP, DA? *SLAVE LABOR* CAMP! HA HA HA!

...AND PLEASANTVILLE WAS GIVEN ITS FIRST DOSE OF "SOCIALIZED MEDICINE."

TAKE TWO OF THESE. IF PAIN CONTINUE, *DIE!*

IF I GET SICK ONCE MORE, I GO ON VACATION.

FLORIDA?

SIBERIA!

PLACEBOS GRADE "C" NET WT. 60 KILO

OF COURSE, IN ANY TOTALITARIAN STATE, FREEDOM OF EXPRESSION IS NOT A RIGHT...

COMRADE SMITH! YOU HAVE **FAILED** TO PRINT YOUR QUOTA OF **LIES** AND **PROPAGANDA!**

B-BUT COMMISSAR! I'VE ALWAYS FOLLOWED THE *"FIVE W'S"* OF **HONEST JOURNALISM** — WHO, WHAT, WHEN, WHERE, AND WHY?

~~STALIN~~
~~PLEASANTVILLE~~ TELEGRAF
~~TELEGRAPH~~

TOM SMITH, EDITOR

A **COMMUNIST** PAPER ALWAYS FOLLOWS THE *"FIVE D'S"...*

...*DECEIT, DECEPTION, DERISION, DESTRUCTION, AND DON'T EVER TELL THE TRUTH!*

SPLASH!

...BUT A CRIME!

OUR PRECIOUS AMERICAN HERITAGE WAS PUT TO THE TORCH....

DA! DA! NOW THROW IN ALL THE **VOTING BOOTHS** AND THE **WRIT OF HABEUS CORPUS**, TOO! ALSO, MAKE A NOTE TO **CANCEL CHRISTMAS!**

THEN, LET'S KNOCK OFF AND COMMIT SOME **ATROCITIES!**

NONE DARE CALL IT TREASON

John Birch Society Blue Book

MASTERS OF DECEIT

CITIZENS WERE FORCED TO CONFESS TO TRUMPED-UP "WAR CRIMES"...

PSSST! DOUGIE! WHAT DOES "GERM WARFARE" MEAN?

...AND THOSE WHO REFUSED WERE SUBJECTED TO THE MOST INHUMAN FORMS OF "BRAINWASHING!"

...AND THEN MY SISTER-IN-LAW AND I DROPPED SIXTY DIPHTHERIA BOMBS ON A NORTH KOREAN ORPHANAGE....

ALWAYS WATCHED, ALWAYS OVERHEARD, THE JONES'S LIFE WAS A NIGHTMARE COME TRUE....

POP! POP! THEY SHOT **FRECKLES!**

I'M SORRY SUPPER'S LATE, BUT THESE MICROPHONES TAKE LONGER THAN I THOUGHT!

THE FILTHY **SWINE!**

THEY HAVE NO SENSE OF DECENCY...

I HEARD THAT, **DOGS!**

BUDDA BUDDA

...THEY'RE JUST **AARRGH!**... NOT HUMAN...

THE STATE NO LONGER HAS ANY **USE** FOR YOU, **COMRADE BILL JONES!**

SUDDENLY, EVERYTHING SORT OF... FELL APART, AND I HEARD MYSELF PLEAD "DON'T SHOOT! *DON'T SHOOT!*"

BUDDA BUDDA

NYET NYET NYET

BUDDA BUDDA BUDDA BUDDA BUDDA

..LIKE BEASTS *GAAAH!*.....JUST *HUNH!*.....NOT NICE....

DON'T SHOOT! *DON'T SHOOT!*

DON'T...SHOOT... ...DON'T...

POP! POP! WAKE UP! *WAKE UP!*

BILL! IT'S ONLY A *BAD DREAM!*

YOU MUST'VE CLOSED YOUR EYES FOR A MINUTE AFTER FRED LEFT TO LOOK FOR WORK!

*SOME* PEOPLE HAVE HAD THEIR *EYES CLOSED* FOR A *LONG TIME,* HONEY...

...AND I THINK IT'S TIME FOR *ALL* OF US...

...TO WAKE UP...

...BEFORE IT'S TOO LATE!

WELCOME TO PLEASANTVILLE, U.S. POPULATION: 3,564 SPEED LIMIT: 25 MPH

THE END

# Pharmacopoeia

## by Chris Miller

BROOKLYN CENTRAL HOSPITAL
BIRTH REPORT

Date: March 1, 1942
Name of Baby: James Willie Fish
Name of Mother: Margaret Perkins
Fish
Medication: Morphine, for pain

———— • ————

High Harold, a thirtyish freak, was worried sick about his growing impotence. He finally screwed up his courage and made an appointment with his dealer.

"You gotta help me, man," Harold told him. "My old lady is taking this thing personally. She claims I'm being hostile toward women."

"I've got just the thing for you," said the dealer with a sly smile. He opened his leather dealer's bag and withdrew a rapier-thin joint. "Smoke this together during the last ten minutes of Cavett and woo-woo!"

"Outstanding." Harold paid and departed.

The following morning he returned to the dealer's office and burst angrily into his stash room, surprising him at his triple-beam scale.

"What the hell was in that joint?" he demanded.

"Why, Michoacán buds," said the dealer. "What's the matter? Didn't you get potent?"

"Potent? I got so potent I could have hired out as clapper for the Liberty Bell. Sunshine says she may be permanently stretched out of shape. And the head of my dick looks like a cheese grater from being repeatedly punctured by her intrauterine device. Michoacán buds, huh?"

Stunned, the dealer turned his bag inside out and examined closely the spilled contents. Abruptly, he looked up at Harold.

"Good Lord, man, I gave you the DMT by mistake. You owe me a buck-fifty."
—*Playboy* party joke, September, 1976

———— • ————

Willie pauses at the closed bathroom door and listens for tinklings. If there are tinklings, it means Mommy is making siss and he is not allowed in. But he hears no tinklings.

He opens the door and sees Mommy put something in her mouth and drink two swallows from a glass of water.

"What ya doin'?"

"Mother is taking a pill, dear. To make her feel better."

Willie digests this intelligence, then holds out his hand.

"Me too, Mommy."

———— • ————

Scored an ounce of pure, uncut smack,
Copped it from a French refiner,
Took a quick blow an' then I hid it
real good
To find it takes a lamp like a miner's.

Flyin into ol' Boston, Mass.
With a finger stall stuck up my ass,
Don't check my can if you please,
Mr. Customs Man.
—Pop song lyric, 1967

———— • ————

Willie's parents get up at nine or ten o'clock on Saturdays and make pancakes for Willie and his little brother, Benny, and Bloody Marys for themselves. While Willie and Benny listen to *Big John and Sparky* on the radio, George and Meg drink several more "bloodies," as George calls them.

When Willie returns from play in the afternoon, the bloodies have been replaced by long-stemmed martinis. After dinner, it is scotch on the rocks, and George takes out his New Orleans jazz records and listens intensely, occasionally saying, "Yeah!" It is the happiest George is all week. It is when Willie can most nearly love him.

———— • ————

The acid that Abbie intended for the reservoirs was intercepted by Daley, who cut it with five pounds of very impure Methedrine and dumped it into the water tank at the assembly point of his special convention police force.
Street rumor, Democratic National Convention, 1968

———— • ————

Dr. Mossbacher has his face right up close to Willie's. He is picking gently at Willie's teeth with the instrument that has the pointy metal question mark on top. The dentist is the only man Willie can think of who gets this close to him without smelling bad, and Willie likes him.

"Lots of holes, pal. You'll need four or five appointments, at least."

"'Our or 'ive a-ointments?" Paranoia blossoms in his belly. Having his teeth drilled is the worst thing in the world.

Even with Novocaine he sits stiff as rigor mortis, cringing at every change of pitch in the whine of the drill. Paralyzed with fear, he awaits his injection.

"Ever heard of laughing gas?" asks the dentist.

"Uh, I saw it in *Son of Paleface*. People breathe it and start laughing?"

"Medically incorrect. The reason they named it laughing gas is because the king and his court laughed like hell at the behavior of the poor page, who the king had volunteered for demonstration purposes, the day the doctors brought it to show to him."

"What *does* it do then?"

"It makes you not afraid."

The rubber nose-mask smells sickly sweet, but the gas makes Willie feel terrific. The dentist drills and drills, and Willie never moves. He is picturing birds and willows.

———— • ————

Fishcakes and Jerry were sitting on the front porch of their commune. Fishcakes pulled a joint from his pocket, lit up and passed it to his friend. Jerry had taken three hits when a mutant pigeon chanced to fly overhead and release its daily bowel movement. Approximately the size of a medicine ball, the turd splatted to the ground directly before the porch.

"My God," cried Jerry, "where'd this shit come from?"

"Colombia," said Fishcakes proudly.
—Neobebop joke, 1973

———— • ————

Alfred is holding an ounce of cocaine, which he is dealing for $45 per gram. He scores a half ounce of superfly for $700, which he would have to deal for $60 per gram to make anything on it. How much of the $45-per-gram coke should Alfred mix with the superfly to make grams that will sell for $50?
—Question from New York State Algebra Regents, 1970

———— • ————

Willie slouches against the grimy brick wall of the Brooklyn Paramount, hoping his poor suburban charade of toughness will keep him safe from the many real hoods all around him. Willie's pals, Steamin' and Ned, slouch beside him. They are waiting in line for the box office to open and grant them access to the day's first performance of Alan Freed's Second Anniversary

Rock-'n'-Roll Jubilee. Soon they will be rockin' an' reelin' to an endless string of snazzy, choreographed black vocal groups.

The hoods are cool in the early morning chill. Many smoke cigarettes and drink coffee from paper cups. It is time for Willie's little melodrama. He takes a pack of Camels from his jacket, carefully withdraws a cigarette, and places it between his lips. Steamin' is starin'. Ned is agog. They know Willie has always been afraid to inhale but is probably even more afraid merely to let the smoke dribble lamely from his mouth before real hoods, who would detect this uncoolness immediately and whump him with their belts. What can he be thinking of?

Willie lights up real quick, like the hoods do, and flips the match to the gutter. He draws on the weed—and inhales. Yes, he breathes in and breathes out, and when he breathes out, smoke comes out. Steamin' and Ned are massively impressed, which they do their best to hide.

Willie never tells them that his Camels were actually disguised Sanos.

———— • ————

Answer to Regents Question

Alfred saves the cheaper coke and steps on the superfly twice with lactose, thus creating 42 grams, which he sells for $50 per gram. He makes a profit of $1400.

———— • ————

SUPERCOOL: Hey, man, you ever hear 'bout de Bungo tribe?
SLICK: De who?
SUPERCOOL: De Bungo tribe. Dey a little-known tribe of Pigmy in Central Africa. Dey got an asshole instead of dey nose, an' dey very, very mean.
SLICK: An asshole instead of dey nose?? Den how does dey snort coke?
SUPERCOOL: Dey don'! *Dat's why dey so mean!*
—Harlem nightclub joke, 1971

———— • ————

First Handwriting: I LOVE COCAINE
Second Handwriting: MY MAN!!!!
—Elevator grafitti, New York City, 1971

———— • ————

Willie is sitting in the formica-and-simulated-pine basement of Joyce Retch, a freshman he has noticed in the halls of Nozzlin High. It is a Friday night. Though he has just sort of dropped in, Joyce doesn't mind. Willie is a Senior. With credentials like that, he doesn't *have* to call first.

Joyce's parents are out for the evening and she is starting to let Willie get a little. They have been dry-humping with great zeal for some time, and now she is getting slower and slower to re-

move his hand from her breast. Willie has had a hard-on for over an hour. His balls feel as if they have migraine headaches.

They separate to smoke cigarettes. Willie ponders the situation. Joyce is really young, hardly more than a kid. Maybe, if he can get her to drink, say, half of one of his beers, he can convince her she is drunk and not responsible for her actions. It's worth a try. If she swallows it, he'll ask for a hand job. He offers her a swig.

"Ik!" She makes a face. "I hate the taste of beer. I'd rather drink my mother's stuff." She disappears up the stairs, returns with a quart bottle of hundred-proof vodka.

"Holy shit," breathes Willie.

"What's the matter? Isn't this good?"

"Oh, yes, it's *very* good. Sort of like a mild wine. Allow me to pour you a glass."

It's an uphill fight all the way, but gradually, to his stunned disbelief, he actually gets all her clothes off except for her panties. At that garment, her resistance stiffens. Willie is half-mad with frustration. His balls feel like cantaloupes. If something doesn't give soon, he'll be forced to go to the bathroom and jerk off.

But wait. Joyce appears to be fading in and out of consciousness. If he can time·this correctly … there. She closes her eyes and, quick as a reptile's tongue, Willie tugs the panties down.

*"Yoo-hoo, dear! We're home!"*

Good God. A boulder rolls over in his stomach. He lurches to his feet. The room whirls around him the way the dock whirled around Marlon Brando at the end of *On the Waterfront*. He is halfway to the back door when he remembers his coat and darts back for it.

Joyce is snoring softly on the sofa, her panties bunched about her knees. Willie remembers the incredible blue balls she has given him. Suddenly, he smiles. Moving quickly, he places the half-empty vodka bottle in Joyce's right hand and closes the fingers around its neck. Then he takes her left hand and inserts the middle finger into her vagina.

*"Joy-oyce! Are you in the basement?"*

Whoops, the father. Like speeded-up film, Willie grabs his things and is out the door. Behind him, he hears heavy footsteps on the stair.

———— • ————

I looked. And looked again. Mrs. Roistacher was lying as if flung on a low divan. Tight, green lounging-pajamas encased her like a stem, and her face, daubed with glistening pink and sticky lavender, was framed by a teased burst of fiery hair.

She was scary as hell.

Then she sat up, and, through the cloud of pale-green gauze gathered at her bust, I glimpsed lazily shifting enormities. Beneath my thickly waffled underwear, I felt myself begin to perspire.

Smoothly, Mrs. Roistacher withdrew a cigarette from a slim, silver box and fitted it into a black ivory holder. Watching me intently through the prison windows of her lowered false eyelashes, she lit up and inhaled deeply.

"You must be warm in that parka," she purred, allowing thick driblets of smoke to issue from her mouth and nose. "Why don't you—" She broke off, seized by a fit of sudden coughing. "Shit," she said, wiping at her eyes.

—Excerpt, *National Lampoon* story by Chris Miller, 1973

———— • ————

The music ceases. Disquieted by the sudden silence, several of Willie's fraternity brothers move unsteadily to the jukebox and start pushing buttons. The bar fills once more with tranquilizing Motown ooh-wahs.

Houseparties Weekend has ended, but the Delta Alpha Hard Core drinks on. Their beery vigil is just entering its fifth day. Willie has been there from the start, sleeping only when the keg was turned off. His last meal was a peanut-butter-and-mayonnaise sandwich sometime Friday morning. He has urinated 347 times. He feels about like a turnip.

In walks Fred Mules, carrying a cardboard carton under his arm.

"Oh, Jesus," mutters someone, "the rag box."

On big weekends, the brothers vacate the House and dates stay in their rooms. Before the brothers leave, and not without much snappy banter, they place in each bathroom a carton with a slot cut in the top. It is one of these very cartons that Fred is setting on the bar.

Fred's date has left and now he feels he can be sick again. He's been taking shit all weekend for not getting drunk and perverse with the guys and is anxious to regain their good graces. He opens the box.

The brothers gather close to peer inside. They behold a sparse pile of red-splotched toilet-paper bundles. Fred removes one and unwraps it. A tampon! He runs it beneath his nose as if it were a cigar. "Mmmmm," he says.

Two pledges go pale and a third leaves. Fred is doing very well.

The second bundle yields a highly soaked napkin. Fred glances at his audience. He puts the napkin in his mouth and begins to chew.

Willie is one of the three who do not vomit. He feels equivalent to a football hero.

———— • ————

### The Origin of MDA

A hippie chemist in Ohio produced 1,000 tabs of a new drug he'd invented called MDA. He took them to the two heaviest dealers at Ohio University, explaining that he'd been very drunk when he made them and had no idea what they were but suspected they would be far-out. The heavy dealers glanced at each other and purchased the lot.

They decided to taste their new product before selling it, to guard against dispensing a bummer. An hour later, wreathed in beatific smiles, they left their off-campus pad and gave the entire thousand pills away free.

That weekend, the whole university seemed to be tripping. Students gamboled through the streets of Athens, giving away their belongings and hugging one another. Virtually everyone got laid. MDA was quickly nicknamed "the love drug."

The original formula was never rediscovered.

—Drug tale, 1970

———•———

On a summer night in '63
Willie has his mind set free
By half a pipe of marijuana
His brother copped in Tijuana.

The weed is delightful, the music
   divine,
His taste buds are awed by the taste
   of the wine.
His girl friend is with him and after
   the grass
They repair to his bed for a fine piece
   of ass.

And after it's over, no hangover blues:
The death knell has sounded for
   Willie and booze.

———•———

Robbie Numberwriter was tooling happily along the Long Island Expressway, stoned on hash, when he was pulled over by a cop. Large and mean, the trooper climbed from his car and strode deliberately to his window.

With a sudden terrible sinking feeling, Robbie remembered that he wasn't carrying his wallet. By reflex, his hands continued to move vainly from pocket to pocket. His fingers touched his hash. Inspired, he tore off the aluminum-foil wrapper and compressed it into a small metal lozenge.

"Sorry not to be carrying my license, officer," he said, dropping the foil into the policeman's waiting hand, "but this silver bullet ought to identify me."

—Drug tale, 1969

———•———

In the army, they put Willie in an impermeable rubber suit and make him decontaminate toxic chemical agents. The heaviest of these is nerve gas, which can seep right through your skin, causing convulsions, paralysis, and death within fifteen seconds unless you are together enough to snatch an atropine Syrette from your mask carrier and jab it into your thigh. But since atropine also makes you high, the Syrettes are never issued.

In a class Willie sees a filmed demonstration of an experimental new gas called BZ. A tough, no-nonsense sergeant is run through a simple obstacle course, a feat he performs with contemptuous ease. The timer tells him to rest ten minutes, then try to better his time. While the sergeant is resting, they expose him to BZ.

When the timer returns and asks the sergeant to begin his second run, the sergeant giggles and tells him to go fuck himself. He picks his nose for awhile, then crawls on his hands and knees to observe a squirrel. As the film concludes, he is trying to get at his penis but can't figure out how to work the buttons on his fly.

"What a neat gas," Willie says to Sergeant Nutall. "While the enemy is incapacitated, we can go in, take his guns away, and capture him."

"Capture him?" says Sergeant Nutall. "You stupid troop! While the enemy is incapacitated, we go in and blow his brains out."

———•———

And so we emerge from the breathtaking experience of "peaking" into the wonderful world of Plateau. If you are "having a bummer," that is, if you are experiencing anxiety or panic as a result of your electrically simulated peaking experience, now's the time to "cool yourself out." Gentlemen, look to your left. The oiled and willing Ne-gresses you see have been programmed chemically to serve your every whim, from body massage to ... well, you name it. And ladies, the same applies to those rippling Korean muscle fetishists on your right.

Insert credit cards into the arm slots of your ride-a-chairs. Thank you. Thank *you*. Thank you very much. Thank you ....

—Canned spiel in the Acid-
Trip ride, Dope World
Amusement Park, 1976

———•———

Willie studies his companion for the evening, a tasty Bennington chick eight years his younger. They are high on pot and she has her eyes closed, rapt on the music issuing from his sound system. Her braless tits are full and heavy, electrically wanton. Willie can hardly restrain himself. Is the THC they dropped never going to hit?

"Fuck it," he says. "Let's smoke some angel dust."

"What's that?" she says, blinking.

"Taste it. You'll dig it." He hands her the pipe.

"It tastes *funny.*"

They begin to feel very spaced. The music seems to be reaching them from a great distance. Willie kisses her. Her lips are thick, her tongue swollen. It nearly fills his mouth. He descends to a breast and puts the nipple in his mouth. She sighs.

Then the THC hits.

Willie looks at the breast. He realizes he is perceiving it as a separate entity, unconnected to the girl. And the music sounds fucked-up. The individual notes do not connect. Each stands

JULY, 1971

*"That's a terribly tacky uniform. You look like you've gained weight ... my how you've aged ... I understand your brother is making a lot of money ..."*

alone, unrelated to the others. Willie is stuck in an ever-changing now, the individual moments of which make no sense. His mind has rejected continuity.

"Hey," says Willie. He has forgotten the girl's name.

"SNORK!" she honks, her voice greatly amplified. "BLURG ZEEBLE FLUP!" She begins to cry.

———•———

*Open on funky young dude in opulently hip pad. Visible in background is his dapper, smiling dealer.*

DUDE: (in Brooklyn accent) I go to my dealer's to score two caps of organic mesc. He says. "You're headin' for a *biiiig* bummer." (Behind him, the dealer nods knowingly.) I says, "Whaddaya mean, a big bummer? I *love* organic mesc." He says, "You're headin' for a *biiiig* bummer." I says, "Hey, c'mon, y'know? Gimme the fuckin' pills already." He says, "You're headin' for a *biiiig* bummer." But he gives me the pills. And they were cut with strychnine. I had a *biiiig* bummer. Took two Valiums.

*Cut to beauty shot of two Valiums being poured from bottle into hand.*

ANNOUNCER: Valium—with power to mellow the worst bummer you'll ever have. Now available over the counter.

DUDE: Don't have a big bummer. Take Valium.

—Television commercial, 1975

———•———

Spencer the Garbagehead had dropped some very powerful Owsley Purple an hour or so ago. It didn't matter exactly when. Time was illusory. Only vibrations mattered. He was at one with the All.

His gaily painted hearse was just chugging onto the Golden Gate Bridge. The sun was setting. All was red and gold, flashing, flashing. The sun was God. *He* was God. All the people in the shiny fruits and vegetables chugging next to him … *they* were God.

He heard a siren. A cop car pulled him over.

"Just how fast you think you were going?" the cop asked Spencer.

Spencer, peaking and flashing, attempted to gather his wits. He'd better play it on the conservative side. He couldn't have been going that fast.

"Uh, sixty-five?"

You were going four miles an hour," said the cop. "Get out of the car."

—Dope tale, 1970

———•———

Willie doesn't take acid. Acid takes Willie.

———•———

## BUSTED DEMONSTRATORS TRIP IN THE CLINK

LOS ANGELES—Beaver Logan's eyes still shine with the memory:

"There we were, five hundred freaks, tripping our brains out in the LA City Jail. You wouldn't believe the energy level we got to. One guy from Topanga was so high he could vibrate right through the bars of the cell. They had to keep putting him back."

The LSD swallowed by Ms. Logan—and the hundreds of other antiwar demonstrators busted during Spiro Agnew's Colosseum appearance earlier that day—was smuggled into jail in somebody's urine. It was immediately dubbed bladder acid.

—News item, *Rolling Stone*, June 10, 1971

———•———

Willie is marching on Washington, crackling on speed. Rank upon rank of scary-looking people, arms linked, jog with heavy boot thuds down Pennsylvania Avenue.

ONE, TWO, THREE, FOUR.
WE DON'T WANT YOUR FUCKING WAR!
STOMP, STOMP, STOMP!

Willie's heart pumps and pounds. The perimeter of his vision is sparkling like broken mirror shards. He rolls his eyes to clear them and sees men with cameras stationed on the building tops. Press? No, FBI. Fuckers. Probably have guns, too.

STOMP, STOMP, STOMP!

It's cold. Willie shivers. A voice like a harpie is shrilling into his ear. He turns to look. A girl with metal on her teeth, running at his left.

"What?"

"How militant are you? We're gonna trash the Justice Building." Her eyes flash inside like an artillery duel at night. She is carrying a sign saying YOUTH AGAINST WAR AND FASCISM.

"You gotta down?" Willie asks her. His blood is pumping through his veins in clumps. He is going to coagulate to death.

STOMP, TROMP!

"Drugs are counterrevolutionary," shouts the girl. She stabs him with a dirty look and runs elsewhere.

HO, HO, HO CHI MINH,
THE NLF IS GONNA WIN.

"Fuck this shit," says Willie. He pulls from the march, returns to his car, and drops a Librium, his final political act.

———•———

SENATOR HORSESHIT: You actually expect the committee to believe that you thought the fifty kilos of refined heroin your spaghetti company imported from Turkey at a cost of $225,000 was organic *tooth powder?*

WITNESS ZUCCHINI: You wanna believe, believe. No believe, no believe.

—Excerpt, transcript of Congressional Rackets Committee hearings, 1974

———•———

Willie lies on a bed of pine needles, back propped against a tree, gazing into the misty profundity of the Rocky Mountains. They are beautiful and alien, and he loves them the way you love someone who doesn't love you.

The woman sitting beside him, however, does love him, and he loves her. Marrin and Willie have spent three weeks living together in her Colorado cabin. Tomorrow he will be leaving to go on about his trip, so they both are

feeling some pain, but it is a sweet pain.

A few hours ago Frank the Poet came by with a gunny sack of peyote, and they each ate six buttons…all seventeen separate poisonous alkaloids of them. Marrin threw up, and Willie had fierce cramps, but then they got very high and Frank showed them the face of the peyote god on the top of one of his remaining buttons before wandering off to commune with the One.

Marrin glances at Willie. She sees that he is brooding and starts to tickle him. Willie defends his ribs briefly, then starts tickling back. They get into one of those giggling things where every time you look at each other you start laughing all over again. Finally, the laughing gives way to fucking. A cool mountain wind, perfumed with pine, caresses their naked asses.

———— • ————

"Hello?"

"Peter? This is Tim."

"Timmie! Hey, man."

"Listen, I'm looking for some fiction editions, and I wondered if you had any in stock."

"Well, no…no fiction. But I have some very fine nonfiction."

"Um. Is it really *interesting* nonfiction?"

"Oh, yes. In fact, it reads like fiction. Haven't been able to put it down, y'know?"

"Well, how long are they?"

"For you, 250 pages. Get three or more, and I'll make it 235 each."

"Sounds good. Of course, I'll want to see the first few chapters."

"Of course."

"Now, what about obscure pieces? Say, eighth century?"

"Ah, yes, I have some superb obscure pieces. From Peru! The eighth-century ones are 175 pages."

"I can get behind that. See you later?"

"You bet."

"*Ciao.*"

—Telephone transaction, *New York City, 1972*

———— • ————

Dope Daniel, Willie's dealer, whisks the ten of diamonds into the glistening heap of cocaine, withdraws a small quantity, and spills it onto the mirror top. The card beats a tiny tattoo on the mirror as, French-chefwise, he slices the rocks into powder. With the edge of the card, he drags the powder into four slim rails and hands the mirror to Willie.

Snurt. Snurt. Two of the rails disappear through a rolled-up fifty into Willie's nose, striking the roof of his nasal cavities like sweet ak-ak.

"Mmph!"

"Lotsa rocks," observes Dope Daniel.

"Yeah." Willie snorts the second two rails, leans back, and closes his eyes. "Yeah!" He sits back up. "I'll get it together for a half-ounce. Meet me at my apartment at midnight."

"Solid. But, listen, don't have anyone else there, okay? That's *really* important." At his feet, Evelyn, his Doberman pinscher, yawns toothily.

"Sure. See ya later."

Willie finds three friends who want eighths, gets $150 from each, adds $50 of his own, and goes home to wait. It is eleven o'clock.

At 11:10, his doorbell rings. Puzzled, he goes to the door and finds Frank the Finger and Bernie Boom-Boom from Brooklyn.

"My man!" says Frank. "Fantastic that you're home. Mr. Chiba has come to town!"

"Chiba?" This is good news indeed. Chiba, the Colombian grass, has been the number-one high-quality weed in the city for the last few years, and Willie has been wanting some. "Come on in, but you can only stay for a few minutes. I have a thing to do at midnight."

"Not to worry," says Bernie. They sit on Willie's sofa, and Frank withdraws a Baggie of chiba from an inner pocket of his embroidered blue-jeans jacket.

"All tops and buds," he points out, handing the bag over. The weed is brown and red and smells like a fresh country breeze. It seems to Willie to have its own inner glow.

"Here's a joint of it," says Bernie. He eases the tip into the flame of the candle on Willie's left speaker and hands it to him. Willie tokes.

The doorbell rings.

"Holy shit," says Willie. "I'm supposed to be alone."

"Come on," says Bernie, pulling Frank by the arm. "We'll hide in the bedroom."

Willie goes to the door and peers through the peephole. It is Hash Henry!

"Willie? I got ounces of Moroccan red at European prices. Lemme in."

Willie had been about to ask Henry to come back later, but…

"Henry baby! Come in! But you can only stay a couple of minutes. I got a…chick in the bedroom."

"Right on. Just taste this." He pulls a slim hash pipe from his handwoven Greek dealer's bag.

Willie takes two tokes, and the doorbell rings again.

"Good Lord. Look, Henry, go into the bathroom for a few minutes, willya? I'm sorry, but I have to be alone to do a short number here."

"Sure, man." Hash Henry sidles into the can. Willie goes to the door.

It is Carol McHashoil!

"Listen," says Willie, opening the door a crack, "I can't…"

"Willie," she stage-whispers, "I've got Afghan oil at thirty a gram."

"…*say* how pleased I am to see you! Come in!"

Carol hands him a cigarette with a thin line of green painted on it. Willie already had a chiba joint in his left hand and a hash pipe in his right. He transfers the pipe, takes the cigarette, and inhales.

*Ring!*

Stammering quick, meaningless noises, Willie hustles Carol into the kitchen, hurries back to the door, and opens it.

It is Molta Hector and his old lady, Miranda!

"Willie," cries Hector, embracing him Hispanically. "*Numero uno,* man. I jos get eet thees mornin'. An' deeg—only thirty dollar a gram, twenny-fife eef joo take more dan whun!"

"*Amigo!*" Willy takes the proffered joint and tokes.

*Ring!*

Hector and Miranda help Willie stand up again. "Joo okay, man?"

"Please, don't ask me to explain, but get in the closet here for a few seconds, willya?"

"Uh, chure."

Willie takes three deep breaths and goes to the peephole.

Dope Daniel.

Willie opens the door. Dope Daniel steps into Willie's apartment, carrying a motorcycle helmet, followed by Evelyn the Doberman and Mary the old lady, who likes dwarfs and hunchbacks. Willie glances at the clock. Midnight exactly.

"Hey, man," says Dope Daniel, giving Willie a hug. "Mary's gonna make us some C."

"I'll go in the kitchen," says Mary.

"No!" says Willie. "I mean, the kitchen is disgusting. Full of roaches. You'd hate it in there."

"I'm hip," says Mary. "We'll fix it in the living room. But you'll have to close your eyes."

This is a new one on Willie. "Why?"

"Mary wants to *present* it to you, man. Just close your eyes for a couple of seconds, okay?"

"Oh, okay." Feeling like he has totally lost control over his own life, Willie sits on his sofa and closes his eyes.

He hears coke being chopped and matches lit. Finally, Mary says, "Open!"

Willie opens. Dope Daniel and Mary are smiling at him. He looks down and finds on the table before him a cupcake tin, filled to the brim with sparkling white cocaine. There is a small, lit candle in its center.

"Surprise!" cry Dope Daniel and Mary.

From every door of his apartment issue dealers waving gaily wrapped packages. "Happy birthday! Happy birthday!"

"WOOF!" says Evelyn.  □

# FOTO FUNNIES

LOOK, SUPPOSE YOU HAD NEVER EATEN A STEAK BEFORE, BUT YOU HAD HEARD IT WAS REALLY GOOD...

...WHAT YOU'RE DOING IS SAYING THAT YOU'RE GOING TO STARVE YOURSELF AND NOT EAT ANYTHING SO THAT WHEN YOU EAT THAT STEAK, IT'S REALLY GOING TO BE DELICIOUS...

...THE TROUBLE IS--AND HERE'S THE PITFALL A LOT OF YOU GIRLS FALL INTO-- THAT WHEN YOU FINALLY SIT DOWN TO EAT THAT STEAK...

...AFTER STARVING YOURSELF FOR SO LONG, YOU'VE BUILT THAT STEAK UP IN YOUR MIND SO MUCH...

...THAT NO MATTER HOW GOOD IT TASTES, IT'S NEVER GOING TO MEET UP WITH YOUR EXPECTATIONS. SEE?

NOT TILL I'M MARRIED.

98

**FIREBLAST!**
*Twice the car you'll ever need—and that goe for the new four-door FunTop!*

written and illustrated by Bruce McCall

## *Fireblast for '58!*
Take exclusive new Darestreak styling! Add improved DynaJet Thunderamic 6000 V-8 power! Include AutoFlite Touch-N-Go Shiftmatic, now 4 percent smoother with Triple-Turbine Surgemaster Drive! Toss in new Gyro-Cloud Full-Spring Suspension, now newly refined. Add new PowerDive Foot Command brakes! New Turbo-Glare Dual Headlights! Pan-O-Wrap Full-Vu Windshield design! Mister, you just found a whole new way of going—not to mention a whole new way of saying you've arrived!

Fireblast is crafted in WondaWeev, new double-strength material-like substance available in 4,569 color combinations!

Milady will adore Fireblast's new space-age-type Revolvomatic passenger chair!

New way to go: AutoFlite Touch-N-Go Shiftmatic!

Models shown: New Fireblast Custom Fleetflair SporTop four-door Special Deluxe Coupe de Grace 4000 in Thuringian Indigo, Tijuana Gold, and Cloudmist White; background, new Firewood Deluxe Special five-door Custom Flairfleet six-passenger Country Cousin Landscape Cruiser 2000 in Abyssinian Mauve and Foamfroth White.

ouble

Flashbolt thrills with sumptuous details like a full-length glove compartment at no extra cost!

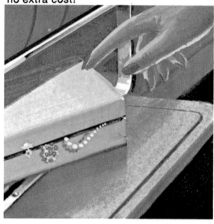

Flashbolt chills—or warms—with Ultra-KlimaTron Interior Weather Control Unit. You'll want to order two!

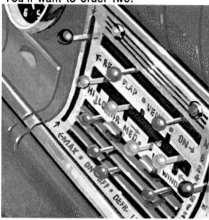

Flashbolt wills its way around curves with new SofTouch Steering!

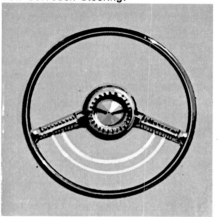

Model shown: New Flashbolt Special Custom Flairwing SkyTop two-door Deluxe Supreme Sport Coupe 3000 in Bessarabian Plum, Omdurman Yellow, and Tundra Frost Silver.

# FLASHBOLT!
## The latest look in timeless elegance meets

**Flashbolt!** From authentic-type front air-scoop to dramatic Double-Delta Sweptail fins, this baby growls "Drive Me!" And who could refuse, with that special DynaJet Thunderamic 6000 Super-Fire-bomb V-8 up front and a heritage borrowed from the Grand Prix? Sport lovers, you got it all! AutoFlite Touch-N-Go Shiftmatic! Adjustable rear-view mirror! Up to 32 percent more trunk room! Built-in turn signals! If it isn't on new Flashbolt for '58, it hasn't been invented yet!!

Flashbolt fills rear lounging area with richly simulated Wonda-Weev fabric-like material, adds scrumptious extras like Full-Vu glass and new Ejecta-Matic ashtrays.

# pirit inspired by the road tracks of Europe!

# FIREWOOD!
## For the man who has everything and just

### Firewood!
Versatile—that sums up Bulgemobile's new world of Landscape Cruisers for '58—as much at home in front of the country club as they are at the polo match or the fox hunt! What gives 'em their special sizzle 'n' style? Here's a straight answer: magic! The magic of new Darestreak Styling, jetswept and sweptwinged and rarin' to go! The magic of Gyro-Cloud Full-Spring Suspension! The magic of Bulgemobile Quality-Crafted Value that gives you extras you don't want to pay for at prices of the future! Firewood! If you didn't know it was 1958, you'd think you just wandered into 1984!

Open wide and say "Aaah."
That's what you'll do when you lift up
Firewood's tailgate and look at all
that storage space!!

104

Model shown: New Firewood
Deluxe Supreme Flairthrust five-door,
six-passenger Special Custom
Country-Cousin Landscape Cruiser Super
5000 in Golden Buttermilk Sunset
Sienna Ochre with Daredash side-
spear of Cameroon Teak Inlay in
genuine Processite.

# eeds something to carry it in!

## Somebody mention safety?
## How's about this?

You're looking at the biggest safety breakthrough in all
Bulgemobile history—or should we say you're looking *through* it!
It's new C-Thru Windshield Glass, now up to 63 percent more
transparent! And it comes on every Bulgemobile you can buy!
Doesn't that say a lot about how much Bulgemobile cares about
you and your driving safety? You bet your life!

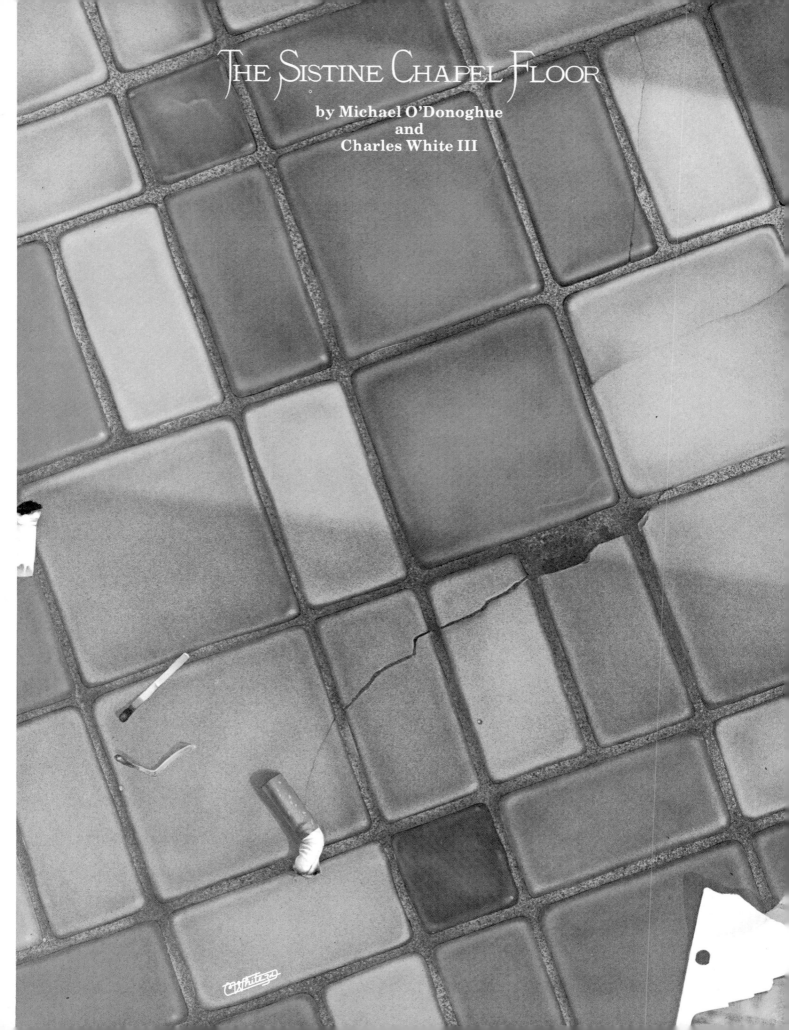

# Surprise Poster

## The Delegate from Chappaquiddick

by Michael O'Donoghue

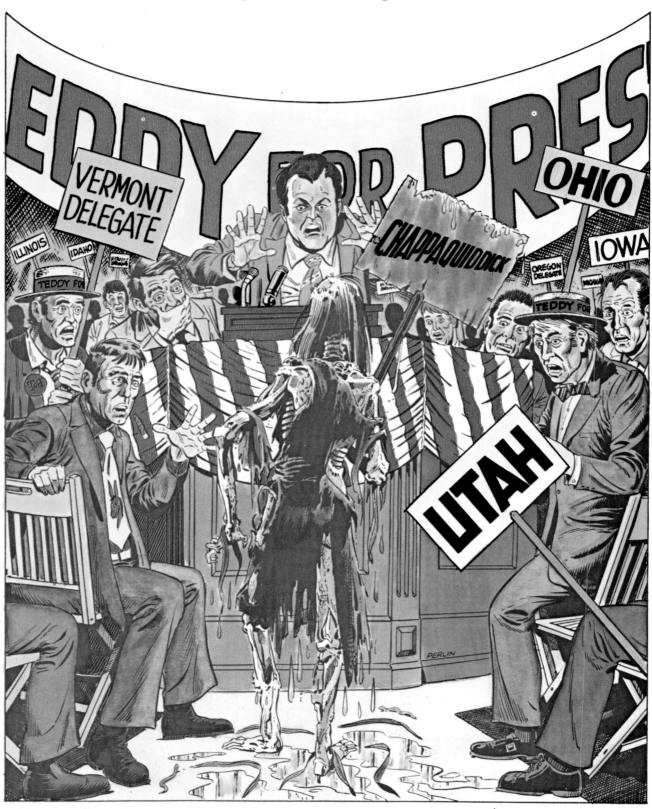

THE OTHER SERVICES SOON LEARN NOT TO TANGLE WITH THE TWIN-FISTED DENTAL CORPS....

HEL-**LO**, DREAMBOAT! HOWZABOUT YOU AN' YER GALFRIEND DITCHIN' THESE CREAMPUFFS AN' JOININ' US?

WHAT SAY WE **DRILL** A LITTLE SENSE INTO THEIR HEADS, MEL?

YOU MUGS JUST **BIT OFF** MORE THAN YOU CAN **CHEW!**

SECONDS LATER...

The Blue Boar

HOLY MOSES! SOME NUMBSKULL MUSTA RILED THEM CRAZY DENTISTS AGAIN! WON'T THEY EVER LEARN?

THIS SAME FIGHTING SPIRIT MAKES THEM A BATTLE-FIELD LEGEND, FROM THE STEAMING JUNGLES OF BATAAN...

TAKKA! TAKKA!

THE TINFOIL FROM THIS CHEWING-GUM WRAPPER SHOULD SERVE AS A TEMPORARY FILLING UNTIL WE CAN GET YOU BACK TO THE BASE, SON!

DUB DUB DUB

...TO THE BULLET-RAKED BEACHES OF ANZIO....

HMMMMMMM! WELL, IT APPEARS AS IF YOU NEED SOME WORK ON THE UPPER RIGHT MOLAR AND...LET'S SEE...

BUDDA BUDDA

SOME WON'T BE COMING HOME....

AND REMEMBER, BRUSH REGULARLY AFTER EVERY ME—

PHLUUUUUEEEE

# Click

### by Gahan Wilson

PHIL: This first slide here shows Madge and Bill standing right there in front of the New York Space Authority building, ready to start our trip. You can tell it was a pretty nice day on account they're not wearing any protective clothing except for goggles and a mask. The old guy got hit by our taxi—that was some wild driver we had—and the kid's playing a trick on him. Cute, hah?

MADGE: If he hadn't of done it someone else would of. *CLICK.*

PHIL: Now this here was some lucky shot. I was going to take a picture of Billy there, when this guy steps on the Hijacker Sentinal and *pow*, huh? What I mean is it really got him good. I asked why it done it and they said it was on account of he looked suspicious and if you study the expression on his face you can see how they got to wondering about him.

MADGE: It turned out he didn't have no gun or bomb or anything.

PHIL: Look, all they can do is the best they can and I'm glad they got those things up there protecting us, anyways. *CLICK.*

PHIL: Well then, after we got settled in our cabin and the ship took off and all, we went up to the observation lounge and I mean they had the place really fixed up swell. No less than sixteen TV sets all going at the same time, each on a different station, of course, and a bar and every kind of a slot machine and game like that you could wish for. Back there through that window you could see the universe out there if you wanted.

MADGE: I won a whole lot of credit at the Lucky Astronaut game but I lost it all on the Zodiac Wheel. *CLICK.*

PHIL: Just a day out from Mars they announced everybody had to come and see the indoctrination lecture, and I hadn't been looking forward to that. It was something those stiffs at the United Nations had whipped up to teach you all about the Martians' customs and way of life and even their goddamn religion, for Christ's sake. But then I saw it was our social director, Earl, going to do it, and I relaxed right off.

MADGE: That Earl!

PHIL: You see, those UN creeps had given Earl a whole bunch of pictures and graphs and stuff he was supposed to teach us with, and I guess they'd bust a gut if they ever saw what he done with them. Here he is pretending to explain the sex life of a Martian, can you beat it? Only they don't have no sex life on account of they haven't had any babies in thousands of years. He sure had us all laughing. *CLICK*.

PHIL: Right at the space port they got these weird Martians trying to sell you pots and statues and stuff. Nothing but a lot of junk, if you ask me. Anyhow I was taking a picture of one of them when Billy did this here. It's a good thing those Martians can't talk or this one here would have really given the kid a couple of bad words I bet you.

MADGE: It's not that they can't talk, it's that they've taken an oath of silence. Don't you remember the joke Earl made on that, honey?

PHIL: Well, anyhow, the way that stuff broke up, he had a nerve trying to sell it. *CLICK*.

PHIL: Right outside our hotel there, they had this wall which goes on practically forever and has all these religious pictures on it, and our guide told us a lot more than I was interested hearing about it. Anyhow it's supposed to be very holy and all like that.

MADGE: That right there behind me is supposed to be the sun. *CLICK*.

113

PHIL: The next day we went out on a fishing trip, and here's the baby I come up with. What do you think of that, hah? They asked me did I want it stuffed and that handed me a laugh on account of where would I put it once I got it home, right? I don't think you could get it through the street out there. Then they asked me did I want some of it to eat it and I told them they had to be kidding. I mean who could eat something like that, for Christ's sake, and you could smell it starting to rot. Anyhow, it was something, my catching it, cause there's hardly any of them left. *CLICK.*

PHIL: Now this was a really terrific place and the fellow who run it one of the funniest fellows you'd ever care to meet. A really swell souvenir shop and we bought a whole bunch of stuff there. You saw that thing in the bathroom, hah? What'd you think of that? And a whole bunch of other stuff, too.

MADGE: That's Billy there, wearing the mask. He got sick in it on the flight back. What a mess.

PHIL: Anyhow, that fellow that run the souvenir shop was a hell of a funny guy. *CLICK.*

PHIL: So on the last day of the tour they took us to the Holy City there, which was out in the desert away from the town. There were these Martians at the entrance playing what was supposed to be a song of greeting, our guide told us, but it sounded to me more like a bunch of cats in heat, right, Madge?

MADGE: I had to laugh. *CLICK.*

PHIL: Speaking of laughing, here's Mr. Parker again. Seemed to me he was always laughing at something or other.

MADGE: Sometimes he'd laugh at nothing at all.

PHIL: Well here he is fit to bust on account he can't break off any of these statues right. I don't know how many he tried, must have been at least twenty, but he never did get one to break at the feet like he wanted to.

MADGE: He was going to make it into a lamp stand.

PHIL: See the stone they use there is very porous and light and what with the gravity and all being what it is you can make like Superman. Really a lot of fun. *CLICK*.

PHIL: Here's Billy, pushing over a whole, entire wall! Hard to believe, isn't it? Boy, that kid really went to town. Oh yeah, and this picture cleared up a little mystery we had all the way on the flight back which was: whatever happened to Mr. Parker, and if you look down at the left-hand corner of the picture there you can see what happened to him.

MADGE: Billy mustn't have seen he was there. *CLICK*.

PHIL: So here's Madge and Billy and we're all leaving the Holy City and Mars and I'm not ashamed to tell you we were a little choked up, you know? And it wasn't just the dust and all, it was knowing we'd probably never live to see Mars again.

MADGE: Now, Phil . . .

PHIL: No, it's true, Madge—hell, we might as well admit it. We're not kids anymore. That was our last chance. I just wish we'd done more while we were there.

MADGE: There's always Billy, dear.□

FOTO FUNNIES

TRANSCENDENTAL MEDITATION?

NO.

KUNDALINI YOGA?

UH-UH.

ASTRAL PROJECTION?

NOPE.

PSYCHOKINESIS?

GETTING COLDER.

TIBETAN MANTRAS?

WRONG, IT'S...

...HEMORRHOIDS!

# Dodosaurs

## Dinosaurs That Didn't Make It
### by Rick Meyerowitz

Millions of years before the dawn of man, the earth was ruled by giant reptiles whose scaly likenesses are familiar to any fan of natural-science journals or cheapo Japanese ick flicks. However, every standard model *Tyrannosaurus Rex* or *Brontosaurus* that rumbled off Mother Nature's assembly line was preceded by dozens of evolutionary Edsels who finished dead last in the race for survival and were soon consigned to behemothballs. On the following pages, NatLampCo Science Foundation lizard wizard **Rick Meyerowitz** pays homage to these passé paleoliths. Behemothballs?

The **Preposterosaur**, a tiny-headed carnivore of the Early Sciatic Period, towered seven inches above the ground and, understandably, found it difficult to convince anything to allow itself to be eaten. Thus, the Preposterosaur pooled its resources with the **Ridiculadon** (two and a half inches) to become a nine-and-a-half-inch **Thesaurus** (literally, "terror of the mud puddle") and quickly starved to death, decease, demise, departure. See EXTINCT.

Swampy shorelines wer[e]
the temporary habitat o[f]
the short-lived **Ptoitysaur**
Primarily a harmles[s]
muckraker along coasta[l]
marshlands, this "Comod[o]
dragon's" moment in th[e]
slimelight (3,000,002–
3,000,000 B.C.) was cut shor[t]
by fellow bog-dweller[s]
who could not ptolerat[e]
its breath

The **Tricyclatops** was [a]
Darwinian uh-uh tha[t]
resulted from the matin[g]
of a *Tricercetops* and [a]
*Bicycladon* on a listles[s]
rainy Sunday afternoo[n]
approximately four millio[n]
years ago. Their traine[d]
wheeled offspring domi[-]
nated the Cohassett Perio[d]
until late Wednesday

Little is known of th[e]
**Winosaur** (*Deliriu[m]
tremendus*) beyond its die[t]
of fermented fruits (se[e]
page 56) and its natura[l]
enemy, the Pin[k]
Mammoth

In an attempt at aerodynamic compensation for its vast bulk, the **Pterrible-dactyl** (*Kamikasus bonzai*) was equipped with a tri-wing anatomy that gave this evolutionary SST a top speed of 144 feet per second. Once.

The only dinosaur lacking even a vestigial brain, the **Lesser Moronodon,** or "Dunder-lizard," lived out its brief life-span (twenty-eight minutes, thirty-five seconds) as one of Mother Nature's crueler jokes. The entire species quickly fell prey to its intellectual superiors, which included the Trilobite and a number of advanced ferns.

Time has passed the **Masturdon** by. So shall we.

Carrying the protective carapace of the Anklyosaurus to further lengths, the heavily armored **Tanklyosaurus** (*Panzerus claustrophobus*) is thought to be the ancestor of the common tortoise. Although invulnerable to attack from predators, the Tanklyosaurus never surmounted its instinctive urge to stay asleep.

The **Homosaur** minced the earth simply ages ago, but, like the reader, never lived to be as old as it looked. You bitch. □

Here, a pair of one-legged **Pogosaurs** have joined forces, linking forelegs to avoid their tendency to fall over. It is ironic to think how these unfortunate creatures might have flourished had they lasted until the Dawn of Hopscotch, which evolved somewhat later. Ironic to some, anyway.

# LET'S GET
# AMERICA OUT OF DUTCH

Occupant
635 Madison Ave.
New York, N.Y. 10022

AMERICANS UNITED TO BEAT THE DUTCH
POST OFFICE BOX 6041, WASHINGTON, D.C. 20109

KNOW THE ENEMY!

FLORID FACE          SHIFTY EYES
WEAK CHIN            BEER AND/OR
                     CHEESE BREATH

CHOCOLATE UNDER
FINGERNAILS

**D**ike-building schemes

**U**nrest everywhere

**T**ulip scourge

**C**heese-mongering

**H**ex signs

# The A.U.T.B.D. Newsletter

PRICE--50 CENTS

# ACTION!

*

We're happy to welcome all you new tile-smashers to the fight against Dutch subterfuge. Our movement is growing by leaps and bounds every day, and although we cannot disclose the exact number of our members to prevent infiltration from certain persons who feel more at home in footwear made out of trees, we can say that it is very large indeed and getting larger! Politicians be warned!

You will ignore this aroused brotherhood of true Americans at your peril! And if you don't believe us, take a wishy-washy position on Government-supported elm-seeding programs and stiff tariffs to protect our razor-makers, breweries, dairies, diamond mines, and chocolate manufacturers next Election Day and SEE WHAT HAPPENS!

\* \* \* \* \* \* \* \* \* \* \* \* \* \* \* \* \* \* \* \* \* \*

by Henry Beard and Christopher Cerf

I regret to say that I must begin this month's issue of the A.U.T.B.D. newsletter with an important piece of unfinished--and unpleasant--business.

I am referring, of course, to Mijnheer Duane Van Der Vincent and his band of Soestdijk Palace hirelings who lick the hollandaise from the wooden jackboots of Prince Bernhard while pretending to be fighting the Bane of the Benelux! All of us true Americans at A.U.T.B.D. had him and his cheese-loving crew spotted from the moment they tried to infiltrate the organization three years ago, and we were just playing along with them, waiting for them to try their power grab. Now that they've shown their chocolate-smeared hands by forming their transparent front group at the bidding of the Big Burgher in an effort to confuse and divide American opposition to the Low Country's highjinks, we can expose them for the delft double-crossers they are! Do not be fooled by their claims of militancy against the Nederlander menace! They are not true opponents of the nemesis of the North Sea! They are in the pay of the Bandit Prince! They loll in their plush offices, eating grilled-cheese sandwiches, swilling creme de cacao, and reading Dutch pornography! We must unite to oppose these vicious upstarts! Ignore their crude propaganda and laughable attacks on real foes of the tyrants of Rotterdam! They are beneath contempt! They stink of Edam and Gouda! The lewd litanies of the Dutch Reformed Church are ever on their lips! SHUN THESE SINISTER IMPOSTERS! REPUDIATE THEIR BASE LIES! THE INFECTED ELM MUST BE CUT DOWN TO SPARE THE HEALTHY TREES!

    --Leading Dike-buster Raymond Petri

xxxxxxxxxxxxxxxxxxxxxxxxxxxxxxxxxxxxxxxxxx

# Tulips Take Lead

## WILL HE FALL FOR IT?

FORT WAYNE, IND., Aug. 14 (UPI) —According to statistics released here by the National Flower Growers' Association Convention, tulips are the nation's number-one Easter gift-flower, with sales of over 14,000,000 individual blooms last year alone.

Lilies, which used to be the favored holiday flower, are now in second place in the potted-plant category. The popularity of the distinctive Dutch import, long a familiar part of the Easter scene, has been growing steadily for years, in spite of the fact that it has practically no scent.

No scent? No, just the odor of conspiracy and the foul smell of deceit!

xxxxxxxxxxxxxxxxxx

The Bandit Prince and his evil Queen, the Grand Dike Juliana, enlist more willing dupes into their vicious drainage schemes.

xxxxxxxxxxxxxxxxxx

**sab•o•tage** \ˈsab-ə-ˌtäzh\ *n* (fr. *saboter* to trample on with sabots, the wooden shoes worn in European countries, chiefly Holland) **1**: destruction of property or hindering of manufacture by discontented workmen **2**: destructive or obstructive action carried on by a civilian or enemy agent designed to hinder a nation's war effort **3**: an act or process tending to hamper or hurt.

*Sabot*

    —Webster's American Dictionary

Thanks, Mr. Webster--that's all we needed to know!

A big vote of thanks is due to the staunch zee-protectors who braved the rain to picket the notorious Concertgebouw Orchestra during its appearance at the Bushnell Auditorium in Hartford, Connecticut. In spite of the inclement weather--and it's no accident we've been getting so much bad weather, either, since the natural process of evaporation has been thrown out of kilter by the Bandit Prince's relentless drainage projects carried out behind wraps on supersecret "wildlife preserves"--more than half a dozen loyal Americans were on hand to alert the audience to the insidious manhood-robbing melodies scheduled by Mijnheer Joachim Ruyter and his "musicians." As usual, the police had been bought off with boxes of Dutch Slavemasters cigars from Mijnheer Fidel Van Der Castro's plantations, and they prevented the hardy band of cheese-grillers from greeting the Maestro of Maastricht backstage with a good old-fashioned American "review" of his performance.

Still and all, a good day's work, and a potent reminder to some people who shine their shoes with shellac that this country isn't about to be sweet-talked into swallowing the Soestdijk Palace line with a few phony low-country lullabies!

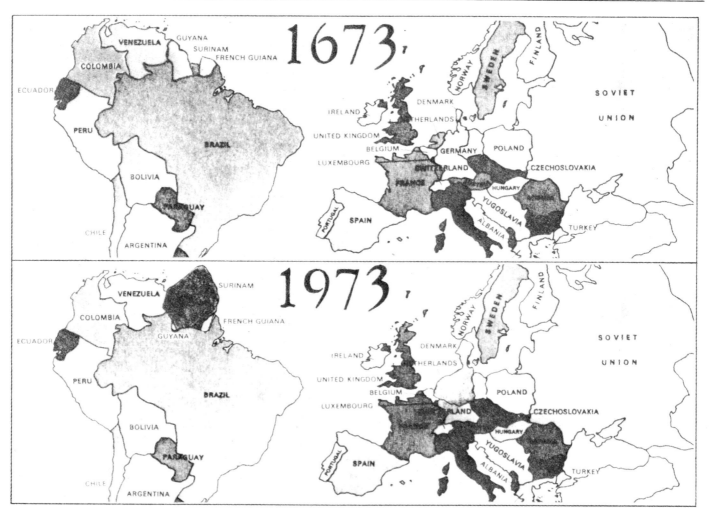

Fellow travelers in the U.S. government are trying to keep you from seeing these maps, but reliable State Department sources released them to us. The Dutch imperialists plan to conquer the world by expanding Surinam and the Netherlands with their insidious system of dikes. Eventually the two areas will join up, cutting off all shipping between the Old World and the New, and the Soestdijk murderers will control the high seas. As you can see, they've already made remarkable progress. They must be stopped! Now! BOMB THE DIKES!

XXXXXXXXXXXXXXXXXXXXXXXXXXXXXXXXXXXXXXXXXXXXXXXXX

VITAL BOOKS

THE PROTOCOLS OF THE LEARNED ELDERS OF THE HAGUE. These are the minutes of a secret meeting of Dutch leaders to plot control of the Benelux countries...................$6.00

ROTTERDAM: HOTBED OF PORNOGRAPHY. Over 100 magnificently reproduced photographs proving that Rotterdam is indeed a hotbed of pornography. (What less would you expect from the people who gave <u>American</u> towns names like Climax, Intercourse, and Blueball?) This is the best book on our list for converting new people...................................$15.00

BETWEEN SACRILEGE AND BLASPHEMY: THE STRANGE STORY OF THE DUTCH REFORMED CHURCH. What, if anything, was so awful about the church that the Dutch should feel called upon to reform it? This horrifying book asks that question and, as you might suspect, fails to come up with the answer.........................$5.00

NONE DARE CALL IT GOUDA...and neither will you, once you've read the shocking facts about what really lies beneath that innocent-looking outer layer of red wax.......$4.00

OLD MASTERS OF DECEIT. The astonishing facts about how the so-called Dutch Masters--Rembrandt van Rijn and Jan Vermeer--cheated unsuspecting art dealers of their own and later times out of hundreds of thousands of dollars --by dashing off cunning forgeries of their own work...............................$4.00

THE DIKES OF HOLLAND. It's a little-known fact that female homosexuality was invented in the Netherlands, but it's true, as this book proves through a breathtaking series of photographs.........................$20.00

THE DIARY OF ANNE FRANK: PREPOSTEROUS FORGERY OR OBVIOUS LIE?........................$4.00

MIJNHEER MIES VAN DER ROHE: DESIGNER OF DEATH TRAPS OR ARCHITECT OF DOOM?............$3.00

While we're at it, it's high time to blow the whistle on the whole sly scheme of the gnomes of Zeeland for world economic domination. With the help of the Stuyvesants, the VanDerBilts, the Roojkefellers, and other double-dealing Dutch cousins who are big cheeses in Nieuw York banking circles, these guilder-grubbers use promises of diamonds---and shares in the vast profits from their perfidious trade in narcotics made from Flanders poppies and opium tulips---to woo greedy Wall Street tycoons into backing their plan to put the financial world onto the discredited cheese standard. At the same time, they labor long and hard to ruin confidence in gold by flooding the Free World with gold coins that on close inspection turn out to contain nothing but chocolate. And every time some money-hungry fat cat, his brain fuddled by their flourine-laced liqueurs, falls for one of their dirty Dutch deals, millions more pour into the coffers of the Bandit Prince and his robber-burghers. And where does it go from there? It goes to finance Royal Dutch Shell, which at this very minute, under the ridiculous pretense of drilling for oil in the North Sea, is actually pumping dry this vital ocean highway, sending billions of gallons of water into the already dangerously swollen English Channel.

The Dutch timetable for conquest is clear. It's the eleventh hour on the flower clocks of the Hague. Yet while good Americans loll in their bone-crushing van der Rohe chairs, unknowingly allowing their bodies to be poisoned by radioactive Dutch Boy paints and foolishly subjecting their delicate facial follicles to the same deadly Phillips razors used by Mijnheer van Gogh to cut off his ear when he flew into a fury after learning that his plan to foist off forgeries of his work as his own had been discovered, our politicians are being seduced by buxom milkmaids at wild cheese-tasting parties at the Dutch embassy and bought off by promises of huge estates in the New Holland they'll build once the Great Lakes are drained!

---
*
---

```
XXXXXXXXXXXXXXXXXXXXXXXXXXXXXXX
X                             X
X     KEEP OUT OF THE REACH   X
X                             X
X         OF CHILDREN         X
X                             X
X    AVOID CONTACT WITH EYES  X
X                             X
XXXXXXXXXXXXXXXXXXXXXXXXXXXXXXX
```

This label was reproduced from the side of a can of Old Dutch Cleanser. The Surgeon General obviously considers this product too hazardous to be used by America's youngsters, and, apparently, the things it can do to your eyes are just too horrible to describe! And yet in the name of "good sportsmanship" our snivelling, vote-seeking politicians make no move to take Old Dutch Cleanser off the market. We say, "To hell with Old Dutch Cleanser! To hell with Juliana and Bernhard and their treacherous American puppets! The spirit of Leopold I of Saxe-Coburg-Gotha will prevail!"

# Dutch Gets Boost

UNITED NATIONS, N.Y., Feb. 12 (AP)—A report issued by the U.N. Information Office shows that Dutch has moved from 14th to 13th on the list of the world's most commonly spoken languages.

The shift puts it just ahead of Malay and behind Tamil, a Hindu dialect. U.N. offiicals attributed the change to a previous error rather than to any significant growth in the number of people speaking the oddly lilting European tongue.

The only "error" is on the part of our leaders, who are so blinded by promises of chocolate-covered diamonds and other Hollander gewgaws that they can't--or won't--see the handwriting on the dike!

**********************

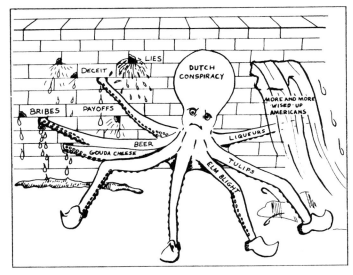

"A touch. A smile. A shared memory of a special time. That look that says more than a volume of poetry. The kiss that says you are a dream come true.

Diamonds are more than a promise. Diamonds are forever."

--De Beers Consolidated Mines ad

Just another of the many open invitations to adultery and lustful behavior planted in our popular publications by the Bandit Prince and his greedy gem-lords to weaken our will, so that when we hear the sound of a chain saw cutting our doors in half in the middle of the night, we'll be too sated with sickening pleasures to resist!

---

Here's a poem from a little girl in Buffalo, New York, which should give us all a lot of hope for the future!

---

Roses are red,
Tulips are bad,
I hope Prince Bernhard
Chokes on a shad.

(Shad are a kind of fish they have in Holland which I read about in geography class and we couldn't find the Frisian Islands on the map, either.)

## DUTCH JOKES

Q. Why do Dutchmen wear red suspenders?
A. So they can use them to strangle helpless, enslaved Frisian Islanders.

Q. Who was the Dutch lady I saw you with
   last night?
A. That was no lady.  That was a dike.

He: I just ate some Dutch cheese.
She: Was it Gouda?
He: Jesus, no.  It was awful! God knows
    what was in it.

He: There were several Dutch cheeses on
    that plate.
She: Edam?
He: Are you kidding? I might have been
    poisoned.

Q. What did the Dutch tulip farmer do when
   the traveling Frisian asked to stay overnight at his windmill?
A. He made him sleep with his Dutch elm
   disease-ridden daughter, then baked him
   alive in his delft-tile kiln.

Q. Why did Hitler firebomb Rotterdam, Gomorrah
   of the North?
A. Because he liked his burghers well done.

Q. Why did the chicken cross the road?
A. Because land-hungry Dutchmen had turned
   its precious marshy habitat into barren
   tulip fields.

Q. What's white on the outside and black and
   blue all over?
A. A defenseless Flemish nun who was tied to
   a windmill arm, then whipped by a vicious
   Dutchman with a cat-of-nine-tulips.

He: Who is the smartest Dutchman?
She: Senator Jacob Javijts.
He: But he's Jewish.
She: He fooled you too, didn't he?

Q. Why don't they have baptisms in the Dutch
   Reformed Church?
A. Because they drained all the fonts and
   planted them with tulips.

   "Knock, knock.  Knock, knock."
   "Who's there?"
   "Amsterdam."
   "Amsterdam who?"
   "Answer the damn door, you slimy cheese-
   gobbling zee-drainer! Either you come out and
   take your medicine or I'll bust it down and
   come in there and beat you into a pulp like
   any right-thinking American should."

Q. How many Dutchmen does it take to torture
   a hapless Frisian?
A. One to stoke the kiln and six to turn the
   spit.

Q. What has eighteen legs, eats cheese, smells
   bad, and has a florid complexion?
A. A Dutch baseball team playing with the head
   of a decapitated Belgian.

xxxxxxxxxxxxxxxxxxxxxxxxxxxxxxxxxxxxxxxxxxxxxxxxxxxxxxxxxxxxxxxxxxxxxxxxxxxxxxxxxxxxx

Question: Is it any wonder the Netherlands and
surrounding area are known as the "low countries"?

Answer: No.  The name is only too appropriate,
as millions of victims of Dutch perfidy will
readily attest.

# The World Wildlife Fund—
# Blueprint for Global Domination

The Royal Dutch Imperialists and their international front, the World Wildlife Movement, are winning the battle for men's minds. They make a special effort to feed on the compassion of our bird and animal lovers, and to destroy the will of all who resist their land-reclamation efforts.

"The power and influence of the World Wildlife Fund," wrote Prince Bernhard of Lippe-Biesterfeld in the semiofficial Royal Dutch political journal *Animals*, "and of the conservation movement generally has grown steadily. More and more people now support conservation activities around the world; governments, too, are beginning to appreciate the importance of conserving wildlife and wild places."

Much as they have done with their dike-building programs in the low countries and in Surinam, the Dutch want to expand their territory through the deceptively simple twin practices of landfill and drainage. Every cesspool that is drained to be a bird sanctuary, every dump that is cleared to extend a meadowland is noted gleefully by the Dutch in the Soestdijk Palace who can see how thoughtless and vulnerable these "conservationist dopes" really are.

GIVE COPIES OF THIS ARTICLE TO
ANYONE WEARING THE ECOLOGY SYMBOL;
ALSO TO THE PERSONNEL AT
YOUR LOCAL RECYCLING CENTER.

ONE CENT EACH--100 for $1.00

Authentic photo showing Mijnheer Richard Mil-
hoous Van Der Nijxon and Mijnvrouw Pat taken
by courageous photographer in the White Haaus,
or Soestdijk West, as it has come to be known.

# Elm Periled

Some of the vile Gouda cheesecake with which the Dutch daily sap our moral vibrancy to make us pushovers.

———————— * ————————

Question: Should we continue to allow dishonest, vote-seeking bureaucrats TO TAKE JOBS IN THE TULIP-GROWING, WINDMILL-TECHNOLOGY, DIKE-BUILDING, WOODEN-SHOE-CARVING, AND ZEE-DRAINING INDUSTRIES AND GIVE THESE DESPERATELY NEEDED SOURCES OF NON-HOLLANDER LIVELIHOOD TO A GANG OF CHEESE-CRAZED DUTCHMEN?

Answer: Not if we can help it!

———————— * ————————

A BUM DEAL?

In the infamous Treaty of Breda, signed in 1667, England and the Netherlands swapped Surinam and New York even-up. Thus, the English acquired a filthy harbor city where waters were badly situated for drainage and in which the scoundrel Hollanders had already built the steaming ghettos of Harlem and Bedford-Stuyvesant.

In return for this, the Soestdijk tyrants received 63,037 square miles of territory full of mixed-blood Creoles (39 percent), East Indians (30 percent), Indonesians (16 percent), indigenous Indians (10 percent), and Chinese (2 percent) just waiting to be mercilessly enslaved and abused.

We say it was a bum deal, and we say to hell with it!

WASHINGTON, D.C., Sept. 12 (AP) —The Department of Agriculture has announced a $15,000,000 program of research, removal of infected trees, and spraying in an effort to halt the spread of Dutch elm disease.

Assistant Secretary of Agriculture Reuben Toms warned that unless measures are taken immediately to control the blight, the common American elm will be "effectively extinct" by 1980. Over 2,000,000 of the stately shade trees have been killed by the mysterious fungus since it first appeared in 1958.

THE HAGUE, NETH., Jan. 4 (Reuters)—Prince Bernhard and Queen Juliana celebrated their 15th wedding anniversary here today. They were married in 1958.

NEED WE SAY MORE!!!!!

CORNWALL, ILL., May 4 (AP)—A huge dead elm tree fell on a house trailer during a thunderstorm here. A family of four sleeping in the trailer escaped injuries.

<u>This</u> time!

———————— * ————————

Yet another example of the sickening perfidy of the Dutch interloper has been sent to us by Mrs. Edith Flemson, a faithful tulip-stomper in Flagstaff, Arizona:

"I've seen these here mijnheers traipsing down Main Street pumping the Indians full of Bols liqueurs and egging them on to acts of barbarity and worse, and I'm not fooled one bit by their hoity-toity linen caps and cute baggy trousers. They may dress up like our beloved circus clowns to deceive us, but all decent, wide-awake folks who take pride in our country's many lakes and other bodies of water and don't cotton to weirdo drainage schemes fresh off the drawing board of Bernhard and his dike-happy crew can see right through their fake Vandyke beards to the Face of the Enemy that lurks beneath. But we'd better act fast, because in this state alone there are seven dams, or Van Dams, as I call them, because if you ask me, they're just dikes in disguise, and one day we're going to wake up looking down the business end of a blunderbuss and our precious American waterways will be just so much grist for the Dutchman's evil mills!"

**********************

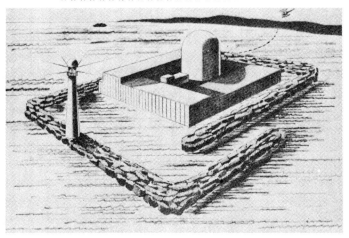

The first step in the nefarious Nederlander scheme to turn our precious continental shelf into prime tulip-land--huge landfill islands with nuclear windmills disguised as reactor coolers. We're supposed to benefit by getting "electricity." Tell that to the Frisians!

AMERICANS UNITED TO BEAT THE DUTCH
POST OFFICE BOX 6041, WASHINGTON, D.C. 20109

DUTCH PERFIDY THROUGHOUT HISTORY #15
Mijnheer Martin Van Buren
Why did Mijnheer Martin Van Buren, propelled into the White House by Dutch interests, oppose the annexation of Texas? Because its oily soil was unsuitable for tulips and it was situated too close to Surinam for comfort! The Dutch don't like anyone peering over their shoulders when they do their dirty work! Mijnheer Van Buren, dubbed "The Red Fox of Kinderhoek" by vigilant Americans, was chucked out of office and sent packing by alert voters, who saw through his insidious scheme!

\*\*\*\*\*\*\*\*\*\*\*\*\*\*\*\*\*

# Wetlands Shrink

BOSTON, Jan. 20 (AP)—A survey by the Audubon Society reveals that 12,978 square miles of wetlands, marshes, swamps, and other bird-nesting grounds, an area equal in size to Holland, have been covered by landfill since 1950.

## AMERICA, WAKE UP!

\*\*\*\*\*\*\*\*\*\*\*\*\*\*\*\*\*

Dear Fellow Patriot:

Many citizens are not aware of how their leaders have taken positions on national security which weaken America's defense against the twin scourges of Dutch Imperialism and its bandit prince, Bernhard of Lippe-Biesterfeld.

We need you to participate in our National Security Issues poll. We want to release the results of our poll to President Nixon, the Congress, and the national press in a few weeks, so mail us your filled-in questionnaire as soon as possible.

Thanking you in advance for helping preserve our great nation, I am,

Raymond Petri

P.S. We believe that most Americans support a strong national defense against the Koningkrijk der Nederlanden, but we can't prove it without your cooperation in this poll.

- - - - - - - - - - - - - - - - - -

We've just heard from Corpus Christi dike-buster Ron Clafey. Ron is working on a courageous book that he says will rip away the pat delft glaze from the report prepared by World Court puppet Earl Warren on the Kennedy assasination. He's come up with a lot of unanswered questions that should disturb a lot of people, like: Why was the grassy knoll covered with tulips? What was Mijnheer Van Der Zapruder doing along the motorcade route? What was the source of the pungent odor of rotting Edam in the Texas School Book Depository? Was Oswald's first name Lee or Leeuwenhoek? Who was the lady in the traditional Dutch polka-dot dress? And why was the Bandit Prince Bernhard cowering in Soestdijk Palace when EVERY OTHER MAJOR HEAD OF STATE was attending the Kennedy funeral?

Keep up the good work, Ron. A grateful nation will one day go down on its knees to thank you for sparing it from the pitiless scourge of cheese-maddened Nederlanders.

---

NATIONAL SECURITY ISSUES POLL

Please check the one box which most nearly represents your position on each of the following issues:

1. Do you believe the United States should have a policy of military superiority over the Netherlands?

   ☐ A. YES      ☐ B. NO

2. Do you feel strongly or not very strongly about that?

   ☐ A. STRONGLY   ☐ B. NOT VERY STRONGLY

3. Have you ever known anyone who went to the Hague and came back?

   ☐ A. NO      ☐ B. YES

   ☐ C. NOT SURE

# Tony Hendra's
# Wide World of Meat

Photocollage by Ron Barrett

From the moment God cooked Adam's goose with a sparerib to the time his Son served Himself for supper, through all the ages in which fat was rendered unto Caesar and Sir Loincelot rode to the Meate d'Arthur, honest Dutch burghers ignored the Rump Parliament and millions of tons of perfectly good ground round was buried in the poppy fields of Amiens while children starved in China, fundamental questions have been raised regarding meat. As the German pessimist Flanken has it in his monumental *Meataphysics,* "Are we not merely meat arranged to facilitate the passage of irrelevant electric currents? And if so can we not eat our sister?" Other questions crowd the plate. Will the meat inherit the earth? In a tight spot should you sell your chicken stock? What is a sweetbread? Perhaps we shall never know, but of one thing we can be certain: meat was never meant to fly. Thus on May 6, 1937, the 7,630,000-cubic-foot, 804-foot-long Hindenbird, largest turkey ever to cross the Atlantic, caught fire at its moorings in Lakehurst, New Jersey, and burned to a crisp.

From the ashes of tragedy comes forth a rib roast. In 1963 meat finally makes the grade in its long journey from humble pie to *prime inter pares.* Sworn in by the successor to Frankfurter and precursor of Burger, Chef Warren, the Bird made Flesh embarks on a stomach-boggling Administration, including the war in Meatnam, the Grade-A Society, and, with the help of his First Lady, herself a toothsome 140 pounds of choice Texan tartare, the Meatification of America.

*Above:* Recipe for relaxation: Loin lies down with limb and weenie with wahine to grill gently in a moderate Florida sun.

Visitors to the fabulous redmeat forests of Northern California examine a steak (*left*) that has been aged for more than five thousand years. Conservationists are concerned that the redmeat trees, widely used in the manufacture of Americans, are not being replaced as fast as they are being logged.

Elsewhere in the redmeat forests youngsters smack their chops over the amazing Petrified Hamburger (*below, left*), discarded countless millennia ago by a bronto-saurus with the blahs. Paleontologists have as yet failed to unearth the amazing Petrified Sesame Bun it came on.

*Above:* Taste the classic elegance of American design. General Meats' top-of-the-line for '73. A sleek roaster, boned and rolled throughout. Lays lard with the best of them, yet boasts a specially tenderized interior for the ultimate in comfort. Revolutionary safety snout built to withstand up to 10-m.p.h. impact. Body by Butcher. Live high off the hog in '73. You won't regret it.

Is there intelligent meat on other planets? At Cape Carnivoral (*left*), a team of experts labor round the clock to prepare Pollo I for its historic flight in search of the answer to this and other timeless secrets of the universe, answers that cannot but have the profoundest implications for the future of all meatkind. □

# Whiffers and Cooties and Lungers on Strings

## These Are a Few of My Favorite Things

### by Doug Kenney

**Chapter 1**

*"You can pick your friends, and you can pick your nose, but you can't pick your friend's nose."*—Benjamin Franklin

What is wrong with this picture? You are waiting in a Greyhound terminal and observe an aged gentleman, bracketed by worn shopping bags, reading a *National Enquirer* and quietly mining for nose gold. You know, picking a winner. Striking paydirt, he disappears with the swag behind his paper and reemerges a moment later, pages rustling guiltily and his snakey little eyes darting every which way.

Careful now, don't be fooled. Despite the front page pix of two-headed starlets and freeze-dried toddlers, the *real* headline reads OLD GEEK IN BUS STATION EATS OWN BOOGERS AND LIVES!

*Shocking*, you say? *You mean some people actually...?* The words stick in the throat. Well, so would that yummy rope of butterscotch if he didn't rewind occasionally, so have some compassion. (Bronchitis, America's number one appetite crippler!)

Just stop at any traffic light, watch the guy alongside, and you may be surprised, certainly nauseated, by the rampant ambergris poaching on our nation's highways.

Yes, mucus recycling—once thought to be the exclusive province of tots and dotards—is enjoying new interest among sensual adventurers. Bored with hand-held oscillators, rubber torsos, and clever chimps, today's jaded thrill-seekers often feel that they have "lost touch" with themselves and yearn to return to their roots. Tiring of that, it is a small step to sexual reversions such as loogie-hoarding.

Symptoms appear early, often as a marked fondness for rolling up and saving those little balls of rubber cement. But with practice, this childhood pastime may blossom into such elaborate reversions as the Incredible Sticking Booger. Simply, the nose nugget is rolled around on the fingers until the proper consistency is obtained. Then, it is passed from finger to finger, from hand to hand, and from hand to ...other areas. Distinctly personal styles soon evolve, ranging from rigid formalism reminiscent of Japanese tea ceremonies to inspired improvisations recalling the ball-handling of Meadowlark Johnson.[1] Calorie counting? Then play *bombe plastique*. Stick it anywhere! Under the theater seat, on a taxi door handle, between a firm handshake (don't be timid—he just planted one on your coffee spoon).

Disgusted? So were the reactionary bluenoses who banned Joyce's *Ulysses* and hounded Thomas Edison into an early grave. Be a bold explorer, and rediscover the pleasure garden growing right under (or, as with our elderly friend above, in) your nose. Any quiet grotto or untraveled nook can be a gold mine of exotic delight. Take your search inward toward those marshy undergrowths where a treasure-trove of yeasty and intriguing foreign matter awaits. Mine workers of the world, unite! You have nothing to lose but your lunch.

**Chapter 2**

*"In the permissive atmosphere of the '60s, the news media were avid chroniclers (and some believe, instigators)* of the much heralded 'sexual revolution.' Any Tom, Dick, or Abbie with a mouthful of obscenities and a headful of LSD was practically guaranteed a nightly audience of twenty million viewers on evening network news.

*"Many Americans now hold Mario Savio's Berkeley-based 'Free Speech' movement as primarily responsible for later public acceptance of such porno flicks as* Deep Throat *and* Behind the Green Door. *'These campus messiahs of the "Free Smut" philosophy,' Billy Graham recently stated on Barbara Walters 'Not For Women Only' television program, 'have led millions of impressionable young people into a moral cesspool. Sometimes it gets me so angry I have to stalk the park and suck off a Seeing Eye dog just to shake the jitters.'"*— Time Essay, "Where Have All the Flower Children Gone?" Oct. 38, 1973.

I can't exactly explain why I wrote that. This article is supposedly only about Fun with Mung, but until I run through this Jamaican I received in quantities under one ounce from my good buddy Jon Jones, it may tend to ...wander a little.

Also, the tube just reported that they ruled *Behind the Green Door* obscene. Jesus, I saw it and they weren't kidding, it really *is*. Don't get me wrong, though. I personally would eat out Marilyn Chambers after eight laps around the track on a muggy day. Nine maybe. And as obscenely as possible—rrrrraaaaawwwwrrr you eat so good oh baby oh God *you eat so good gimme eat God please gimme gimme.*

Oops. Tony Hendra said this was supposed to be under two thousand words...probably afraid that if I had enough space I'd blow the whistle on

---

1. The *Guinness Book of World Records* gives the nod for jam-juggling over time to Scotty Peterson, eleven, of Orlando, Florida. Peterson kept it in play for 117 hours, 37 minutes, excluding naptime.

the Atomic Mole People. *Yes...strange visitors from another zip code and who, disguised as* perfectly harmless fire hydrants *are secretly plotting to turn us into human Roto-rooters and slaves and living toilets and*

The headaches again. Please...no more, please...yes, I'll stop *I said I'll stop*

There. Better now. Physical pain...how well they know our individual weaknesses.

Leaving the nose for a moment (just pausing long enough to remind listeners that nose *polish* does wonders for doll furniture), let's drop in on the wide world of coprophilia. Coprophilia, as you already may know, is *not* what Adam Troy (Gardner McKay) used to haul on "Adventures in Paradise," but the infantile infatuation with one's own uh-uh's. If discovered in time, the doo-doo dabbler may be diverted to modeling clay and an interest in the plastic arts. In fact, the noted sculptor Brancusi privately referred to his most famous work as *Turd in Space* and often remarked on the striking similarity between Michelangelo's *Pietà* and a big pile of dingleberries.[2]

Closely allied to feces-fiddling is another interesting bowl game known as...

### Chapter 3
*Operation Turdwatch, or, Return of the Black Banana*

There are some of you sitting at home right now who will deny ever having actually even *looked* at it. Even once. But who can resist the impulse, when flushing, to follow that long hypnotic spiral down to the Other Place? Frankly, does a more suspenseful moment exist in daily life than wondering if it will...aarrrgggh...*come bobbing back at you?*

This is no laughing matter. In Victorian times, more than one society hostess found herself cruelly brownlisted for the presence of a single anonymous "floater" in her footbath. To overcome such unreasoning squeamishness in yourself, get to know your plumbing on non-verbal levels with such Esalen-developed techniques as "commode-hugging," and invite that little nerd in the miniature sailboat out for a breath of fresh air. Lastly, remember that even the fabulous Kohinoor diamond was once a homely lump of coal, and the way things are going lately, yesterday's breakfast might well be the president of tomorrow.

Actually, while we're in the neighborhood, let's touch for a moment[3] on your rosebud, its care and cleaning. *Scorchmarks, flashburns, skidmarks,*

brown outs,...whatever you called them, carelessly hidden underwear could once make you the laughingstock of the dorm, but no more! There is no social stigma connected with this familiar household disaster. Just make sure you don't get fresh ones out of my drawer. I will kill you.

### Chapter 4
*"If you pick it, it'll never heal."*—Earl Scruggs

Looking for something slightly kinkier? Try scabfarming. You know, worrying that big scrumptious four-by-four-inch playground knee injury. Never letting it alone.

Scabfarmers roughly divide themselves into two schools. The first allows his boo-boo to ripen slowly until it can be picked at peak maturity. "Winter wheat" enthusiasts, however, prefer to harvest the same patch repeatedly, knowing that the festering green corruption below is capable of multiple (though admittedly decreasing) yields. The first technique requires great patience and, should reaping be delayed too long, may lose the entire crop through sudden and massive flaking. Picking too soon, however, is equally chancy and may ruin the knees of your new khakis.

Those who have mastered the "winter wheat" method may wish to graduate to tick bites. Natural, long lasting anticoagulants on the little fellow's fangs can keep your wound putrefying

NOVEMBER, 1974

S.GROSS

month after month and, if properly tended and cultivated, a single bite can produce enough sloughings to fill a pint basket!

Had enough yet? No? I'm so numb by now I can just keep on typing, but don't blame me if *you* just pick at your supper tonight.[4]

Peeling is a related practice. Everyone, of course, has experienced the wordless bliss of despoiling the lifeless hulks of summer blisters, but how many of us have acquired the skill to *not go too far?* It takes a sharp eye and a steady hand.

Perhaps the commonest form of erotic self-mutilation is finger-eating. Not mere nail-biting, but honest-to-God finger-eating. (A correctly eaten finger should, after extended immersion in the bath, closely resemble a flayed stalk of albino broccoli.) An alternative form of such self-abuse is palate-stripping. This rather baroque reversion requires only your mouth and a ball of hard candy. As any child knows, a ball of hard candy, when sucked with enough masochistic intensity, quickly deteriorates into a mass of jagged, razor-sharp edges which score and gouge out little runnels of flesh from the roof of your mouth. For an added treat, once the candy is gone, you can vie with playmates for the longest skin streamer!

### Chapter 5
*A dog never smells his own."*—Hopi proverb
*"Qui est-ce qu'a coupé le fromage?"*—François Villon
*"Softee, but deadly."*—Lao-tzu

If you like to smell your farts, smile. That settled, you can come out of the water closet and dive right into some elegant spin-offs of this entertaining blast from the past. While repressed peers still stifle them against the upholstery, blush profusely, or try to frame somebody else, accomplished Whiffers exist in a rarefied atmosphere where, as Father Flannegan often chuckled, there is no such thing as an ill wind.

While flatulence between consenting adults is still illegal in many states, literally millions of young moderns are finding self-realization in such simple games as the "Dutch Oven," i.e., pooting in bed and *sticking your little brother's head under the covers.* The modified "Dutch Oven," commonly known as the "Bessemer Furnace" or the "Wolf-Spider's Revenge," involves stepping on a frog in the hall closet, then pouncing on a member of the family and locking them inside until all sounds of struggling have ceased. Sound like fun? Try it and see! (You'll be glad you did.)

Whiffers, however, are by no means

---

2. See also, *The Phlegmish Painters: One Wop's Opinion*, C. Brancusi, (New York: Random House, 1965); idem, *The Clinker in Art*, (New York: Random House, 1967).

3. And *only* for a moment, sickie.

4. Or get blown by a piranha.

restricted to their own olfactory whistles. Women, for example, have told me in confidence that they often sample their used paper ponies, and who is to say that these fine Americans, many of them successful professionals in their chosen fields, are to be branded as "sick" or "twisted"? Besides me, I mean.

Whiffers, the legendary descendants of the first seat sniffer and the first bubble snapper, are found in all walks of life. Many respected businessmen and high government officials, under the guise of "seeing what time it is," *deliberately smell under their watches.* Golda Meir, in her autobiography, remembers that as a small pig in Milwaukee she used to lick her kneecap to *perfectly reproduce the odor of sour milk.* Billy Kidd, the famous skier, is often photographed smelling the inside of his turtleneck, and for centuries Eskimos have occasionally put their hooded parkas on backwards "by accident" to *smell the backs of their own heads!*

Sometimes, sexual reverts find themselves straddling the line between two forms of reversion. Peefreaks "checking the oil" have much in common with Whiffers in that, after having achieved micturition, Peefreaks *smell* their trigger fingers to see whether they *really* need washing. Peefreaks may be easily recognized as the ones who liked to perform "visiting fireman" or "fighter plane" from a standing position. (You are the fighter plane. Mission: destroy that flotilla of Daddy's cigarette butts! *Buddabuddabuddabudda!*)[5]

## Chapter 6

*"My wife has a little asshole. Me."*—Napoleon Bonaparte

Napoleon didn't really say that. I lied. My buddy Peter Ivers says it all the time, but he lives in L.A. and probably won't know I ripped it off so fuck him. He also does things like throw his arm around a parking timer and say, "Hey, I got a new girl friend. Wanna meter?" or "Hey, didja hear about the big party? It's in your mouth—*everybody's* coming!"

Jesus, he's funny. I really wish you could meet him. Then I could stop pounding this cocksucker and go check out that recipe for fish oil surprise in the new *Oui....*

By the way, I saw *Last Tango in Paris* finally, and I, for one, thought that the languorous pacing combined with the semi-improvisational characterizations and tactical naturalism really bit the bag. Didn't like her tits, either. (I find big tits oddly threatening, don't you?) The butter-bugger was okay, though.[6]

---

5. Tinkle Tip: If your urinal is big enough to share with a pal, why not try an impromptu "swordfight"? Just remember not to touché the Snoopy poster, the *Jokes for the John* book, or, unless you're really ready for it, each other.

6. Word has just come from the tube that NASA thinks Jupiter may actually be a giant, severed testicle. Any of you honchos lose something?

## Chapter 7

*"A people's song in a nation's heart. A nation's heart in a child's eyes. A person's foot in his little brother's sneaker by accident. Ouch."*—Dag Hammerskjöld

*"I am as the sound of one clam humping."*—T. S. Eliot

*"Officer! I think someone just sucked off my Seeing Eye dog!"*—Al Hibbler

One last thing. Snowstorms. You will need: a dark-colored or black piece of construction paper, a light-colored crayon, and a near-fatal head of dandruff. What you do is, while you're waiting for Miss Walker to pass out the paste, draw a little woodland scene on your paper with your crayon, with a log cabin and a chimney on top. Then, lean your head over the paper and give yourself a double Indian-burn. Real hard. As your scalp flakes off, a beautiful winter scene will appear as if by magic. When your little scene is completely snowbound, and if it's a first period class, beginning around, say, 6:45 A.M. or so, you may wish to add a festive miniature snowman made from three graduated balls of eyegorp.

Another interesting finding from the Federal Drug Report was that longterm use of marijuana "greatly erodes an individual's drive, general attentiveness, sense of responsibility, and pride in appearance. He lacks get-up-and-go, and has difficulty in completing his work, turning in assignments half- (continued on page 439) ☐

*"We're not so bad, are we now, kids?"*

SGT. SHRIVER
CUTOUTS
1. Tie Clip
2. Picture Card
3. Badges
4. Stand-Up

*Sgt. Shriver*

EAGLETON

PT 109

1.

2.

3.

Is This Glass
Half-empty or Half-full?

Join the Peace Corps

SHRIVER'S BLEEDING HEARTS CLUB BAND

4.

Lee Sturdivant

# Sgt. Shriver's Bleeding Hearts Club Band

### by Sean Kelly
#### with a little help from Tony Hendra and Henry Beard

### Side One

SGT. SHRIVER'S BLEEDING HEARTS CLUB BAND

Just a dozen years ago today,
Sgt. Shriver taught the clan to play
Once they played for Bobby and for John
Now they're guaranteed to raise a yawn.
We now reintroduce to you
The act we've blown for all these years,
Sgt. Shriver's Bleeding Hearts Club
Band.
We're Sgt. Shriver's Bleeding Hearts
Club Band,
The martyred brothers' kith and kin.
We're Sgt. Shriver's Bleeding Hearts
Club Band,
Sit back and watch the votes roll in.
Sgt. Shriver's bleeding, Sgt. Shriver's
bleeding,
Sgt. Shriver's Bleeding Hearts Club
Band.
It's wonderful to be here,
It's certainly a thrill.
You're such a dumb electorate,
We'd like to take you home with us.
America, come home!
We don't really want to stop the war,
But that's what you'll all be voting for,
You'll forget amidst this stupid sham,
We're the ones who got you into Nam.
So let us introduce to you
The once and future Tommy—who?
And Sgt. Shriver's Bleeding Hearts
Club Band.

A LITTLE HELP FROM MY FRIENDS
(TEDDY'S SONG)

What would you think if I told you a fib,
Would you go out and vote GOP.
Give me four years and if nothing goes
wrong,
I am certain you'll turn back to me.
I got off with a little help from my
friends,
At the trough with a little help from my
friends,
I don't scoff at a little help from my
friends.
What makes you think you can carry
the South.
(I'm a shoo-in in a three-way race)
How can you speak with your foot in
your mouth.
(Well it helps to have another face)
And a little help from all my
well-heeled friends,
Do you need anybody,
I need some fascist for Veep.
Could it be anybody
A down-home little red-neck creep.
What about all the wild oats that you
sowed,
In four years they'll be underground.
What did you see when you turned off
the road,
I can't tell you, but I think it drowned.
Oh I get by with a little help from my
friends,

Yes I can lie with a little help from my
friends,
With a little help from my friends.

JACKIE IN THE ISLES WITH DIAMONDS

Picture yourself on a yacht on an ocean,
With gold-plated plumbing and dozens
of maids
Somebody calls you, his voice thick and
moldy,
A Greek wearing wraparound shades.
Sell the same powers that made you
our queen,
Glowering, over-inbred.
Marry the Greek with the shades on
his eyes,
And you're gone.
Jackie in the isles with diamonds,
Follow him off to a junta-led nation
Where coarse-talking people get
busted, and quick,
Everyone waves when you drive past
the prisons,
You're oh so impeccably chic.
When paparazzi appear on the shore,
Wanting you for Photoplay,
Climb on their backs, give their heads
a few clouts,
And you're gone.
Jackie in the isles with diamonds,
Picture yourself in a Halston creation,
The spray-net madonna of gay
masquerades,
Sullenly someone pays up while you
learn style,
The Greek with the wraparound shades.

FOR THE BENEFIT OF MR. KIKE

For the benefit of Mr. Kike
There will be a missile strike on Lebanon
The Hebrew guns will flame and flare
The Arab countries which were there
will be gone!
Over Aden, Sinai, Jordan, Gaza
Blasting all those wogs dead with real
fire!
Then you'll see George McG. will
capture the vote!
The celebrated Golda Meir
Ends her war by Saturday near
Zion's Gate
For ancient Hebrew laws deplore
The flight of Phantom jets for more
than six days straight.
Messrs Sarge and George assure
B'nai B'rith
Air protection that is second to none
Toe to toe, Gary and Joe dish out
the shmaltz.
Campaigning starts in old New York
When Sargent S. renounces pork and
eats a blintz
Before a Bronx Hadassah group
George eats ten bowls of chicken soup
without a wince
Gott in Himmel, man, they've got
Kimmelman
Footing the bill!

### Side Two

IN WITH YOU OUT WITH YOU

We were talking—about the space
between your ears
And the people—who find themselves
behind the walls of institutions
Never told the truth—now it's far
too late—votes are pissed away.
Tried to compromise us and yourself
But your brain cells took that charge
Now you see you're really only very
small,
And life goes on without you, Tom,
without you.

LOVELY DITA

Lovely Dita memos made.
Everything that Geneen does,
We can invoke to put some folk away.
Though she could have been discreeta,
Glad we got that tip from Dita,
All about the contents of her little
black book.
Lovely Dita, poorly paid,
May I suggest discreetly,
Give us a leak,
And pique the GOP.
Then you'll be free to flee
The ITT.

A DAY ON THE LEFT

I saw the news that day oh boy
About a lucky shot Lee Harvey made
And though the news was rather sad
I found it kind of droll
I saw the grassy knoll.
They blew his mind out in a car
Nobody noticed that the film was
changed
Commission witnesses declared
That to their great dismay
Nobody could really say
If he was from the CIA.
I saw a press release oh boy
The Peace Corps had just put an end
to war
A crowd of peacenik volunteers
Were quickly sent away
Wearing green berets.
Woke up, fell out of bed,
With a ringing in my head
When I realized it was the
phone,
Picked it up and heard McGovern's
drone.
Gabbed a bit then took the bait
Made the ticket twelve days late
Found my way upstairs and told the
wife,
Who asked about insurance on my life
I saw reports today oh boy
Ten thousand craters in the DMZ
And though that count might be
impugned
The country heard and swooned
Now we know how many holes it takes
to make an exit wound.
I'd love a term like John's....

137

# OFFICIAL SHIP'S GUIDE
## 1922 SEASON

written & illustrated by Bruce McCall

# R.M.S.
## 'THE BIGG

NEW YORK–LIVERPOOL

# TYRANNIC'
## ST THING IN ALL THE WORLD' LIVERPOOL—NEW YORK

# SUP, VOYAGER, AT TABLES
# 'O TYRANNIC, THY M

We can here but peep at Tyrannic's labyrinth of Public Rooms. They are 103, not including the Kandahar Verandah Grill. First Class passengers are reminded that all meals, excluding teas, must be ordered three months in advance of sailing. The Maitre d'Hotel will signal conclusion of dinner. Persons without references cannot be considered for the Captain's Table guest list.

Foyer of Palm Court Salon, A—Deck

Second Cla

# D MAKE NEPTUNE BLUSH
# AME BE BACCHUS!'

An area equivalent to Hindustan is devoted to food and its preparation aboard Tyrannic. Forty tons of Stilton cheese are consumed on every crossing, as are 214 miles of sausage and melons sufficient to fill the Grand Canyon of Arizona. All excess livestock is thrown overboard on sight of landfall. Steerage is reminded that eating toffee in bed is forbidden.

Gentlemen's Smoking Lounge, D–Deck

lon, F–Deck

"The right crowd, and no crowding." The Boat Deck is

# 'PRAY, GAMBOL

Gentlemen are requested to refrain from riding
ponies through the Steerage after 8:00 P.M.
While the Captain emphasizes the rules of
proper attire at all times, gentlemen may remove
their spats in the Gymnasium. Golfers from the
First Class have right-of-way through
the Steerage. The Chariot Race in the Grand
Ballroom is held on the eve of
disembarkation. Off limits to Steerage.

"A tennis match."

ed for First Class, with harsh penalties for interlopers.

# TYRANNICALLY!"

Lifeboat drill is conducted on the first day out at
3:00 P.M. for First Class, and on the last day out
at 3:00 A.M. for Second Class and Steerage.
One circuit of the Promenade Deck is equivalent
to walking from Aix to Paris and return. More
ammunition is expended during the skeet
shooting on a single voyage than was used in the
Crimean War entire. There is a
deck of cards in the Steerage Tuck Shop.

"A brisk swim."

# 'SAIL ON, O MIGHTY MAMMOTH'

The Tyrannic is so safe that she carries no insurance.

Among many advances in her design and construction is the pneumatic bulkhead that seals off Steerage from the rest of the ship in case of flooding. Her wireless equipment is powerful enough to reach Brisbane, Australia, from the vicinity of Greenland.

Total length of Tyrannic's hot water piping in First Class alone is estimated to exceed the distance in nautical miles from Lisbon to Durban.

A routine voyage uses up six thousand mops, four hundred acres of table linens, and a fifty-gallon drum of Mercurochrome. Kept in the Stores are ten miles of shoelaces, one half-ton of flea powder, two hundred caskets, a like number of hummingbirds, and a spare funnel.

The ship's newspaper, issued daily, enjoys a larger circulation than the Times of Bombay. More musicians are employed aboard Tyrannic than in the entire city of Vienna. The chandelier in the Grand Ballroom weighs more than the Eiffel Tower, and gives off more light than that structure's host city of Paris.

Steerage passengers who board at Liverpool often fail to reach their quarters before Tyrannic has safely berthed at New York. They are advised to run.

Tyrannic abuilding, 1909.
The Duchess of Plinth views
her triple screws.

# ORDERS TO THE STEERAGE:

Do not make loud noises on Sundays. Remove shoes or boots before retiring. Steam, smoke, or heavy fumes in the Steerage area should be disregarded. If sick, stay in your cot.

Mutton is taken, X–Deck.

Steerage: "No Smoking, Spitting, Etc."

A CHILD'S CHRISTMAS IN ULSTER

BY SEAN KELLY

*with woodcuts by Randall Enos*

One Christmas was so like another in those years around Waterside now, that I can never remember whether there were twelve Papish killed on the twenty-fourth or twenty-four Papish killed on the twelfth.

All the Christmases roll like an armoured patrol down Shakhill Road, ricochet round my brain like rubber bullets in a bogside boxcar, and into the Donneybrook I dash to salvage whatever I can find. Into the gas cloud bottle bomb melee of Belfast memories I scramble, and out I come with Mrs. Shaughnessy, and the Tommies.

It was in the aftermath of the day of Christmas Eve, and I was in Mrs. Shaughnessy's back alley, waiting for Catholics, with her son Tim. Patient, cold, and callous, our faces covered with nylon stockings, we waited to clobber the Catholics. Wild-eyed and drunk as lords and horribly whiskied, they would stagger or slink, saying Aves and Paters and rattling their beads down the cobblestones, and the sharp-eyed gunners, Tim and I, King Billy's dragoons from the battle of the Boyne, off Crumlin Road, would fire our deadly dumdums at the red of their eyes. The wise Catholics never appeared. We were so still, black and tan marksmen lying in ambush for the Mayo Flying Column, that we never heard Mrs. Shaughnessy's first scream. Or, if we heard it at all, it was, to us, the far-off lament of a Sinn Fein banshee over the smoking ruins of Cork. But soon the cry grew louder. "I.R.A.!"

cried Mrs. Shaughnessy. And we ran down the alley, our guns in our hands, toward the house; and glass indeed was shattering out the windows, and automatics were rattling, and Mrs. Shaughnessy was howling bloody murder as was appropriate to the time and place.

This was better than all the Catholics in Ulster with targets pinned to their greatcoats standing in a row. We crawled to the threshhold, cradling our rifles, and peered into the door of the pitchblack room.

It was pitchblack with reason, and so was Mrs. Shaughnessy, who was rumored to be very high up in the Women's Auxiliary of the local Orange Lodge. She was sitting in the middle of the room, saying, "A fine Christmas," and clawing away at the smouldering tar with which she was smeared top to toe. "Call the Constabulary!" she bellowed, a surprisingly talkative tar baby.

"They won't be here," said Mr. Shaughnessy. "It's Christmas."

There were no I.R.A. men to be seen, only Mr. and Mrs. Shaughnessy, and she black as sin and scrubbing away at herself like Aunt Jemima playing Lady Macbeth.

"Do something," she said.

We let go a round or so out the back door—I think we missed Mr. Shaughnessy—and ran out of the house to the telephone box.

"Let's call the army as well," Tim said.

"And the B Specials."

"And Ian Paisley, he likes riots."

But we only called the Royal Ulster Constabulary, and soon the paddy wagon came and the tall men in helmets rushed into the house with Thompson guns and Mr. Shaughnessy got out just in time before they opened fire.

Nobody could have had a noisier Christmas. And when the policemen ran out of ammunition and were standing in the destroyed and bloody room, Tim's aunt, Miss Shaughnessy, came downstairs and peered in. Tim and I waited, very quietly, to hear what she would say to them. She had the gift of the gab, for sure.

She looked at the three tall policemen in their brass and helmets, standing among the smoke and rubble and her expiring sister-in-law, and she said: "Would yez care for a drop o' the crayture, at all, at all?"

Just yesterday, just yesterday, when I was a boy, when there was trouble in Ulster, and the night sky was bright orange as a twelfth of July flag, we ran riot day and night down streets that reeked of fear and pee, and we chased with tins of petrol the superstitious nuns and leprechauns through the wassailing streets of Christmas in the North, when it rains. And rains.

But here a small boy says: "It rained last year, too. It washed my whitewash slogans off the walls, and I cried."

"But that was not the same rain. Our Christmas cloudbuster rain was wet as martyrs' blood, our rain roared down the gutter like beer from a blown-up public house, our rain glistened on the mackintoshes of the patrolling B Specials till they glittered like Christmas trees in the flare light, and it swept the bits of bodies and such down the true blue sewers out to the Protestant sea."

"Tell about the presents."

"Ah, the presents. After the dour and sour smelling service, the presents. There were Useless Presents: toys and dolls and King James Bibles, crayons in various shades of orange, red, white, and blue; never, of course, green; and a pair of socks or some candy . . ."

"Go on to the Useful Presents."

"Plastique bombs and ammo belts, spring knives and knuckle-dusters, blackjacks and cherry bombs, ski masks for tugging over your mug till your own mum wouldn't know you at a mugging, toy guns that looked realer than real ones, and a shrill whistle to summon your friends to call the Tommies to save your hide; and a booklet that warned in big bold type NOT to make incendiary devices out of the accompanying batteries, blasting caps, wires, bottles, rags, petrol, and powder, with instructions and detailed diagrams, oh! easy for little guerrillas!"

And on Christmas morning I would walk the rain-wet streets with Tommy, conjuring whistle and a bundle of weapons under my coat, scouring the town for mass-happy Catholics, saluting the local patrols as they slithered by on the slippery streets, till I rounded a corner and out of a rain-veiled lane would come a boy, the spit of myself but a Dogan for certain, misshapen and grim as a Galway spud. I hated him on sight and sound, and reached for my gun to blow him off the face of Christmas when suddenly he reached into his coat, whipped out his revolver, and we sprayed the street with a volley of shots so quick, and so exquisitely wild, that tinseled windows shattered all down the block and a half-dozen goose-gobbling citizens fell face forward into their Christmas dinners, instantly concocting a traditional Ulster recipe, brain stuffing. The young gunmen, he and I, unharmed, ducked and were gone before the echoes were.

And when I got home, as often as not, there was a crater where the dining room had been, and Uncles like burst balloons and Aunts like broken teacups would be festooning the ruins of the feast. And I would squat amidst the rubble and nibble bits of what I hoped was the turkey, carefully following the instructions for little guerrillas, and produce what might be mistaken for a battery-powered nuclear device.

Or I would go out, my shiny new pistol cocked, into the Bogside, with Tim and Dan and Mike, and prowl the still streets, leaving little bullet holes in the fences and people.

"I bet people will think there's been provos."

"What would you do if you saw a provo coming down our street?"

"I'd go like this, bang! I'd throw him over the railings and roll him down the embankment and then I'd kick him behind the ear and he'd pack it in."

"What would you do if you saw two provos?"

Trenchcoated and terrible provos strode and strove through the sputtering snow toward us as we passed Mr. Grogan's house.

"Let's post Mr. Grogan a fire bomb through his letter box."

"Let's write things on his walls."

"Let's write Mr. Grogan looks like a Dogan all over his front door."

Or we walked by the freshgrave patchwork cemetery.

"Do the corpses know it's snowing?"

A bogside cabbage-smell fog drifted in from the docks. Now we were crack troops of Cromwell, scouring the fens of Fermanagh, eagle-eyed and English armour-plated, and cowering Catholics fled before us to hell or Connacht. And we returned home through the poor streets where only a few children scrawled Free Derry on the charred walls and fired a few aimless rounds at us as we scampered across the bridge above the troopship bobbing docks. And then, at home, the Uncles would be solemn, and toast the Queen and absent friends which in this case meant half the family and most of the neighbors, now deceased, for the old cause.

Bring out the tall tales now that we told while the peat fire made fairy pictures of King Billy, his white horse like a ghost of flame, and the blazing battle of the Burning Boyne. And the gory ghosts of slaughtered Sinn Feiners listened at the blacked-out windows and the Tommygun spirit of Michael Collins lay in ambush under the bed I must climb to trembling in the dark.

And I remember we went out terrorizing once when there wasn't by chance a building burning to light the terrifying streets. Flush to the cobbles was a big brick house. And we stood before its black bulk with our safeties off, just in case, and all of us too brave to say a word. The wind came round stone corners, cold and sharp as the blades of invisible pikes.

"What shall we give them? The Protestant Boys?"

"No," Mike said, "The Auld Orange Flute. I'll count three."

One, two, three, and we began to sing, our voices high in the darkness round the house full of baby-eating Catholics maybe.

*In the County Tyrone in the town of Dungannon Where many eruptions meself had a hand in . . ."*

Then a big red roar, like the sound of a muzzle loader that has not been fired for a long time, slammed against the door; a loud, old Gaelic gun blew shot through the keyhole. And when we stopped running, we were outside *our* house; the parlor was lit for Christmas and everything was bright and clean and Protestant again.

"Perhaps it was a priest," Tim said.

"Perhaps it was the College of Cardinals," Dan said, who was always reading.

"Let's go in and see if there's any gelignite left," Mike said. And we did that. □

20¢

GLOOMY TUNES presents

# KIT 'n' KABOODLE

MICE BURGERS

COOK BOOK

SALT

STORY: BRIAN McCONNACHIE   ART: WARREN SATTLER

1

3

# The Goyspiel According to Bernie

**as transcribed by Gerald Sussman**

Where you going? The Waldorf? Right. I bet you're going to a convention. You're wearing one of those badges on your jacket. National Conference of Christians and Jews. *Oh, yeah...oh,* sure...I know those guys. I see your name is Bernard Schwartz. That's a coincidence—my name is Bernie, too. Listen, Bernie...we got a long ride to the hotel from the airport. Before you get to that convention I want to tell you a few things you should know...so you don't walk in like Joe Schmuck, y'know?

First of all, just between us Yids, that whole National Conference of Christians and Jews is full of shit. It's a big front that the goyim are using to try and fuck us. Don't argue with me, Bernie, I know what I'm talking about. I been driving a cab for forty-five years and I seen it a million times...the Gentiles are no fucking good and they never will be. It's us against them, Bernie...believe me. You think I'm bullshitting you? Listen to this...last night I pick up three of your fucking friends from the Conference, three priests or ministers or whatever the hell you call them. They're drunk out of their fucking skulls. They can't see straight. First they start singing these religious songs with dirty words ...about Jesus and Mary and Joseph and God knows what else. About Jesus fucking a shepherd up the ass...the Virgin Mary getting gang-banged by the disciples...stuff like that. I've heard some dirty songs in my time, but this was disgusting. I mean, I don't give a shit personally—he's *their* God, not ours. But they shouldn't talk like that about one of their own.

But then they start carrying on about the Jews. Seems like they never saw so many fucking Jews in their life. Everywhere they turn in New York

they bump into a Jew. Jews are pushing them, conning them, robbing them, taking their money at every turn. Each time they think they see a Jew on the street they take potshots at him with these BB pistols they're carrying. They almost took a guy's eye out.

So they're talking and giggling and carrying on like a bunch of kids about the tricks they're playing on all the rabbis that are attending the Conference with them at the hotel. They've done stuff like "Frenching" the rabbis' beds, whatever the fuck *that* means— they put matzoh crumbs all over the bedsheets—they're dropping water bags on them—all that classy stuff that the Shriners and the American Legion used to do. The rabbis think some gang of anti-Semitic kids is doing this. And of course, the ministers are putting on this big front about living together in brotherhood. Meanwhile, I'm driving along like I'm Joe Schmuck—like I don't hear a word.

Then one of these scumbags starts talking about how all these tricks are just kid stuff—and if they really wanted to do something important, something their superiors would be proud of, they should carry out the plan. The other guys agree. They're going to do the plan tonight. They talked it over in my cab and I heard the whole fucking thing. The plan is to arrange a social evening with the most prominent rabbis at the conference. Jews are not big drinkers, y'know. It doesn't take much to get them a little tipsy. So while they're tipsy the ministers will put some kind of a pill in their drinks and drug them real good. Then they're going to take them up to their rooms and have a bunch of fags fuck them, blow them, make them blow the fags, etc., etc. And while all this is going on they're going to take pictures.

A real bunko scheme. Only the fucking ministers are not going to give the rabbis the incriminating pictures in exchange for big money. Oh no. They're going to release the pictures to all the media. Get it? The gist of the plan is to destroy the rabbis' reputations. These are the biggest, most respected rabbis in the country. Can you imagine what Jews all over America will think when they see these pictures? Especially the young people. You know how sensitive we are about homos. Then with all our top rabbis in disgrace, they're going to walk in and feed the young kids a nice line of propaganda and convert them all to Gentiles. That's the plan.

Naturally, I could've stopped the cab at any time and kicked the shit out of those lowlifes with one hand tied behind my back. And believe me, Bernie, I was tempted to do it a hundred times. But then I had a better idea. What if the rabbis got wind of the plan and played possum? They could make believe they were drugged and when they got up to the hotel room they could really lay into those ministers and turn the tables on them—make *them* go down on the fags, which those guys like to do anyway. Then they can crease them up a little bit — y'know,... wrinkle them a little, to teach them a lesson.

So I'll probably tell the rabbis about the plan as soon as we get to the hotel. Unless you want to do it. You know them all, I suppose. I'll leave it up to you. One thing I know...there's going to be plenty of Gentile blood flowing in the Waldorf tonight, kid.

As long as we're talking about Gentiles, I might as well fill you in on them. We got millions of them in New York—all kinds. And for some reason, God wants to punish me. He brings them all to me. That's all I get in my

cab all day long—fucking Gentiles—the cream of the crop. I know them all. The Irish, for instance. When they're not killing each other, they do have one great talent, I got to admit—they really know how to get drunk. You don't know what a drunk is until you get a fucking drunken Mick in your cab. They're always singing some stupid song and you can't understand a word of it because they got so much phlegm in their mouths. So what they do is clear their throats and lay their lungers in my change compartment. It's always a nice feeling to stick your hand in there and come up with a half

a dozen Irish oysters.

As disgusting as the Irish are, the best drunken pukers are the Italians. Must be that greaseball food they eat and that wine they make in the basement out of cow's blood. They don't sing and they don't talk. They eat and drink until they're going to explode. Then they hail my cab, get in, and puke in it. What am I supposed to do? They could be Mafia, the fucking clowns.

You know what the fucking Greeks like to do? They like to bargain with me over the fare. They got all these cards in their pockets that they want

to give me instead of money. These cards are supposed to give me big discounts on all kinds of merchandise that their cousins sell. I'll give them discounts...right up their fucking keisters.

Every once in a while I get a Polack. You got to stop for a Polack. Y'know why, doncha? He always hails a cab by walking right into it while you're driving. You got to stop on a dime. Even if you crease them a little, they don't feel it. Polacks never heard of tips. They don't tip for anything. They see the price on the meter and that's it. You can't explain to them that you work on

tips—that you don't make much in salary. One night a Polack took a shit right on my back seat. That's what he left me for a tip. I guess when they have to go, they have to go.

There's only one Gentile worse than a Polack that I had in my cab. I don't even know what they were. They were talking a language I never heard of and they were wearing those clothes the English singers used to wear about ten years ago. I think they were from a soccer team or a hockey team or something, from someplace like Latvia. They were carrying on something terrible. When they got out of the cab

they ripped out the back seat and took it with them. I started to go after them and one of them laughed in my face and I swear to God he knocked me unconscious with his breath. It made the Polack's shit smell like Chanel Number Five. To this day, whenever I think about it I get dizzy and I have to stop the cab for a few minutes.

What's the sense talking about spades and PRs? I never pick them up. I don't care how respectable they look. I figure I'm still too young to die.

There's one bunch of Gentiles that really drive me up the fucking wall. The big shots. I get 'em in my cab all

the time—on Wall Street or Park Avenue, coming out those clubs. They're supposed to be the smart ones, the ones that own everything and run everything. You can see how smart they are by how fast this country is going to the shithouse. The only thing smart about those fucking closet queens is what they're doing to Jews like me. Those millionaire cocksuckers are driving me to an early grave. Because of them I'm going to get a heart attack. And not just me. All my friends who drive cabs. All the Jews. I'll tell you what I mean.

A couple of weeks ago I'm cruising

down Park Avenue about ten, ten-thirty at night when this woman hails me. She's wearing a mink coat that must have cost more than I make in five years. She looks like Grace Kelly when Grace Kelly was in the movies. I was never crazy about that type. I go more for the Sophia Loren type. But you wouldn't throw this broad out of bed, believe me. She wants to go to the Village. About ten blocks later she changes her mind. Now she wants to go uptown. O.K., fine. But a few minutes later she changes her mind again. I tell her, lady…it's your money, but I wish you'd make up your mind. She says she's still not sure, so how about driving through Central Park while she thinks it over. We get into the park and she starts talking to me—about how driving a cab must be a dangerous business—how you have to be brave to drive a cab at night. Then she asks me if it's O.K. for her to sit up front with me so we can talk better. Shit, I don't want to be unsociable and I'm not sure if she's O.K. in the head, so I figure I'll play along. She tells me she feels very restless—at loose ends—that's why she doesn't know where she wants to go. Then she starts telling me about her home life, about her husband, how he's busy all the time with business and golf and squash and all that shit—and how they got separate bedrooms and she never sees him and how she never knew marriage could be such living hell. I looked at her in that coat and you can imagine how sorry I felt for her. Then all of a sudden she starts stroking my leg and playing with the back of my neck and telling me how sexy I look and how she likes older Jewish men who don't shave every day. By now she's zipping down my fly and playing with my shvance. When she sees how big it is she goes crazy and begs me to find a quiet spot somewhere in the park. This kind of thing happens to me all the time with the broads. They must have a sixth sense about the size of my joint. Anyway, I figure she's too clean to be working a Punch and Judy act, so what do I have to lose? Besides, if I don't throw her a few fucks she might go to a nigger. So I take her to this spot I know where all

the cops go and I fuck her till her ears bleed. I must have come about twenty-nine times and I can't remember how many times she came. You'd need a fucking adding machine to figure it out.

She's so fucking grateful she wants to give me a couple of hundred bucks. Money is no problem, she says. Her husband is president of one of the biggest banks in the country and he owns this and has stock in that, etc., etc. If I told you his name you'd shit purple. What could I say? She made me take the money and then she made me promise to fuck her and her two friends tomorrow, which I did, to everyone's satisfaction.

Well, I'm feeling pretty good about this deal I fall into. And pretty soon this broad has a whole group of friends that I'm fucking, almost every day of the week—all these beautiful blond shiksas with small tits and nice long legs and flat asses. They can't keep their hands off me. They got to have a big Jewish cock. Their husbands are fags or they can't get it up anymore or it's too fucking small or whatever. But when my cabbie friends at the Belmore cafeteria tell me the same story I smell a fucking rat. Those fucking Gentile cunts are really working for their husbands all along! They know that Jews can fuck all day and all night so they seduce us and make us fuck our brains out until we're all going to get heart attacks!

So I call up all these broads I been fucking and tell them I'm through—that I smelled out their fucking plan. They all cry and scream and beg me to change my mind. They said that it started out as a plan to kill us—that their husbands made them do it—but they could never go through with it because now they're desperately in love with me—they know what real sex is and they would die rather than give me up. My answer to all that was "up your hole with a Mello-roll." The next day I read in the papers that twelve society ladies committed suicide. Fuck 'em. I didn't even shed a tear. It was their own fault. All those fucking shiksas are spoiled. If they don't get their way, they go right to the fucking

sleeping pills.

Of course, your basic American Gentiles come from out of town. I always get cursed with a Gentile family at the airport. They're on vacation. First time in New York. They all come from Indiana, Ohio, or someplace like that. The husband wears red pants and a yellow Banlon shirt with two little golf clubs on it, and white shoes with gold links. His wife wears a pants outfit with weird color combinations. She has a big, square ass and her pants are always too short. She wears a scarf because her hair is in curlers. They have two kids—always boys—about ten, twelve years old with blond hair and no features on their faces. The kids never talk. All the kids in Indiana, Ohio are mutes.

All of them have those little cameras but I never saw one of them take a picture. The father has this big fucking leather pen holder on his pants with all kinds of gadgets in it. He likes gadgets and he always shows me his combination tire gauge and shoehorn. Sometimes one of the blond, mute kids takes out a bolo knife or a hand grenade from a plastic shopping bag and starts playing with it. And the father says, "Edna, why do you let them pack all that junk whenever we go on vacation? We won't have room for anything we're going to buy." The kids always send away for that kind of stuff—that's their favorite toys.

Naturally, they always ask me the same questions. "Is New York really as dangerous as they say?" It all depends on the neighborhood and the time of day, I say. In Harlem it's always safe. Fifth Avenue, Madison, Park—those are the dangerous streets—especially in the morning. They're not sure whether to believe me or not so they try to make a little small talk. These people are so fucking boring they're almost dead. The wife reminds me of the Gentiles you see on those TV commercials. They're always testing a paper towel against another doochbag who has the good towel. She talks like a zombie while her towel is doing a shitty job, getting all stringy and gummy looking. You notice they never use a Jewish girl in those commercials? Only

"…And now we will hear the dissenting opinion."

S. GROSS

Gentiles from Indiana, Ohio. Can you imagine what a broad like that must be in bed? I'd rather fuck the wet towel. They're worse than boring, those assholes. They're creepy. These are the ones that scare the shit out of me, and there's millions of them out there.

Did you ever notice how many Gentiles walk around with a stupid look on their face, with their mouths open? Y'know why, doncha? It comes from eating so much fucking peanut butter on Wonder Bread. When they were kids they were always scraping that peanut butter off the roof of their mouth, but they could never get it all off. Eventually they got a permanent wedge of peanut butter up there that keeps their mouth open. It gets as hard as a brick. I had a dentist in the cab once who told me all about it. He says you could have an operation to cut it out but it's very dangerous. So they all walk around with their mouths a little open. It's just right for drinking beer and eating Big Macs, which is all they eat when they get older. I swear to God I think a Jewish mongoloid is ten times smarter than a Gentile.

But let's face it...the main reason the Gentiles are so fucking dumb is they were born that way. I once had a very big rabbi in my cab, a very learned man. He told me the real story of the Jews and the Gentiles. First of all, he said, you can always tell the difference between a Jew and a Gentile because the Jew has the Holy Crystals in his blood. The Holy Crystals are like kosher salt. When a Jew is born these Crystals appear in his blood. They're supposed to be very beautiful, like snowflake designs, only they're invisible. The Crystals stay in the blood until the Jew dies. Then they fly out of his body and go back to heaven, where God can use them again in another Jew's blood. God put these Holy Crystals into a Jew's blood to make him smarter than anyone else. That's how He made us the Chosen People. But since He was a just God, He had to do something for the rest of the people, the Gentiles. So He made them the *shtarkas,* the strong ones, like animals they were, with thick heads they could use like helmets. The Gentiles were allowed to eat anything, even pigs.

But when God made us His Chosen People we became too smart for our own good. We strayed from Him. He always wanted us to be perfect and it was very hard. Finally He lost patience with us and had us kicked out of Palestine and scattered all over the world. His parting words were something like, "You're smart enough to fend for yourselves. I'm not going to fight your battles for you anymore. Your punishment is you must live with the Gentiles for

all time, or until I send a Messiah for you. They hate you like poison because you're much smarter, so they will make your lives miserable or kill you all."

Meanwhile, the Gentiles were trying their best to imitate the Jews, even going to the trouble of making up their own God. They made up a crazy story about a God being born from a virgin. Can you imagine a Jew making up a story like that? Then they went crazy with their new religion and made all kinds of rules and regulations. They even made a lot of money and bought a lot of fancy churches and fancy clothes and jewelry for the priests. If the Jews had a God and a church, they were going to have a better God and a fancier church. That's how we got the Catholics. And then everybody wanted to get into the act and now we got a million different Gentile religions. The rabbi calls them all "The Chosen Assholes."

Speaking of Chosen Assholes...I'll give the first prize to the Catholics. Those fucking Catholic priests really take the cake. I nearly killed one of those guys once. I'll never forget it. I had this priest in the cab with two boys, about ten, eleven years old—two really nice looking boys. I'm taking them to Saint Patrick's on Fifth Avenue. We don't go more than three blocks when one of the kids starts crying. He says he won't go. He says his older brother hated it and told him how disgusting it was and he didn't want to do it. The priest has this very soft voice. He was trying to calm the kid down, saying it was a privilege, an honor, that the kid was too young to understand how important it was for him, but that he should trust the

Church and he would always be taken care of. But the kid got more upset and said he didn't care—he just wanted to go home. Meanwhile the other kid is giggling and says there's nothing to it, that it tastes like a cucumber with a little salt on it. Now the kid is really crying and the priest is getting annoyed. He keeps telling the kid what an honor it is, that he was chosen from hundreds of kids that were dying to do it—that his parents are proud of him and that he was going to get a scholarship to Notre Dame. And all he had to do was give up an hour or so of his time a few days a week.

The other kid is a spiteful little bastard. He says that Kevin, that's the one that's crying, is really afraid of the other thing. Now the priest switches back to his soft voice. He's a beauty, this guy. And he says something like..."Kevin lad...I was once in the same position as you. I was terribly frightened. Do you know why? I was thinking of myself, not of the Lord and what He wanted of me. When the priests took me and blessed me and offered a prayer of thanks to the Lord, I wasn't frightened anymore. And do you know something, Kevin? Those were the happiest hours of my life."

Kevin is wiping his eyes and giving the priest a look that says you're full of shit. He says his older brother used to come home in pain all the time. It was so bad he had to stay in bed, lying on his stomach. The priest says that it was truly unfortunate—that Kevin's brother was a great favorite and would always be invited to the special parties for the bishops and the cardinals and whatever and sometimes things got a little out of hand. He would make sure that this wouldn't happen to little

## The Joys of Motherhood

WHAT DOES IT LOOK LIKE I'M DOIN'? I'M CALLIN' THE POPE TO COME BABY-SIT!

© 72 —SHARY FLENNIKEN—

Kevin.

By now I'm beginning to put two and two together. I always knew this kind of shit was going on in the Catholic churches. Those fucking priests got homo written all over them. I happen to be one of the best fag detectors in New York. The cops use me on tough cases, when they want to get something on a guy. Nobody can spot a fag faster than me. But when it's going on right under your nose it takes a little while to sink in. I figure that this priest must be pimping for whatshisname...Cardinal Spellman.

I'm thinking that this poor kid is going to be ruined for life. Even if he *is* a Gentile, he's still a human being, right? By now I'm pulling up to the side entrance of Saint Patrick's. The priest pays the fare and takes the two kids out. All of a sudden Kevin makes a run for it. And just as I was about to get out and kick the shit out of that priest so he couldn't put the chase on the kid I see two big Irish cops come out of nowhere, grab the poor kid, and carry him into the church. What's the sense in tangling with a couple of Jew-hating cops over one little Gentile kid? But I couldn't help feeling sorry for him. That's what those fucking Catholics do with a lot of their kids —millions of them. Today Kevin is probably cruising around Times Square with all the other Catholic kids. He probably has gonorrhea or the syph...if he's not dead already.

You know what the really scary thing is? The fucking Gentiles are at it again. They're showing their true colors. They want to kill all the Jews again. You don't believe me? They're already starting it. You don't read about it in the papers because the goys control all the media. Already, a lot of Jews are disappearing in Florida. The Gentiles are trying to wear us down from all sides. And do you know what they're doing in the neighborhoods?

The butchers are selling different kinds of meat, depending on whether you're a Jew or a Gentile. The Jews get the shittier cuts of meat. They always did this in the German neighborhoods, but now they're doing it everywhere. They're doing it with all kinds of food. Yesterday I stopped at this diner for a cup of coffee and a roll. The coffee tastes like piss warmed over and the roll must be a week and a half old. I knew something funny was going on so I said to the Greek, "Give me a cup of coffee from the *other* urn and give me a roll from that *other* bin over there." The fucking Greek gives me a dirty look. He knows I got his number. I said, "Don't worry, asshole, I'll pay for the two coffees and two rolls. Just give me a pair from the same place you took it for your other customers." So I taste the other coffee and roll and sure as shit they're both fresh. The fucking scumbag is trying to get rid of stale food on the Jews. I heard it's happening in all the restaurants and stores now. They want to get us undernourished, so we'll become weak and defenseless.

I had a guy in my cab yesterday that used to work for the government, a Jewish fella, very smart. He told me that something terrible could happen to all the Jews in America soon. He said Nixon made a deal with the Arabs before he resigned. The Arabs said they would give America all the oil they wanted, for free, if the Americans kill all the Jews living in their country. It would have to be done fast—like in one day. It should look almost like an accident. Well, it just so happens that J. Edgar Hoover, who was the biggest anti-Semite of them all, once devised a perfect plan to get rid of all the Jews in one day. He had a master file on every Jew in America—their names and addresses and apartment numbers—everything. On the orders of the president he would send out his men to

every place where a Jew lived and they would fix the water system so that poisoned water would flow into the taps of Jewish homes only. In one day almost every Jew would drop dead. Hoover tried to sell his idea to all the presidents. Nixon was absolutely ready to buy it and then he had his own problems. This guy who used to work in the government told me that President Ford is just about ready to carry out the plan.

So what are we going to do about it? We got to use our water, and we don't know exactly when that cocksucker could feed poison into our plumbing systems. I say the only thing we can do is get guns and go to Washington and kidnap Ford and make him tell us his plan. We got to be like the Israelis. Hit them before they hit you. The only way we can win is to use surprise tactics because they got us outnumbered. Meanwhile I wouldn't mind mowing down a few hundred Gentiles and busting a few of their stupid heads. They got away with killing millions of us in Europe but they're not going to get away with this one, not if I got one drop of life in me.

What? What did you say? Why don't I start by trying to bust *your* stupid head? Why should I do that for? We're in this together. This is the time for all the Jews to stop arguing and fight back fast. What are you talking about...you're not a Jew. Your name is Bernie Schwartz. It's right on your fucking card you got pinned to your jacket. What's that? Your name is Barnhard Schwarz? How do you pronounce that? Barn...hard... Schvaarrzz. I thought you said Bernard Schwartz. My hearing is getting bad. What kind of name is that? German? It *is* German. You want me to stop the car and go out to that field over there and settle this once and for all...you want to pick a fight with me, right now, in the middle of this highway? You got a good case. Why don't you pick on someone your own size? I'm half your size, you fucking scumbag. I got a weak heart and I can't even make a fist, I got so much arthritis in my hands. You're all the same, you fucking Gentiles. You can only fight Jews who can't fight back. I'd like to see you try the same shit with my nephew. He'll beat the shit out of you with one hand. What? Take you to my nephew right now? You must be crazy. What am I, your slave? Your chauffeur? Even if he was right here I wouldn't let him waste his breath on you. Get your fucking hands off me, you Nazi! I'll yell for the police! I got a police radio in the car! Stop hitting me or we'll crash the car! Help! Police! Help! Somebody...please help! God...please...anybody...Oy! Oy! Oy! Oooooooy...

MAY, 1970

*"There's one thing that money can't buy, Mr. Grotberger, and that's good health!"*

JUNE • 25¢

# Boys' Real Life

## FOR MOST BOYS

**INDOOR CAMPING**
A Bonfire in the Basement

**LET DAD BUILD YOUR
SOAPBOX DERBY RACER**

**LEARNING TO SMOKE**

162

**FOR MOST BOYS**

# Boys' Real Life

JUNE

P. J. O'Rourke
Editor in Chief

David McClelland
Articles Editor

Dean Latimer
Color Section Editor

Brian McConnachie
Fiction Editor

Henry Beard and Doug Kenney
Research Assistants

## Use High-Strength BONEX

## FICTION

## ARTICLES

## REGULAR FEATURES

*"This is more serious than I thought," shouted Dr. Pinky, Junior Medical Technician. "Prepare the garage."*

# Young "Dr." Pinky in
# NO BONES ABOUT IT

The doors of Madisonville Elementary School burst apart like a crumbling dam no longer able to contain the flood of fleeing children. As they poured down the front steps, their joyous shouts unmistakably marked the end of school. Another year of formal education was behind them, but to Pinky Fisher, the learning process was not about to take a vacation.

"Mary Beth, Mary Beth. Wait up. I have to talk to you. The tests are back from the lab," called Pinky.

Mary Beth spun around in anger. "You stay away from me, Pinky Fisher. My baby sister was spying on us last time, and now I have to take her everywhere or she'll tell my parents. . . ."

"Your baby sister, huh . . . how old is she?" asked Pinky.

"She's five and she's a real brat," answered Mary Beth.

". . . Ummmm . . . you mean she acts like a real brat. She's probably got ovarian cysts . . . makes kids act bratty. Better bring her around to my garage and I'll have a look at her," said Pinky.

"No. No more going to your laboratory," declared Mary Beth.

"*Pleeeeeaaaaassseee.* You have no idea how serious these things are. I want to make the whole neighborhood safe from ovarian cysts. One kid gets them, then everyone catches them. You just gotta come to the garage. *Pleeaaaassseee.*"

"No. But I'll meet you by Donally's barn and we can peepee together."

"Okay."

As Pinky waited, leaning up against the barn, the thought of peepeeing with Mary Beth began to bore him. You had to put your head practically against the ground before you could see anything, he remembered. He was certain Louis Pasteur had more cooperative patients. The carefree shouts of Mary Beth and her little sister Cathy soon brought Pinky back to reality.

"Be quiet, you two. You must save your energy. You're both dying of ovarian cysts. Hurry, get your dresses and panties off," directed young Fisher.

"No. I don't gotta and I'm going to tell Mommy on you."

"Now Cathy, it's for your own good. We want to save you. Come on now, get your dress off and you'll be all better soon."

"Let go. Let go of me. Let go. *Help. Owww.* Let go," cried Cathy.

Reaching for a rock, Pinky lunged at Cathy. Mary Beth stumbled back in shock and horror as Pinky swung the rock against her baby sister's head.

"You killed her!" yelled Mary Beth.

"No I didn't. Just a local anesthetic. Shut up. Stop yelling and help me get her clothes off. You're in this as deep as I am. Do what I tell you."

Pinky reached for the skirt hem and began pulling it over Cathy's limp head as Mary Beth nervously drew down the panties along the firm stubby pink legs. Upon seeing the nakedness explode against the shaded green grass, Pinky dropped his end and began pressing his hands to the still

(*continued on page* 194)

THE TARTAR TWINS **PAT + MIKE**
by O'ROURKE & SATTLER

HERE COMES ANOTHER JAP, MIKE! HIT HIM WITH A FLAME-THROWER!

GAS

NOW LET'S TEST HOW FAR THE CALICO CAN WALK ON THE EXPERIMENTAL SPARKLER STILTS!

FFEEOW

OH-OH... IT'S GRAMPS!

BURNIN' KITTENS, ARE YA?

YEP, REMINDS ME A' WHEN I WAS YOUNG. ME AND JEFF DAVIS AND PAUL BUNYAN AND THEM USED TA RIP THE SHIT OUTTA ALL KINDS A' CATS.

...'COURSE THEY WAS MOSTLY MOUNTAIN LIONS AND COUGARS IN THEM DAYS, BUT I'LL NEVER FORGET A CERTAIN RUBBER-HEADED TOM.

IT WAS WHEN THIS COUNTRY WAS YOUNG. LITTLE GENERAL CUSTER AND BENNY FRANKLIN AND MYSELF WERE PLAYING OUT IN FRONT OF BETSY ROSS' HOUSE WHEN HER OLD TOM-CAT GOT ITS HEAD STUCK IN THE WINDOW.

YEOW! YEOW!

CHUCKY LINDBERGH AND I DECIDED TO HAVE SOME FUN AND STICK THE VOLUNTEER FIRE BRIGADE'S PUMP IN ITS EAR.

WELL, THAT CAT'S HEAD BEGAN TO SWELL UP, AND IT SWELLED AND SWELLED AND SWELLED!

WE DIDN'T KNOW WHAT TO DO...I GUESS IT WAS TED ROOSEVELT WHO FINALLY WENT INSIDE AND JAMMED A MUSKET UP ITS ASS.

WHEN HE PULLED THE TRIGGER, THAT TABBY'S HEAD TOOK OFF LIKE A GIANT ROCKET AND BOUNCED AROUND ALL OVER NEW YORK STATE, BUSTIN' THE CRAP OUT OF EVERYTHING.

AND TO THIS VERY DAY, THE DAMAGE THAT HEAD DONE IS CALLED THE CAT-SKULL MOUNTAINS!

WHY, DAD!! YOU LET THAT CAT ALONE!

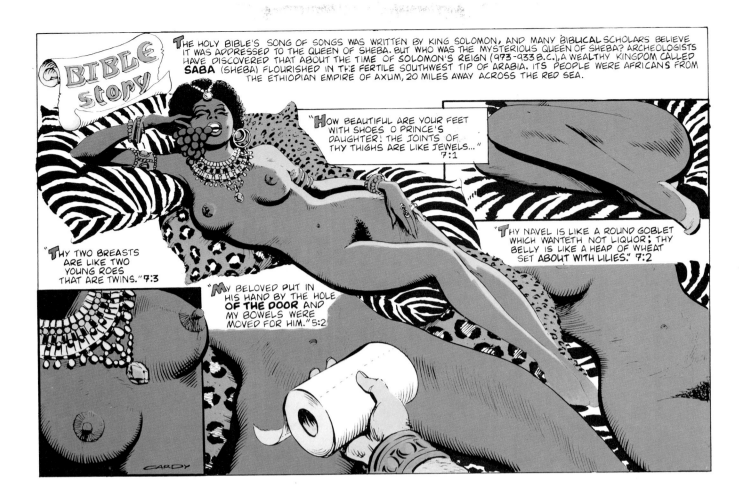

BIBLE Story

THE HOLY BIBLE'S SONG OF SONGS WAS WRITTEN BY KING SOLOMON, AND MANY BIBLICAL SCHOLARS BELIEVE IT WAS ADDRESSED TO THE MYSTERIOUS QUEEN OF SHEBA? BUT WHO WAS THE MYSTERIOUS QUEEN OF SHEBA? ARCHEOLOGISTS HAVE DISCOVERED THAT ABOUT THE TIME OF SOLOMON'S REIGN (973–933 B.C.), A WEALTHY KINGDOM CALLED **SABA** (SHEBA) FLOURISHED IN THE FERTILE SOUTHWEST TIP OF ARABIA. ITS PEOPLE WERE AFRICANS FROM THE ETHIOPIAN EMPIRE OF AXUM, 20 MILES AWAY ACROSS THE RED SEA.

"HOW BEAUTIFUL ARE YOUR FEET WITH SHOES O PRINCE'S DAUGHTER! THE JOINTS OF THY THIGHS ARE LIKE JEWELS..." 7:1

"THY NAVEL IS LIKE A ROUND GOBLET WHICH WANTETH NOT LIQUOR; THY BELLY IS LIKE A HEAP OF WHEAT SET ABOUT WITH LILIES." 7:2

"THY TWO BREASTS ARE LIKE TWO YOUNG ROES THAT ARE TWINS." 7:3

"MY BELOVED PUT IN HIS HAND BY THE HOLE **OF THE DOOR** AND MY BOWELS WERE MOVED FOR HIM." 5:2

CARDY

# TORTURES
## OF THE INDIANS

ALAN E. KUPPERBERG

@UR STORY SO FAR: THE OBA-AH-NEE PEOPLE OF THE CHICKASAW NATION HAVE WELCOMED THE GREAT HERO CHATHAT. TO CELEBRATE HIS VISIT, THE SHAMAN CONDEMNS TWO CHOCTAW CAPTIVES TO SLOW AND PAINFUL DEATHS.

BEING THE INFERIOR SUBJECT, THE GIRL IS TORTURED FIRST. A CLAY HELMET IS PLACED ON HER HEAD TO PROTECT HER VALUED SCALP. THEN THE CHICKASAW WOMEN ATTACK HER FROM ALL SIDES WITH WHIPS AND TORCHES, WHILE CHATHAT AND THE BRAVES LOOK ON AND LAUGH.

LOUDER AND LOUDER GROWS THE MERRY-MAKING AS THE CHOCTAW MAIDEN'S SKIN BLISTERS AND PEELS AWAY. EACH TIME SHE FAINTS SHE IS SPLASHED WITH WATER AND REVIVED. CHATHAT HIMSELF HELPS HER UP, AND EVERYONE LAUGHS.

SOON THE GIRL HAS HAD HER ARMS AND LEGS PULLED OFF AND THE TORTURE OF THE BRAVE BEGINS. THIS IS THE MAIN EVENT OF THE CELEBRATION, FOR, NO MATTER HOW MUCH THE WOMEN AND CHILDREN TORMENT HIM, HE MUST PRESERVE THE SILENCE AND DIGNITY OF A TRUE WARRIOR.

THE TORTURE OF THE BRAVE GOES ON INTO THE NIGHT. FINALLY, THE LAUGHING OF THE CHICKASAW WARRIORS DIES DOWN AND IS REPLACED WITH A RESPECTFUL FUNERAL DIRGE; FOR THE CHOCTAW BRAVE EXPIRED WITHOUT A SINGLE CRY.

IT HAS BEEN A LONG DAY. AT DAWN CHATHAT WILL BEGIN A JOURNEY TO VISIT THE CHOCTAW PEOPLES ON THE OTHER SIDE OF THE GREAT **MISHA SIPOKNI** (MISS-ISSIPPI RIVER). THE SHAMAN ASSURES HIM THAT THE CHICKASAW CAPTIVES WILL BEHAVE WITH EQUAL VALOR.
**CONTINUED NEXT MONTH.**

# HOW TO MAKE TROUBLE

## KNOW YOUR BRIDGE HEIGHTS

### SUCCESS IS IN YOUR SIGHTS WHEN CAREFUL PLANNING CALLS THE SHOTS

RATE OF DROP IS IMPORTANT OFF HIGHWAY OVERPASSES. A COMPLICATED MATHEMATICAL FORMULA IS REQUIRED TO FIGURE IT OUT EXACTLY, BUT HERE ARE SOME HANDY APPROXIMATES WHICH YOU CAN MEMORIZE:

OBJECT FALLS FROM 10-FT. OVERPASS IN SLIGHTLY LESS THAN 3/4 OF A SECOND
FROM A 15-FT. OVERPASS IN ALMOST 1 SECOND
FROM A 20-FT. OVERPASS IN 1 AND 1/10 SECONDS
FROM A 25-FT. OVERPASS IN SLIGHTLY LESS THAN 1 AND 1/15 SECONDS
FROM A 30-FT. OVERPASS IN 1 AND 1/4 SECONDS

CARS TRAVELING AT 60 MPH ARE COVERING 88 FT. PER SECOND. SHARPEN YOUR TURNPIKE SKILLS BY MULTIPLYING DROP TIME IN SECONDS BY 88 TO GIVE YOU A RULE OF THUMB FOR THE NUMBER OF FEET A CAR SHOULD BE FROM THE OVERPASS WHEN YOU YELL "WATER BALLOONS AWAY!"

*EXAMPLE:* A 20 FT. BRIDGE HAS A 1.1 SECOND DROP TIME. 1.1 TIMES 88 IS 96.8, THEREFORE YOU SHOULD PACE OUT ABOUT 97 FEET FROM THE ABUTMENT AND PLACE A VISIBLE BUT UNOBTRUSIVE MARKER AS A "SIGHT" TO ASSIST YOUR TIMING.

ADJUST "88" FIGURE TO CONFORM WITH LOCAL AVERAGE SPEEDS.

FOR 70 MPH USE "103"
FOR 65 MPH USE "95 1/2"
FOR 55 MPH USE "80 1/2"
FOR 50 MPH USE "74"

*(image labels: 20 FT. / SIGHT TO PIECE OF "LITTER" OR OTHER INCONSPICUOUS OBJECT. / 95 FT. / 97 FT.)*

## A REAL SHOCK

*REVERSE THE POLES ON YOUR MODEL TRAIN TRANSFORMER FOR SOME HIGH VOLTAGE FUN!*

*ONE POSSIBLE APPLICATION*

DETONATES IN SECONDS WITH "THROTTLE" ON "FULL SPEED AHEAD"

SHOTGUN SHELL

TRANSFORMER CORD WIRES (WIRE TO PERCUSSION CAP HELD IN PLACE WITH TAPE)

ATTACH BARED ENDS OF EXTENSION CORD WIRES TO TRACK WIRE TERMINALS.

*BONUS HINT:* EVEN AN UNALTERED TRAIN TRANSFORMER MAKES A GREAT "LIE DETECTOR"

PLUG EXTENSION CORD INTO WALL SOCKET.

CLIP PLUG FROM TRANSFORMER CORD, STRIP INSULATION, AND WIRES ARE READY FOR ACTION.

## QUIZ: CAN YOU IDENTIFY THESE EIGHT IMPORTANT TYPES OF FIREWORKS?

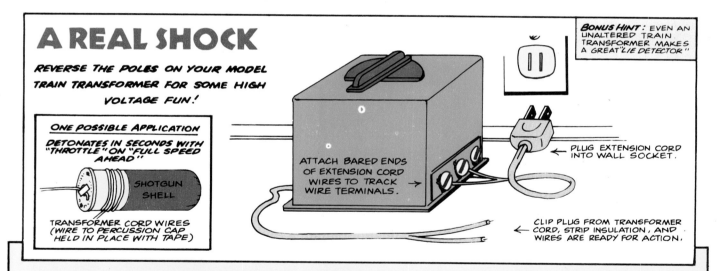

ANSWERS

1. M-80 (ALSO CALLED HAMMERHEADS, BLOCKBUSTERS, OR ASH-CANS)—IT HAS THE LARGEST POWDER CHARGE OF ANY EASILY AVAILABLE FIRECRACKER IN AMERICA, THOUGH MEDIOCRE CHARGE SHAPE MAKES IT MOST EFFECTIVE IN CONFINED SPACES. 2. CHERRY BOMB—ALTHOUGH IT CONTAINS SLIGHTLY LESS EXPLOSIVE THAN AN M-80, THE CHERRY BOMB'S SELF-TAMPING SHELL, EXCELLENT SHAPE, AND WATERPROOF QUALITY MAKE IT. 3. TWO-INCHER—IMPRESSIVE LOOKING AND NOISY BUT LACKING IN REAL STRENGTH. EVEN SO, THE TWO-INCHER AND ITS INCH-AND-A-HALF SMALLER BROTHER ARE THE WORK-A-DAY FIRECRACKERS FOR MOST OF THE WORLD. 4. LADYFINGER—STRICTLY FOR GIRLS, BUT LETTING ONE GO OFF IN YOUR HAND IS A MORE PAINFUL DARE THAN IT LOOKS. 5. BOTTLE ROCKET—MODERATE RANGE FUN WITH SERIOUS AIMING DIFFICULTIES. 6. ROMAN CANDLE—ARMCHAIR FIREWORKS. 7. SKYROCKET—NUMEROUS VARIETIES, ALL INCENDIARY, ALL AIMABLE, AND SOME CARRY A PUNCH EQUIVALENT TO TWO OR THREE CHERRY BOMBS. 8. TORPEDO (ALSO CALLED ATOMIC PEARL)—A SELF-DETONATING FOIL BALL FULL OF BLACK POWDER AND SMALL SHOT, OFTEN THOUGHT OF AS A KIDS TOY BUT VERY USEFUL IN COMBINATION WITH THE SLINGSHOT. BUT USEFUL AS A COMPONENT FOR LARGER PROJECTS.

# Frog Baseball

By T. D. OLINSEN

Tom Latimer winds up after brother Dean singled on a ground ball with a freak hop.

If you're looking for something to keep your troop or gang of guys active and interested this summer—something that combines team sport skills with hiking and nature study—why not try some slow pitch frog ball?

It may look simple enough, but frog baseball is a real crack game the way Life Scouts Tom and Dean Latimer of Crary Mills, New York, play it. "First of all," Tom explains, "you can't use real baseball equipment of any kind. That's cheating, and anyway it'd look dumb to carry gloves and bats and chest protectors and all that junk out into the field where the frogs are. Why, Dean and I have been doing such a good job on the frogs around here that it's getting so you have to go all the way down to the creek a mile back of the barn to find any decent number of frogs."

Yes, there's a good deal of plain old hiking involved in frog baseball, not to mention frog chasing and pouncing—and that's just to get the frogs! "You have to be careful not to hurt them in any way, picking them up," Dean cautions. "For frog baseball you need whole frogs. Any kind of frog, or even toad, will do, and of course the bigger the better. But we don't pass up the little frogs either—that's a real *challenge*, the little ones!"

The only other equipment necessary for frog baseball is a bat of some sort, which by the rules must be procured from the fields themselves—that is, you can't take a bat into the fields with you. "This way you get a real variety of equipment," Tom points out. "One game you'll be playing with a skinny little length of slat busted off a haywagon, the next game it'll be a whole fence post so long and thick you can hardly lift it. It keeps a fellow on his toes."

The object of the game, naturally, is to keep the frog in play for as long as possible, while hitting it as far as possible with the bat. The pitcher addresses the batter from a fixed spot about twenty feet from the "plate" (any particular stone or bush), tossing the frog in to him with an easy underhand delivery. The batter then must hit the frog over the pitcher's head to score a "run," which makes him eligible to hit again. If the frog falls short of the pitcher, then the positions are reversed, pitcher becoming batter and vice versa. The one who scores more "runs" than the other before the frog is taken out of play is the winner of that "inning."

"The first batter has an obvious advantage," Dean notes, "so we flip a coin to see who's up first. If you have a good-sized frog, you can generally get three or four good runs out of him before he starts falling apart, so you have to be careful. The first couple of times, he'll just be kind of flattened out, with his tongue sticking out, one eye closed maybe, but still mean and kicking and solid enough for a good swat. After a couple more good clouts, though, he'll be kinda *shredded,* going all to flinders with the guts trailing out of his mouth and his legs twirling around loose, and this increases the wind resistance, giving him a real *spitball* effect—not only does the pitch shake and flop in the air, but there's no telling where he's gonna go when you hit him. And you don't want to hit him *too* hard when he's in that kind of shape, or the inning's over."

The end of the "inning" is signaled by the frog's losing of one or both legs. A real measure of artistry is required, after the third or fourth "run," to keep this from happening. Once the sides change after the first few runs, the pitcher, having started with an automatic disadvantage, has to exercise special skill and caution in playing catch-up ball.

"That's where the thrill of the *sport* comes in" affirms Tom. "It takes a real surgical-type delicacy to come up from behind in frog baseball. But then frankly, when you get right down to it, who gives a fart? The *real* fun's whacking the living shit out of these goddamn frogs and watching the poor bastards go flying through the air all busted up. Christ, you can keep it up for *hours,* chasing frogs around and playing baseball!"

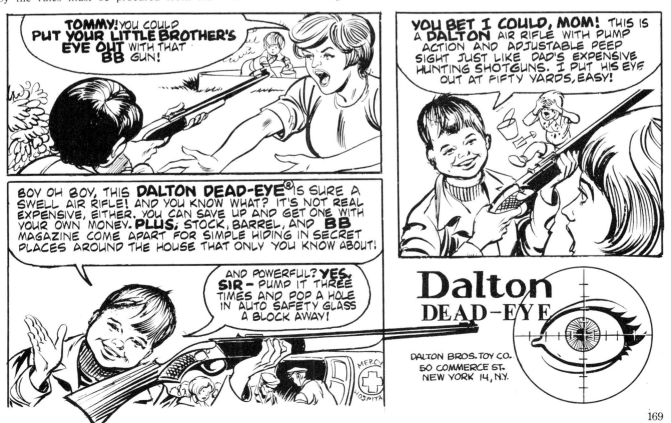
illustration by Annivette/Insite Studios/Larry Schwinger

# LADS' LAFF

A man hears that his wife is screwing the colored handyman. She denies it, but he tells her that if he ever hears that she does it again, he's going to pull out every one of her cunt hairs. People keep telling him that she's screwing the colored handyman and she keeps telling him that she isn't and one day he comes home and he's sure she has been, so he throws her down on the bad and starts pulling her cunt hairs out one by one. And he gets every one of them but one little black one which won't come out. He pulls on it and pulls on it and finally he yells, "Goddamn it, come out, you little black bastard!" And from up inside his wife's cunt, he hears this voice saying, "I'se comin', I'se comin', Boss!"—*David Standish, Oxford, Ohio*

A man who's got an eighteen-inch dong wants to join the Long Dick Club. He tells a friend of his who's already a member that his dong is eighteen inches long and asks him what he has to do to get in. "Eighteen inches!" says his friend. "Why, you see this flower in my buttonhole? Well, that's the tip of my dong, and I'm only the doorman!"—*Dan Riorden, King of Prussia, Pa.*

This is the ballad of Joe McClock,
A guy who was born with a corkscrew cock.
He spent all his life in a fatal hunt,
For the only girl with a corkscrew cunt.

He found the girl and then fell dead,
For her corkscrew cunt had a left-hand thread. —*John Rothschild, Orlean, Va.*

Three boys hear about a contest that a widow is having where if you can climb to the top of a greased flagpole you get to screw her. So they go over to her house and she shows them the greased flagpole and tells them that if they climb it all the way to the top she'll let them screw her but if they don't make it all the way to the top they'll have to pay the consequences. The first boy starts to climb the flagpole and he gets about halfway up before he slips down again. "What does your father do for a living?" the widow asks him.

"He's a butcher," says the first boy.

"Take out your dong," says the widow; and she chops it off with a meat cleaver. Then the second boy starts to climb the flagpole and he makes it three quarters of the way to the top before he slips back down again. "What's your father do for a living?" asks the widow. "He's a tailor," says the second boy. And she cuts it off with a pair of scissors. Then the third boy starts to climb the flagpole and he makes it almost all the way to the top before he slips down. "What's your father do for a living?" the widow asks him.

"He's a lollipop maker," says the third boy, "what are you going to do, lick it off?"—*Chuck Maypole, Wilmont, Wis.*

A guy with a huge dork is invited to go to a party, but he's scared to go because when he gets hard ons, his dork is so large that there's no place he can hide it. So a friend tells him that he should wrap it around his body. He wraps it around and around his chest but it's so long that the tip sticks out at the front of his shirt collar and he has to pretend that it's a tie. As soon as he gets to the party, a girl comes over and tells him how much she likes his necktie, and she's just picked it up to take a closer look when somebody across the room yells, "Hey, I didn't want cream in my coffee!"—*Bob Buckley, Montreal, Canada*

A boy named Johnny Fuckerfaster is playing with a girl underneath the front porch of his house when his mother comes out to look for him. "Johnny Fuckerfaster!" she yells. "Johnny Fuckerfaster!" And from under the porch, Johnny screams, "Jesus, Mom, I'm going as fast as I can!"—*Bill Hart, Concord, N. H.*

A man is screwing a woman with a hole so big that when he lets go of her tits for a second he slips and falls in. He stumbles around in the dark for a long time and finally he runs into a guy with a flashlight and asks him if he knows the way out. "No," says the guy with the flashlight, "but if you'll help me find my motorcycle, we can ride around until we see daylight!"—*Ray Shultz, Bronx, N.Y.*

## MILDRED

LION

"Sure she's mad. How would you like it if you had to wipe with your nose?"

# The Paranoid Abroad

## by Gahan Wilson

**I think those people are lepers.**
Chznashk dwak ekaki bor shlek.
*Sooz-nah-sak twah ah-gah-si buh slah-eek.*

In preparation
for his trip,
the paranoid
studies his phrase book, and sentences such as "I have
been clubbed and am bleeding profusely," and "Please
send someone to my room as I am trapped and it is aflame"
set him to thinking on what he knows will happen.

First, of course, the stevedores
will abuse and defile his luggage.

The passage will set records for foul weather, the
man in the upper berth will die after
a terrible coughing fit, and the
paranoid will have difficulty
discouraging the man in
the lower berth, who
will fancy him.

The customs officer will point
out that his picture in
his passport does
not in the least
resemble him.

The taxi will take him on a lengthy, roundabout route through strange parts of town.

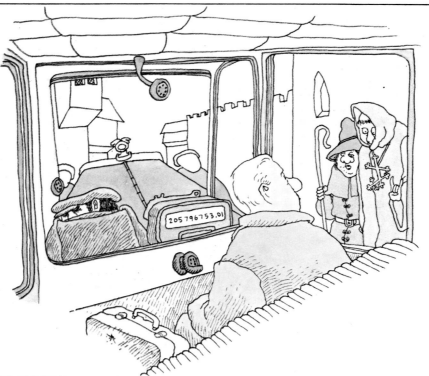

He will find the country's money incomprehensible and be unable to fit it into his wallet.

The desk-man at his hotel will suspect him of things.

People will spy on him.

The bathroom will be full of strange devices.

His voltage adaptor will not work and his razor will be destroyed.

He will order the national dish, *Lakle Bes Cherzdny*, and find it is rats in white cream sauce.

He will try a local medicine to counter the effects of the *Lakle* and will regret it.

The next morning he will take a shortcut and become lost in a dangerous neighborhood.

A whore will attach herself to him for blocks and then shriek curses at him.

A guide will give him mis-information about a tomb, insult his shoes, and insist on an exorbitant fee.

He will inadvertently go into the ladies' room.

He will rent a car, fail to work the gears properly, and be heavily fined.

The maps and road signs will confuse him.

When his car breaks down he will try to telephone the rental agency, but give up.

In asking directions to the railway station, he will unaccountably infuriate passersby.

Whereas his fellow passengers in the train compartment will find his appearance hilarious.

On the way to the airport, a small boy will offer to carry his suitcase and steal it.

Just before leaving, he will buy his sister's youngest daughter a souvenir doll, unaware that it will make obscene gestures when wound.

He will discover the economy flight his travel agent arranged was a serious error and that instead of returning home, his trip has barely started.

ANOTHER "TRUE LIFE" WESTERN ♥ ROMANCE

BY M·K·BROWN

WITH

LOLLY BARROW, ADOPTED DAUGHTER OF CECIL & MAE.

BILLY BARNS, LOLLY'S FIANCE, — STOLEN BY INDIANS AND BELIEVED DEAD BY ALL BUT A FEW.

THE BARROWS (CECIL & MAE), MARRIED SINCE EARLY CHILDHOOD AND DEVOTED TO HELPING "OTHERS".

BABY AMANDO, BORN TO CECIL AND MAE ONLY MINUTES AFTER LOLLY'S ADOPTION. A SMALL BUT FORCEFUL CHILD.

The Barrow's Ranch in Texas where Lolly keeps her lonely vigil

LOLLY! OH LOLLY! LAND SAKES! WHERE IS THAT GIRL? LOLLY!

COMING MOTHER

OH LOLLY! LOLLY!

LOLLY, DON'T WORRY! BILLY WILL BE BACK. HE ALWAYS COMES BACK. REMEMBER THE FIRST TIME HE WAS CAPTURED AND HE CAME BACK THE NEXT DAY?

I KNOW, MAMA, BUT GEE! WHY DOES HE KEEP GETTING CAPTURED LIKE THAT?? OTHER PEOPLE DON'T GET CAPTURED ALL THE TIME, AND WHAT IF HE GETS CAPTURED AFTER WE'RE MARRIED?

RELAX! I HEAR SOMEONE COMING!

GOO!

ONE WEEK LATER

Lolly and Billy spend the night in a cave eating squirrels. Early the next morning Billy is captured by Indians, and Lolly returns home to the Barrow's Ranch in Texas to keep her lonely vigil. Four days later Billy is sent home free, this time with useful gifts made of bark and moss. In his absence, Lolly reunites with her mother, who recognized her at the wedding.

THE END

# BAR ASSOCIATION OF THE STATE OF NEW YORK

## 1975

# EXAMINATION FOR ADMISSION TO THE BAR JULY 21, 1975

This examination is designed to test knowledge of the laws of the State of New York.

Time allotted: Eight hours. All questions must be answered.

STOP! Do not turn page until instructed to do so by the examiner. Your examination paper has been assigned the following code number. Do not write your name anywhere on this booklet.

Congratulations, _John "Jake" Sussman, Esq._ !!!!!!

You have just passed the New York State Bar Exam. You are now privy to one of the best-kept secrets in the nation. You're in. You're it. You're one of us.

Do not look up. Do not cheer. Keep quiet and keep reading.

For the last three years, we have been following with satisfaction your progress at _Yale Law School_. You have shown yourself to be amply qualified to practice law in this, the best of all possible states. Needless to say, it would be superfluous to force you to take another examination now, *or at any time in your career.*

## Sssshhhhh.

Sixty-three percent of the people in this room are reading what you are reading. Thirty-seven percent are attempting to answer intricate questions covering points of law which, as we and now you know, are insoluble. Rest assured that the Negroes in this room are among that 37 percent (except for the tall buck in the corner, whose father was Commissioner of Sanitation under Governor Harriman. And you don't have to worry about him because he's slated for Legal Aid).

## Don't worry. Keep your head down. We will tell you when it is safe to look up.

Perhaps you are wondering how we arrived at this percentage.

Each year, the Board of Examiners gathers at a small country club outside of Albany to determine the number of new lawyers the state can absorb without disturbing the economics of the prevailing attorney-client ratio. And, irrespective of qualification, *you made it!!* Perhaps you are also wondering, given all of the above, why this charade is necessary. As we and now you realize, this organization must preserve its public image of screening would-be entrants to the profession in order to ensure that the finest legal assistance is provided for the good people of the great state of New York.

## Don't laugh!

Now then. In order to maintain the fiction that you are, in fact, undergoing a grueling examination of your legal expertise, you must stay in the room for the next eight hours. During this time, you will have to display various forms of emotion: frustration, elation, anxiety, determination, fear, etc. We leave the delineation of these emotional pyrotechnics in your already capable hands, as a prospective courtroom lawyer.

## Go on, give it a try. Try frustration. How did it go?

We and now you realize that this kind of silliness is not going to get you through the next eight hours. (You can fool the jury but you can't fool yourself.) So we've put together a few time-consuming tidbits to help you through. Remember one thing, however. You're in. You're it. You're one of us. Nothing you do on these diversions will make any difference in the way we feel about you.

# Have fun.

**Across**

1. What your client does to the corner candy store.
4. If you defend one of these, remember: The attorney gets paid before any of the creditors.
6. *My_____Lawyer:* Harvard Law School Revue of 1966.
9. Little-known 1932 case upholding compulsory Hail Marys.
11. The first man to handle his own case.
12. What 13 across completed all his opinions with.
13. Mr. Justice_____: Brandeis, Frankfurter, Goldberg, Fortas, and probably a few others.

**Down**

1. What Daniel Webster got the morning after.
2. What you sit on if you're the prosecution.
3. Everybody's doin' it, doin' it, doin' it.
5. _____Rico: Wasn't he the lawyer who defended Trujillo?
7. Association of Ventriloquists (abbr.)
8. Stupid American lawyers traveling in London try to book a room at Lincoln's _____.
10. What you yell when you fry.

In order to get you started, here is a case for you to work on. We do not mean that you are being examined on this case. This is a real case. You can make money on this case—lots of it—the minute the exam is over.

*A*, a welfare mother who has just won the New York State Lottery, is on her way to the corner of a busy midtown intersection. When she reaches the corner, she calls across the street to her child *B*, who is begging on the opposite corner of the intersection, to inform him of this fact. *B* puts down his cup and crutch and runs across the street towards *A*. A car driven by *C* is approaching the intersection. Fearing that the car will strike *B*, *A* screams a warning. *C*, startled by the sudden noise, loses control of his automobile and mounts the sidewalk, striking *D*, President and Chairman of the Board of the Chase Manhattan Bank, in the ankle. Simultaneously, another car driven by *E*, a film star, strikes and kills *B*. *D* had been informed by his physician a week previously that he was slightly overweight, and had been advised to play polo at least three times a week, which he is unable to do due to his ankle injury. This results in an additional weight gain on *D*'s part, which in turn results in the appearance of an editorial cartoon depicting *D* and titled, "Inflated interest rates or what?" in a local newspaper. *D* alleges severe mental distress and professional anguish, and seeks to recover damages in the amount of $250,000.

As you remember from your days in law school, *A*'s scream is clearly the "but-for" cause of the injury sustained by *D*. Coincidentally, the amount of money won by *A* on the day in question was $250,000. *D* is looking for a lawyer. His number is 555-4070.

## Warning!

Although it has never yet happened, it is possible that you may be tempted to share this privileged information with unauthorized persons. Needless to say, this indiscretion would work a hardship on all past, present, and future members of the New York State Bar Association. If you shoot your mouth off:

1. Your estate will be immediately probated.
2. Your personal property will be attached, liens will be slapped on your real property, and you can kiss your chattels good-bye.
3. We will hound you to death.

**O.K., that's it. You can raise your head. Have a nice practice, and remember—one hand watches the other.**

This examination has been a service of the New York State Bar Association.

Mar. 19, 1975

# THE NEW YORKER

Price 60 cents

# GOING ON AND ON
## A CONSCIENCELESS CALENDAR OF EVENTS OF INTEREST

### THE THEATRE
#### PLAYS AND MUSICALS

**ADD HUE TO YOUR VEHICLE**—A tired, thinly-disguised reprise of the old musical, "Paint Your Wagon." With Rogers Peet and Georgette Klinger. (Desi Arnaz, 209 W. 45th St. Nightly, except Sundays, at 8. Matinees Wednesdays and Saturdays, at 2.)

**AMUNDSEN, AMUNDSEN**—Kurt Remark plays the gloomy introspective Polar explorer in Norwegian playwright Ringes Lager's classic study of human pride and foolishness set in an igloo at 45° 34', 2° 7'. (Asbury Park, 145 W. 48th St. Nightly, except Sundays, at 8. Matinees Wednesdays and Saturdays at 2.)

**AN EVENING WITH JOHN PAYNE**—The star of many a Twentieth Century Fox musical with Alice Faye and Betty Grable does readings from these movies, plus several arthritic song-and-dance numbers. Payne proves once and for all that he can act his way out of a paper bag. (Herman Badillo Playhouse, Madison Ave. and 60th St. Matinees every day.)

**ATTACK OF THE ANTBEARS**—Absolutely enchanting and in Yiddish. Screeching actors planted in the audience effectively add to the suspense. The ending should be kept a secret, but it goes like—the antbears all agree to put on their skates and go fight Hitler provided the townspeople will never again accuse the antbears of being selfish and overly sentimental. Sorry. (Playmobile. Various nights at sunset. Various locations. No matinees.)

**BANQUO AND THE WITCHES**—Shakespearean adaptation of *Macbeth* done by Earl Wilson, Sr. It takes on the two elements that made the show "the hit it was." Funniest scene is when Richard III enters frantically, willing to trade anything for a horse, and Lady Macbeth says, "... well, you'll just have to see for yourself. (Duff/Lapino Theatre, 80 West 41st St. Every night, seven matinees. Will play parties and small rooms.)

**BAWDYHOUSE BAXTER**—One of Tennessee Williams' earliest efforts. Baxter is an enigmatic young Englishman who refuses to pay the rent to his New Orleans landlady. She informs him that as a landlady she has the power to have him shot for nonpayment. He informs her that he is the King of England and he can have *her* shot for asking him for money. It's all happily resolved when he finally brings down his trunk containing his royal raiments and the crown jewels. (Ed Sullivan Theatre, 52nd St. and Broadway. Nightly except when CBS needs the studio to tape giveaway shows.)

**CATARACTS**—Patty Meat as the iris and Jeff Fishbank as the cornea in a penetrating tale of an eyeball gone to seed. Michel Outré directed, and Lou Fusco made the marvelous mechanical peeper that almost steals the show. (Better Vision Institute, 1790 Broadway. Nightly, except Sundays, at 7. Matinees, except Sundays, at 2:30.)

**CLEMENT OF ALEXANDRIA**—Robert Bolt's latest historic drama about the somewhat confused second-century philosopher. Clement is angry about all of the philosophy he has to learn but is at the same time happy about all of the philosophy that he doesn't have to learn because it hasn't been written yet. Now enter Diana of Europe, and Clement closes his books once and for all. (Theatre in the Dark, 265 W. Vanderbilt. Nightly, except weekends, at 7:30. Matinees at 2:30.)

**COLORADO**—This year's big, splashy musical, which is a direct steal of "Oklahoma." The hard-working cast includes John Stitt, Mary Jane Pythe, and Lou Anders. Music and lyrics mostly by Richard Rodgers and Oscar Hammerstein, III. (Mario Biaggi Theatre, Fifth Ave. and 59th St.)

**THE HUNCHBACK OF NOTRE DAME**—Israel Surfeit's archly unsentimental play about four college sophomores who bet that they can stay up all night and what happens when they have visitors, among

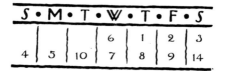

| S | M | T | W | T | F | S |
|---|---|---|---|---|---|---|
| | | | 6 | 1 | 2 | 3 |
| 4 | 5 | 10 | 7 | 8 | 9 | 14 |

them a derelict Pulitzer Prize winner and a Negro ventriloquist with a sore throat. The cast is able, but the surprises are few. Directed by Marc Mersky. (Vito Battista Theatre, Park Ave. and 45th St. Nightly.)

**I SAY, OLD CHAP**—A petty little comedy by the English playwright Alun Smallpox, which ran in the West End for nine years. The exceptionally obese cast includes Jennifer Rutherford and Miles Melvin. (Rose Ann Scamardella Theatre, Fifth Ave. and 57th St. Nightly.)

**MOTHER!**—Multitalented Melvin Van Peebles has rewritten the Oedipus story in black street slang, with Dorothy Dandridge as the mother and Ben Vereen as the mother-finder. Powerful, jazzy. (The Butterfly McQueen Center for the Performin' Arts, Broadway and 100th Street. Nightly at 7.)

**THE SHMENDRICKS**—Tim Toomey's musical is about a file clerk who goes to see a man about a dog. There

isn't much more. The music is by Stephen Blomberg and Bart Huff wrote the lyrics. (Malcolm Wilson Playhouse, Fifth Ave. and 56 St. Weekends and Tuesdays at 5.)

**STRANDED IN DE JUNGLE**—Stanley meets Livingston, Stanley loses Livingston, Stanley gets Livingston. The old story, retold from the African's point of view, with a "rock 'n' soul score" (that's what it says in the program) provided by Melvin van Peebles. Fast-paced, but presumptuous. (The Grand, 233 W. 46th St. Tuesdays through Sundays at 7:30, Matinees Wednesdays and Saturdays at 2.)

**STRETCHMARKS**—Sondheim scores again as he brilliantly underscores the joys and frustrations of dumb, fat people in New York. "Sup-hose I Loved You" and "Nice Piece of Fish" both show-stoppers. (Colostomy, 346 W. 46th. Reopens Tuesday, March 22nd.)

**SYNJO LIVING PUPPET THEATRE OF LATVIA**—Latvian folk tales brought to life by people masquerading as puppets. Perfectly ordinary entertainment· for anyone age 6 or age 60. (Harrison Goldin, Fifth Ave. and 44 St.)

**TOO HOT TO HONDLE**—The Yiddish-American Theater's latest potpourri of gutteral gibberish, served up in a seemingly endless array of unintelligible skits, saliva-sprayed songs, and pachydermatous production numbers. Most memorable moment:

## TABLE OF CONTENTS

COVER: *Bruce McCall*

DRAWINGS: *Ted Key, Buck Brown, Tom Wolfe, Candy Bergen, Walter O'Malley, Al Vargas, Peter Max, Jules Feiffer, Walter Keane, The King Family, Robert Wagner, Dorothy, Margaret Chase Smith, Charles Schultz, Georgie Jessel, Rally Fingers, Knuckles O'Toole, W. C. Handy*

## THE NEW YORKER
### 25 WEST 42ND STREET, NEW YORK, N.Y. 10036
#### PIED-A-TERRE ON EAST 82ND, (212) OVERSHOE 8-4070
#### STUDIO APARTMENT IN GRAMERCY PARK, (212) WELSHRARBIT 6-1212

## CHANGE OF ADDRESS

In considering a change of address, the traditional dictum of "no more than a quarter of one's available income toward lodging" may still be said to hold true, though this should not be taken as a hard and fast rule for the modern young couple.

# GOING ON AND ON

the pastrami ballet from "West Side Tsuris." These people are their own worst enemies. (The Sholem Aleichem Little Theatre, 342 2nd Ave. Evenings and Matinees every day but Saturday.)

**Ubangi Blackface Big Mama**—Lonny Hayward's folk farce is broadly based on "Othello," but no one has told the actors, who are having a wonderful time, especially John Paul Jones, who is not even in the play. Lloyd Wainright's halfhearted direction is perfect. Blackamoor Repertory Company. (Abe Beame Theatre, Madison Ave. and 55th St. Nightly at about 8 or 9-ish.)

**Viva Gorboduc!**—A long-overdue revival of Norton and Sackville's blank verse tragedy. Uta Hagen shines as Gorboduc in a novel transsexual rendition of the title role, and Daniel Seltzer is superb in the moving dumb shows that precede each act —a Sackville innovation that seems as fresh today as it was in 1561. (Margaret Dumont Theatre, 221 W. 46th St. Nightly, except Sundays, at 8. Matinees Wednesdays and Saturdays at 2.)

**White Pastures**—A David Merrick revival, in much altered form, of Marc Connelly's 1934 classic, *Green Pastures*, with an all-white cast and folk-rock score by ex-Chad Mitchellite John Denver. Merv Griffin is amusing as "de Lawd." (The Crackerbox, Broadway at 42nd. At 8:30 nightly, except weekdays. Dark Saturday and Sunday.)

## NIGHT TOWN

### SMALL AND CHEERFUL

**Downstairs in the Back**, 80 Lafayette St.—An upholsterer's warehouse that doubles as a cabaret and showcase for sundry rock, folk, pop, jazz, and whatever. The Proctor-Silex, a rock group that plays electrified appliances, appears Nov. 9. On Dec. 8, Sean McGullicidy presents his latest collection of off-speed polka records and travel slides. On Thursday, April 2, Blind Willie Siegel and Arthur "Jellybones" Weiss start playing and singing the same monotonous stuff they've been doing for thirty years. The Majestic Magenta Messiahs of Motown, a gospel 'n' cheese group, take over in June. BYOB.

**Plaza**, Fifth Ave., at 59th St.—Watery drinks and Sonesta ashtrays in the **Persian Room**, along with beat-out, black-rooted chantootsie Mimi Hollandaise. In the **Oak Bar**, some swell wood paneling, acrylic rugs, and two loud salesmen from Cleveland. **Trader Vic's** is now featuring Muzak by Arthur Lyman and a dollar off all drinks normally served in plastic blowfish.

**Village Idiot**, 24 Grove St., near Christopher St.— Miles Renfro brings his accordion and his highly nervous quintet into this oppressively small, humid, and generally unsafe room. On Thursdays, Cloudy and Cool, a soul food duo, make an appearance. There is a large Black bartender who answers to the name "Sir."

**Stork Club**, 3 E. 53rd St.—A good address, just off the avenue. Used to have tea-dances back when people had money and neckties. Not like now, though.

### SLEEPY AND BASHFUL

**Dumbbell's**, 10 Mott St., at Pell St.—Red checkered tablecloths and broken glass line the floor of this neighborhood bar, formerly an opium den. A desultory trio led by Herman Rubin, Jr., offers Moravian hymns. Vocalist Judi Neale takes over on Wednesdays and doesn't go home. Beers and wines only. No smoking.

**The Eagles' Nest**, 1146 Hudson St.—A *gemütlich* roost for rough traders and civilized S&M. Come as you are, as long as you are stuffed into a black leather space suit with more chains than Marley's ghost and can fart nails on command. Watch yourself.

**The Village Dump**, at the corner of Sixth and Bleecker—Exposed brick and N.Y.U. students with exposed brick complexions set the downbeat for this long-lived boho bistro, said to have been a favorite of Dylan Thomas, although management changes more often than the tablecloths and it's hard to be sure *who* they let in, what with the new drinking age. Folk music by Leonard Simpcus and the New Youths.

**Hotcomb's II**, First Ave., at 84th St.—Bobby and

the Bodyshirts recreate future gold and every Wednesday is Ladies' Night with free Harvey Wallbangers to any patron in hotpants or Ms.-ing her bra. Some rugby team pretty much takes over after eleven, free popcorn and check. Fairies beware.

### DOPEY AND SNEEZY

**Sheraton-Krupsak**, Fifth Ave., at 60th St.—Les Ludlow's trio holds forth for dancing until ten, when Dimitri Trentini's violin takes over. At eleven-thirty, pianist Jules Martel and vocalist Patricia Zinty provide smoothly agreeable sounds until one-fifteen, when Herb Lofiere's harp holds the floor until two-forty-five. On Tuesdays and Fridays, Bella Romano's viola alternates with the Anthony Campobello orchestra. Steven Schwemmer's piano follows on alternate weekends, between ten and eleven. Closed for renovations until next year.

**Table d'Hote/Leftovers**, 56 E. 53rd St.—On even-numbered days, this elegant little Eastside dining spot operates under the name **Table d'Hote** and serves the finest in French haute cuisine. On odd-numbered days, it cuts its prices by eighty percent, changes its name to **Leftovers**, and serves up whatever was left behind by the previous night's diners. Fun, but not for everyone. Double-check your calendar before making reservations.

**Strydelle's**, 198th St., at Broadway—A silly-looking room that doesn't know whether it's supposed to be mock-Tudor, or pseudo-Venetian, or what. Etta LaPierre gives us a lesson in rhythm, harmony, and needlepoint with a sporadic trio (Roy Tripe is on drums). In the front room Benny Bush leads a twenty-two-piece Dixieland band. Both groups like to play at the same time.

**El Monaco**, 154 E. 54th St.—Not what it used to be. Doors nailed shut, tarpaulins over what's left of the furniture. Gee.

**Le Club Soda**, 920 First Ave., at 52nd St.—The smoky Tonette of Babs Tuckahoe and Vern Cudahy's engaging impressions of a variety of barnyard animals combine to weave a subtle spell over this snug, pleasantly frowzy *boîte* just a snap from Turtle Bay. Not for the tenderfooted— it's strictly stand-up (the chairs are nailed upside down to the tables, in keeping with the maître d's practiced yawns and the chic, can't-be-bothered atmosphere), and unless curling and uncurling your toes is your idea of tripping the light fantastic, there's no dancing. Shows begin at eight-thirty and ten-thirty. Snacks, dips, and funny-looking crunchy things in dishes.

**Fantod's**, 145 W. 46th St.—Visitors to this sullen cabaret are quickly confronted with the smell of sizzling shashlik, won ton soup, and home fries, the house specialties, and the glint off the walls of smashed lightbulbs stuck into slabs of hardened butterscotch. Presently, Freddy Herb is coaxing vaguely bell-like noises from his xylophone and comedian Buddy Brazo keeps visitors in stitches with his knock-knock jokes. Dining.

## MOVIES

**Sideswipe**, the world's smallest disaster movie. Lots of shots of cars speeding along highways, cross-sections of humanity and little dramas in each car, all leading up to an accidental sideswiping of two cars that brush against each other when the two lanes narrow into one. No one is seriously hurt. Directed in what seems like slow motion by Ted Glish. Stars Charlton Heston, Glenn Ford, Ava Gardner, and Ernest Borgnine. (It was at the Amherst Theatre, last we heard).

Enchanting figurines from...

# Poubelle

Wee Willie Wee Wee, a bewitching
little cherub handcrafted
from the finest porcelain
by our old world masters.
Slip down the little rascal's shorts
and learn why Willie
will be "number one" among
discerning collectors everywhere.
Height, 7½ inches.
In a limited edition of fifty thousand.

*Price, Four dollars and thirty-nine cents*

# TOWN ON THE TAKE

## Nuts and Currents

TWO items in the newspaper caught our eye last week. One was a report from Kandy, in Sri Lanka, which is the tag Ceylon has been asking everyone to use lately. It told of the beaching of a giant squid on a strip of sand on the east coast of the lush island republic. The aquatic behemoth, which reportedly measured a full fifty feet from its head to the tips of its ten, sucker-studded arms, had been dead for several days, and was apparently washed ashore by the powerful tides typical of the Indian Ocean at this time of the year. We imagined the scene : a large crowd of curious Sri Lankans who had come to see the antique and alien creature, which even in death must have seemed threatening and malevolent, a reminder, perhaps, of some ancient terror ; children frisking around the massive carcass, daring each other to run up and poke it with sticks and then scampering away when a stray roll of surf moved its massive tentacles in a slow mime of once mighty thrashes ; and, at last, after a day or two, when amazement passed, and with it fear, and the momentary respect that man accords the large, the novel, and the physically forbidding, a handful of scavengers stripping the great fish for bait, and even for food ; for Sri Lanka is still as poor as it was when its name was less cacophonous.

The other item described the passage by the Michigan legislature of a law requiring drivers in that state to make clear and complete hand signals to indicate turns, stops, and lane changes, regardless of whether the electrical direction indicators on the rear of their automobiles were in working order. It sounded like the kind of statute that is headed for some pretty widespread public disrespect.

It's hard enough to pilot a motorcar through the endless maze of highways that writhe and squirm around the country like the arms of a squid without letting go of our steering grip and shifting mechanisms to wave and waggle a tentacle out the car window, and at the same time keep our eye, semantically Cyclopian, an echo of the cephalopod that navigates the horrid depths as we drive through the thick smog sea, cased in sheet metal, not scales and slime, but heavy and glistening, and like that primordial beast, speeding perhaps toward some unimagined shore—sand for him, concrete, of which it is a constituent, for us—where, beached and mute, we suffer, ignorant of it, the serried gaze of an idle crowd come to view a more modern demise, fearsome, though all too familiarly so, and like the departure of that grand submarine denizen, final.

• •

## Up In Fred's Room

SETTING our hat at a jauntier angle than usual, we went up to the Hotel Pierre bright and early the other morning to renew acquaintances with Mr. Fred Astaire, the dancer. All we could hear from behind the Astaire door was "zzzzzzz," so remembering

a trick taught us by Mr. Willie Sutton, who was not a dancer, we gingerly let ourselves inside. We decided that Mr. Astaire in the flesh looks ten years younger than he does on television talk shows. We also decided that even when he's dead to the world, Mr. Astaire has style. We liked the way he lay there in his blue silk pajamas, as poised and graceful in repose as in a dance number. We also liked Mr. Astaire's wafer-thin gold Patek Philippe wristwatch, which had been carefully placed atop a black alligator Mark Cross billfold on the bedtable. When it comes to your average billfold, we can take it or leave it, but since this was Fred Astaire's billfold, we decided to take it, and we were glad we did, because inside, among other things, was two hundred and forty dollars in crisp new twenty-dollar bills. As if Fred Astaire would be caught carrying rumpled old currency around !

Down on the street again, we decided we liked Mr. Astaire's billfold just as much as we liked his watch, the way he sleeps, and Mr. Astaire himself.

• •

## U.N. Me, Babe

LAST Wednesday morning at the United Nations General Assembly, Resolution #A648 was signed, unseating the Israeli delegation and replacing it with a group from the Palestine Liberation Organization, who would henceforth represent "all residents of the territories hitherto erroneously referred to as the sovereign state of Israel."

After the signing, we overheard the following conversation between two U.N. ambassadors :

"Let's e-e-e-eat lu-lu-lunch. We p-p-p-put in a b-b-big mo-mo-morning."

"Well, that's very easy for you to say."

## Pillow Talk

THE first thing to do before entering the famous **Manhattan** Hotel on Seventh Avenue, we were solemnly informed by its doorman, is to transfer your money from your hip pocket to your front pocket. "Do *not* stuff your money into your shoe," admonishes the elegantly-liveried Mr. Hamilton; "for whereas the common 'foist' will most likely accept frustration after soliciting an empty hip pocket, the more determined and temperamental 'hitter'—the one who carries a gun—is generally too impatient to wait for his 'mark' to toe off his Oxford, and typically opens fire at any unexpected gesture."

With this point well taken, we were guided by the miscellaneous odor of recycled alcohol and *hors d'oeuvres* to the **Manhattan's** magisterial Final Curtain Cocktail Lounge, where, in the intimate glow of vermilion neon on polyethylene palm leaves, pass continually the moguls and tyros of the contemporary Times Square set. As we expected, we were immediately saluted by our old friend, Detective Alfred Infantino of Vice, Gambling & Pornography, who was wreathed in a smile so bright it fairly reflected from the shiny tips of his $86 Bally-of-Italy shoes. "Oh, it's a bumper year all around for this industry," he exulted confidentially. "The Recession may be putting the marks out of work, but what little they've got left, they're handing it over to our people like it burned them."

AFTER further pleasantries, we were introduced to one of the Detective's latest *ingenues,* a willowy young trace of *café au lait* decked out in nostalgic *apres-mini* scarlet hot pants and jeroboam-sized blue suede purse, named Honeycakes Sayer. We inquired if the improved profits inspired by the crunch had filtered down to her level yet? "Listen," she articulated through a virtual occlusion of Juicy Fruit, "I got no time for honky-talk. You wanna go out?" Was she attached to a recognized *salon,* or was she merely paying court to Vice, Gambling & Pornography? "You talk too much, you know that? You goin' out or ain'tcha?"

So out we went, or rather up two floors, to her studio, a utilitarian alcove evoking the last scene of *Days of Wine and Roses,* and eerily redolent of—what was it?—rubbing alcohol? Ah no, it all became clear when she fished into her ten-gallon purse, extracted a cylinder of grey aluminum, and carved it deftly open with one sanguineous fingernail: *eau de Fourex,* that curious amniotic premoistening solution. "Lay down."

FROM here it was all monosyllables: "Head, right? Ten bucks. Five more for the room. Open up. Here. You put it on. Ik. Pfu. Tastes shit. Mumph. There. Done? Right." (*A knock on the door.*) "Stay here, I'll see who it is. Ham? That you, Ham? No, man, I'm not hooking again. I'm not, really, Ham honey, I'm all alone. I'll let you in, just a minute. Hey you, honky, get in the closet. Get

in there, turkey, you'll get us *killed.* It'll just be a minute. No man, don't take your clothes, just get in there. *Now!* Okay, Ham, honey, c'mon in."

She left with Mr. Hamilton, and the contents of our pockets. But our Cartier cufflinks were still in our shirt (we had been wearing it), and thankfully, Ham, a sizable specimen of livery, had no use for our size ten oxfords. Our friend Detective Infantino thanked us volubly as we left: "I try to take care of my girls," he explained. "This isn't a charity industry, but I do my best."

## Grandma's House

RUMMAGING through our top drawer the other day, we came upon a knitted pair of left-handed mittens, and realized with a start that we had not seen our grandmother in an age. With almost no effort, we recalled that some years ago, she had been transferred from the cramped quarters of her farm in Connecticut, and installed in the peaceful bosom of the Shin-Bet Nursing Home on upper West End Avenue.

Shin-Bet occupies some dozen floors of one of those unpleasant yet irreplaceable buildings which date from the days when the West Side was the financial nexus of the city, rather than, as now, merely the progressive.

Happily, in these straitened times, the home does not skimp on security. The doorman, severely dressed in coveralls and a handkerchief, told us to go away, as did the elevator operator, the janitor, and a Miss Gertrude Baum in the frosted-glass and steel-paneled reception cubicle. Miss Baum added, after some ninety minutes of scrutiny and questioning, that our grandmama was dead. A brief mental riffle through the obituary pages of the *Times* led us to the opposite conclusion, and with what seemed to be a struggle against her better judgment, Miss Baum let us in.

Our new friend satisfied herself that we were not bearing any

*"For the love of God, please help me. I think my friend is dead."*

unsuitable gifts, such as cameras or tape recorders, and led us past a series of dark green doors. Over each was a flashing light and the sign "Do Not Enter—Surgery in Progress." Our confidence in Shin-Bet rose. At the end of the corridor was a steel and glass barrier, beyond which could be heard the sound of senior voices raised in revelry, and through which Miss Baum disappeared. It was watched over by a large orderly named Washington, with whom we got onto the subject of working at the home. "It's O.K.," he allowed, "except when the stiffs get uppity." What, we asked, happened then? "They get set up," he replied with a grin, "or spiked."

Three times Miss Baum returned, and three times we asked her to look further. On the fourth try, she appeared, wreathed in smiles. "You mustn't be surprised if your grandmother's changed," she said. "People sometimes develop new personalities."

Grandmama had indeed changed. She was wearing trousers and an undershirt and what looked like a wig. We asked her if she missed the farm and thanked her for the mittens. "What farm?" she said. "What mittens?" We explained about the farm and the mittens. "Give me a cigarette," yelled Grandmama, tearing off her wig. Grandmama certainly had lost her inhibitions, not to mention her hair. We said as much. "Your ass," she replied.

"Just one of her little jokes," chipped in the lady of the gate. "She's the life and soul of the seventh floor." We smiled fondly at Grandmama, who was getting quite noisy about the Battle of the Somme.

"Time for your sleep, Fred," said our friend to our ancestor.

"Up yours, beanbag," said Grandmama, in a splendid spirit of defiance. "Gimme back my teeth."

## Shop Talk

AT the Brooks Brothers' Madison Avenue address we found no garish signs in the window, only the familiar husky and headless tweed torsos which, legend has it, come to life each All Hallow's Eve at the stroke of twelve, and throw one heckuva board meeting. Inside, we were greeted by a graying Warner Oland look-alike who proved to be a perfectly nice man named Mr. Campbell. He showed us his selection of English striped silk and

"We're all out of food. Scram."

• •

polyester rep neckties, now $6.95 to $7.50. A fine selection they were indeed, our eye particularly held by his array of solid-color foulards-with-the-little - things - embroidered - on - them. Sporting motifs mostly, plus little bulls and bears and crossed automatic pencils. Mr. Campbell was especially enthusiastic about a tie with little neckties on it, which, frankly, gave us the willies.

Our salesman excused himself to get more patterns; more seductive, however, were the solid colors, and we selected a brace of them, one off-burgundy and the other a deep maize, and not wishing to trouble Mr. Campbell further with wrapping and sales slips, briskly pocketed them and headed for the shoe department. Here we would find a wide assortment of those shoes-with-the-little-holes-all-over-the-toes at, if not next to cost, certainly something closer to our Fayva budgets than normal.

THE shoe department proved disappointing; someone had already cleaned out the shoes-with-the-little-holes, leaving only odd sizes behind, and we had to content ourselves with replacements for our worn, adhesive-mended Weejuns (which we left in a drastically reduced Cold Duck cooler/ice bucket).

Better luck on the fourth floor: luggage and ready-to-block hats in seductively vague beiges and pommy grays. We picked up a nice set of matching English leather carry-alls and, deploy-ing ourselves at either aisle end to watch for floorwalkers, stuffed them full of headgear to be blocked at home with the wonderful Abercrombie & Fitch Home Hatblocker received from Aunt Eleanor in lieu of our usual Old Spice gift pack assortment (we still don't know how much she got when Uncle Rudolf's insurance finally came through—and they're still pretty suspicious about that second set of tire tracks—but mum bets it was a bundle).

Sportswear proved equally fruitful. Wool tweed sports jackets normally $115 to $235 were now a low-low $92 and $188, and considering what the same money buys some poor yid up the Avenue at Paul Stuart, these fine Shetlands and lambswools would have been a steal at twice the price.

After selecting a rich rust number from the rack, we picked up a super double-breasted camel's hair overcoat reduced to $299 and headed for the third floor dressing rooms to try them on, along with some nifty blue oxford Brooksflannel pajamas and a dozen pairs of Brooksknit undershorts which fit neatly, if a bit snugly, under the tan whipcord cavalry-twill trousers which we temporarily cuffed with straight pins from those terrific Brooks button-downs.

SUDDENLY feeling a bit warm, we decided to skip Sportshirts and Knits and proceed to the last stop of the day: those white Irish linen handkerchiefs whose handrolled softness so reassuringly bulks out a new

W. Satta.

• •

camel hair's ample pockets.

On our way out, we encountered our friend Mr. Campbell again. He seemed disappointed that we had not waited, so we paused a moment to admire a fine silk four-in-hand peppered with little embroidery necktie salesmen. As he turned to answer another shopper's query, we impulsively stuffed it in our jacket and hastily re-buttoned our overcoat.

"You should see the ties we've got coming next month," Mr. Campbell whispered with a conspiratorial wink upon returning. "Women. Nothing indecent or anything like that. Just famous ones like Jacqueline Onassis and Mrs. Angier Biddle Duke. Real doozies."

We thanked Mr. Campbell for the tip and headed casually for the exit. Once outside we found the crisp March air a tonic after the stuffy atmosphere within and, much refreshed, decided to skip lunch and see what looked good at Saks.

### Bum's Rush

THE hand-lettered invitation that turned up under our desk the other day read:

HELP
(signed) PUNK

and we couldn't resist. The punk in question was our old Bowery friend, Mr. Punk Purna. Whenever we get a note like that, we know he has something special up his well-tattered sleeve. We canceled all appointments, slipped the aerosol mace into our pocket, and hopped a cab down to lower Third Avenue.

Before we knew it, we ran into Mr. Purna. Indeed, our Checker and Mr. Purna collided—sharply—as he was attempting to give our windshield a spit-and-polish shine with his colorful rag. The cab left before we had time to pay the fare, and we found ourselves escorting Mr. Purna, who had apparently suffered a slight spinal fracture, to the sidewalk. We propped our friend against a hydrant, made ourself comfortable, and asked him what was up.

"Mmmmmph!" he began, lunging for a pint container of Tiger Rose which had slipped from his pocket. We watched as he quaffed it enthusiastically, a good deal winding up on his lap. "Aaaaaaaaarrrh! Skuuuhhh!" exclaimed Mr. Purna. "Mmmmhuh. Them suckin did *puke* got no time for them got what the hunh, cocksucker." You hear that sort of thing a lot these days, but when Punk says it, you know he means every word.

We inquired about his windshield buffing business. By way of an answer, he produced eighteen cents and three cribbage pegs—one black, two metallic —apparently collected earlier that day. "Faaarh. Runhh, comin no bastard some gimme fuckin' cock wha." We noted that Mr. Purna had opened his trousers and was relieving himself, ap-

parently so engrossed in the conversation that he neglected to stand. Soon he was sitting in a fair-sized puddle, gesturing vigorously.

We interrupted his monologue to show him the note we had found under the desk. He studied it with interest, then placed it in his mouth. The next thing we knew, the note, along with a fair quantity of Mr. Purna's mucus, had landed square on our lapel. About that time, three young men toting a bright orange gasoline can rounded the corner. We saw they had business with Mr. Purna, and wished him a good afternoon.

### Talk is Cheap

AS the clock on the wall struck five-thirty, we crossed our final *t*, and decided to take ourselves downstairs to Eddie's to renew our acquaintance with our old friend John Barleycorn.

We slid gratefully into the overstuffed armchairs which make Eddie's *the* place to unwind after a "hard day at the office." A wave of our hand to Eddie, who had once gone one minute thirty seconds with Sugar Ray Robinson at the Garden, soon produced the "ticket"—a pitcher of stingers and five little bowls of our friend Mr. Peanut's finest dry roasts.

After several more "rounds," as the ex-pugilist proprietor liked to call them, we felt our muscles relax and grow loose. At this point, a gentleman at the next table suggested that our tongues were keeping pace with our muscles, and recommended that we shut up. Emboldened by the cups of cheer which we had quaffed, we waved at him gaily, told him to sit on a pickle, and ordered up a half dozen martinis. The drinks came straight up, a position we had had more than a little trouble assuming when we requested them, and after dispatching them briskly, our talk turned to a subject which often preoccupied us at this time of evening—our employer and editor, Mr. William Shawn.

WHY, we wondered aloud, did Mr. Shawn, who had a *reputation* for being a fair and generous man, insist that our gemlike little pieces appear in his magazine *sans* signature? Could it perhaps be because an author whose name was familiar to the public might be in a position to demand compensation somewhat more reasonable than the slave wages we were currently receiving?! Could it perhaps be because Mr. Shawn was in fact a penny-pinching, double-dealing son-of-a-bitch? We honestly weren't sure, but since we had apparently advanced the possibility in a loud voice while standing on our chair, Eddie walked over and suggested that we continue our considerations elsewhere. We promised Eddie that we'd behave and tried to order a pitcher of old-fashioneds, but Eddie was adamant, and before we knew it, we'd been thrown out onto Forty-third Street.

Rather than risk provoking the wrath of any of our other favorite bar-keeps, we purchased a bottle of our own, and retired to our offices, to confront Buccaneer Bill himself with our dilemma. Whiskey in hand, we poured gleefully out of the elevator and rushed down the hall to our Editor's private lair. Hooting like banshees in the hopes of disturbing his usually unflappable composure, we kicked open the door to his office and found him—gone! We speculated that Old Slyboots had hidden himself in order to avoid our righteous wrath, and we had just begun a thorough search of his digs

## INVOCATION

Upon my soul, neat as a photo album
Of shore summers and stark urban peregrinations,
Descend, Muse of Gentility, and in lines
That never reach the margin
And occasionally rhyme,
Inspire me to sexless dithyrambs.

I could use a little irony, to offset
The perhaps self-indulgent style of that last stanza,
Maybe a metaphor right at the end,
A punch line almost, that makes the whole thing
Universal, and yet in a way personal, and please,
Help me find a place to use that lovely word
I came across in the dictionary while doing the *Times*
Crossword puzzle.

—Marion St. Vincent Javitts

• •

when we heard the grandfather clock in the corner strike twelve. We cursed our miscalculation, for we realized instantly of course that we had missed our man by some six or seven hours.

Throwing our feet up on his Chippendale desk and opening a box of his Cuban panetellas, we settled back to decide on an appropriate course of action. After several pulls at our bottle, we determined that our visit should not be a total loss, and after switching all the papers in his *out* box to his *in* box and crushing our cigars out on his oriental rug, we sang three choruses of "Mussolini Bit His Weenie" into his dictaphone and ran out of his office giggling at our cleverness.

*"Well, if you can't find the goddamn things, we'll just have to use the thumb of your catcher's mitt again."*

## The Other Day

THE other day, we went to visit a friend of ours who is a psychiatrist. He has an office in a building on Park Avenue in the nineties, just south of 96th Street, "the D.M.Z.," as he calls it, because Spanish Harlem begins there. Arriving a few minutes early, we sat down in a standard-looking waiting room and instinctively picked up an old copy of the *National Geographic*. We were just getting interested in an amusing-looking piece entitled "Burma—Mysterious Land of Rubber and Magic" when our friend emerged. He was ushering a brown-haired, youngish-looking girl towards the door. She had obviously been crying, and her wrists looked like they were smiling. "I mustn't suppress," she said uncertainly. "That's it, isn't it?"

Our friend produced a noncommital affirmative of some sort, and with a firm gesture that must have come from years of practice, opened the door, propelled the young lady through it, made a gesture of salutation, and closed the door again, all in the space of five seconds. "This has been one of those days," he said, as we went into his office. "Sometimes I think I should just give them all loaded pistols and tell them to you-know-what or get off the pot."

HIS office was a more expensive version of the studio backdrop they use for television patent medicine ads, in which a man who is no longer allowed to dress like a doctor half sits on the edge of a desk in front of a bookshelf full of *Reader's Digest Condensed Books* and busts of demised greats, takes off his glasses in a very doctorish kind of way, and speaks frankly about afflictions in parts of your body that a more tasteful Creator would not have included in His Plan.

"Well," he said, as he settled into a swivel chair behind a desk that fell just short of the surface area required to qualify it for admission to the United Nations, "how are you *all*?" We said that we were fine, and plumped ourselves down, a bit nervously, on the very edge of his tufted, black leather couch.

"Schizophrenia is an interesting thing," he said, his hands automatically forming into a sort of finger Rorschach, which looked to us like two daddy longlegs spiders toe-to-toe, or perhaps one on a mirror, an observation we thought better not to mention. "It's far more common than most people realize. Perhaps it is a need for anonymity and self-effacement, for a reduction in the force of our identities, for a little internal company for our misery, a need to share the blame with ourselves, that leads us to retreat into a polypersonal way of being and thinking. You know, I've always had a theory that writers who use pen names are definitely schizoid, as are those, I think, who use the editorial *we*."

We found ourselves reclining on the couch without a very clear recollection of how we got from a sitting position to one more recumbent in nature. "Are most of your patients schizoid?" we asked a little nervously.

"Oh, easily half," he said. "Actually, schizophrenia usually comes with something else." He made it sound like a sandwich that would naturally arrive with a side order. "My most interesting case is that of a man with a triple personality, a Napoleon complex, and advance paranoia. He thinks he is the First Triumvirate—and that Cato is plotting to have all three of him murdered by thugs in the Forum."

We asked him what the cure, if any, for schizophrenia was. "In most cases," he said, "the only certain cure is electroconvulsive therapy, what is popularly known as electroshock treatment. Anywhere from eight to fourteen severe electrical impulses are sent directly into the brain of the disturbed individual. No one is quite sure why it works, but it does. Of course, there is usually some memory loss and disorientation, but that's a small price to pay for normality, isn't it?"

We had the feeling that we were being looked at, and quickly gauging the distance between ourselves and the nearest wall socket, we got up, invented an appointment, and after bidding our friend farewell, we put on our hats and coats, went out the doors, and walking briskly, headed down Park Avenue and into the cold nights.

*"It was that noise he kept making. That 'Cccaaaaaaahhhkkk, cccaaaaaaahhhkkk' noise he kept making with his throat. It was driving me crazy. And it was driving you crazy, too, wasn't it, Brennan?"*

# ❃ ❃ P R O F I L E S ❃ ❃

## EAVES TROUGHS

AT approximately six thirty-two on the crisp morning of March 14, 1953, a Wednesday, a twenty-eight-year-old Harvard Business School graduate and casual collector of stones, pebbles, sea shells, and fossils, Loring H. (for Hargreaves, the name of his maternal grandfather, now deceased) Humboldt, dressed in an old gray-green tweed jacket, slate-colored slacks, a light blue button-down Oxford cloth shirt, silk four-in-hand necktie featuring tiny gray scarabs in a small pattern on a maroon background, black calf-length socks, and brown, moccasin-style loafers, parked his six-year-old Studebaker Champion coupé, purchased in used condition the previous summer for four hundred dollars cash from an elderly Flushing, New York widow named Mrs. Bea Havemeyer, and finished in a nondescript beige color with grey upholstery, blackwall Firestone tires, and a small ding on the left rear fender just over the wheel well where Humboldt had backed into a fire hydrant while trying to locate parking space during a visit to the home of his parents in Melrose, Massachusetts, about thirteen and a half miles from the Boston city limits, the previous July 12, a Tuesday, noticed out of the corner of his eye that the hanging metal sign about ten feet away read "No Parking, 9 A.M. to 3 P.M.," realized he was well within the law, since the small Westclox pocket watch he always carried in his right jacket pocket and which had been given him as a gift in 1951 by his Uncle Ben, a lawyer who played varsity football at Rutgers and now spent most of his spare time bird-watching after the sudden death in 1952, by a myocardial infarction, of his wife of thirty-seven years and four months, Grace, whose family had moved in 1917 from Portland, Oregon to Lynn, Massachusetts, where she had met Ben Sullivan, then a struggling small-claims lawyer, showed the time to be not quite seven o'clock—something of a surprise to young Humboldt, who had set out an hour earlier in the Studebaker from his small but cozy two-room apartment at 362 Runciman Street in Wellfleet, Massachusetts, a small town whose origins dated back to the Puritan Colony of 1653, but which had come down in the world from its giddy days

as a major whaling and shipbuilding center and now functioned as a sleepy suburb, indistinguishable except to residents from a dozen similar communities radiating out in all directions from the city of Boston; a town of white clapboard that was slowly yielding, even in 1953, to the ersatz Colonial style of A&P supermarkets and Pancake House restaurants, and assumed from past experience in making the drive that he would arrive no earlier than six forty-five, or perhaps even seven, since a considerable section of the highway he normally traveled, Route 86, believing it to be the most direct route and infinitely better for a man in a hurry than the old Route 7, with its forty-two stoplights and notoriously poor grading on curves, a legacy of its having been one of Massachusetts' earliest paved north-south routes, was currently under the ax, or more accurately the steamshovel, the State in its wisdom having let a contract six months previous for road widening and repaving, part of a major ten million dollar Massachusetts highway improvement program passed through the State Legislature in December, 1951, on a unanimous vote (although the ensuing two years found only six and one-half miles of road

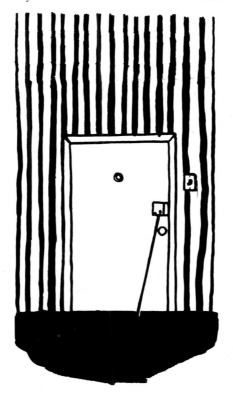

actually "improved" and the Massachusetts State Department of Highways receiving ever-increasing condemnation from newspaper editorials, the Republican opposition, and the kind of perpetually angry Massachusetts *doyenne* who writes to her State Senator complaining about such things), making Humboldt, normally cautious to a fault, wonder briefly if, in his haste, he had not exceeded the legal speed limit of sixty miles per hour (fifty miles per hour for trucks) during the run from Wellfleet, thus reducing the time he had traveled; or, the thought skipped across his mind, perhaps his watch was again acting up, as it had done a few months ago when he found himself late for an important luncheon appointment in Lowell, Massachusetts, sixteen miles northeast of the city of Boston, although he had made doubly sure of his punctuality, of which he was uncommonly proud and which had been drilled into him in youth by his late Uncle Frank, a former Marine Corps major, who after his retirement from the Corps in 1949 on a medical, or "D-4" basis, had moved to Hingham, Massachusetts, forty-four miles west of Boston, where he bought a home and spent much of his time reading *National Geographic* magazines on his front porch, or, during the hard New England winter months when a man could quickly freeze to death sitting outdoors unless bundled up in parka, earmuffs, thick sealskin boots, and woolen mittens, in his forty-six by sixty-one-foot living room, where the house's previous owner, a Swede, had installed an oil heater some twenty years before, and taken a great interest in his nephew Loring; but perhaps he had, after all, simply driven a bit faster than usual this morning, inspired by a remarkably bright sunrise and the buoyant sense of nature stirring that always made March, for him, a favorite month, perhaps not so stimulating to a young man as June or July, when tennis was beginning to reach that easy, rocking pace after the jerky fumbling of spring, but nonetheless a time of year when the Loring Humboldts of the world could luxuriate in the long and almost impossibly exciting prospects ahead, and then saw something that made him stop dead in his tracks.

(This is the first of a six-part profile.)

# LETTER FROM SCOTLAND

NOTHING could have been more welcome in these gloomy times of inflation and unemployment than a visit from Marcel Marceau, generally acknowledged as the world's greatest mime. Mr. Marceau, or Fafa, as his friends call him, is making a nationwide tour on behalf of his new Schools of Mime, which will take him from Glasgow to the Hebrides to John O' Groats, our northernmost town. The schools are operated as franchises, which are granted to those who possess the requisite capital ($112). For this, the school owner receives the official Marcel Marceau franchise, which includes the Marcel Marceau School nameplate, a pair of mime leotards boldly emblazoned with $MM$s, and a two-volume set of Marcel Marceau long-playing records. The actual space for the schools must be provided by the franchisee. While the school nameplate and the leotards are handsome and the mime records are useful, Marceau readily acknowledges that they are not worth $112.

"You are paying for the right to use my name," he said. "To me, that is worth at least $81.75 out of the $112. I figure that the leotards retail at $7.75, the records at $10, and the plastic school nameplate at about $12.50. That leaves $81.75, which I really think is an excellent price for the prestige value of getting the name Marcel Marceau for your mime school."

Mr. Marceau is gambling that Scotsmen and women will take to his venture, despite the spectre of gloom that hangs over the economy. He travels in a large lorry filled with his school supplies, and stops at every town, no matter how small. A public address system is built into the lorry, and Marceau announces that he will make a public appearance and perform at the town auditorium or public square or whatever area is most suitable for a large crowd to gather. Although many Scots have never heard of him, his bright orange and black lorry with the school name on it attracts a pretty fair amount of attention. Besides, Marceau does not charge for these performances, since they are part of his presentation to the public of his franchise plan.

His appearance in Altnaharra, a town in the far north, was typical of his tour. About thirty townspeople showed up to see Marceau open his presentation with a four-hour performance called "The History of Mime, from Egyptian Times to the Present." Marceau had recently broken his leg in a mountain climbing accident, but still managed to perform adequately with the leg in a full cast. He did his classic pieces, "Man walking up a staircase," and "Man walking up a staircase against the wind," which were received fairly well. He closed the program with his new number, "Calisthenics," perhaps the finest, purest example of his art—a forty-five-minute set of rigorous exercises, including push-ups, sit-ups, and a beautiful cartwheel to bring the piece to a close.

While his audience is still entranced by the stunning beauty of his "Calisthenics" piece, Marceau begins his sales talk for the mime school franchises. In his charming Gallicized English, he explains how easy it is to be a mime, how everyone is born a natural mime, and can use this talent for both fun and profit. He reminds the audience that a mime school can be set up just about anywhere—no special equipment is needed. It is a strong and persuasive sales pitch that seems to interest a good number of the townspeople until Marceau reveals the price for one of his franchises. At this point, the legendary Scottish respect for money takes over and Marceau must either fold his tent and leave gracefully or try to make special deals and concessions. He admits that his only sales so far have been to slightly deranged widows and a few gentlemen of dubious sexual affiliation, but to be sure, he has not covered the cosmopolitan cities of Edinburgh, Glasgow, Dundee, and Aberdeen. He also anticipates eventual success in the oil-rich towns of the North Sea, and so far, is not discouraged by his reception in the rural areas.

It is difficult to predict how well Marceau's mime school franchise plan will fare, but one thing is certain—he is definitely a most providential attraction for the Scotsman—a man who will attend any kind of show, whether he understands it or not, as long as it's free.

— HARRY LAUDER

# MUSIC
## *Jazz*

AFTER some years absence from New York, Wynton Mosely has returned to midtown's newest jazz showcase, the Cotton Club. Mr. Mosely, whose series of quintets were a mainstay of city nightlife during the fifties and early sixties, appeared ill-kempt and disreputable, and, but for his saxophone, might have been mistaken for one of the legion of narcotics addicts who mass about the Cotton Club's front entrance, harassing passersby. However, his thick, chocolatey lips caress the mouthpiece of his tenor in as endearingly suggestive a manner as ever and, happily, he has lost none of his chops. In an attempt to reach the contemporary audience, Mr. Mosely played few of his jazz classics, concentrating instead on new arrangements of current pop hits. On "You're Havin' My Baby," he fashioned a long, blistering solo, leaping with sudden, salmon-like upstream runs which often plummeted to lower-register honks that were like the moans of the lonely aged. During "You Little Trustmaker," whose muddy, medium-tempo ensemble sections suggested a powerful buttocks inches from your face, Mr. Mosely's chopping, scudding solo, broken by abrupt, unexpected cough-clusters, was like angry bear traps moving willfully through a stranded commuter train.

Nor was the playing of Mr. Mosely's sidemen without metaphoric possibility. Red Powell, whose worried attention to his piano keyboard was like a frightened foot patrolman scrutinizing a rooftop for snipers, produced pillars of shimmering block chords, suggesting anarchistic Slinkies in pursuit of gravity's antidote. Meanwhile, the continual clinking of glasses, at the bar and around the room, made for an embarrassment of Chinese rhythm accompaniment, and the Cotton Club's busy, tray-laden waiters contributed numerous jaunty, rattling passages of their own. At one point, a tall woman with decollatage like dusky avocados, scarcely held, sat uninvited at my table and ordered champagne in a voice that was like unlined taxi brakes. My startled, upper-register protests to the extra $30 this added to my bill quickly slid to gentle, behind-the-beat meanderings as two large bouncers stood before me creating staccato, arhythmic knuckle crackings.

# World's Longest Truck Jump, 55' 7", March 12, 1975

Wayne McLoughlin in a Peterbilt Tandem semitractor-trailer
at the Mt. Carroll Fairgrounds, Mt. Carroll, Illinois.

photographed by Chris Callis

# All Creatures Even Bees

**by Ted Mann**

It wasn't easy for a newly qualified veterinarian to get a job in 1952. So you can imagine how pleased I was to be offered a job at the Farmer Animal Hospital, even though the pay was only three dollars a month with room and board.

When the bus dropped me off in front of the hospital, I stood for a moment wondering just what the future held in store for me there. Then, shaking my head, I made my way up the path between the potted geraniums and rapped loudly on the door. After some minutes had passed, it was opened by a flustered middle-aged lady who breathlessly introduced herself as Miss Nora Wills.

"I'm the bookkeeper here. Wolfgang Farmer is out on a house call...a cage call, actually. This time it's a canary with an impacted anus. It shouldn't take him long to clear *that* up. Though you'd never guess that from the way he was cursing when he left." She led me down a hallway and into Farmer's comfortable consulting room. "Land sakes, all he has to do is heat up some number seven gauge copper-coated

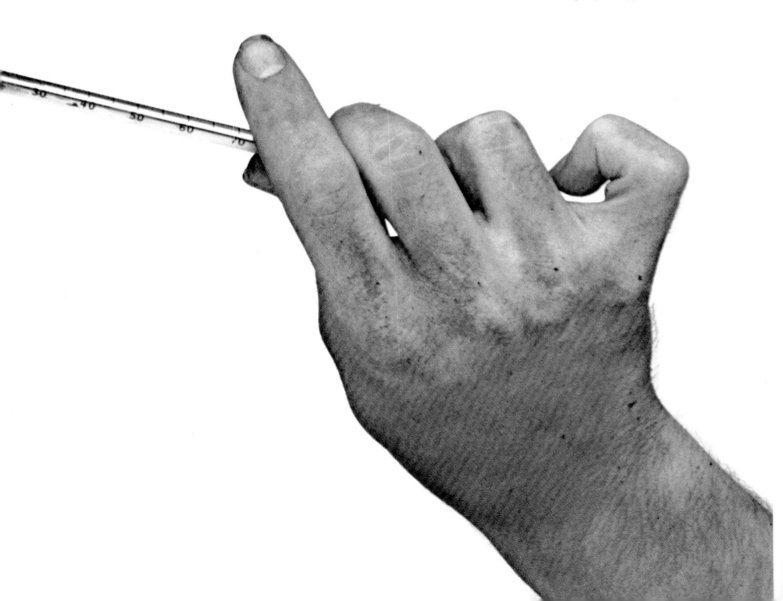

wire with a blowtorch and push it up birdie's butt ... honestly, to hear him talk, you'd think it was the end of the world."

I nodded sagely in agreement, even though I knew that Miss Wills' treatment hadn't been in use for twenty years. Still, these folk remedies tend to linger on. People are often quite startled to see a young vet treat their constipated canary with sophisticated new techniques, like blowing down the bird's gullet with a flex-i-straw, or probing the rectal region with a tiny corkscrew. "When will Mr. Farmer be back?" I asked politely.

"God only knows," she said, throwing her hands up dramatically. She had been out of the room only a few moments when a young man with a puckish grin and cheeks like a matched set of rotting apples stuck his head in the door.

"I don't suppose you'd care for a smash of Gordon's gin," he said. "It's certain Gordon won't mind, hah-hah." He must have seen me glance at my watch, for he added, "Don't worry about the time. Anytime's the right time to blow your brains out on Gordon's. Hah-hah. We're dissipated as hell here, don't you know?" Then, producing two glasses, he banged them on Wolfgang's desk and filled them to the brim. I sipped politely at my drink while he poured his down with one smooth flick of the wrist.

"So," he said with a satisfied cough. "You're to be the new assistant. That's fine with me; it means I'll have less work to do. I'm Terry Farmer, Wolfgang's brother. I'd remember that if I were you. Most people just call me

Twisted. It's kind of a nickname, don't you see?" He poured himself another glass of Gordon's, and then, deftly blocking one nostril with a fat finger, he blew a grimy booger square in the center of the *Codex Ethacarium Vetenerice*, which had been stapled to a piece of plywood and mounted on the rosewood-paneled wall.

I mumbled under my breath and took another sip of gin. Twisted appeared to take no notice, but, leaning forward, whispered conspiratorially, "We have to be careful around here, you know. We were investigated the other day. It was all Wolfgang's fault. He tossed a lump of cement in a dissecting tray, and after dumping steak sauce all over it, he tried to convince a customer it was his pussy's gallstone. The customer was a doctor and went straight to the ASPCA. They were around here thick as flies on a dead dog's eye."

Just then, a merry peal of laughter shook the room. A squat, swart, bald man of about fifty stepped through the door. "I'm Wolfgang Farmer," he said, holding out about five pounds of heavily veined top ground round for me to shake. "I see Twisted has been telling you some of our troubles. Honestly, sometimes I don't know how we keep going." He chortled and dragged four square feet of terry towel across his perspiring brow. Then, clearing his throat loudly, he hawked into his left front shirt pocket. "Do you know, I've even had to build a phony surgery out front so they don't find out what the real one looks like?"

"That's right," said Twisted, butting in. "It cost us thirty bucks. I bought a

clean bedsheet and we spread it over a picnic table Wolfgang stole from the adventure playground one night. Then we lined the shelves with preserve jars full of colored water so they'd think it was medicine...."

"That was my idea," said Wolfgang, snatching at the gin bottle.

"Yeah, but it was my idea to put those Q-tips in a jar of piss. That really throws them for a loop."

Miss Wills, who was passing by the door, sniffed loudly. "Who suggested hanging the gin bottle upside down from the hat rack? Mercy me, I don't know where they think we're going to lay our hands on dog blood."

"Sure," said Twisted, "I never heard of one walking into a blood donor clinic...." We all burst out laughing, and the room became infused with a feeling of warmth, a human warmth that filled the room and spilled out into the hall, almost as if someone had set a wastepaper basket on fire. It was then I realized that I was going to enjoy working at the Farmer Animal Hospital. We sat in the consulting room over our gins and recounted many a merry story. Twisted's tales were the funniest. He told us the one about the flinty old Scotch vet, Angus McHebrides. It seems McHebrides was called out late one night to attend the calving of an old milk cow by the name of Blossom. This cow was famous for the power of her vaginal sphincter, which was said to have been able to bend a two-inch bar of cold rolled steel or snap a rake handle like a pencil. And it was into this cow that Angus had to stick his skinny arm to drag out a twisted calf.

MAY, 1975

S. GROSS

But the canny Scot was not about to get his arm broken by a cow's cunt. "Oi'll create a diversion, and while the bonny beastie is distracted, Oi'll insert me arm and yank out the calf." So saying, he stuffed a lit cherry bomb into the stunned cow's mouth. When the blast had gone off and the cow stared, stupified, at her teeth lying in the manger, the highlander reached in and snared the calf's foot with a binder twine noose. The cow never lived that could best Angus McHebrides....

We all laughed loudly. Twisted began yet another story, when he was interrupted by the cheerful dingle-dingle of the bell on the waiting room door. "That'll be your first case!" Wolfgang hollered as his chair went over backwards.

I stepped self-consciously into the waiting room, and was surprised to see a small girl standing uncertainly in the midst of that linoleum prairie. She started when she saw me, then wordlessly held up a scummy Baggie of brown water in which floated an upside-down goldfish. "Dear me," I mumbled, "it does look as though your little fish has..."

Just then I noticed Miss Wills beckoning frantically at me from the surgery door. "Excuse me for a moment," I said, and stepped over to see what she wanted.

"Tell her you'll fix it," she hissed.

"What?"

"Tell her you'll fix it. Get five bucks from her and slip out the back door to Woolworth's. Goodness gracious, they've got Goldy's twin brother on sale today for 39 cents."

I took Miss Wills' advice and the little girl's money, and after some argument with a clerk at Woolworth's (who suspected I was buying the fish for my cat), I managed to obtain a fine, healthy specimen for a bargain price.

The little girl was overjoyed when I presented her with the new fish. "Oh, Goldy! Now that the nice man has made you all better, I promise I'll never let that old Marsha Hildon take you to school again. I don't care if she gives me *two* new pencils."

Rejoining Wolfgang and Twisted in the consulting room, I flipped the five bucks onto the table with a studied casualness. Wolfgang broke off in mid-sentence and stared at me. I told him what had happened and awaited their hearty congratulations. Nothing doing.

"We get kids like that in here all the time," said Wolfgang. "Just the other day, two kids came in with a half-dead, tick-ridden pigeon they had found in the street. Son-of-a-bitch. That fucking gutter eagle looked like it had been run over by engine company number three. Hell, what could I say? I like kids as much as the next guy. I told them I'd do everything I could for sick

birdie and after they left I tossed it out back."

"What do you do when they come back for a visit?"

Twisted spoke up. "That's where I come in. I give them the sorrowful doctor routine. I tell them that the sewer falcon must have lost his will to live somewhere along the line even though Wolfgang here," he gestured at his brother, "did everything he could, including installing brand new lungs and a liver that cost $49.50."

"And," added Wolfgang, "if the kids should feel like offering us their next three years' allowance, we don't complain. Do we, Twisted?"

"Nofuckingway," said Twisted.

* * *

The next few weeks passed quickly for me as I gained that practical experience so necessary to a young vet just out of school. I still remember how strangely thrilled I felt watching Wolfgang at work in his back room, cutting the nuts off doggies and flinging them carelessly over his shoulder into a greasy oil drum which stood in the corner.

"Once a week we sell that crap to the Mandarin Palace," he explained.

When the waiting room bell tinkled, I would duck out to see the clients. Often I would find an elderly lady perched nervously on the edge of Wolfgang's naugahyde couch, clutching a small, timid dog whose two eyes glowed like cigarette ends from beneath tufts of silky hair. "I—I'd like to have Philip...altered. It won't...hurt him, will it?"

I thought of Wolfgang out back, a cigar clamped between his yellow teeth, a pair of bloody tin snips jutting from the back pocket of his coveralls, and a rusty hacksaw slung carelessly

around the neck of a gallon jug of Gordon's gin.

"They never know what hit 'em, ma'am."

"Oh, that's nice. I don't want to hurt Philip, but he ruined a Shiraz carpet the other day, and lately I've been worried he'll get to the guest towels."

"Yes, I quite understand." Then I'd scoop the bowser up under one arm, and before I could get halfway out of the room, I'd hear Miss Wills' strident voice. "That'll be $27.50, ma'am."

Twisted was always around, weaving through the surgery and consulting room like a sperm in a petrie dish, throwing off jokes and breaking the tension. He'd claim that he knew a vet who would deworm poodles with a crab fork, or maintain that the best way to remove a cat's gallstones was to press them out with a rolling pin. Once he told me a joke that made my trocar slip and pop a German shepherd's aorta. I was horrified. The dog belonged to one of our wealthiest customers, Mrs. Rudy Dufus.

Wolfgang put on a serious face when I told him the news. "Dear, dear. So Fritz has gone to heaven," he said, picking up the phone. "We'll have to put him in intensive care." He dialed Mrs. Dufus' number. "Hello, Mrs. Dufus? I'm afraid your Fritz's illness is more serious than we thought. It wasn't just a cold after all. No, he's suffering from engorged blood, and his heart's swollen up to the size of a balloon. We're going to put him into intensive care. Perhaps you should come down right away. There's no saying how long he will last. Right, you'll be down right away. Very good."

"Grab the dead mutt!" he shouted at me and headed off down the hall. "Miss Wills, I'm afraid we're going to have to use your office again. Intensive

JUNE, 1972

care, you know...." With much grumbling, the old spinster gathered up her invoice pads and ledgers, and headed off to make the consulting room her temporary headquarters.

"Right," said Wolfgang, seemingly galvanized to action. "Twisted, get the oxygen tent in here. And the plasma, don't forget the plasma. Oh, and the TV, and hurry up, will you!"

Twisted bustled into the room and began arranging a bunch of dry cleaner's bags stuck together with scotch tape over a coat hanger frame across the dead pooch's body. "Oxygen tent," he explained, and began to hum "How Much Is That Doggy in the Window." He ducked out of the room for a minute, and reappeared with an old TV chassis on a brass stand. He quickly stuffed some multicolored wires leading from it under the dead dog's body. "Monitors heart beat and respirator."

"How is our patient doing?" shouted Wolfgang down the hall. "Is it all right if Mrs. Dufus sees him now?"

"Well, as long as it's only for a minute, and she doesn't touch him. That could put him away for good and all."

Mrs. Dufus came to see the dog twice a day for two weeks before Wolfgang gave her the bad news. "He slipped away from us in the night. We can be thankful it was a peaceful passing...." Mrs. Dufus sent us a lovely present. She was very happy that we had done everything we could to make Fritz's last hours comfortable.

Days passed into weeks at the Farmer Animal Hospital. Gradually, I began to get used to the routine. However, there were still a few surprises in store for me, as I learned one morning when I heard a terrible shrieking out in the hall. Wolfgang was shouting at the top of his voice.

"Go on, you filthy old rat sack, I told you never to disturb me when I'm taking my nap! I'll show you...a little taste of the fire poker will help your memory!"

I could hear Miss Wills' terrified screams right through two pillows and my bedroom wall. "But it's the zoo! The zoo! You've got to go or we'll never make the premium on the malpractice insurance this month!"

"Go yourself, you old bitch!" he bellowed, and I could hear Twisted's laughter echoing above all the confusion.

Suddenly, there was silence. The next thing I knew, Wolfgang was dragging me off the couch, where I had been sleeping. "Come on," he said, "we gotta go to the zoo. Say, what are those fag pajamas you're wearing? Hah-hah."

"Fuck you," I mumbled under my breath, and took a sorrowful glance at the clock, which read just 11:00 A.M.

Minutes later, we were zipping across town in Wolfgang's Thunderbird. "Good business, the zoo," he said, chatting merrily. I could barely keep my eyes open. The night before, Twisted had invited a bunch of vets over to see his "Dogarama Sex Review," and we had stayed up drinking till four in the morning, watching one of our patients, a great Danish bonerhammer, slip the pink steel to another of our patients, a tiny Scotch terrier. My head still hurt as I remembered the merry peals of laughter that had rocked the hospital as the bonerhammer hop-skipped around the surgery with the little terrier screwed onto his tool.

"Are you listening to me?" said Wolfgang, swerving the car at a squirrel that was trying to find its way across the road.

"Uh-huh," I said, but he didn't hear me. He was looking backwards at the squirrel.

"Hah! Nailed the nasty, nut-eating son-of-a-bitch. One more acorn tree will grow in the wild wood. Hah-hah."

We pulled into the zoo parking lot, and a few minutes later, I stood by Wolfgang's side in the curator's office while the man explained his problem. "It's the snakes this time, I'm afraid. They just don't seem to have any zest for life. People don't want to watch a deadly Afrikaans Head Ripper just lie there. They want to see some snapping and thrashing on their day at the zoo. I thought that after how you perked up MGM, you might be able to come up with something."

Wolfgang had told me a few days earlier how he had put some pep into the zoo's mangy old lion. He fed the friendly old thing some candy pills, and then, when the curator wasn't looking, he shot the king of beasts in the ass with a squirt gun full of turpentine.

"Oh, look," said the curator, "he's chasing his tail...." You would be, too, if it felt like somebody was running a belt sander over your butt.

"I think I can help you with the snakes," said Wolfgang, looking thoughtful. "Just toss a gerbil into the cage with them and let them chase the bouncing rat for a while."

"But snakes only eat once a month," said the curator timidly.

"No problem. After the snake swallows the rodent and starts to snooze it off, you grab the sleeping serpent by the tail and crack him like a whip. The partially digested spring rat will fly forty feet in the air, and the snake will be left with a powerful rumbling in his food tube that will see him flying around his cage the next day like the loose end of a fire hose. Hah-hah."

\* \* \*

As we walked toward the car afterwards, Wolfgang turned to me with a smile. "How do you like being a vet so far?" he said. "Was it worth all the studying?"

I hated to spoil the moment by telling him I had picked up my credentials from a mail-order firm for five bucks. I just smiled, and said nothing. □

*"Heck, no! We're not crazy! Why? Do we look crazy?"*

MAY, 1975

# Learn religion straight from *God*

**Thanks to the magic of the computer, for just $11.95.**

When you Dial-a-Prayer, do you get a busy signal? Want to improve your chances for an uptown train on Judgement Day? Uncertain where the path of your belief lies? If you're discouraged at your lack of devotional improvement, you need the advice of a proven professional. But where can one go for such advice?

The Pope makes fewer and fewer house calls these days. Even the Wailing Wall has been turning a deaf brick.

Well, brothers and sisters, NOW . . . due to a recent miraculous discovery in computer technology and automation, it is possible to receive expert advice direct from the Judeo-Christian Heavenly Being of your choice. ELIMINATE THE MIDDLEMAN!

Not face to face, of course. But in the next best form—by way of direct, one-to-one written communications straight from the shoulder.

Your lesson from GOD runs 8,000–10,000 words, and will show you in illuminating detail how to find enlightenment.

For over a year now, GOD and a group of communications experts have been programming a computer with everything GOD knows about religion. At the same time, the group also worked out a series of questions through which every man can profile his religious life.

The advice you receive is the creation of GOD and computer to responses received from your questions.

With regular reference to the lesson you receive (in a fire, flood, and plague-resistant cover) from GOD, you too will be able to make friends, impress people, and decimate your enemies in a very short time. Act now.

## THEY DID IT!

St. Dismas: "It's a steal!"

Mary Magdalen: "Sure turned the trick for me!"

Adolf Eichmann: "A real gas!"

Moses: "This is no bullrush!"

St. Joan of Arc: "It really burned me out!"

---

## QUESTIONNAIRE

**CAUTION: Please pay your VERY BEST ATTENTION when completing this questionnaire. The value of the guidance you receive will be in direct proportion to the value, honesty, and accuracy of all your answers. (Besides, we'll know if you lie.)**

Dear GOD:
To help you make my enlightenment more meaningful, here is some information about myself.
**CIRCLE APPROPRIATE ANSWER**

1. My age is:
   A. under 20 years
   B. 20–35 years
   C. 36–50 years
   D. over 50 years
   E. waiting for the last rites

2. I am a:
   A. Male
   B. Female

3. My religious persuasion is:
   A. Catholic
   B. Jewish
   C. Protestant
   D. Not sure

4. I go to a house of worship:
   A. Never
   B. Once a year
   C. Once a month
   D. Once a week
   E. Once a day
   F. I live there

5. I go to Church or Temple because:
   A. I like the music
   B. To look at the stained glass windows
   C. My family makes me go
   D. Hebrew and/or Latin make me laugh

6. I consider myself basically a:
   A. Sinner
   B. Saint
   C. Martyr
   D. In between

7. I share this much of my daily bread with GOD a year:
   A. $1,000 or more
   B. $100
   C. $10
   D. $0

8. I use this money to
   A. Buy Christmas presents
   B. Plant a tree in Israel
   C. Balance my tax forms
   D. All of above

9. The sin that tempts me most is:
   A. Adultery
   B. Murder
   C. Pride
   D. Possession or use of graven images

10. I feel closest to GOD:
    A. Watching Pat O'Brien movies
    B. Making love
    C. Firing machine guns
    D. Shooting heroin

Send $11.95 to Compreligious Inc., Heaven, Neb. $$$$$

Name _____

Street/Apt./Cell Block _____

City _____ State _____ Zip _____

Signature _____

NO C.O.D. Please allow two weeks for delivery.

by Elias Teiber

ACCORDING TO SEAN KELLY · ILLUMINATED BY NEAL ADAMS

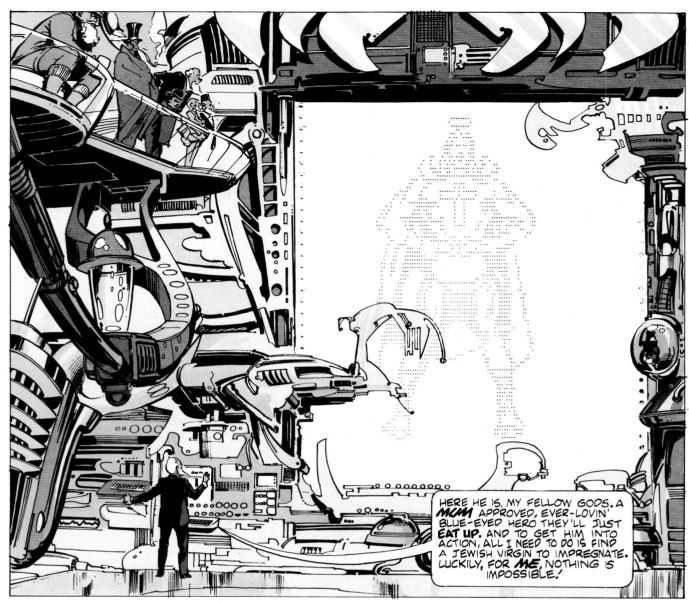

HERE HE IS, MY FELLOW GODS. A *MGM* APPROVED, EVER-LOVIN' BLUE-EYED HERO THEY'LL JUST *EAT UP.* AND TO GET HIM INTO ACTION, ALL I NEED TO DO IS FIND A JEWISH VIRGIN TO IMPREGNATE. LUCKILY, FOR *ME,* NOTHING IS IMPOSSIBLE.!

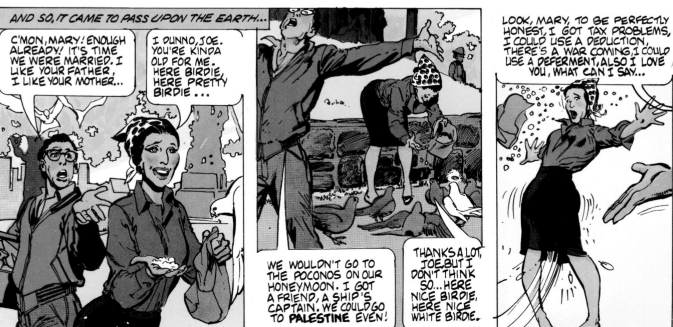

AND SO, IT CAME TO PASS UPON THE EARTH...

C'MON, MARY! ENOUGH ALREADY! IT'S TIME WE WERE MARRIED. I LIKE YOUR FATHER, I LIKE YOUR MOTHER...

I DUNNO, JOE. YOU'RE KINDA OLD FOR ME. HERE BIRDIE, HERE PRETTY BIRDIE ...

WE WOULDN'T GO TO THE POCONOS ON OUR HONEYMOON. I GOT A FRIEND, A SHIP'S CAPTAIN. WE COULD GO TO **PALESTINE** EVEN!

LOOK, MARY, TO BE PERFECTLY HONEST, I GOT TAX PROBLEMS, I COULD USE A DEDUCTION, THERE'S A WAR COMING, I COULD USE A DEFERMENT, ALSO I LOVE YOU, WHAT CAN I SAY...

THANKS A LOT, JOE, BUT I DON'T THINK SO... HERE NICE BIRDIE, HERE NICE WHITE BIRDIE.

AND HE CAME UNTO HIS OWN, AND HIS OWN DIDN'T KNOW WHAT TO MAKE OF IT. MR. AND MRS. DAVID ONLY KNOW THAT THEIR **STRANGELY BEGOTTEN** SON IS... SOMEHOW... DIFFERENT...

MOM, CAN I HAVE A **HAM SANDWICH** AND A GLASS MILK?

WOULD YOU MIND HITTING THIS CHEEK, TOO? I KINDA **LIKE** IT.

AND, IN THE EIGHTH GRADE...

BUZZ OFF, **BENNIE!** YOU **CREEP!**

GOODBYE, LAURA LEVY, I'M DYING FOR LOVE OF YOU!

HEY! THIS IS GONNA HURT! **JESUS CHRIST!**

SHALOM

BENNIE TAKES **THE NAME**...

AND IS TRANSFIGURED INTO **SON-O'-GOD!**

WHY?

WHY ME?

GET THAT TRASH OFF THE TRACKS!

GOD? WHY **ME?**

HONESTLY, KIDS TODAY!

DRIVER, RUN HIM OVER!

CRUCIFY HIM!

MEANWHILE, IN HEAVEN...

HAHAHAHAHA

HOHOHO HOHO

TEEHEE TEEHEE

YUCKA YUCKA YUCKA

JEHOVAH, YOU'VE DONE IT AGAIN!

**Our Insides**
Each human body has more wiring, tubing, insulation, filters, and circuitry than the entire Bell system. Our digestive tract alone, if stretched out in one straight line, would allow us to have dinner in Fort Lauderdale, Florida, and pass our wastes in Lexington, Kentucky.

# OUR WONDERFUL BODIES
## by Brian McConnachie

photographed by Ede Rothaus

For a moment, mentally picture yourself standing in front of a full-length mirror. Behold the body. Let's, for the purpose of example, imagine ourselves as a national park. Our eyes are two ranger stations on the constant lookout for forest fires and rampaging bears. The face is our own private Mt. Rushmore, which serves as our identification. Our arms and legs, giant redwoods; and the tufts of hair at the top of each, foliage. Toes and fingers are knotty roots, and there are additional bushes growing on the top of the monument. Standing firm and serene, we are Nature's trophy and a woodsman's paradise. But now, imagine a motorcycle gang or some of those rampaging bears invading our picnic area (the stomach). Knocking over trash pails and zooming along unauthorized paths, they have disturbed the serenity of the park, and official action must be taken. The rangers in the ranger station are helpless to do anything for two reasons. First, because they cannot see the trouble (it is

directly below them), and secondly, it is not their job. They are forest rangers assigned to survey everything and they cannot leave their posts. What will happen? How will this mayhem be stilled? Just then, a glacier of late-melting winter snow falls into a nearby stream overflowing the stream which in sequence flushes the motorcycle gang and the rampaging bears with the force of a Niagara right out the front of our Rushmore.

It all seems quite simple; but it isn't.

The human body is probably the greatest marvel in the wonderful world around us. In our wildest understandings, we can just begin to comprehend the myriad, complex functions which go on ceaselessly, from the day of our birth to the day when it all just stops. For as much as we have come to know about the body, there is that much again to learn. But thanks to modern techniques and the official cooperation of state hospitals, nursing homes, and prisons, our scientific explorers are,

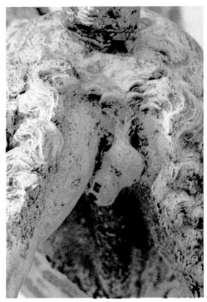

**The Fifteenth Islet of Langerhans**
Magnified 2,000 times. Its job is to
make sure that the little shelf that your
heart rests on gets enough to eat.

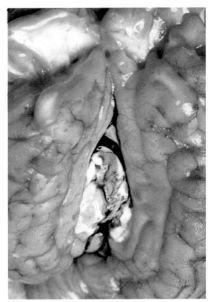

**The Hernia**
Located in the lower abdomen, it is
considered by many as Nature's
retribution to men for already having
given women the menstrual cycle.

**Green Corpuscles,**
resting. An important part of our body
when we lived in the sea, green corpuscles once did a thriving business
manufacturing our scales. Displaced
by their more imaginative red and
white colleagues, there is not much
left for them to do.

day by day, closing in on the mysterious, uncharted
territories that abound within us. Perhaps one day we
will know all there is to know about the body; but until
that day comes, we must content ourselves with the
wonders of how the liver makes bile, the miracle of
wisdom teeth, and the timely function of sweat glands.

It has been often said and it is true: We take our
bodies for granted. Though we pay rapt attention to our
outside shell, we expect our inside to do its job, as we do
our jobs, and not complain like older parents who sometimes feel neglected and whine about their condition.
We live our lives relatively unaware of all the unbridled
inventiveness going on inside. Only when we are forced
to defecate or expel a mouthful of mucus or remove
congealed darkened phlegm clinging to our nostril hairs
do we outwardly share in the wondrous process. Silently
and efficiently, the body does what it must do to keep us
on our feet in search of further nourishment. It is per-

haps that the body's quiet labors are conducted with
such stealth which eventually lulls us into our understandable neglect. We can't see the functions and we
certainly can't hear them. If our bone marrow made
whizzing and churning sounds when it produced blood
and our muscles made ripping and snapping noises and
our white corpuscles gave out maniacal banshee cries
every time they attacked invading bacteria, we would,
no doubt, be comforted by the industrious sounds of
craft. But that would be impractical, and the body must
have reasons of its own for conducting itself the way it
does. Save for the faint beat of the heart and the barely
perceptible exchange of our breath, there are no out-
ward signs of the diligence within. One could almost
believe it didn't want us to know. It is always so quiet.

But when the body wants something, there is no end
to which it won't go. It wakes us up in the middle of
the night if it is thirsty and makes us get it a glass of

**The Eyebrow**
Magnified fifty times, no two eyebrows are alike. Though they are
exactly alike when magnified only two
or three times.

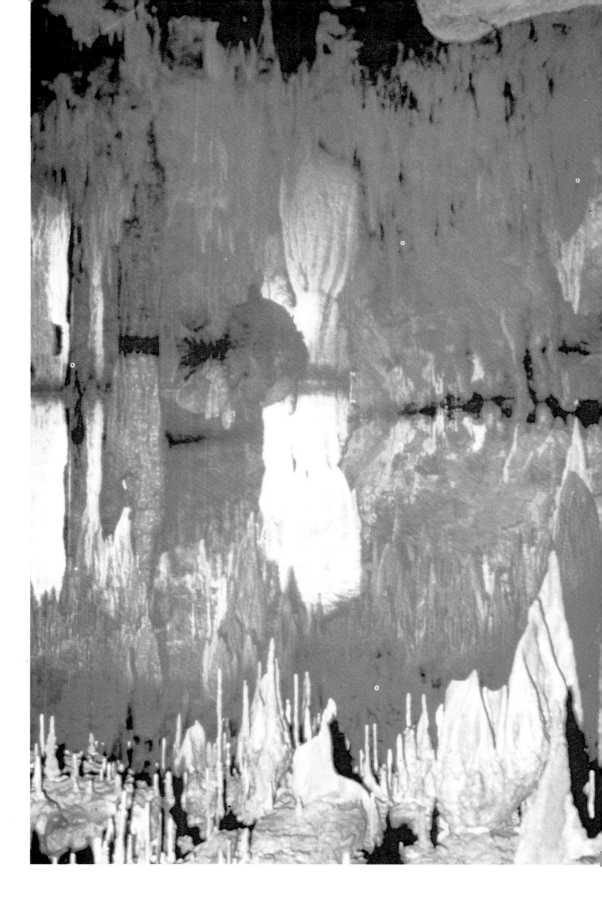

**The Liver**
The object of the raging debate whether the liver was a muscle or an organ has finally been settled recently when the liver was declared to be a gland.

water. If it is in need of sexual release, it'll march us all over town until it finds its own brand of fulfillment. If for some reason it becomes angry with us, its recourses are seemingly endless: inflate the appendix, manufacture gallstones, leave the air passage open when we are eating bulky food, to name but a few. It can make us walk into doors, hit ourselves in the thumb with hammers, make us jump into freezing cold waters. It can humiliate us in front of our friends by urinating in our clothing. It can make us fall asleep when we don't want to fall asleep. And while asleep, it can scare us half to death by conjuring up monstrous images, tossing us off of a cliff or out of a tree. On a capricious whim, it can make just our legs fall asleep, or our eyes cross, or lower things out our nose. It can do anything it wants. It makes up 94 percent of us, and there is nothing we can do about it. Our meager 6 percent shell just has to go along. It can make us run till we drop from exhaustion, swim till we about drown, and get us into punching fights with one another. These are the cold, indisputable facts, and there is no way around them. If we attempt to take control by drugging our bodies with liquor or pills, its defenses simply release all of our muscle tension, and we drop like a placenta. But our small percent is an important percent, and our insides know this. As the container, we keep it from slithering off in several directions at once. It is truly a *good* symbiotic relationship. And we should be happy. Happy because our insides are not wicked or mischievous by nature.

One has only to imagine what it would be like if we had, say, the insides of an elephant. We would all be walking around with tusks, a big funny looking trunk, and a silly little tail. No, our bodies, as a whole, are quite serious. Sometimes they frustrate us, sometimes they give us joy, but we always should love them because they are *our wonderful bodies.* □

**The Head**
Captured on film is the inside of a Chinaman's brain while the Chinaman was attempting to pronounce the letter *l*.

**The Soul**
Once believed to be everlasting and the source of our interest in religion, the soul now busies itself with helping us pick out flashy clothes and R & B records.

**A Healthy Pancreas**
is the hardest working organ in the body. It filters blood, digests food, cleans up your stomach after meals, regulates the heartbeat, supervises over the small and large intestines, controls the muscles, produces calcium for the bones, keeps us walking in an upright position, and was responsible for inventing the opposable thumb.

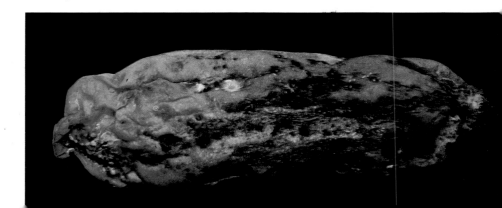

# FOREIGNERS
## AROUND THE WORLD

A Brief Survey of the Various Foreign Types,
Their Chief Characteristics,
Customs, and Manners

### by P.J. O'Rourke

## AFRICANS

**Racial Characteristics:** Probably not people at all. Probably some kind of monkey. They eat each other and worship bundles of sticks and mud. You can never remember the names of their countries, which have a new Main Nigger every half hour and too many snakes and bugs anyway. They eat those, too. They put bones in their noses and wear plants for clothes.

**Good Points:** Don't feel pain the way we do.

**Proper Forms of Address:** *Jig, coon, fishmouth, soot-back, shitskin, boy.*

**Two Ancedotes Illustrating Something of the Negro Character:**

A traveling cattle barterer asks to stay the night at a root gatherer's hut. The root gatherer agrees but says the cattle barterer will have to sleep with the root gatherer's daughter. The cattle barterer goes to get onto the mat with the root gatherer's daughter and sees that she's very dead, so he spends all night eating her. In the morning, the root gatherer asks the traveling cattle barterer how he liked sleeping with his daughter. "She was wonderful," says the cattle barterer, "especially those delicious maggots in her mouth."

"Those weren't maggots," says the root gatherer, "those were just some grains of rice. She's only been dead since yesterday."

Then there was an African pervert who ate women before they were cooked.

## AFRICANS

## ARABS

**Racial Characteristics:** Wear bed sheets and put bags over their women's heads. They burp and fart during meals and wash themselves in sand. They bugger little boys and practice some stupid religion that they're trying to get all our Negroes to believe in. Disorderly cowards when they have to fight anyone else, they nonetheless quite courageously murder each other and chop off people's hands for littering. They plant bombs everywhere they go and own all the earth's oil, which is why you can't buy high-test if you're wearing a yarmulke. They hate Jews because Jews are the only people in the world with noses uglier than their own, and they're cornering the Cadillac market so that the Hebes will have to drive Buicks.

**Good Points:** If they had any country clubs, they wouldn't let Jews in.

**Proper Forms of Address:** *Camel jockey, tent-head, soggy Arabian, desert Irish, gas-ass.*

**An Anecdote Illustrating Something of the Arab Character:**

During the Yom Kippur War, Syrian armored units were preparing to charge several fortified positions in the Golan Heights when the Israelis canceled their credit rating.

## AUSTRALIANS

**Racial Characteristics:** Violently loud alcoholic roughnecks whose idea of fun is to throw up on your car. The national sport is breaking furniture and the average daily consumption of beer in Sydney is ten and three quarters Imperial gallons for children under the age of nine. "Making a Shambles" is required study in the primary schools and all Australians are bilingual, speaking both English and Sheep. Possibly as a result of their country's being upside down, the local dialect has over 400 terms for *vomit*. These include 'technicolor yawn,' "talking to the toilet," "round-trip meal ticket," and "singing lunch." It is illegal to employ the aboriginal inhabitants as anything but toilets, and some of the peculiar forms of native wildlife have up to nine assholes. The recent destruction of Darwin by a hurricane was actually a cover story for the regrettable coincidence of paydays on three separate sheep stations.

| ARABS | AUSTRALIANS | CANADIANS | CHINESE |
|---|---|---|---|

**Good Points:** Amusing zoos.

**Proper Forms of Address:** *Steady there, Cool off, For Christ's sake, not in the sink, Stay back, I've got a gun!*

**An Anecdote Illustrating Something of the Australian Character:**

An Australian fellow asks his girl friend to fight, but she says she doesn't want to because she isn't feeling well. "Whatta ya mean, not feeling well?" he says.

"You know," she says, "I've got my time of the month."

"Whatta ya mean, time of the month?" he says.

"You know," she says, "I've got my period."

"Whatta ya mean, period?" he says.

"You know," she says, "I'm bleeding down here." And she opens up her pants to show him.

"Jesus," he says, "no wonder you're bleeding! They've gone and cut your cock off!"

# CANADIANS

**Racial Characteristics:** Hard to tell a Canadian from an extremely boring regular white person unless he's dressed to go outdoors. Very little is known of the Canadian country since it is rarely visited by anyone but the Queen and illiterate sport fishermen. It is thought to resemble a sort of arctic Nebraska. It's reported that Canadians keep pet French people. If true, this is their only interesting trait. At any rate, they are apparently able to train Frenchmen to play hockey, which is more than any European has ever been able to do.

**Good Points:** Still have plenty of Indians to abuse.

**Proper Forms of Address:** *Bud, mac, mister, hey you.*

**Some Examples of Canadian Repartee:**

Two Canadians are talking in a bar. One Canadian says, "Who was that lady I saw you with last night?"

"That was my wife," replies the other.

A lady is shopping in a Toronto drugstore and accidentally leaves the bottle of aspirins that she bought on the counter. She gets on a bus and the minute the bus has pulled away from the curb remembers leaving her purchase behind. "My aspirins! My aspirins!" she yells.

And the bus driver says, "Maybe you left them in the drugstore."

A little Canadian boy named Johnny Fuckerfaster is screwing a little girl under the porch of his house. His mother comes out the door and yells for him, "Johnny! Johnny Fuckerfaster!"

"I'll be there in a minute," he says.

# CHINESE

**Racial Characteristics:** Hordes of incomprehensible rat-eaters with a peculiar political philosophy and a dangerous penchant for narcotic drugs. No one can possibly know what dark and grotesque things pass through the minds of this hydra-headed racial anomaly which is, after all, more like a monstrous colony of flesh-crazed carpenter ants than a nation of rational men. Only a fool would deal with two-legged insects such as these. Our only hope is that the farsighted leaders of our own land will join with those of at least nominally Caucasian Soviet Russia and that together they will treat us to the welcome spectacle of a thermonuclear obliteration of this yellow menace.

**Good Points:** They're almost as far away as it's possible to be.

**Proper Forms of Address:** *Zipper head, Chink, slant, ching-chong Chinaman, yellow peril.*

**An Anecdote Illustrating Something of the Chinese Character:**

Nine hundred million Chinese walk into a bar. They order a beer, pay up, and then just sit there, sipping their drinks, not saying a word. Finally, the bartender can't stand it anymore. "We don't see many Chinese in here," he says.

"And with this atmosphere of hedonistic individualism capitalistically exploiting the labor of the masses and wasting the people's agricultural resources," say the Chinese, "you won't see many more."

# ENGLISH

**Racial Characteristics:** Cold-blooded queers with nasty complexions and terrible teeth who once conquered half the world but still haven't figured out central heating. They warm their beers and chill their baths and boil all their food, including bread. An intensely snobbish group, but who exactly they're snubbing is an international mystery. Lately they've been getting their comeuppance world power-wise, as their shabby, antiquated, and bankrupt little back alley of a country slowly winds down like the ill-crafted clockwork playthings of which their undersized children are so fond. In fact, last year their entire government had to kiss the ass of the fat aboriginal nig-nog who runs Uganda to retrieve a single flit hack writer from the clutches of that august nation. They all have large collections of something useless like lamp finials or toad eggs, and they would have lost both world wars if it weren't for us. They like to be spanked with canes and that's just what they deserve.

**Good Points:** It's relatively easy to make yourself understood with them.

**Proper Forms of Address:** *Limey, lime-eater, pom, poof, sister-boy.*

| ENGLISH | FRENCH | GERMANS | GREEKS |

**An Anecdote Illustrating Something of the English Character:**

In his unpublished memoirs, Benjamin Disraeli tells the story of a political conference with then-Prime Minister William Gladstone, who habitually conducted such private discussions while being fellated by an able-bodied seaman of the Royal Navy. At one point during their talk, the sailor suddenly looked up from Gladstone's penis and said, "Excuse me, Sir, but you've come."

"By Jove, so I have," said Gladstone, and he gave the tar a sovereign.

# FRENCH

**Racial Characteristics:** Sawed-off sissies who eat snails and slugs and cheese that smells like people's feet. They take filthy pictures of each other with cheap cameras, wash nothing but their cunts, fight with their feet, and perform sex acts with their faces. Utter cowards who force their own children to drink wine, they gibber like baboons even when you try to speak to them in their own wimpy language.

**Good Points:** Invented the blowjob.

**Proper Forms of Address:** *Froggy, froggy-wog, frog-eater, French-lips, Franco fuck-face, clit-lick.*

**An Anecdote Illustrating Something of the French Character:**

A Frenchman goes home with his best friend and they find the friend's wife laying naked on the dining room table with her legs spread apart. The Frenchman takes a close look at her cunt and says, "Zees *looks* like zee menstrual blood!" Then he bends down, takes a deep whiff, and says, "Zees *smells* like zee menstrual blood!" Finally he gets down on his knees, eats her out for about twenty minutes, and says, "Zees *tastes* like zee menstrual blood! Without a doubt, it *eez* zee menstrual blood!

*Mon dieu,* I am glad zat we did not *fuck* her!!"

# GERMANS

**Racial Characteristics:** Piggish-looking, sadomasochistic automatons whose only known forms of relaxation are swilling watery beer from vast tubs and singing the idiotically repetitive verses of their porcine folk tunes—both of which amusements probably hark back to a prehuman state. Germans have never been successfully Christianized. Their language lacks any semblance of civilized speech. Their usual diet consists almost wholly of old cabbage and sections of animal intestines filled with blood and gore. Once every two or three decades, they set forth, lemming-like, on pointless military adventures during which great numbers of them are slaughtered—much to the improvement of the world in general. Their lardy women have long, tangled masses of sticky hair under their arms, and the men shave the sides of their heads.

**Good Points:** Kill a lot of French.

**Proper Forms of Address:** *Kraut, Hun, Heiny, spike-head, sausage-breath.*

**A German Joke of the War Years Illustrating Something of the German Character:**

If your sister married a Jew—that will make you sauerkraut.

If your son married a Jew—that will make you bratwurst.

If your mother married a Jew—that will make you soap.

# GREEKS

**Racial Characteristics:** Degenerate, dirty, and impoverished descendants of a bunch of la-de-da fruit salads who invented democracy and then forgot how to use it while walking around dressed up like girls. Today

they bugger sheep and are engaged in an international campaign to take over all the world's small, filthy grocery stores. They eat the insides out of goats with their fingers. Their toilets are mere holes in the floor. And they cringe at the least threat from the imbecilic, taffy-yanking Turks next door.

**Good Points:** Cute alphabet.

**Proper Forms of Address:** *Feda-face, sheep dip, dog fashion, Geeko-European, eek-a-Greek!*

**An Anecdote Illustrating Something of the Greek Character:**

An ignorant peasant girl marries a man who's been in the Greek navy for twenty years. After their third anniversary, her mother starts to worry because the girl still isn't pregnant. "Why are you not with child, daughter?" she asks. "Does not your husband make the love to you?"

"Of course," says the girl, blushing deeply, "but…but…to tell the truth, Mother, I just can't keep from shitting afterwards."

# INDIANS

**Racial Characteristics:** Dismal, obsequious deminiggers whose gods have too many arms and legs and about whom entirely too many articles have appeared in the Sunday *New York Times Magazine.* They wrap their heads in towels and wipe their asses with their hands. They are unable to feed themselves and what food they do have tastes as if it was mixed with the offal from muskrat dens. Their culture is moribund, their politics dictatory, their economy stagnant, their skins sebaceous, and their social order loathsome to the minds of decent men everywhere. "Sub-" is no idle prefix in its application to *this* continent.

**Good Points:** Dirty statues.

**Proper Forms of Address:** *Wog,*

| INDIANS | IRISH | ISRAELIS | ITALIANS |
|---|---|---|---|
|  |  |  |  |

*towel head, curry-dipper, human refuse.*

### Three Important Questions Concerning the Future of India:

What do you feed 563,490,000 Indians when you only have 300 pounds of wheat?

*Leftovers.*

What's the difference between an Indian toddler and a regulation NFL football?

*A football has to weigh at least fourteen ounces.*

What's the literal translation of the Hindi phrase for "take a shit"?

*"Nothing to do."*

# IRISH

**Racial Characteristics:** Pie-faced, neckless, bandy-legged sots who almost never fuck. Ignorant and superstitious, they are in utter thrall to the vile, conniving priests of their dark and barbarous religion. Their women have their legs on upside down and no man in the country eats anything but potatoes, and only eats them when he's out of strong drink. The principal delights of the Irish are in quarreling and fighting and killing each other with bombs. They can be trained to do nothing useful that a dray horse can't accomplish in half the time, and they spew out a continuous stream of mumbles and grunts which they fancy to be "poems." They sell their children for whiskey.

**Good Points:** Many Irish are dead.

**Proper Forms of Address:** *Bogmouth, peat-face, Mr. Potato Head, nun-buns, dumb Mick.*

### An Anecdote Illustrating Something of the Irish Character:

There once was an Irishman who got so drunk while he was in Rome that he kissed his wife and beat the Pope's foot to a pulp with a coal shovel.

# ISRAELIS

**Racial Characteristics:** Living proof that money can't buy love, these greedy, usurious, scheming Christ-killers, who won't eat pork because it reminds them of their parents, go around moving into other people's countries and buying up all the pawnshops and delicatessens. They were personally responsible for the fall of the Roman Empire, the 1929 stock market crash, and the loss of World War II by a prominent European country. Now they're ruining show business. Their fiendish heathen religious rituals include mutilating the penises of their own sons and drinking the blood of Christian babies during Lent. The world's nations have historically competed with each other to see who could get rid of them fastest. They control the legal, medical, psychiatric, and accountancy professions, and are the force behind international communism, freemasonry, sex education, the media, and the Catholic church.

**Good Points:** Clean women.

**Proper Forms of Address:** *Yid, kike, sheeny, Hebe, nickel-nose, knife-nose, gabardine stroking mockey, clip-tip.*

### An Anecdote Illustrating Something of the Israeli Character:

A pious rabbi in Tel Aviv had to give up adultery for business reasons. He kept losing interest on his wife.

# ITALIANS

**Racial Characteristics:** This least appealing of the European peoples combines natural criminal propensities with an attitude of slavish idolatry toward that Whore of Rome, the Pope. When speaking, the Italians gesture frantically with their hands in an attempt to distract your gaze from their ugly faces—upon which are clearly etched the marks of their moral and intellectual degeneracy.

They cannot stop stealing, and will sometimes go so far as to steal money that is rightfully theirs from the pockets of their own trousers even as they wear them. Worse yet, they rarely catch themselves doing so. (Not that it matters, since their currency is worth nothing.) Otherwise, they amuse themselves by kidnapping the neighbor's children, voting for Communists, and staying out on strike, where they've been since the 1940s. On the field of battle they are abject cowards, and in the kitchen they're enthralled with bruised tomatoes and the noodle only.

**Good Points:** Big tits.

**Proper Forms of Address:** *Ginzo, guinea, dago, spaghetti-bender, wop.*

### A German Joke of the War Years Illustrating Some Points Concerning the Italian Character:

During the campaign in North Africa, an Italian tank and a German tank accidentally collided and the two surprised drivers jumped out. The Italian yelled, "I surrender! I surrender!" The German shot him.

# JAPANESE

**Racial Characteristics:** Resembling the Chinese in many respects but mercifully less numerous. Their idea of a good time is to torture people, preferably by inserting a glass rod in the penis, then doing the predictable thing. And this is only for captured business competitors. During time of war, they resort to more drastic measures entirely. They have no new ideas of their own or any native creativity, but they are able to copy everything we do quite nicely, considering the color of their skin. Their diet consists principally of fish, which they do not cook or even, in many cases, kill. It's rumored that they know of sex acts peculiar unto themselves, and with any luck, so it will stay. The most

| JAPANESE | MEXICANS | POLES | RUSSIANS |
|---|---|---|---|

frightening thing about the Japanese is that we've tried the atomic bomb on them twice and it doesn't seem to have much effect.

**Good Points:** Frequently commit suicide.

**Proper Forms of Address:** *Nip, Jap, dink, gook, yellow rat.*

**An Anecdote Illustrating Something of the Japanese Character:**

There was once a half-Japanese, half-Polish businessman in Tokyo who attempted to export miniaturized dildos.

# MEXICANS

**Racial Characteristics:** Resembling the Spanish in all their more loathsome characteristics except lazier, dirtier, and more thieving. A large percentage of American Indian blood in the average Mexican deprives him of any natural human sympathies or moral sense and makes him a wholly unmanageable drunk. The principal industry of Mexico is the production of pornographic playing cards that depict their women corrupting the morals of donkeys. Completely untrustworthy, the Mexican will make food out of anything that will hold still, feed it to you, and charge you for it besides. An attempt to conquer and hence eliminate this pesky breed of miscegenators was launched by our government during the last century, but wholesale nausea on the part of our troops, when they'd witnessed Mexican home life prevented our doing as thorough a job as we should have.

**Good Points:** You can buy their twelve-year-old daughters.

**Proper Forms of Address:** *Wetback, beaner, chili-dipper, taco turd, flap hat.*

**Three Important Questions Concerning the Mexican Economy:**

What do you call all thirty-eight members of a Mexican family packed into one Cadillac?

*Grand theft auto.*

How did they get all thirty-eight members of a Mexican family packed into one Cadillac?

*They picked the lock.*

What's hot on the outside, brown on the inside, and stinks like hell all over?

*All thirty-eight members of a Mexican family packed into one Cadillac.*

# POLES

**Racial Characteristics:** A nation known as the Rudimental Reading Class of Europe. Its citizens are turkey-loaf look-alikes descended from a barbarian horde that took a wrong turn on its way to sack Rome. They spent the Middle Ages trying to fight Vikings on horseback and invented breech-loading artillery by pointing their cannons the wrong way around. They didn't know about sexual intercourse until the tenth century, having previously reproduced by raiding warthog litters. In 1947, the Poles became a Communist country under the impression that it was a rite of the Catholic church, and today their principal exports are snow tires manufactured from their own native deposits of snow.

**Good Points:** Easy to beat at contract bridge.

**Proper Forms of Address:** *Polack, dumbo, lug wrench, kielbasa brain.*

**An Anecdote Illustrating Something of the Polish Character:**

A Polish queer was recently arrested in Warsaw for trying to blow his wife.

# RUSSIANS

**Racial Characteristics:** Brutish, dumpy, boorish lard-bags in cardboard double-breasted suits. Lickspittle slaveys to the maniacal schemes of their blood-lusting Red overlords. They make bicycles out of cement and can be sent to Siberia for listening to the wrong radio station. Their Communist party cuts the dicks off of high school boys to get women athletes, and shoots losing chess champions in the kneecaps. They shine their shoes with shit and spread Shinola on their wheat fields.

**Good Points:** They aren't allowed to leave their country.

**Proper Forms of Address:** *Redski, Russki, Commie scum, stinking Red slime, puke-gutted Bolshevik asshole-sucker.*

**An Anecdote Illustrating Something of the Russian Character:**

Three Russian kids were looking at a couple of pairs of blue jeans on a clothesline and discussing what they wanted most in the world. "I want a big box of turnips," said the first kid, "so I could have enough black market rubles to buy a pair of blue jeans like those."

"I want a big box of Shock-Worker's Medals," said the second kid, "so I could have enough People's Hero privileges to buy a pair of blue jeans like those."

"I want a big box of parents," said the third kid.

"A big box of parents?! Why do you want a big box of parents?!" said the other two.

"Because," said the third kid, "I only have two parents and my sister turned them both in to the Secret Police and now she owns *both* those pairs of blue jeans!"

# SCOTS

**Racial Characteristics:** Sour, stingy, depressing beggars who parade around in schoolgirls' skirts with nothing on underneath. Their fumbled attempt

| SCOTS | SPANISH | SWEDISH | SWISS |
|---|---|---|---|

at speaking the English language has been a source of amusement for five centuries, and their idiot music has been dreaded by those not blessed with deafness for at least as long. The latter is produced on a device resembling five flutes that have grown a piss bladder. Formerly, the Scots painted themselves blue and ranged far and wide over the British Isles, but good fortune prevailed and they were conquered by their betters. What passes for an alcoholic beverage in the dreary province to which the Scots have been driven has enjoyed a short vogue among fairies and advertising types, but this appears to be giving way to cocaine.

**Good Points:** Attractive plaids.

**Proper Forms of Address:** *Scotty, Jock, legs, plaid ass.*

**An Anecdote Illustrating Something of the Scots Character:**

In recent years, the small Scottish Nationalist movement has become so desperate that it's been kidnapping money and ransoming it for people.

# SPANISH

**Racial Characteristics:** As hot of blood as they are dim of mind, a national situation dating back to the fifteenth century when they expelled the last of the Moors, and with them the only people south of the Pyrennees who could count above twenty. The deep-seated strain of masochistic homosexuality manifested in their love for watching ritualized forms of stooptag played with large male cows needs hardly be commented on, except to say that Ernest Hemingway's fondness for this country and its neolithic pastimes was enough to keep most educated people away through the better part of the present century. Spiritually, the Spanish are disfigured beyond help by a particularly greasy sort of religious fa-

naticism that manifests itself in morbid visions of the type in which our Savior is seen swallowing the menses of his Virgin Mother and so on and so forth to an extent that turns sensible people ill. The Spanish are largely notable for having set out some 500 years ago and found the only people on the face of the earth primitive enough for them to conquer. (See *Mexicans.*)

**Good Points:** Only one book that has to be read for Comparative Lit. courses.

**Proper Forms of Address:** *Spic, greaser, tight pants, hankie-crotch.*

**An Anecdote Illustrating Something of the Spanish Character:**

In 1536, the explorer Cabeza de Vaca brought an Antarctic penguin back to Spain and displayed it to the mother superior of the Carmelite Order in Madrid, who thereupon had 1,300 nuns burned by the Inquisition trying to obtain a confession.

# SWEDISH

**Racial Characteristics:** Tedious, clean-living boy scout types, strangers to graffiti and littering, but who are possessed of an odd suicidal mania. Speculation is that they're slowly boring themselves to death. This is certainly the case if their cars and movies are any indication. They eat a lot of fish, and perhaps this is more brain food than their modest cranial endowments can cope with. In other points they resemble Canadians, though better looking. Not that that's saying much. Maybe they're depressed because they have the silliest sounding language west of the Urals. Or maybe it's that they have the ugliest famous actress of any civilized nation. No use asking them; what with their silly-sounding language and ugly actresses, it's almost impossible for them to get anything across to anyone. Swedes

fuck a lot, but only in the missionary position.

**Good Points:** They're white.

**Proper Forms of Address:** *Herring-choker, herring-knocker, squarehead, Swede.*

**An Anecdote Illustrating Something of the Swedish Character:**

At a wedding party in Stockholm, the inebriated groom stumbles into a bedroom and finds his bride getting fucked by the best man. He laughs uproariously and calls all his friends over to the door. They tell him he's drunk. "You think *I'm* drunk?" he yells. "Take a look at Sven! He's so drunk, he thinks he's *me!*"

# SWISS

**Racial Characteristics:** Mountain Jews in whose icy clutches lay the fruits of grave misdeeds committed in every clime. Under cover of their sanctimonious Red Cross organization, they have penetrated all the governments on the planet and, concealed by a flutter of blood drives and nurses' caps, lie sucking like leeches at the marrow of the gold, chocolate, clock, and army knife industries of nations beyond number. Pathologically clean, they sterilize their children at birth, which accounts for their low rate of population growth and leaves them more room to hide heaps and piles of money in their tiny, Alp-ringed repository of snow-covered sin.

**Good Points:** They rarely yodel in the home.

**Proper Forms of Address:** *Butter balls, cheese knees, big fat Swiss.*

**An Important Question Concerning Switzerland's Economy:**

What do you call a Swiss banker who likes Italian *lire* better than *Deutsche marks?*
*Queer.*                            □

# DOGFISHING
## IN AMERICA

**by Gerald Sussman**
**photographs by Matthew Klein**

The jukebox at the Pez Dorado on Second Avenue and 116th Street has a surprisingly eclectic selection for a bar deep in the heart of Spanish Harlem. Between your basic salsa we find such foreigners as Frank Sinatra, Otis Redding, Bob Marley, LaBelle, even Paul Simon. It's Friday night. The noise is happy—classically orchestrated. No random violence. Maybe later. Just lots of cheap rum, cheap beer and Puerto Ricans. And tucked between your basic PRs we see jet-setters, chamois-suede safari-suit types, jock superstars, groupies and party people (yes, there's Jimmy Caan with Lauren Hutton and Herman Badillo). This is why the jukebox has broken the ethnic barrier. The Pez has gone cosmopolitan and, dare we say it, chic. It has become *the* hangout for the dogfishing set.

Roberto Valdes, known as "the baboon" because he likes to wear animal costumes, is the unofficial host and mayor of the Pez. Roberto has an odd walk—a hop, actually. His right leg is stiff and extends off the ground. He is a man who likes to mix street *patois* with high-class words picked up God knows where. For a double Ron Llave, Roberto will tell you how dogfishing started.

"The Puerto Ricans started the whole dogfishing sport, you see," said Valdes. "You know why? Because of the dogshit. The fa-ha, we called it. We couldn't walk in the streets for all the dog *merde*. We're clean people. It was those canines that made our streets dirty. So we bought some cheap fishing rods and used *cuchifritos*, that's fried pork stuff, for bait. We used to catch hundreds of dogs casting from the windows of our cars. We caught the newspaper dogs. You know, those cheap little mutts you see in the window of the pet shop on the cut-up newspapers. That's mostly the kind of dog my people could afford. You throw out your line and pretty soon, bow-wow, you got a newspaper dog. Then we drive like crazy to someplace like the East River and dump them.

"One night I am with my friend Willie Mofongo and we are cruising up Third Avenue and we spot a real funny-looking mutt tied to a parking meter. I throw out my line and the little bitch grabs the bait. Seems like it wasn't tied up right so it sprang loose. It put up a nice fight for a tiny dog, but we finally caught it. Very cute dog. Looked like it took tiny shits, cute ones, you know. But you can step on a tiny turd even easier than a big one. It's the tiny ones you got to watch out for, *n'est-ce pas?*

"Well, we really did a dumb thing by catching that little dog. Turned out it belonged to a very dark Cuban by the name of Reuben Olivar, or Angel Eyes, as he was called. Angel Eyes was second in command of the drug business in Spanish Harlem, plus he dipped into other highly illegal activities. We had snared and dumped his favorite possession, a very fancy kind of dog, a King Charles spaniel named La Paloma, after his favorite song.

"Angel Eyes found Willie and me soon enough. He looked like the actor Jack Palance, only darker. A very menacing chap who told us that our lives were worth less than his dead dog's fa-ha at that very moment. Thinking I had about four minutes to live, I went into a big story about how I didn't care if I died because I had already experienced the biggest thrill in my life, the battle of man against dog. I had read a little Hemingway, James Dickey, you see. I had a subscription to *Sports Illustrated.* I'm not a dumb PR. I don't read Spanish love comics in the subway. So I gave him this shit about dogfishing being the ultimate sport, with more kicks than surfing, skiing, car racing, whatever.

"Well, the son of a bitch swallowed it, dug it, you see. But he was already thinking of bigger game. He wanted to fish for German shepherds, Saint Bernards, huskies, Dobermans. Yes, Angel Eyes started the whole big game thing. He went into the parks and fished from his chauffeur-driven Rolls-Royce! And that's how all these movie stars and jet people and millionaires got into it—through Angel. He's their drug dealer, you see. He gives them a taste of underworld chic.

"So, Willie and me were saved. He forgave us. Except he had to do one little thing in memory of his beloved Paloma. He broke my right leg so I could never set it on the ground again. That's why I hop. 'For the rest of your life you're going to pee like a dog,' he said to me. 'So you'll never forget what you did to Paloma.'"

Roberto's story is just one of the many claiming to be the origin of this remarkable sport. Ask any of a dozen Pez regulars and they'll have a swell yarn for you. They all knew the guy who started it all, just like everybody in the Dublin pubs knew James Joyce.

By two A.M., cheap rum goes down as easy as good rum, and the madness of the night before the big dogfishing tournament sets in. Everyone is wasted. Little boy macho antics ensue. Someone sets Jimmy Caan on fire. Roberto is summoned to piss on him and put it out. For perverse reasons, of course. They want to see him do it doggie style.

**D**issolve from Roberto doing a long beer piss on Jimmy Caan to a big sleek Doberman doing a wee-wee on a gingko tree in Central Park. Cut to: a Dodge pickup about a half mile away. Cut to: close-up of Billy Derveen, who has been eyeing this dog through his Zeiss binos. Billy is a veteran dogfishing spotter. He sits alongside dogfishing driver-guide Orris Cooper, another old hand. Billy and Orris are from Moultrie, Georgia, where they use similar techniques fishing for wolf. They're part of the dogfishing team put to-

*Stenreuther accidentally bumps into a school of Pekingese and Chihuahua in his hunt for the Doberman—a distraction that could lose him the big one. "They're undersize and you have to throw them back, of course," he said. "Or you can use them for live bait if you're going for Saint Bernard."*

*Après the Central Park Tournament. Stenreuther tries a little sidewalk dogfishing and scores a monster of a Great Dane.*

gether by Jack Stenreuther, a wealthy gynecologist and dogfisherman from Chicago. They've been out for six hours and have finally spotted a prize catch.

This is Stenreuther's third attempt to win the CPIDFT, the Central Park International Doberman-Fishing Tournament. The Doberman is the ultimo game dog and the Central Park affair is one of the glamour dogfishing tournaments on the circuit. There are teams entered from Mexico, Canada, Jamaica, New Zealand, plus four American groups including one headed by actor Jimmy Caan.

Stenreuther feels that Derveen's and Cooper's country smarts will fare better in the hills and dales of Central Park than the usual urban guide street smarts. He may be right. Or he may not. Stenreuther looks like a stereotype of the millionaire sportsman—and he is. A ruggedly handsome, highly skilled, dedicated man who is also a tournament caliber chess player, an ex-Olympic equestrian, a squash champion, and the author of a highly regarded history of wind instruments; he is quite a fellow.

**D**erveen is studying the Doberman carefully as Cooper puts the Dodge pickup in low and drives slowly up a grassy hill which will partially hide the truck from the dog's view. Derveen looks for earmarks first. High, firm, perky ears denote a great Doberman, a strong runner, a true fighter, and a possible grand prize winner. He talks to Stenreuther through a walkie-talkie. Stenreuther is sta-

tioned in the open part of the truck, ready to make his cast. "Unleashed Dobie sighted near 75th Street and Central Park West. Good ears, plenty of leg," says Derveen, making it sound almost exotic in his south Georgia drawl. Stenreuther acknowledges the message and adjusts the drag on his Pfister Special. He must make a fast decision on what kind of bait to use. Conservative dogfishermen still rely on fresh meat. Stenreuther isn't sure. "A prize Doberman is never overfed by its master," he says. "He doesn't always go for meat just because it's put in front of him."

He looks over his lures—the fake dog turd, the plastic vomit. "Good sniffing stuff, but it only fools the stupid ones," he says. There was also live bait to be considered. A big dog likes to play with a little dog or a kitten. Stenreuther had a toy Pekingese and a cute alley kitten on the truck. "With live bait, it's all in the chemistry," he says. "Will the dog be interested in fooling around with a cute little nipper? He may not be in the mood."

In the end, Stenreuther chooses a prime sirloin steak, well-marbled with fat. He's hoping this big beautiful Dobie is as hungry as a bear.

**S**tenreuther does a picture book cast with his sirloin, and the Dobie is all eyes and nose for it. At the same time, another piece of bait is cast toward the dog, an aluminum foil box that suddenly pops open to reveal a plate of calf liver and onions. It is a new kind of bait developed by the

General Foods company, that overpowers a dog with the appetizing aroma of freshly cooked meat. It is supposed to be irresistible. The Dobie now has two baits to choose from. The liver and onions belong to Jimmy Caan, who had sighted the dog from a different vantage point. He is wearing a shit-eating grin.

Stenreuther is angry but does not lose his cool. He maneuvers his raw steak skillfully around the steaming box of liver, poking it away each time the Dobie tries to bite into it. Caan is annoyed, then frustrated. The liver gets ice cold and rubbery. The onions slither off the plate and disappear. The Dobie has had enough teasing He goes right for Stenreuther's juicy sirloin and is hooked. Stenreuther's crew gives out their first yelp of victory. It looks like a clean strike.

The Dobie takes out about two hundred yards of Stenreuther's line when suddenly Caan leaps off his truck and sprints to the dog and attempts to wrestle him to the ground, rodeo style. It looks like Caan has gone berserk. He is well-known as a fanatical competitor in sports. He simply hates to lose. Even if he has to violate the rules. He is trying to get that Dobie any which way. The Dobie is having none of him, however. The animal seems to have the strength of a runaway horse, and he is dragging both Caan and Stenreuther's line up and down the hills of the park. Stenreuther is exhilarated and concentrating totally on keeping his line at the perfect tension. He wants the Dobie, with or without Caan at the end of it.

For three hours, Stenreuther stays with the Dobie and the crazy but persistent Caan—a total weight of perhaps 250 pounds. His hands are blistered and raw. Sweat pours through his flannel shirt. At exactly 7:35 in the evening, the Dobie breaks off, snapping the line, leaving a semiconscious Caan on the ground. It is all over. Stenreuther casts a lure to Caan and reels him into the truck. He gives the

actor a look of weary disgust, then sighs, shrugs his shoulders, and throws him back to the ground. "Not worth keeping," he says. "I'd sooner hold on to a poodle puppy."

Derveen and Cooper are quiet, subdued, in need of a Jack Daniels. But Stenreuther regains his good humor. "Hell, it's the fight that counts, isn't it? I still have the memories even if I don't have the dog."

# The Other Side of Dogfishing

Sammy Rodriguez is a sidewalk dogfisherman who uses a Hardy bamboo flyrod he bought by mail from London. He ties his own turds. "I do wet and dry. Real ones from a poodle I keep as a pet," he said. Rodriguez also keeps tiny pieces of garbage and other baits and lures in neatly stored mason jars. Sammy looks like he stepped out of an Abercrombie & Fitch window display, complete with waders, fishing vest, wicker creel, and a corncob pipe. "I don't smoke, but it looks so fine to dogfish with a pipe in your mouth," he said. "I saw a picture on a calendar once of a trout fisherman smoking a pipe while landing a big one. I wanted to look just like him."

Sammy is a member of an elite group of dogfishermen who shun the big game park stuff and never use trucks or cars. They prefer extremely light flyrod equipment and fish right on the street. Sammy uses parked cars as a cover or "blind" and will cast his turd or perhaps an exquisitely made dry or wet cockroach into a spot where he thinks a stray dog will show up. He only fishes for strays, the wild, lost mongrels of New York City who roam the streets looking for food in the manner of a school of trout swimming in a stream. Sammy wouldn't dream of wresting a dog from its owner.

Catching a stray is the only pure form of dogfishing, as far as I'm concerned." said Sammy. "It's you against the dog, one on one—with no unfair advantages—no trucks or cars to help you, no guides. Besides, I always throw the dogs back. Only time I keep one is when I'm really hungry. Then I like to panfry the dog on the spot. I skin it, dip it in flour, salt and pepper, and fry it up in butter. I've got this little barbecue pit I dug near the river, under the West Side Highway. My buddies and I have a dog fry down there sometimes. Next year when I get a little extra money, I'm going to buy a tent and a sleeping bag and we're going to camp out so we can get a real early start in the morning. That's the best time to fish for the real good strays, the dogs that roam around wild."

Roberto Valdes thinks Sammy Rodriguez is a *putz*, which is not a Spanish word. It is a Yiddish word for prick, a word he no doubt picked up in the garment center where he toils. Who is to say who is the real purist? Even Valdes admits that the exciting part of dogfishing is not the catch, but the intricacies of maneuvering the dog into your car amidst heavy traffic, pedestrians, police cars, fire engines, taxicabs, and other mysterious urban impedimenta. "Sammy's dogfishing is too faggy. And I can't afford that big game shit," said Valdes. "But try snaring a tricky little fox terrier on 125th Street and Lenox Avenue on a Saturday night. *That's* dogfishing." It's all dogfishing, Roberto. That's what makes it the best fucking sport in America.

*With New York City's hopeless financial problems, there is no money in the budget to hire a staff of dogfishing wardens. And so rooftop poachers have an easy time of it. All they need is a dropline, a Colonel Sanders chicken bone, and a bottle of Wild Irish Rose to keep them company.*

# Dogfishing, Compleat

Dogfishing can be done with just your basic equipment—a rod and reel and some bait. Even a dropline, if that's your game. But somehow it's much more fun dressing up a bit for the sport. It's a bit pretentious, but it makes you feel good to wear a pair of hockey goalie's gloves when you're handling an angry dog. Or a goalie's mask if the dog attacks you before you net him. And a big heavy-duty ocean spinning reel gives you a nice secure feeling when you're battl-ing a Doberman or a huskie. It's not that you can't catch them on a twenty-dollar reel. It just won't feel the same. Get the best stuff you can afford. Cheap stuff always costs more in the long run. Be an equipment snob. Especially if you're going for the big game dogs. Don't skimp on the proper protection. Remember: The catch isn't over until that dog is thoroughly subdued on your truck.

*Jack Stenreuther is ready to subdue an angry Doberman in his complete dog silencing outfit. His face is completely protected by an Acme goalie mask. For handling an un-cooperative dog before the kill, he wears hockey gloves by MacPherson and Smith. His nylon rubberized waders by Leach Brothers are bloodproof.*

*The essential tool in dog skinning is an extremely sharp knife. Unlike gourmet cooks, there is no argument here over carbon vs. stainless steel blades. Only the finest carbon steel knives kept at a haircutting edge by a professional sharpener can do the trick. Jack's knife by G. Herschel of Solingen, Germany.*

*A beautifully skinned Schnauzer ready for spit-roasting. Stenreuther's recipe: Marinate your Schnauzer in a mixture of oil, vinegar, soy sauce, garlic, chili powder, and cloves for two days. Then baste it with the marinade as you spit-roast it for three hours. Serve it with rice or potatoes, a green salad, and a big Bordeaux such as a Calon Segur or a Cheval Blanc.*

223

1

2

3

4

5

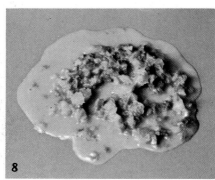

6

7

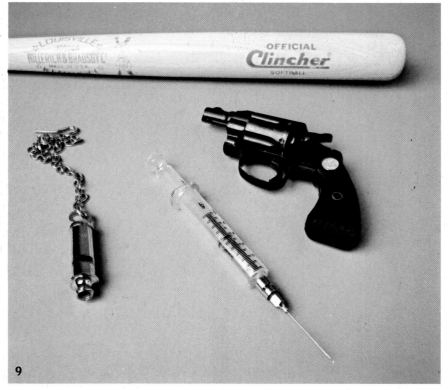

8

9

1. New York Times. *Good for the larger game. Use tabloids for medium-size dogs;* People, Oui, *other slim magazines for small dogs.*

2. *Fake turd also effective for dogs mentioned above and will work with small and medium-size Labrador retrievers and Airedales as well. Both lures by Bliddon.*

3. *Stuffed toy by Stenleitz. Appeals to playful dogs, especially mongrels.*

4. *Basic black postman's shoe complete with white sock. An old favorite that is still used in small towns. Shoe by Moblee, sock by Diamond Brothers.*

5. *The old reliable dog biscuit still works. A good steady lure for suburbs and shopping centers.*

6. *Garbage can be used as bait and also goes very well when attached to an artificial lure to create authentic smells.*

7. *Kitten. Named Rollo, out of Cleopatra, sired by McGinty. Used for live bait or as a dog tease.*

8. *The "hot lunch" fake vomit in superrealistic plastic. Ideal for terriers, dachshunds, cocker spaniels.*

9. *Snub-nosed .38 revolver handles vicious types. Official "Clincher" softball bat will subdue most small and medium-size dogs. Heavy duty hypodermic by Meditronics is perfect for instant tranquilizing. Whistle by Zemco works wonders, can be heard by dogs from miles away.* ☐

On the top of a hill on a tropical island in the South Seas, there was a statue of an airplane, all made of twigs and leaves.

Every day, Douglas Aircraft flew back and forth over the South Seas. With a blue sky around him and blue water below him, he flew over that little green island. But he was always too busy to notice things like the sky or the water or the island. He had work to do.

When there was a war, Douglas carried necessary things and important people to and from the battles. It was hard work, and dangerous, but Douglas always did his job, and he never expected any thanks.

He had one flying buddy, whose name was Curtis. Curtis was a melancholy twin-engine bomber with creaky landing gear. "I'm tired," Curtis was always saying. "What's it all about, anyway? I mean, who cares?"

"Do your job, and don't ask questions. Business is business, I always say," was what Douglas always said.

One day, during a very important mission, Douglas and Curtis flew together into a big white cloud, but only Douglas came out. "Tough luck, Curtis," thought Douglas, "but that's the way it goes. Good-bye, old pal, there's work to do." And on he flew.

After the war was over, Douglas went right on working hard. He got a job as a cargo plane, flying poppies to and money fro, across those same South Seas.

One morning, Douglas happened to look down, and he saw that the natives on one of the islands below had built what he was sure was an airplane statue in honor of him. "Isn't that nice!" he thought. "They have seen how hard I work, and they appreciate it! I will give them a real treat, and fly down close."

"They love me!" thought Douglas. "Some-day I must find time to visit them on their island. But not right now, because there is still a lot of important work to be done."

And there was, indeed, work to do, because soon there was another war. Douglas was busy carrying bandages and bullets and chocolate bars and officers and high explosives and famous comedians to and from the battlefront. It was just like the good old days.

All through this new war, Douglas worked hard every day, although it wasn't easy, considering the monsoons and the typhoons.

But now, whenever he flew over that special island where his statue was, he would look down and promise himself a holiday, just as soon as he was finished dodging rockets and not asking questions and doing his job.

Then, one day, as he was taking off from the battlefront, Douglas noticed that all of his passengers were generals and other brave leaders. So he knew that somebody had won the war, and that his job was over.

When the special island was below him, bright green in the sunshine, he thought, "This is my chance to pay a visit to those wonderful islanders, who love me!"

As he came in for a landing, the excited natives rushed out to greet him, with their arms full of fruits and flowers. Even Douglas's very important passengers seemed excited at this turn of events. "Perhaps there will be a feast!" thought Douglas.

And there was.

On the top of a hill on a tropical island in the South Seas, there are *two* statues of airplanes, all made of twigs and leaves.

# CLOO ®

**FOR 3, 4, 5, OR 6 PLAYERS/TERMS 6 MONTHS—LIFE.**

## Introduction

This game is unlike any other. All the characters are for real—even the victim. It is like real life.

The scene opens in Mr. Charley's vast real estate holdings. Mr. Charley is apparently the victim of foul play and is found in one of these locations.

The object is to find out the answer to these questions:
**1. WHA'S HAPPENIN'? . . . 2. WHERE AT? . . . 3. WIF WHA? . . . 4. WHO CARES?**
All players are assumed to be guilty until proved innocent. The player who, by someone else's deduction, absence, bad luck, stupidity, an act of God, physical disability, or any other reason cannot prove his innocence, loses the game.

This is accomplished by the players moving around the various locations and making blind guesses as to what they believe is the location, person, and weapon or combination of weapons connected with the doing in of Mr. Charley. This may reveal which cards are in the other players' hands and which cards are missing, or it may not. In any case, the cards are of little use, except that they may give a player something "on" another player. They may be bought or taken by force at any time. "Accusing" a suspect therefore has little to do with any of the original information.

One of the answers lies in the little glassine envelope resting on the abandoned lot in the middle of the board. There are, however, certain penalties associated with it, which may prove to be no answer at all.

## Equipment

The game board showing nine of Mr. Charley's more profitable holdings. Six colored tokens representing the suspects, all of whom are token. The colors of the tokens are closely associated with the names of the suspects:

| Suspects | Tokens |
|---|---|
| Col. Amal Nitrate $6^{7}/_{8}$ X | Black |
| Black Jack | Black |
| Reverend Jamaica Moan | Black |
| Mr. Jesus "Banana" Colon | Brown |
| Ms. Dolores O'Reo | Black |
| Ms. Blowjangles | Black |

Twenty-five moderate sized weapons and dice.

The pack of illustrated cards includes a card for each suspect, one for each of the nine locations, and one for each weapon.

There is also a pad of Detective "notebooks" to aid players in their investigations, which can be thrown away after the first couple of rounds.

Place the tokens anywhere on the board, provided they are not inside one of the locations. Stack the weapons in neat piles in *all* the locations. Place the glassine envelope, sealed, on the spot marked X.

Since the cards represent evidence, at least in the early stages of the game, they give players an advantage over

illustrated by Marty Geller

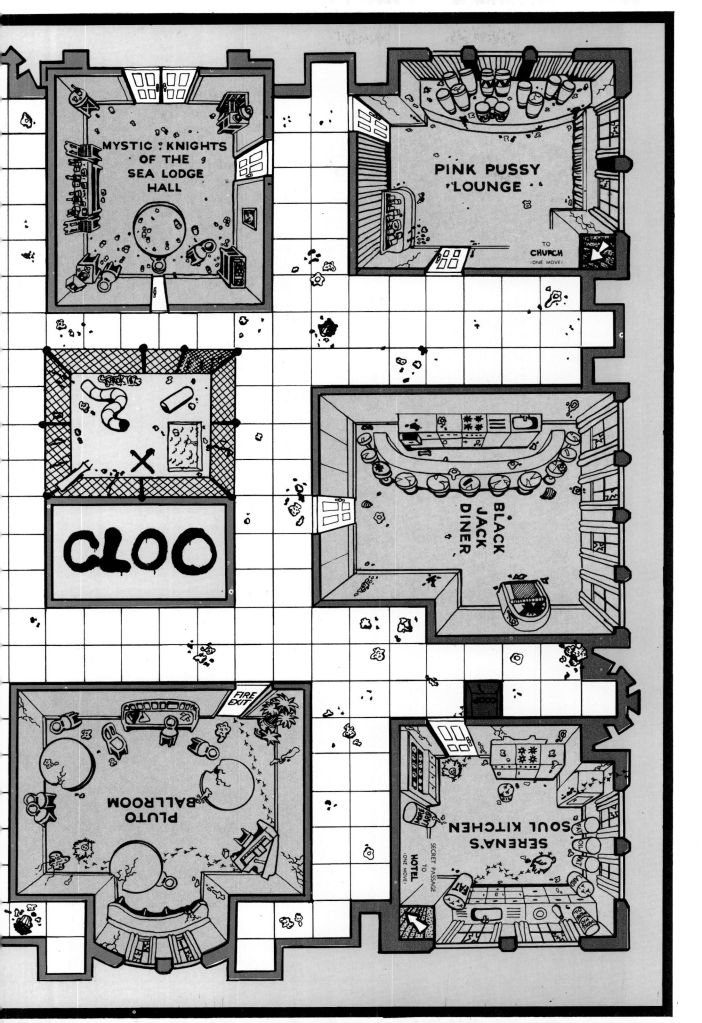

## ÇOLONEL AMAL NITRATE 6⅞ X

COLONEL AMAL NITRATE 6⅞ X

NITE VISITORS

## BLACK JACK

BLACK JACK

## MR. JESUS "BANANA" COLON

MR. JESUS "BANANA" COLON

# WEAPONS

| | | | | | | | | |
|---|---|---|---|---|---|---|---|---|
| blackjack | | | | | | | | |
| straight razor | | | | | | | | |
| shive | | | | | | | | |
| sword stick | | | | | | | | |
| 22. | | | | | | | | |
| 32. | | | | | | | | |
| 45. | | | | | | | | |
| 9mm. | | | | | | | | |
| sawn-off 12 gauge | | | | | | | | |
| sawn-off 16 gauge | | | | | | | | |
| sawn-off 20 gauge | | | | | | | | |
| saw | | | | | | | | |
| fire ax | | | | | | | | |
| ice pick | | | | | | | | |
| brick | | | | | | | | |
| fist | | | | | | | | |
| two-by-four | | | | | | | | |
| baseball bat | | | | | | | | |
| car door | | | | | | | | |
| car trunk | | | | | | | | |
| car antenna | | | | | | | | |
| car | | | | | | | | |
| A-train | | | | | | | | |
| gravity knife | | | | | | | | |
| gravity | | | | | | | | |

## REVEREND JAMAICA MOAN

REVEREND JAMAICA MOAN

## MS. DOLORES O'REO

MS. DOLORES O'REO

WELFARE $200

## MS. BLOWJANGLES

MS. BLOWJANGLES

one another. All the cards should therefore be dealt equally. Once the cards have been dealt, they may be bought, sold, or "seized."

The player who ends up with the most cards rolls the dice first.

# Movement of Tokens

To reach a given location, players may move their tokens on the "alley" squares anywhere on the board, according to the throw of the dice. If a player insists on going further than the number of squares indicated by the dice, or less, or simply refuses to budge, there is not a lot that can be done.

Tokens can move forward, backwards, or crosswise, but not come to rest on or pass through a garbage square.

# Moving Into a Location

There are three ways of moving into a location: (1) legally, through a designated entrance, (2) illegally, by smashing a hole in the wall, and (3) by extradition from another location, a method hard to enforce.

If the space at the entrance to a location is occupied by the token of a player, another player may experience difficulty entering the location, depending on the number of cards held by the player occupying the entrance, his physical size, and his mood.

# Moving Out of a Location

There are three ways to move out of a location: (1) legally, through a designated exit, (2) illegally, by smashing a hole in the wall, and (3) by burning that part of the board containing the location.

# The "Insinuation"

Whenever a player moves into a location, he can, if he dares, make an "Insinuation." An Insinuation consists of naming a Suspect, the Weapon or Combination of Weapons, and the Location into which the player has moved. *As soon as a player makes an Insinuation, the token of the suspect named is supposed to be brought into the location named.* Good luck.

**Example:** The player representing Ms. Blowjangles may reach the Black Jack Diner. She then calls a Suspect into the Diner (if he or she can be found or will cooperate) and the weapon or weapons she is insinuating were used. She might thus say: "I insinuate that it was *Black Jack* in the *Black Jack* with the *blackjack.*"

# Proving the Insinuation True or False

It is at this stage that the evidential or controlled portion of the game usually ends, and the pyschological or uncontrolled portion begins.

The subject of an Insinuation may take either of these two courses. He may calmly attempt to show that the cards he has in his hand, or those he suspects to be present in the hands of others, prove his innocence. Or he may become enraged, attempt to bluster his way out of the situation, and threaten physical violence.

A player wishing to make an Insinuation should bear this in mind; he or she should also remember that consistently *not* making an Insinuation may indicate (*a*) weakness or (*b*) guilt and thus infuriate one or more of the other players.

In any event, all these reactions to an Insinuation can be used in building the case against a potential victim.

# The Accusation

When a player is satisfied that, irrespective of the truth, he can build a case against a specific player, he can, on his turn, make an Accusation. To indicate that he is about to make an Accusation, a player must read the accused his Miranda Rights.

# Miranda Rights

You have a right to remain silent.

Any statement you do make may be used as evidence against you.

You have the right to have an attorney present while you are being interrogated.

If you cannot afford an attorney, one will be appointed for you by the court.

The accusor *must* have finished a reasonably understandable reading of the accused's Miranda Rights for the Accusation to be valid. If the accused can make physical contact with the accusor, or otherwise silence him before he has completed the reading, the Accusation is null and void.

**Note:** For the above reasons, it is usually best to make an Accusation when the accused is in the bathroom, getting a beer, detained by force, or out replacing the envelope (see below).

# Copping a Plea

Upon being successfully accused, the accused may either (1) cop a plea, or (2) protest his or her innocence.

If a plea is copped, the accused pleads guilty to a lesser included offense, loses five turns, and returns to the game.

If innocence is protested, the rest of the players form a jury of his peers, elect a foreman, and decide on the guilt of the accused. The accused may attempt to influence the outcome of this decision by any means he wishes, including money, rhetoric, surrender of some or all of his cards, and the use of force.

If guilt is established, the game is over.

If some other arrangement is arrived at, the accused returns to the game, and it continues.

# The Answer

At any point during the game, if a player is sufficiently confident of his or her position, they may open the envelope in the center of the board and consume the contents. The contents, however, *must* be replaced. The player forfeits five turns or the time it takes to replace the contents, whichever is greater.

Any player taking this course, however, should remember that it may impair his ability to challenge an Insinuation or Accusation, or even to return to the game at all.

# Interesting Notes and Hints

After the first Insinuation has been made, it is inadvisable in most situations for a player to resort to evidential rules. Rage, force, and negotiation are much more likely to achieve results.

It should be remembered that since Mr. Charley is dead, and there is no decisive means of knowing who did what to him, where at, and whif wha', guilt can only be established by agreement among the players. Players must realize that in the larger sense, they are *all* guilty, and that that guilt extends to everyone, even those who are not playing the game, never wanted to, or never heard of it, and if they had, would think it dumb. The crime of the guilty party is our crime, the crime of society, the crime of humanity.

Have fun.

# ZOO TRAMP MARIE GETS PUT AWAY!

by ED SUBITZKY

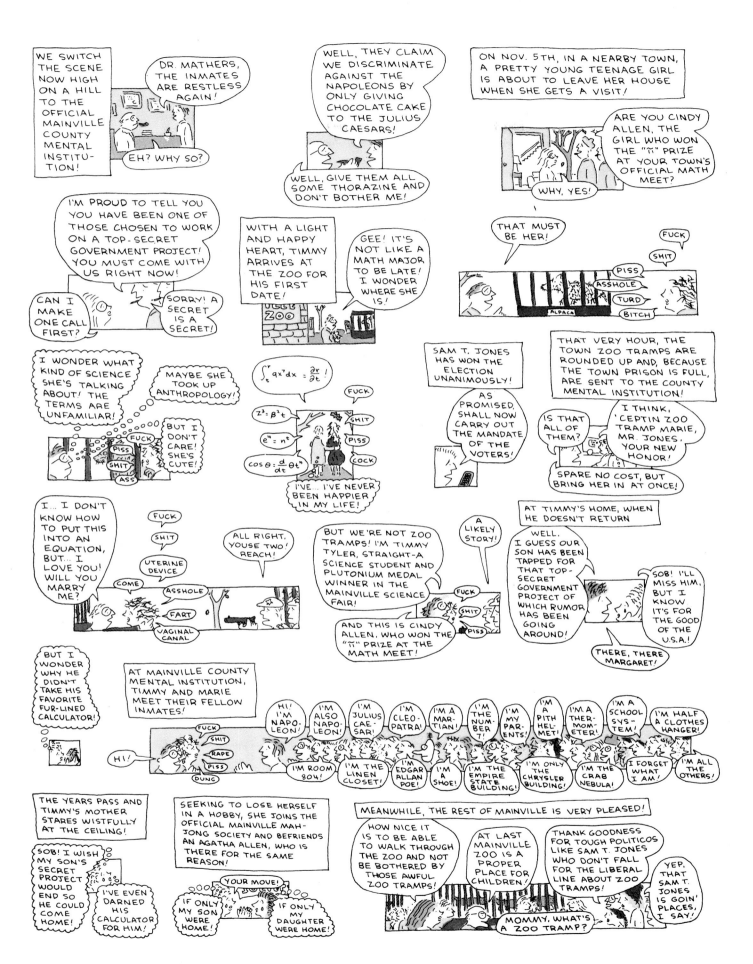

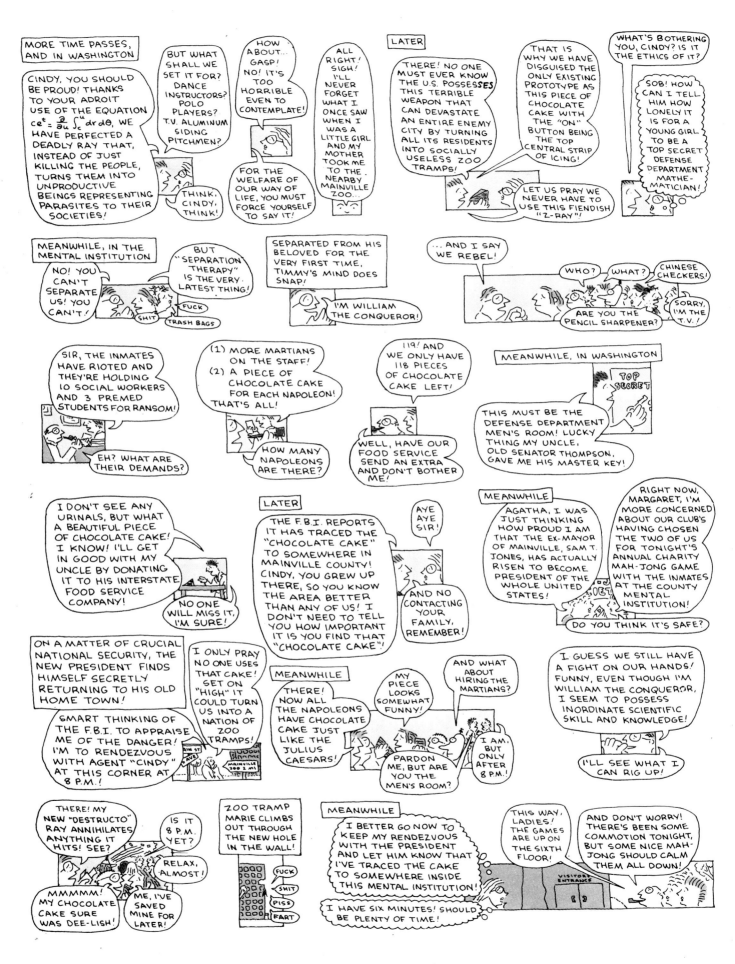

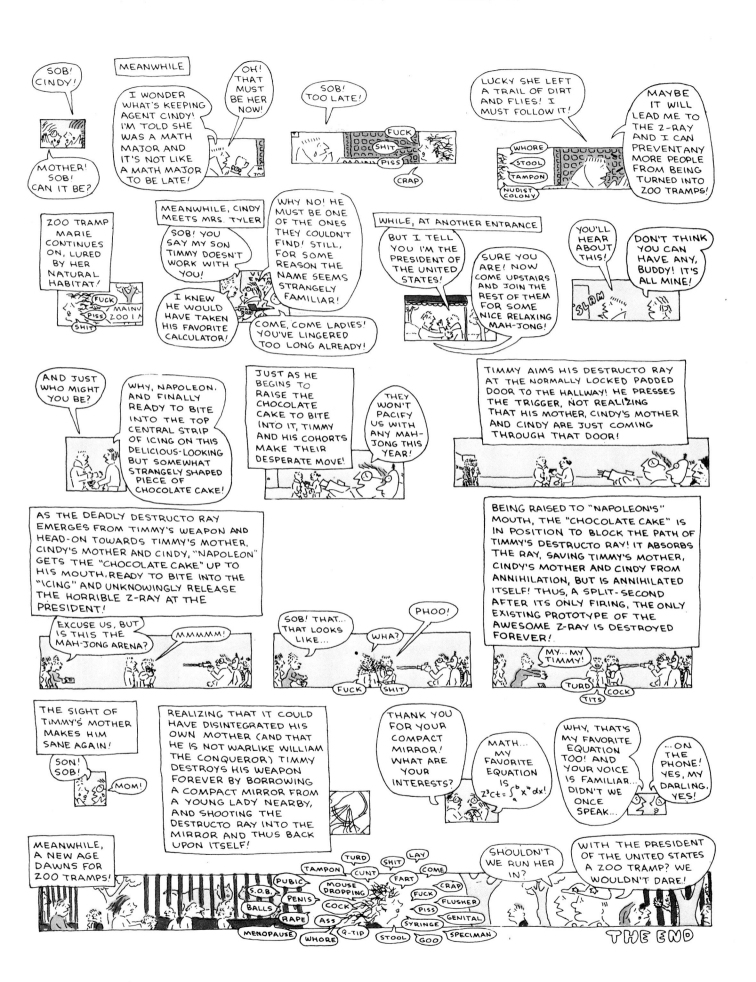

# CONFUSIONS of an ADMAN

**by Jed Cohen
as told to Gerald Sussman**

Hey, you're Gerry Sussman, right?
*Right.*
Jed Cohen.
*Oh yeah. How are ya? You still at J. Walter?*
Yup. You still at the *Harvard Lampoon?*
*National Lampoon.*
How ya doin' up there? Hey, you guys do some really crazy shit. What was that thing you did? That picture of Kissinger naked, like a *Cosmopolitan* spread. Was that your idea?
*No.*
So what are you doin' at P.J.'s?
*Waiting for someone.*
Let me buy you a drink. Jesus, I haven't seen you in what, three years, at least. Since you left J. Walter.
*How is it at J. Walter?*
Same shit. Hasn't changed since you left. You're lucky, man. You're lucky you got out. It's a jerkoff. I don't know what the fuck I'm doing. I don't know what's good from bad anymore. I've got some stuff on the air now that I'm ashamed of.
*What is it?*
I won't even tell you.
*That's O.K. I don't watch much television.*
The fucking business is so *boring* now, man. It's deadly. It's all run by the research people. You can't even take a piss without checking it out with them.
*It was pretty bad when I was there.*

It's worse now, man. Nobody gives a shit about being creative anymore. Your stuff has to test out good with the research people, that's all. That's why most of the stuff on the air now is so deadly. I don't write ads anymore. I write position papers. That's the secret, man. You don't create an ad, you *position* it in the market, and you back up the position with a couple of buzz words. I spent six hours in meetings today with the account people and the research group on some buzz words for Scott toilet paper. That was my day. I wrote one new word. Big deal. Tonight I'll come home and I'll be fucking exhausted. All I do is eat dinner, talk to the wife and kid for a while, and fall asleep in front of the TV set. I'm a zombie. Writing one word takes a lot out of ya.
*When you're bored, you get tired faster. Boredom is very enervating.*
I know, man. I know. That's why I gotta do my screenplay. It's the only way I'll ever get out of this fucking business. I'm tired of being a hired gun.
*What are you writing?*
It's hard to describe. It's like a combination love story and comedy, with a lot of action in it.
*Sounds nice.*
If I tell you what it's about, don't say anything to anybody. You know how easy it is to get ripped off. Anyway, it's

like a takeoff on *Taxi Driver.* Did you see that movie? Great fucking movie. My story is about a pair of identical twin brothers who buy a cab. One drives it by day, the other by night. And they each have these crazy adventures and they fall in love with the same girl who thinks they're one and the same guy. It's a crazy idea. It's still mostly in my head. I got a lot of notes on it. I shpritzed the idea to this movie lawyer and he flipped. He can't wait to get my outline. He says he can get big bucks for me to write the screenplay. Who the fuck knows? It's all a crapshoot, man. One out of a million scores. Everyone I know is writing a screenplay. I'd like to have a dime for every screenplay in every copywriter's drawer on Madison Avenue. Or if they don't have a screenplay, they've got an outline or a treatment or an outment or treatline or whatever they call it. They all want to get out and score Hollywood. They're all working on their screenplays during office time—like me.
*What happens if their boss finds out?*
The boss is working on a screenplay, too. The elevator operator is working on a screenplay with the guy who runs the candy counter in the lobby. I swear some of the cleaning women are using the IBM typewriters at night working on some great new ideas for Jack Nicholson. Anyway, nobody finds

out about it. You just have to be careful. You don't leave your manuscript scattered all over your desk. You work on one page at a time, and that page is in your typewriter. If someone comes into your office, you roll the page down until the words are hidden. You never leave any notes or pages on your desk. You never know when a snooper will come in. You know, the guys who like to poke around your desk, read your memos, look at your copy, your storyboards, whatever. I hate those guys. And if you leave your office, even to go to the john, you put the screenplay in your drawer. Never, never leave anything on your desk that you don't want to be read. Shit, you know that. You wrote in the office, didn't you?

*Once in a while, when it was slow. Listen, why can't you work at home?*

C'mon, will ya? It's impossible to work at home. Do you have kids? You have no kids, right? You're not even married. Then you don't know about distractions. Look, I don't get home until seven-thirty, eight o'clock. Then I got to talk to my wife, my kid, eat dinner, have a few drinks to unwind, maybe a few glasses of wine with my dinner—you know. I got into the habit of drinking a little wine with dinner. They got these great California wines, they're better than a lot of French ones. Then there's always something to do around the house. By the time I'm ready to write, it's after eleven and I'm falling asleep. I used to doze off and bang my head on the fucking typewriter. No decent writer can work at home. I should really have a separate little office. Or a studio apartment in Manhattan, so I can write all night and sleep over. But then I'd be tempted to bring broads in.

*So how are you going to finish your outline?*

I don't know. Maybe I'll get up very early and work from 5:00 to 7:00 A.M. Some guys can do that. Maybe I'll work in the office after six, a few days a week. Maybe I'll just kill myself, I don't know. It's a vicious cycle. I don't know how I got into this fucking business.

Actually, I *do* know how I got into it. Probably the same way you got into it. For the money. You never really wanted to be in the advertising business, did you? Right. You always wanted to be some kind of writer, right? Me, too. I was a creative writing and film major in college. I wrote and directed. I was going to be the next Orson Welles and Stanley Kubrick put together. Did you know I made a short while I was in college that was nominated for the Toronto Film Festival? It wasn't a bad film. It was a satire on the sixties' commune trip. I was into the hippie thing like everyone. I did

this film about a guy who lives in a commune but is very lazy, won't do any work. He's a real eccentric. All he wants to do is grow a penis out of the soil, as if it were a plant. He starts with his little seeds and plants and waters them every day. All the people in the commune make fun of him because nothing happens. But he sticks with his little plant. Then one day, he wakes up and sees his cock plant sprouting something. Every day it gets bigger and bigger, and sure enough, it's a real cock growing. It gets bigger and bigger like the Jack in the Beanstalk story. But this time the people aren't making fun of him anymore. I won't tell you how it ends. It's a cute story. It's a fantasy. I can get a screening for you at the agency if you ever want to see it. It's only a ten minute film.

Have another drink, Sussman. I'm going to have another one.

God, I can't believe it. I did that short thirteen years ago. That means I've been in the advertising business almost as long. I started out by writing free-lance, you know. I told you I majored in film, so naturally I was writing screenplays as soon as I graduated from college. I wrote five screenplays in less than a year and couldn't sell one. Nobody wanted to take a chance on a first script. It's not bankable, they would say. Only established writers are bankable. How the fuck can you be an established writer if you don't sell your first script? It was *Catch 23,* man. It was unreal. I couldn't deal with it. And I wrote some great shit, beautiful dialogue, crazy characters. But nobody reads a script. Nobody can read more than two pages. They got an attention span of nine seconds in Hollywood. Forget it, man. I thought I could make it as a writer...you know...*real* writing. Nobody gives a shit about writing. The movie business is strictly for hustlers, for politicians. You got to be a snake, a cobra to make it in bubbleland. That's what I call Hollywood. I thought I could make it on talent alone. I was naive. So in a year and a half, I was on my ass. My unemployment ran out and I had a wife and a kid. That was my first marriage. So I bump into this old college buddy who's working for Y & R, and he practically begs me to take a job as a copywriter-producer. What the fuck, I say to myself. It's not the end of the world. I was only twenty-three. I'll still be writing and I'll be getting a regular salary every week. I don't have to buy the specials at the supermarket. I can eat anything I want. And I'll stop living like a rubber band that's always about to snap. You know, waiting for my agent to call with good news, or trying to weasel an advance out of somebody. Fuck it. I couldn't take that kind of

rat race. I was starting to get hives, migraines. I was too young to die.

What's wrong with a little security? Especially when you're married and have a kid. So you figure you'll hang in the advertising business for a while and make a few dollars. Meanwhile, you can always write screenplays on the side and go back to Hollywood on your own terms in a few years.

*Everybody promises themselves they'll only be in the advertising business for a few years, but most of them end up in the business forever. That was our mistake, Jed. We should have gotten out years ago.*

Wait a minute, Sussman. Actually, it wasn't so bad in those days. In the sixties, when you went into advertising you weren't exactly working in a wasteland. Don't be so judgmental. I'll tell you something. I didn't have to rationalize that much. I enjoyed myself in those days. The business was incredibly creative. In fact, it was probably the most creative area for a writer to work in, so don't bullshit me about selling out. I don't have anything to apologize for. Man, those were the golden days. Doyle Dane, Wells, Rich. Carl Ally—everybody was doing great stuff.

I got a theory. When advertising is really creative, it's *the* most important art form. Right. I really think it's an art form. Think about what we were doing in those days. We were creating the Existential Minute. That's my name for it. Like everything you do in an hour-and-a-half movie, we did in one minute. In sixty seconds or thirty or even ten seconds, we packed in a fucking human drama, a human comedy, plus music, fantastic sets and great acting, memorable faces. And at the same time we were *selling.* We not only entertained, we sold a product and we sold it well. In those days, a lot of people liked the commercials better than the programs on TV. Remember? We did miniature movies, and we did them better than the real ones. Your script had to be perfect. Not an ounce of fat. Not one extra word. It was like *haiku.* Every gesture, every camera move was designed to convey one thing—the memorability of the product. And we were really far out in those days. A lot of shit we started was picked up by the movies—quick cuts, rack focus shots, throwaway funny lines like Howard Zieff used to do for Alka-Seltzer. You know, his commercials of the sixties are much better than the movies he's making now. He was the master of the throwaway line, the comedy vignette. We were living out our dreams by writing and producing commercials, man. And we actually had fun. No shit. It was the swinging sixties, baby. Everybody was making big money, moving fast from one agency to another, grabbing an Art Director's award here, a Clio there. A young punk in the business for a year, with one award-winning commercial, could go from ten to thirty grand in one move. In six months he could be making fifty grand.

You remember how we used to work in those days? Dope was much cheaper, so you bought five, six ounces a week. You and your art director could get stoned first thing in the morning, drink two double chocolate malteds, eat a box of pretzels, write a couple of wild TV spots, and then go look for someone to ball for the rest of the afternoon. Sometimes you had a meeting with a client, so you sobered up. But you always told the client exactly what was on your mind. You were the expert, not him. If they didn't like your ideas you told them to take their account elsewhere. We didn't need any research people to tell us what was good or bad.

Every major magazine had stories about our ads and commercials. Remember Alka-Seltzer's "Try it, you'll like it" spot? I really made that line work. They wanted to say, "Try it, you'll love it." I told them to use the word *like*. There's a big difference. A lot of my best stuff never went on the air in those days because it was too far out. It was much funnier than the

Alka-Seltzer or Volkswagen stuff. I wrote the funniest commercials in the world in those days. After I won a few awards I was approached by an art director and an account man to form our own agency. Remember that agency I had? Passalaqua, Cushing, and Cohen. Ruggiero Passalaqua, the art director on TWA, and Pierpont Cushing, Pete Cushing, the TWA account man, they approached me after I won a couple of Clios and asked me to be a partner in their new agency. Cushing was this old line WASP with great connections in drugs and package goods. He had a couple of ten, fifteen million dollar accounts in his pocket, and we were pitching five or six more. The plan was to build up the billing to about thirty million in a year, then go public, sell our stock, and make about a million each. I never knew the details, but the idea sounded pretty terrific to me.

Everybody was forming their own agency in those days. We developed our own philosophies of advertising, everybody thought he was really unique. Marshall McLuhan was hot shit. We were like gurus, man. Except nobody knew anything about business. Passalaqua took money from the till to pay for his penthouse apartment and Meledandri shirts and models that he used to take on shoots. Cushing was an alcoholic whose con-

nections all dried up and I was in the middle of an expensive divorce, two very expensive girl friends, a summer house in the Hamptons, and a $10,000 sports car that was in the repair shop every Tuesday and Thursday. So after six months, Passalaqua pulled out and got a job as a director for Screen Gems at a hundred thou a year, Cushing committed suicide when the world discovered he was a transvestite, and I developed a writer's block and a four-day-a-week psychiatrist habit. In six months, P,C,&C was down the toilet and yours truly was out on the streets.

Suddenly, it was 1971, and the fucking recession hit us bad. People were getting fired right and left. The clients were cutting their ad budgets in half. They were checking every penny we spent. The streets were lined with copywriters, art directors, producers, account men—it was wall to wall unemployment. Once in a while a job opened, but in Chicago or Cleveland or Dallas. Who the fuck wanted to go out of town? Everybody went nuts. Everybody got very political, remember? Very protective of their accounts. Very paranoid. The agency business got very uptight. Everybody was afraid of getting fired if they did one commercial that didn't have the product on screen for sixty seconds. Nobody was having any fun anymore. Even the dope supply dried up. Everybody got very serious, or half-serious. Man, I used to get ideas like Niagara Falls. Nonstop. I could do an entire campaign in a half a day. I once knocked off nine print ads in one morning. Three of them ended up winning awards. I thought I was a bottomless well of ideas. And I could design ads as well as most art directors. Between you and me, there's only three or four good art directors in the whole business. Most of them have an IQ of about minus nine and can barely choose a typeface, much less come up with an idea. So when I developed my writer's block, when I started to dry up, I thought I was going to join Cushing and take a pound of Seconals. I was a fucking basket case for three months. Took uppers, downers, and in-betweeners. Had to give up my apartment on East Sixty-third, my car, my summer house, almost everything. I had to move to a tiny apartment on the West Side, and on top of everything I was impotent. I don't mind saying it. I'm not ashamed of it. Happens to the best of them. Couldn't get it up for over three months. Nowadays, no one cares, but in those days it was terrifying. I had nightmares, dreams that I was really a homo and that men really turned me on. I had this strange thing about looking at men's crotches. I couldn't do it. I got very self-conscious about my crotch

MAY, 1971

"They got me, Lennie—I'm wounded."

S.GROSS

or other guys' crotches. I didn't want to even pass my eyes over them. I couldn't take a piss in a public bathroom if someone else was in the room. I was ashamed of my dick, man. I hated it. I thought it let me down. It took me a long time to realize that the sickness was in my *head,* not in my cock. My head was really fucked up, man.

It was all tied together with my writing problem, you know. I mean, my writing was my way of getting a hard-on. You know what I mean? I could always get a hundred ideas a minute. Like, I could always get it up, get the ideas up. That's why I always hated the advertising business. Because it was so fucking easy for me to come up with ideas. I mean, the whole business is like that. It's all so fucking slick and easy. One idea is just as good as the other. There's no real difference. You could just say Polaroid is a nice camera and still sell a million Polaroids a year. You don't have to be clever. But I used to be so fucking clever. I was arrogant. A real wiseass. Because I had contempt for the business. The whole business of advertising as an art was just a big front, a big rationale to cover up the contempt we all had for it. Deep down, we all hated it. So we went out of our way to be clever, to parody old movies in our commercials, or do all kinds of tricky photography. And if you ran out of ideas, you commissioned someone to write a song, a jingle. We told each other how wonderful the business was because we could take so many trips when we shot commercials. We lived for the trips. A lot of us even had steady girl friends in California because we'd go there every month. Remember L.A. in the late sixties? We once had a party that lasted for nine days. We had just finished a long shoot, a two-minute commercial that took three weeks to shoot. I don't remember why. We must have had a lot of rain days. Anyway, we all decided we needed a vacation after that, and we rented a house in Malibu and just partied for almost two weeks nonstop. Somebody told me that Manson and his family showed up at the party. I don't remember. I was too stoned to remember anything.

That's what we really liked—the trips, the long lunches, the expense accounts. We liked it until it was three in the morning and you were drinking Margaritas that were giving you heartburn and smoking dope that wasn't making you high—I mean, that's when we used to look at each other and say, "What the fuck are we doing in this business?" God, I used to sit in the Polo Lounge of the Beverly Hills Hotel at three in the morning and get an instant ulcer just thinking

about what I did that day. What kind of shit I had to go through. Like casting for a butler who would be in a cookie commercial, bringing his master some cookies and milk. Should the butler be English or American? Or should he be a rough, tough gangster type like Mike Mazurki, all dolled up in a fancy uniform? You wouldn't believe how many days we would argue about what kind of character the butler should be. He would be in the commercial for three seconds, three seconds...saying something like, "Your Nabisco scum wafers, sir," or something like that.

And we spent days figuring out what type of butler he should be. As if anyone really gave a shit.

You'd think we were making *Jaws* the way we used to come on. We would audition a hundred guys to find a memorable face, like Fellini does. Except Fellini always found memorable faces and we always ended up using the same half a dozen people. Not too ethnic, but not too bland. Or if you're using a spokesman, he had to be dynamic without being threatening. His face had to be interesting but not quirky. He had to inspire trust but couldn't be too slick. Who was that perfect guy? I never found him. Gregory Peck wanted too much money and Gary Cooper and Spencer Tracy were dead. The client was never really

happy with anyone we chose. And then, after a while everybody in your commercial had to be middle of the road looking with maybe one token spade, and he had to be more middle of the road than anybody.

God, I used to look at my expense account and throw up. Sheer guilt. Jewish guilt. I couldn't believe I was spending all that money over a thirty-second spot with one or two nice camera moves, a moderately interesting script, and a couple of actors who hardly had to do anything. And for this I was getting a nice salary, padding my expense account, getting laid, smoking dope, tripping acid, whatever. Then if I won a Clio for the commercial, I would make believe it was all meaningful. Bullshit. You know those awards are just jerkoffs. They've got one for every category, every type of commercial in the business. Everybody wins something.

That's when we started calling the business a craft. That's what it probably is, a craft. You do have to have some skills and taste, but so does a basket maker. A carpenter has ten times more skill and integrity. A plumber is doing more useful work.

I was using my craft to convince people that Turdley soap is better than any other brand. As if all soap isn't exactly the same. It gets your body clean, right? And when you wash

*"Hey! We eat on that table!"*

it off you're finished with it. And when you sweat you smell a little funny and no soap or deodorant is going to hide it. Who's kidding who? So you have to make up elaborate rationales to explain the fun and excitement of your job, the importance of your *craft*. Shit, you can learn your craft in six months if you're a decent writer. It's a business. That's what it is. All you have to do is suspend any guilt about the shit you're selling. Just tell yourself it's as good as any other shit on the market, which is usually true. So you might as well convince people to buy your brand of shit since they have to buy something, right?

Have another drink, Sussman. Your date isn't here yet.

I don't know, man. I had to learn to live with myself in this business. Especially after my breakdown and my writer's block. That's when I had to make all kinds of adjustments. The fucking glory days were over, man. In '71 I went to J. Walter Thompson with my tongue hanging out, begging for any kind of job. You wouldn't believe it. I won six Clios, four Art Director awards, a couple of Andys. I had commercials in every fucking film festival. But I was lucky to get a job for $25,000.

I got to say that they did treat me with kid gloves at J. Walter. I did have a big rep even though my ideas didn't flow out like Niagara Falls the way they used to. You start repeating yourself when you're in the business too long. Anyway, they gave me fancy assignments. I was too creative to work in the day to day stuff. They would use me on new business presentations or to help out accounts that needed creative, offbeat stuff.

I was a troubleshooter, which is the perfect way to write yourself into a corner and become an orphan. Nobody really wants your help, even if your ideas are better than theirs. Everybody wants to protect their little domain. It doesn't matter how creative you are; if you don't have your power base, your own group working under you, you're shit. And the only way to get a power base is to do some politicking. And you know I was never any good at ass-kissing. Frankly, I was just too good a writer to worry about politics. That's when I really started hating the business, when I knew I had to do some politicking to survive. That took more out of me than working on nineteen campaigns at once.

That's when I started looking at the whole thing as if it were a game. I became very detached, very removed from the whole thing. I was Mr. Cynic. "You want six pounds of ads with this headline, fine." "You want a pound and a half of this type of commercial—you

got it." Don't ask if it's good, just do it, wash up, get your money, and go home. I realized that it wasn't quality that was important. Anything will work and sell the product. It's how you play the game. I started drinking with the big account men. Then I socialized with them. I got invited to parties at their houses. I was divorced and in between wives, so they actually liked me better because I had plenty of girl friends, and if I played it right, I could even fix up some of them—the ones who wanted to be fixed up. I mean, I really did a number—pimp, whore, sycophant—you name it. Finally I was made a VP and group head, and my salary went up to forty-five Gs. So big deal. What did I really gain out of the whole thing? Did I really enjoy playing the game? The whole point of it is that you have to enjoy it. Some people actually enjoy it. You have to get an aesthetic thrill out of it—like playing chess with human chess pieces. Well, I'm not that kind of a game player. My game is tennis, not office politics. What happened was I started gaining weight and getting high blood pressure. I had to go on all kinds of crazy diets and my weight used to go up and down like a fucking Yo-Yo. I also lost most of the hair on top of my head. I had to do the bushy sideburn look. I also went out of one-to-one psychiatry into group stuff and encounter therapy. That worked for a while—you know, yelling and screaming and letting out all the frustrations. But that stuff is only temporary. You can't solve your problems by screaming at people three times a week. You gotta make your big move or get off the pot.

*Why don't you just quit? Take six months and finish your screenplay. What the hell. What do you have to lose? This way, you can concentrate on it full time and really find out if you can make it.*

Great. It's easy enough for you to say. You write for the fucking *National Lampoon*. You can do anything you want and get paid for it. Who the fuck is going to pay me while I'm writing my screenplay? So I've got a little money socked away. O.K., I'm not doing badly right now. Between this, that, and the other thing, I'm good for over fifty grand a year. But I've got a lot of responsibilities, man. I can't quit just like that. I've got to write on my own free time and leave on *my* terms. Listen, I just bought a summer house in the Hamptons. Now I got two mortgages, plus my alimony and other payments to the ex-wife, plus private school for the previous kids, plus education for my new kid. I've become a money-making machine, not a writer. And here's the thing. I *like* my summer house, I like the Hamptons. I

like the quality of my life, and I don't feel like chucking it for a chance to sell a screenplay or a TV series. I've got a lot of fucking responsibility, and frankly, I'm scared to risk it all. Do you blame me?

It's easy for you. You're not married, are you? You have no kids. My kids don't know from screenplays. When they open the refrigerator, they want to see their fucking peanut butter in there. And milk and Twinkies. And I want to see my lox and cream cheese, man. I don't dig starving, especially with the price of food these days.

What about *you*, Sussman? Why don't *you* go write a screenplay or a novel? Your stuff isn't getting any better these days. I think the whole magazine is getting stale. I think you're repeating the same old shit every month. I read it every once in a while. You all used to be much funnier. What happened to all that craziness? You guys weren't afraid to take chances, to dump on anyone. Now the magazine is so fucking tame I can send it to my *bubbe* in Miami Beach. Don't tell me about selling out, man. We all do a little selling out. If we don't, we have to eat supermarket chicken and fatty hamburgers. Fuck you, Sussman. Buy your own drink on the next round.

Shit…I'm sorry. I don't mean to be judgmental about your situation. I'm sure you've got your own set of problems. Actually, it's still a pretty good magazine. I know how hard it is to be funny every month. Look at the "Saturday Night" show. They have to be funny every week. Here, let me buy you another drink. What are you doing later? Maybe we can have a bite to eat. Your person you were supposed to meet hasn't shown up, anyway. Listen, man, I got a few numbers I can call. A couple of girls in my office, these junior copywriters. They'd love to go out with me and a guy from the *National Lampoon*. They love the fucking magazine. They're like groupies. You want to get laid? There's a very good chance you'll get laid.

Fuck me, what am I saying. I really should go home. I'll miss the 7:54 and then I'll really be late and I'll have to make up a phony excuse. Actually, I love my wife. Great lady. Still has a better body than 98 percent of the girls in my office.

Is that your friend over there? O.K.…I guess I better go myself. Give me a few bucks for your share. That's fine. Hey man, let's not lose touch. I'll call you for lunch next week. Wait a minute, next week I'll be in London. We're shooting three commercials in London. It's cheaper than doing them here. No, no. I never take my wife on trips. Business is business. So I'll call you when I get back. Take care, man. Write funny.  □

# The Ballad of Pulp and Paper

*(A tribute to our suppliers.)*

BIG 'BABE' BLUE OX

BIG PAUL BUNYAN

Of the great Northwest where brave men quest
For power and pulp and gold
Where the tales are all like the timber tall
There are many sagas told,
Of the lumberjacks with the singing ax
And the wolf that learned to swear
But the strangest tale on the sawdust trail
Is of Paul and the Crazy Bear.
Now the trees that grow in the Land of Snow
Were put there by You-Know-Who
To be scaled and topped and sawed and chopped
And ground to a mushy goo
Which becomes the stuff to make paper enough
For wrappers for bubble gum
And almanacs and paperbacks
And paper to wipe your bum.
Big Paul was the best in the whole Northwest
At ridding the land of trees
Of all shapes and kinds to enrich young minds
And the paper companies.
But one winter's day as he hacked away
Beside Babe, his big blue ox,
This hideous bear roared out of his lair
And challenged Paul to box.
"You're stupid and bad and money-mad
And your harvest is rack and ruin,
But you'll deal with me before your next tree!"
Cried the ecocrazy bruin.
They fought to the death, and with Paul's last breath
He howled, and the mountains chorused
The touching plea of the industry:
"Only *you* can prevent a forest!"

Cancer Ward

# EARTH MOTHER NEWS

### AN ALTERNATIVE BUNDLE OF SKINS WITH MARKINGS ALL OVER THEM

## THE DANGERS OF FLINT CHIP POLLUTION

### BY SHAMAN HUNGRY ROCK TASTER

THE OTHER DAY AS I WAS MAKING A WALK, I SAW IN MANY PLACES CHIPS OF FLINT WAITING FOR THE FEET OF THE PEOPLE. THESE ARE NOT THINGS THAT PASS AWAY. FLINT CHIPS LINGER LIKE A WOMAN BEFORE HER REFLECTION IN A SILVER POOL OR A MONKEY.

THE CHIPS CUT NOT ONLY THE FEET OF HOLY MEN, BUT THE GULLETS OF OUR NEANDERTHAL BROTHERS WHO TRY TO EAT THEM.

NOT LONG AGO, ONE OF OUR GREATEST POETS, HAIRY FART WOMAN, BROUGHT TO ME HER HUSBAND, WHOM THE PEOPLE CALL "GRUNTER" (HIS NAME IS BRAVELY FORAGE). HE WAS IN TERRIBLE PAIN FROM EATING THE DEADLY FLINT CHIP, WHICH HE FOUND IN AN ABANDONED BARTERIST CAMP NEAR THE SINGING RIVER.

BAD ENOUGH THAT THESE MULTITRIBAL DEATH MERCHANTS SHOULD MAKE A FORTUNE TRAFFICKING IN FLINT AND BRONZE ADZES, BUT THAT THEY POISON OUR NEANDERTHAL BROTHER IS HORRID EVIL BADNESS.

AS I SANG TO THE GODS AND MADE A GREAT SACRIFICE (EATING NO BARK FROM GODDESS TREE THAT NIGHT), BRAVELY FORAGE SQUATTED IN TERRIBLE AGONY IN THE BACK OF MY CAVE, EATING HANDFULS OF MOSS AND YOWLING IN PAIN. AS THE SUN ROSE, HE FINALLY EVACUATED THE FLINT CHIPS, THE MOSS, AND MY CAVE.

IT HAD BEEN A HARROWING ORDEAL FOR MYSELF AND HAIRY FART WOMAN, THE SCREAMS NEAR THE END OF BRAVELY FORAGE'S ORDEAL ATTRACTING MANY CAVE BEARS. IT IS NOT AN EXPERIENCE THAT ANY OF US WOULD WANT TO REPEAT, BUT IT WILL HAPPEN AGAIN AND AGAIN UNLESS WE STOP THE DEADLY FLINT CHIP POLLUTION THAT IS SLOWLY POISONING OUR PLANET. IT DOESN'T MATTER WHETHER YOU WORSHIP SUN, RAIN, RIVERS, OR BIG MUD BALLS, ALL MEN WHO RESPECT GOD MUST JOIN TO OPPOSE THIS TERRIBLE DANGER TO OUR WAY OF LIFE.

SURELY THERE ARE ALTERNATIVES TO FLINT. ROCKS, PIECES OF WOOD, MUD, SAND, DIRT, LEAVES, AND DEAD BIRDS ALL MAY MAKE FLINT SUBSTITUTES. WE MUST BEGIN TO USE SUBSTITUTES AND TO LET THE TRIBAL COUNCIL KNOW WHERE WE STAND.

## ATMOSPHERIC TESTING OF FIRE MAY TURN EARTH INTO A LIVING UNDERWORLD

### BY SPOTTY MUSIC BOY

PICTURE A WORLD WHERE THE TEMPERATURE IS 70 DEGREES, SO HOT NO LIFE COULD SURVIVE. IMAGINE WALKING THROUGH CLOUDS OF INKY BLACK POISON, BREATHING THROUGH HANDFULS OF WET MOSS, STINGING EYES CLOSED AGAINST THE PAIN, EASY PREY FOR TOOTH TIGERS. THIS IS WHAT SHAMANS TELL US MAY HAPPEN IF ATMOSPHERIC TESTING OF FIRE CONTINUES.

SOME SHAMANS ARGUE THAT ALL THE FIRE IN THE WORLD WILL BE USED UP LONG BEFORE DISASTER STRIKES; BUT WE KNOW SO LITTLE ABOUT THE WAY FIRE WORKS — IS IT WORTH TAKING THE CHANCE?

FIRE, WHICH UNLEASHES THE SPIRITS LOCKED WITHIN WOOD, IS CURRENTLY BEING USED BY THE BARTERISTS AND THEIR MULTITRIBAL AGRARIAN ALLIES TO BURN DEAD ANIMALS AND TO DANCE IN FRONT OF. THIS BEHAVIOR CAN ONLY ANGER THE GODS, ACCORDING TO MOST JUJU MEN. WHAT WILL HAPPEN THEN? SOME SAY WE WILL BE EATEN OR CRUSHED BY BIG JAGGED ROCKS LONG BEFORE THE WORLD IS DESTROYED.

THERE ARE OTHER ARGUMENTS AGAINST THE USE OF FIRE. WHY SHOULD WE BE SETTING FIRE TO VALUABLE STICKS WHEN THEY ARE A MAIN FOOD SOURCE OF OUR NEANDERTHAL BROTHERS?

YET THE BARTERISTS WHO CONTROL OUR TRIBAL COUNCIL (ALREADY PEOPLE ARE CALLING THEM "THOSE WHO SIT CLOSE TO THE FIRE") PLUNGE BLINDLY ON TOWARDS DESTRUCTION.

THE BARTERISTS ARE OPPRESSING ALL OF US. TREETOP NO CAVE, A WISE OLD PERSON OF TWENTY-FIVE, SAID, "PRETTY SHELLS ARE THE ROOT OF ALL EVIL." HE KNEW BARTERIST OPPRESSION, AND DEMANDED WE RETURN TO STEALING, THE NATURAL WAY. SO WE MUST, IF WE ARE TO AVOID DISASTER. YOU SAY YOU WANT EVOLUTION? WELL, YOU KNOW....

## PICTOGRAPHS TO THE EDITOR

DEAR EARTH MOTHER,
I JUST THOUGHT I WRITE IN AND TELL THE HORDE THAT IF ANYONE HAS BACK PAIN, IT IS PROBABLY FROM WALKING UPRIGHT. WALKING UPRIGHT IS COMPLETELY UNNATURAL AND IS BOUND TO CAUSE PAINS TO ANYONE WHO TRIES IT.
THE NATURAL PEOPLE, OUR NEANDERTHAL BROTHERS, ALL WALK ON THEIR KNUCKLES AND VERY RARELY HAVE BACK PAIN UNLESS THEY HAVE BEEN SPEARED BY A SPECIESIST FEUD-MONGER. GOOD-BYE NOW,
RUNNING MOSS PERSON
BY SLEEPING TREE

DEAR EARTH MOTHER,
WE JUST HAD A TRAGEDY IN OUR HORDE. MY MAN MATE, WILL-HE-LIE-DOWN, TOOK UP THE DANGEROUS PRACTICE OF BATHING, AND STOPPED MOVING. WE DECIDED TO HAVE A NATURAL FUNERAL FOR HIM WITH NO FRILL. SOME OF US TOOK TURNS HOWLING WHILE THE OTHERS ATE HIM RIGHT WHERE HE LAY. IT WAS A BEAUTIFUL EXPERIENCE FOR ALL OF US AND WE FEEL LIKE MUCH MORE OF A UNITED HORDE NOW. I WANT TO HEARTILY RECOMMEND NATURAL FUNERAL RITES TO ALL MOTHER'S READERS AND ALSO PRAISE MY MATE'S TASTE.
GONE AWAY NOW,
WANDERING SIDEWAYS
NEAR MOUNTAINS

DEAR EARTH MOTHER,
ONE PROBLEM HAS BEEN VERY MUCH ON MY MIND, BUT I AM WRITING TO YOU ABOUT SOMETHING ELSE. THAT IS OVERPOPULATION. IT IS MAYBE OUR WORST PROBLEM BESIDES VANISHING CAVE BEARS. PEOPLE ARE BEGINNING TO CLUSTER IN FIXED DWELLING PLACES. IF THIS CONTINUES SOON THERE WILL BE NO FORAGE. I KNOW THAT EACH MAN NEEDS AT LEAST TWO THOUSAND NEW CUBITS TO SUFFICE A HORDE OF THIRTY. WE MUST SACRIFICE MORE CHILDREN OR WE WILL ALL DIE SOON.
SHAMAN TREE SPIRIT
MUD FLAT

DEAR EARTH MOTHER,
WE ARE SERIOUSLY CONCERNED ABOUT THE BREAK-UP OF THE PRIMAL HORDE. THIS BASIC SOCIAL UNIT IS CRUMBLING RAPIDLY AS THE BARTERIST-CONTROLLED TRIBAL COUNCIL IS DAILY PASSING NEW INCEST TABOOS. IT IS ALREADY ILLEGAL FOR A FATHER TO MATE SONS UNDER EIGHT MONTHS. SOON THERE WILL BE A LAW AGAINST SONS KILLING FATHERS AND MATING MOTHERS. WE MUST SERIOUSLY ORGANIZE TO FIGHT SOMETHING.
ξ16 DIRTY HAIR HORDE
NEAR SINGING RIVER

## THE NEANDERTHAL

HE IS OUR BROTHER
NOBLE KNUCKLE WALKER
HE TROTS FINGERS AND TOES
IN TUNE WITH NATURE
WE SHOULD NOT DISCRIMINATE AGAINST HIM
CALL HIM NO-LOBES
NAME HIM GRUNTER
HE IS OUR BROTHER
AND OUR HUSBAND

— HAIRY FART WOMAN

11 ← PAGE THIS MANY

## EARTH MOTHER NEWS

SHAMAN HUNGRY ROCK TASTER
EDITOR

SPOTTY MUSIC BOY
MANAGING EDITOR

BRAVELY FORAGE, HAIRY FART WOMAN, DENTED SKULL ELDER, WOMAN WITH SORES, COUGHING ONE

PETER BIG OFFICE
ART DIRECTOR

T. MANN, J. GREENFIELD
VERY IMPORTANT ONES

ξILL PISSED OFF
ADVERTISING

A. ANTONOFF
LETTERING

## OFFICES

ALL OVER AND AROUND DOWN BY THE RIVER UP IN THE MOUNTAIN NEAR THE BIG JAGGED ROCK JUST ANYWHERE, ANYWHERE REALLY. THE ENTIRE CONTENTS OF EARTH MOTHER NEWS ARE COPYRIGHT © YEAR OF THE FALLING MUD BY THE HORDE WRITING COLLECTIVES. NO WORDS OR OTHER MAY BE REPRODUCED IN WHOLE OR IN PART WITHOUT PERMISSION OF THE HORDE BOSSES. IF YOU WISH TO BE AUTHOR IN HORDE WITH DIRTY MANUSCRIPT, COME OVER TO OUR OFFICE AND YOU CAN BE AN EDITOR, AND WEAR SKIN ON YOUR HEAD.

## DOMESTICATING ANIMALS: ARE PEOPLE NEXT?

### BY BRAVELY FORAGE

SOME PEOPLE ARE KEEPING AN ANIMAL WITH THEM. THERE IS NOTHING WRONG WITH THAT IF THEY LIVE AS EQUAL. MAKING LOVE IS BEAUTIFUL NO MATTER WITH WHAT. BUT TO MAKE ANIMALS DO THINGS IS WRONG. LIKE THE PEOPLE WHO WANT TO MAKE MY BEAUTIFUL NEANDERTHAL BROTHERS AND SISTERS WALK UPRIGHT, THE ONES WHO WISH TO MAKE ANIMALS CATCH FOOD ARE THINKING WRONG. IF THEY MAKE ANIMALS DO THINGS, SOON THEY WILL MAKE PEOPLE DO THINGS.

BARTERISTS CONTROL OUR TRIBAL COUNCIL, AND UNTIL WE HAVE THROWN THEM OVER, WE WILL BE OPPRESSED BY THEIR ACTING. THEY SAY BASKET WEAVERS SHOULD WEAVE BASKETS. LET ME TELL ALL THE PEOPLE. BASKET WEAVERS OUGHT NOT TO HAVE TO WEAVE BASKETS FOR OTHER PEOPLE JUST BECAUSE OTHER PEOPLE GO OUT AND FORAGE. BASKET WEAVER OUGHT TO SEIZE FOOD AND KEEP THE BASKETS, TOO.

CON'T PAGE NUMBER THIS MANY → 𝍭𝍭𝍭 𝍭𝍭 𝍭𝍭𝍭 𝍭𝍭

---

## WHAT IS GOING ON NOW HERE

### PLOWING DISTURBS BALANCE OF NATURE

SHAMANS ARE SAYING THAT "PLOWING," THE PRACTICE OF TEARING UP THE EARTH AND BURYING FOOD IN IT IN THE HOPE OF SEEING MORE FOOD, IS ANGERING THE SPIRITS OF THE EARTH AND THE TREES.

THIS WANTON INTERFERENCE WITH THE LAND IS UNNATURAL AND UNHEALTHY AND WILL PROBABLY RESULT IN THE COLD COMING BACK AND MORE VOLCANOES LIKE THE ONE THAT BOILED TWO WALKS AWAY NEAR THE TALKING ROCK.

### FIXED DWELLING PLACES ANGER GODS

THINKING PEOPLE ARE DEMANDING STRICT NEW TABOOS AND THE ENFORCEMENT OF OLD ONES TO PREVENT SOME FROM STAYING IN SAME CAVE FOR TOO LONG, OR WORSE YET BUILDING A HUT WHICH RUINS THE NATURAL NATURESCAPE.

WE MUST MAKE SOME GREAT SACRIFICE TO APPEASE THE GODS, WHO ARE ANGRY AT THE FOOLISHNESS OF MEN AND THE "HUTS" SOME BUILD.

### DIETARY LAWYERS FIGHT UNNATURAL FOODS

DIETARY LAWYERS WORKING WITH EARTH MOTHER NEWS ARE LEADING A BATTLE TO PREVENT THE REPEAL OF OLD TABOOS AGAINST EATING BURNED MEAT BY THE BARTERIST- CONTROLLED TRIBAL COUNCIL.

LAWYERS SPOKE TO THE ELDERS, ALL OF WHOM ARE DODDERING OLD ONES PAST TWENTY, BUT WERE UNABLE TO GET TOO CLOSE BECAUSE OF THE FIRE THE BARTERIST HAD BUILT TO DEFEAT THE WORDS.

ELDERS EARLIER REJECTED A PLEA THAT PEOPLE FOUND BURNING SHOULD BE CAST OUT.

---

## SOLAR HEAT WORKS BETTER THAN DANGEROUS FIRE

### BY WOMAN WITH SORES

ALL ABOUT ME I SEE THE BURNING OF FIRES AND MY HEART IS SAD, FOR THE TURNING AWAY FROM THE NATURAL WAYS OF THE EARTH.

SADDER YET, FOR THE SUN IS BY FAR THE BETTER WAY TO THE PREPARATION OF THE FOOD. HERE I OFFER A RECIPE FOR THE PREPARATION OF A GREAT WOLF, USING ONLY THE NATURAL HEAT OF THE SUN — NOT THE FIRE WHICH RENDERS THE AIR POISONOUS.

FIRST, SLAY A WOLF.

DRAG THE WOLF TO A HIGH POINT NEAR YOUR CAVE.

LET THE WOLF SLOWLY BAKE UNDER THE RAYS OF THE SUN FOR THREE WARM DAYS.

YOU WILL FIND THE MEAT OF THE WOLF TENDER; IF YOU COLLECT EIGHT LEAVES FROM A TREE AND PLACE IT AROUND THE WOLF'S CARCASS, YOU WILL SURROUND IT WITH A FLAVOR NO WORDS OR STONES CAN DESCRIBE.

SOME COMPLAIN THAT WHEN THE SUN FALLS BEHIND THE HILLS, THE WOLF MEAT WILL GROW COLD. YES — BUT IT IS THE WAY OF THE EARTH. IF THE GODS WANTED US TO DEVOUR WOLF MEAT WHEN IT IS DARK, THEY WOULD HAVE MADE THE SUN SHINE THROUGH THE NIGHT.

YES, WE STILL MAKE TOOLS THE OLD-FASHIONED GROUND STONE WAYS.
DO NOT BE TEMPTED BY THE CHIPPED STONE AND POLISHED STONE TOOLS THAT ROB
YOUR TOOLS OF THE MAGIC THAT FELLS TREES AND BEARS.
REMAIN TRUE TO THE WILL OF THE GODS!
COME TO THE THIRD CAVE PAST THE CARCASS OF THE MASTODON.
(WE ACCEPT YOUR MATE OR LIVE FEMALE CHILD.)

## CLASSIFIED

BIG BOULDERS OVER HERE. JUST COME AND HELP YOURSELF. THERE'S LOTS. COME OVER ANY TIME. NEAR THE RED CLIFF.

I KNOW WHERE THERE IS GOOD FORAGE. IF YOU WANT SOME, YOU HAVE TO HELP ME MOVE A BIG ROCK. YOU GET HALF OF WHATEVER IS UNDER ROCK. NO FINGER WOMAN.

WANTED: VOLUNTEERS TO TROOP TO AFRICA. EXCELLENT FORAGE, WARM CLIMATE. EVENTUAL PROMOTION TO NEGRO A POSSIBILITY. WANDERING LOON

DOES ANYONE WANT A DEAD BIRD I FOUND BY THE RIVER? I DON'T WANT IT ANYMORE. ANYONE CAN HAVE IT. JUST COME AND GET IT. I WILL BE WANDERING NEAR THE PITS THURSDAY BUT SHOULD BE BY THE BLACK GROVE FRIDAY. I WILL TAKE YOU TO BIRD. "GRUNTER"

BIG UGLY MAN, KNUCKLE WALKER, WANTS INFANTS OR ANYTHING AT ALL TO EAT. FATTIES, PLEASE. SHAMAN X

### WHEN CAVE BEAR IS DEAD

WHEN CAVE BEAR IS DEAD
FOREVER GONE
WILL NOT LIFE BE POORER
MORE AWFUL
WHEN CAVE BEAR IS GONE
WILL NOT WE BE UNHAPPY
WILL NOT GODS BE ANGRY
EARTH BE ANGRY
MOON BE ANGRY
AIEE, WE WILL BE EATEN!
— HAIRY FART WOMAN

### DEATH MERCHANT

THEY COME IN WAR
MEN WITHOUT EXTENDED FAMILIES
TO TRADE IN BRONZE ADZES
(SO THEY'RE CALLED THE SHINING DEATH)
THEY KILL OUR CHILDREN — THE NOISY ONES
THEY KILL OUR CAVE BEARS — THEY KILL OUR
NEANDERTHAL BROTHERS. WOE. WOU.

---

### PRIDEFUL WALKING ON TWO FEET GOES BEFORE FALL
#### BY DENTED SKULL ELDER

BY THE LAST BROKEN MOON, I SAW WALKING BY THE EDGE OF THE WATER A YOUTH WHOSE BLOOD FLOWED WITH THE JUICE OF SPURT-HOPE. HE WAS WITH A WOMAN OF STILL-CLOSED OPENING, AND HE WAS POSSESSED TO SHOW HIMSELF BRAVE BEFORE HER THAT SHE MIGHT LET HIM OPEN HER.

THIS YOUTH TOOK HIS ARMS AND HELD THEM HIGH IN THE SKY, AS IF TO MOCK THE GODS OF TREES AND THE SKY, AND SOUGHT TO MAKE A WALK ON HIS TWO REAR LEGS ONLY. I CALLED OUT TO WARN HIM OF THE ANGER HE WAS MAKING WITH THE GODS, BUT HE LAUGHED AND SCORNFULLY CRIED, "YOU ARE AN OLD MAN OF PERHAPS TWENTY-THREE, AND YOU COULD NOT SPURT ENOUGH TO FILL THE OPENING OF A NORM!"

A FEW BLINKS LATER, THIS LAD LOST HIS BALANCE, PLUNGING INTO THE WATERS WHERE HE WAS SWIFTLY CARRIED AWAY AND DEVOURED BY THE ANGRY GODS.

HEAR ME! OLD I AM, AND NONE THAT I HAVE HELPED TO BIRTH WITH MY SPURTS COME TO ME AND TELL ME OF THEMSELVES, BUT THIS MUCH I KNOW: TO WALK UPRIGHT IS TO MOCK BOTH THE TABOOS OF THE EARTH AND THE WISHES OF THE GODS.

IF YOU WALK UPRIGHT, YOU ARE SUPPORTED BY TWO OF YOUR LIMBS; IF YOU WALK NATURALLY, YOU ARE SUPPORTED BY FOUR; YOU HAVE MUCH LESS CHANCE OF FALLING.

IF YOU WALK UPRIGHT, YOU ARE MUCH FARTHER AWAY FROM THE EARTH AND CANNOT FIND THE ANIMALS TO EAT AS SIMPLY, NOR CAN YOU SEE THE ROCKS AND TREES AND DEAD TRIBE-SKIN AND SO YOU MAY WELL FALL OVER THEM AND KILL YOURSELF.

IF YOU WALK UPRIGHT, YOUR HEAD AND FACE ARE EXPOSED TO ALL OF THE EARTH'S FURY, AND BIRDS MAY FLY INTO YOUR FACE AND SWALLOW YOUR EYE. AND YOU WILL BE SEEN BY THE CAVE BEARS AND THE ENEMIES OF US AND MAY BE EATEN BY THEM AS A WARNING FROM THE GODS.

OUR WAY OF LIFE DEPENDS ON OUR OBEDIENCE TO THE WILL OF THE GODS WHO COMMAND THAT WE REMAIN CLOSE TO THE EARTH. FOUR-LEGGED IS FOREARMED.

# THE HIPE REPORT

## SHEERE HIPE

## A PURPORTED STUDY OF FEMALE SEXUALITY

**3,000 women, ages 14 to 78, describe "in their own words" their most intimate feelings about sex including:**

- What they like—and don't like—and, like, all that
- How orgasm really feels—and how it doesn't really feel
- How it feels not to have an orgasm, sex, fun, or even just a few laughs now and then
- The importance of post-orgasmic cuddling and snuggling
- And, the most unforgettable characters in their sexual lives

**With a few sulking interpretations of female sexuality**

## Questionnaire IV*

*March 1974*

NATIONAL ORGANIZATION FOR
FEMALE PERSONS,†
N.Y.C. CHAPTER
635 MADISON AVE., N.Y.C. 10022

### I. ORGASM

1. Do you have orgasms? Do you have sex? Do you think this is too personal a way to begin a questionnaire such as this?

2. If you do not have orgasms, do you feel sexually or psychologically inferior? Or do you feel it is "all right" to go through life without orgasms? Are you nuts?

3. Is having orgasms important to you? Would you enjoy sex as much without having orgasms? Would you enjoy orgasms as much without having sex?

4. Were you aware that "broads orgasm" was an anagram for "a smorgasbord"? How do you feel about this?

5. During which of the following do you orgasm?
masturbation:_____
intercourse:_____
manual clitoral stimulation by a partner:_____
intercourse plus manual clitoral stimulation by a partner:_____
intercourse with a partner, manual stimulation by yourself:_____
manual stimulation by a partner, intercourse with yourself:_____
oral stimulation:_____
oral stimulation of your partner's hand while he/she manually stimulates you while you have intercourse with yourself:_____
never orgasm, leave me alone and go away:_____

6. Is there more than one kind of orgasm? Do you know of a kind I don't know about? If I send you a self-addressed stamped envelope, will you tell me about it? Quick?

7. Please give a graphic description of what it takes to bring you to orgasm. Be specific. Draw pictures on the back of this sheet if necessary. Or, prepare a dramatic presentation. Feel free to use song, dance, mime, poetry, construc-

*Questionnaires I, II, and III were identical to IV, but I kept tearing the mimeograph master when I tried to put them in the machine.

†This project is connected with the National Organization for Female Persons, New York Chapter, only in that I hung around their offices and was able to steal both a ream of letterhead stationery and a copy of the key to the mimeo room, which enabled me to print the questionnaires. There was no funding involved, although I will return any of the letterhead stationery left over after the project, provided the book sells a lot and I become rich.

tion paper, tagboard, and papier-maché to express yourself.

### II. SEXUAL ACTIVITIES

8. What do you think is the importance of masturbation? Have you ever watched another woman masturbate? Would you like to watch me masturbate? In glorious full color, sixteen mm., for only $12.95?

9. Can you imagine women you admire masturbating? Can you admire women you imagine masturbating? Did you know that Golda Meir masturbates? What do you mean, "How do I know?" Don't you trust me? Do you mean to say that you're going to tell me everything about your secret, furtive, sweaty, depraved sex life and you don't trust me? I think that's rather weird, don't you? Be specific.

10. Do you enjoy masturbating? Physically? Psychologically? Sociologically? Geopolitically? Do you think masturbating is a political act? Who are you kidding, sister?

11. Do you enjoy masturbating half as much as I do? Can you possibly imagine how much I enjoy it? Go on. Guess. Guess how much.

12. How often do you masturbate? Where do you do it, i.e., in what part of the house or other dwelling? Please give a detailed description of your technique. Include everything: fingers, hands, props, positions, what you think about, etc. Can I come to your house or other dwelling to watch?

13. Does your partner stimulate your clitoral area manually? Orally? Do you enjoy this kind of stimulation? Or would you prefer other kinds, such as witty conversation or long walks in the rain?

14. Is breast stimulation important to you? Whose?

15. Do you like vaginal penetration/intercourse? Well, isn't it at least better than watching television? What position do you find most stimulating? What methods do you use to increase stimulation, e.g., long foreplay, "grinding," manual stimulation by a partner, "chopping," indirect stimulation by thrusting, "liquifying," "pureeing," etc.

16. What forms of nongenital sex are important to you? Kissing and hugging? Cuddling and "being nice"? Snuggling and "feeling close"? Have you ever tried nongenital masturbation, i.e., cuddling or snuggling with yourself? Is the best sex genital? Are the best genitals sexual? Do you ever secretly confuse the word *genital* with the word *Geritol?* Has this ever resulted in horribly embarrassing experiences? Please describe them in painful detail.

17. Can you believe that my man never cuddles me after sex? What, never? No, never. What, *never?* Well...hardly ever.

### III. RELATIONSHIPS

18. Rate the following in their numerical order of importance to sex:

passion
romance
candy and flowers
the Battle of Hastings
friendship
nonromantic love (deep caring)
sort of love but not really (very deep caring)
romantic liking (shallow caring)
the publication of *Uncle Tom's Cabin*
desire
economics
history of philosophy
trigonometry
acute hatred
bitter resentment
"triangular trade"
indifference
cuddling and snuggling and being nice

19. What is this thing called "love"? This funny thing called "love"? Just who can solve its mystery? Why does it make a fool of me?

20. Describe the first time you ever fell in love. Was it related to sexual activity, such as intercourse or "69"? Describe the first time you had a "crush" on someone. Was it related to sexual activity such as "making out," "necking," or "heavy petting"? Does a person get a crush only from heavy petting? If the petting were not so heavy, would this prevent the person from being crushed? If you fall in love on a person, will this crush him, too?

### IV. LIFE STAGES

21. How old were you when you first masturbated? To orgasm? To music? Did you know that I was twenty-nine? That I just "got it" two years ago? Isn't that pathetic?

22. How old were you when you had your first orgasm with another person? How old was the other person? How old were you when you had another person's first orgasm? How did you manage that?

23. What were your feelings about "losing your virginity"? How did you feel when you found it again? If not, i.e., if it is still lost, what are your feelings about that? How do you feel about your feelings?

24. Have you ever had sexual feelings for anyone in your family? Brothers or sisters? Parents? Have your parents ever had sex? Have they ever had children? What does this suggest

about you? Isn't it true that you are an orphan, found on the doorstep many years ago?

## V. THE ENDING

25. Have you ever faked an orgasm? Why? Are you at least believable? Have you ever faked arousal? Vaginal penetration/intercourse? Paying attention?

26. How do you feel about fellatio (oral stimulation of the penis)? To orgasm? How do you feel about "performing" cunnilingus (oral sex) on another woman? How do you feel about "performing" cunnilingus on the stage of the Metropolitan Opera?

27. Do you think your vagina and genital area are ugly or beautiful? What other parts of your body do you like or dislike? What are your favorite internal organs? Describe in detail your favorite square inch of skin. Do you think noses are silly, or okay? What about toes?

28. Have you ever been afraid to say no to someone for fear of "turning them off" or "making a scene"? Have you ever been afraid to say yes to someone because they "turned you off" or you "hated their guts"?

29. Do you think sex is in any way political? Do you think politics is in any way sexual? Have you ever had sexual relations with a politician?

30. What do you think of the "sexual revolution"? What do you think of the "industrial revolution"? The "French"? The "Russian"? Were these revolutions in any way sexual? You want to bet?

31. Have you ever had sex with a man simply because you were afraid to say no to him? Would you define this as rape? Have you ever not had sex with a man simply because you were afraid to say yes to him? Would you define this as impotence?

32. Do you live with a man? Is he as insensitive and as frustrating to live with as my man? Can I tell you about it, at length and in boring detail, until you want to scream?

# MASTURBATION

**"Do you enjoy masturbating?"**

**Most women said that they did enjoy masturbating, but that psychologically, it didn't seem like much more than masturbation, really.**

"Physically I enjoy it, yes. Psychologically, I don't know yet. I have tried time and time again to masturbate my psyche, but nothing seems to work. I usually just end up holding a vibrator up to my head and messing up my hair. Am I doing something wrong?"

"It super feels good, and everything, and I like it, because it's me and I'm into liking me."

"I like masturbation, yes, but I don't like the fact that I like it. I do like the fact that I don't like the fact that I like it, however, and the women's movement has helped me in this."

**Some women, however, felt guilty about it, and were thus unable to bring themselves to do it. Supposedly.**

"When I was a child, my twin sister was hit by a train while masturbating. Then the nuns told me I would go to Hell forever if I touched myself. I asked them what I should do, and they told me to touch them, so I did. I have never been able to masturbate since then. But at least I'm not dead, or a nun."

"Feel guilty. Can't do it. Tough shit. Fuck it."

**One woman—myself—was unable to masturbate to orgasm until two years ago.**

"I only thank God I've discovered how at last, and now I do it all the time in various locations throughout the city and the nation."

## TYPES OF MASTURBATION
## TYPE 1A

This was by far the most prevalent technique used. Basically, it entails lying on your back and using a vibrator, finger, hand, etc.

"I lie on the bed with my blouse on and buttoned, but my slacks or jeans open and unbuttoned but not off completely. I pull them down to about my knees—well, not all the way to my knee*caps*, actually, but to just above the caps. I mean that the seam of the jeans, just where the bottom of the belt path meets the rest of the garment, is approximately even with the top of my kneecaps. The belt is open, of course. The zipper is unzipped. Believe me, I've tried it with the zipper zipped, but it just isn't as good. My underpants are also down, but not as far as the jeans. I generally pull them down until the elastic waistband is even with a line segment containing the points which mark the midpoints of a line segment between the center of my kneecaps (assuming that the caps are actual circles, which mine are not) and the center of my thigh, even with the point at the very tip of my vagina. Then I set the vibrator to medium (Regulo 4), and touch it to my clitoris at a point just about an eighth of an inch off center. Then I come and come and come and come and come and scream like a lunatic."

"My parents were both born in Warsaw, so I prefer the 'Polish' technique. I hold my finger out in a stationary position against the clitoris, and have six strong potato farmers move my entire body back and forth in short, quick strokes."

"On back in bed. Vaseline on finger tip. Up-and-down rubbing. Massage breasts with other hand. Legs spread. Slap bare feet together in time to record on stereo. 'Night in Tunisia.' Dizzy Gillespie. Get excited. Squeeze legs together. Bite down on sheet. Orgasm. Do this for six hours."

"My mother was very frank about masturbation, so I have a very healthy attitude toward it. I like to make it an activity for my entire family. I lie on my back with my head propped up with pillows. My children stand to either side of me and toss rose petals all over my naked body. My husband sits beside me and feeds me Pepperidge Farm Milano cookies at regular intervals. I leaf through porno magazines as I stroke myself with one hand and play with a vibrator with the other. Sometimes I stroke the vibrator and my husband plays with me or himself or the children. It's very beautiful."

## VARIATIONS ON TYPE A—IA$_2$—IA$_5$

IA$_1$ Women who, during some of the time they masturbate, enter their vaginas, but leave soon thereafter.

IA$_2$ Women who, during most of the time they masturbate, enter their vaginas and stay awhile, perhaps taking snapshots or doing sketches.

IA$_3$ Women who, *all* of the time, enter their vaginas during masturbation and stay the night, leaving the next day with a promise to return some day.

IA$_4$ Women who occasionally enter their vaginas to obtain lubrication, only to be told that there is none, because "the energy crisis means that there is also a petroleum crisis."

IA$_5$ Women who enter their vaginas at the moment of orgasm, only to be told by a resentful clitoris, "Oh, so *now* you show up! After I do all the work!"

## TYPE II

Type II is the same as Type IA, but instead of lying on your back, you lie on your stomach.

"I lie on my stomach, and with the right hand commence to petting, teasing, urging, tickling, prodding, and stimulating the clitoral area. This is very difficult, since I can't reach the clitoral area when I lie on my stomach. It isn't very exciting, is it? No orgasm, either. No wonder I always fall asleep so quickly."

"Usually I lie on my stomach, with my left hand stimulating my left nipple. I rub myself back and forth on the bed. Sometimes, if I'm really horny, I actually put my nipple into my mouth. Or, I'll put my left hand into my mouth, and my nipple into my clitoris. Or, I'll put my stomach into my clitoris, and lie on my left hand. This last way is the most exciting, but the problem is that when I orgasm, it isn't the clitoris that does it. It's the nipple. Can you help?"

"I lie on my stomach, and use both hands. I sometimes try to use three hands, but cannot, as I only have two."

### TYPE III

Type III is my own personal type, which I am pleased to share with you at this time. I lie on my side, and place a satin pillow between my legs. Then I breathe very carefully to a count of one, two—one, two, three, four, and stroke my clitoris with a piece of fruit (peaches work the best!). But none of this helps until I concentrate on my favorite form of interpersonal stimulation, ie., cuddling and "being nice." After about two minutes of fantasizing about being held and snuggled and everything, I orgasm.

# ORGASM

"Orgasm is wondrous, a renewal of life energies and cosmic union with truest Being and essence, a divine upsurging of love and blissful emotion that makes me one with the utterly ineffable fact of the self-affirming beauty of life, and which makes me a better human being."

"Waves thundering in a chasm …flowers bursting toward heaven with color and fragrance…comets streaking across the mild night sky…trailing fire and magnificence…this is what orgasm means to me."

Sex consists of more than orgasm—there is also kissing, touching, and "feeling up." But now women are "allowed" to enjoy sex "too," and orgasm is "suddenly" "important." The "question," therefore, "is" this: "what" "is" "orgasm," "and" "how" "do" "women" "get" "it"?

### IS ORGASM IMPORTANT?

**Most women said that orgasm was important.**

"Orgasm is important."

"I would say that yes, orgasm is important."

"In terms of importance, I would think that orgasm has some."

"Importance-wise, yes, re: orgasm."

**But some women said they felt "pressured" to orgasm.**

"Sometimes my man stands over me with a horsewhip and says things like, 'You better come, you miserable bitch,' and I feel pressured, sort of."

"I've been with men who demand that I orgasm repeatedly to 'prove' my high degree of 'sexuality.' Fuck that! I don't need to prove *anything* to *anybody!* I'm too intelligent to need that

sort of crap, and anyway, I'm also too sensitive to have to prove how intelligent I am. Besides, I'm much too mature to think that sensitivity is related to intelligence in any sexual way. If men can't see how enlightened I am spiritually, tough. I say the hell with all their macho competitiveness!"

**Some women felt "left out" or even resentful if their partner orgasmed and they did not.**

"I have been married for twenty-two years, and in all this time, I have never orgasmed. My husband orgasms every time we have sex, however, and I do not think this is fair. I have been considering mentioning this to him, but am afraid he will call me a 'castrating bitch,' or other similar epithet."

"Dig this, cause when my lover comes and I don't, I feel pissed off and like resentful, and like I want to kill him, which like I did once. Wow."

In sum, most women feel that orgasm is important and desirable. And, based on the findings represented in the Masturbation section of the study, our conclusion is that women know how to bring *themselves* to orgasm quite efficiently. (I know I do.) Yet isn't it true that, as a rule, we still depend on men to initiate the activities of sex, and to "give us" orgasms? And isn't it true that, more often than not, they fail to do so—whether out of "inability," not caring, or plain ignorance? It is certainly true with the man in my life, let me tell you. And I've tried every way I could think of to communicate this to him. But he won't listen when I tell him face to face; no, he'll only believe it if he reads it in books. It makes you stop and think, doesn't it?

"Yes, it makes me stop and think."

"Absolutely. I have stopped, and now I am thinking."

### WHAT DOES ORGASM FEEL LIKE AND LOOK LIKE?

**"What does orgasm feel like?"**

"Throbbing, pulsating, electrifying, exploding, galvanizing, and so forth."

"Physical well-being, mental health, a positive attitude, and malice toward none."

"Wow! Yow! Ah, yahoo! Yippee! Zowie-zoom! Ka-zoom! Ah, ya-ha-ha-ha-ha!"

"Quite nice, or, rather, nicely."

"A complex of feelings, actually. My breasts seem to beckon through a haze of time. My vagina says yes to life. My clitoris beats out a primal jungle Morse of unleashed wantonness, and my thighs become twin stages on which the vast panoramic spectacle of human history is enacted before my very knees."

**"What do you look like during orgasm?"**

**Some women said they looked like animals.**

"My body arches, my legs flail about, my arms flap up and down, my head spins around in a complete circle, my mouth opens in a hideous grimace, my feet stamp up and down, and horrible noises come out of my nostrils."

"I grow a long tail and a tough, scaly outer skin, and large jaws lined with razor-sharp teeth. I look like an alligator, I guess. At least, that's what my husband says."

**But other women said they exhibited few obvious external signs of orgasm.**

"I look quite composed and self-possessed. At most, my eyebrows rise up. But even this is rare."

"My body becomes completely still, and remains that way for up to three days."

### IS ORGASM DIFFERENT WITH OR WITHOUT INTERCOURSE?

**Some women preferred clitoral orgasms to the "emotional" sort, suggesting that penile penetration resulted in a less satisfying orgasm.**

"Clitoral orgasms are sharp, clean, pure, whole, pear-shaped, complete, well-spoken, smooth, firm, and pleasingly proportioned. The other kind are vague, wide, airy, open-ended, evasive, hypocritical, self-contradictory, and lie while under oath."

"Clitoral orgasms are LSD, Jimi Hendrix, and a machine gun to the gut. Vaginal orgasms are chicken soup, Edith Piaf, and being pelted with bean bags."

**However, many women did enjoy the psychological and generalized body-pleasure of "emotional" orgasms—particularly the post-orgasmic phase.**

"After we make love, I like to lie there and fantasize, and pretend that we've just made love and are lying there fantasizing."

"When I come with Mike inside me, I know he is mine, and I am his, and we are together, and he isn't out banging that blond cost accountant who—oh my God, what am I saying?!"

"Emotional orgasm is nice, too, what with cuddling and snuggling and all."

These findings begin to suggest that orgasm due to penile penetration isn't all it's cracked up to be, no pun intended. This possibility, linked with the findings concerning masturbation, place the activity of intercourse in a very interesting light. Therefore, before we proceed any further, we must find out—once and for all—what women feel about intercourse itself.

# INTERCOURSE

We must now ask whether intercourse supplies sufficient stimulation to trigger orgasms, whether clitoral or "emotional."

### DO MOST WOMEN ORGASM FROM INTERCOURSE?

"I...I really don't know how to say this...I...you see, I...well, um..."

"I've spent two hours staring at this question, and have finally decided to admit it: no, most women do not orgasm from intercourse. I do, though. Sometimes."

"I do not orgasm from intercourse. I am afraid that may mean I am not normal. I would rather be normal than anything. In our society, it is very important to be normal. If one is not normal, one runs the risk of being considered abnormal."

"I find it difficult to have orgasms at all, let alone during intercourse. I grew up in a very restrictive environment, with a mother who was afraid of sex and a father who was afraid of bugs. I've tried many different strategies to get in touch with myself emotionally and all, but nothing seems to help. God, I'm so unhappy. You may not be able to tell, but my child was kidnapped just last week. My husband gave me this questionnaire just to take my mind off my troubles, but it's no use. I don't know what to do. Can you lend me a quarter?"

"Sex in utopia? My goddamn clitoris would be in my vagina, so I could come when I fuck! And my eyes would be in my mouth so I could watch while I eat! And my mouth would be in my urethra, so I could sing when I piss!"

"Frankly, I resent having to play with my clitoris every time I have sex. I am a forty-two-year-old woman, and I expect my clitoris to be grown-up enough to be able to play by itself while I have sex."

"I rarely orgasm when I intercourse, but I often climax when I self-stimulation."

**"Do you ever fake orgasms?"**

"I do fake them. Oh God, I do! I'm sorry! I know I've been living a lie all these years! Please forgive me! I'll never do it again!"

"Yes, I do. I am a very insecure person, and find it necessary to not only fake orgasms, but also to fake arousal, hunger, digestion, and respiration."

"I only do so during masturbation—and it never works. I always can tell when I'm faking it, and then I get insulted and hurt."

"Certainly not! If a man can't give me pleasure, and leaves me frustrated and irritated and keyed up and unsatisfied, let *him* suffer about it!"

**Some women said that they did** orgasm from intercourse, but frankly, I don't believe them. Take a look at these responses:

"Yes, I usually orgasm during intercourse. However, I must tell you that I am a compulsive liar, and nothing I say should be believed."

"Well, as a matter of fact, I do come during intercourse. But then, I also come during ordinary conversation, and from sneezing, too."

"Yes! I do! Is that what you want? Are you happy now?"

"I do come from intercourse. It's easy for me. You know why? Because I'm a man! I sneaked into your office and stole a questionnaire and sent it in! Ha-ha! Fuck you!"

### FINDINGS OF THIS STUDY

Do most women orgasm from intercourse? In fact, the answer is *no*. Only 30 percent of those women who have had intercourse reported that they orgasmed as a direct result of penile insertion and thrusting. The other 70 percent of those who responded said they orgasm from "some other cause."

**"If you can't orgasm from intercourse, what's the story with you?"**

Many women report guilt feelings, frustration, and self-condemnation, due to the fact that they cannot orgasm during intercourse. And so, many fake it. I know what they mean. I have been intercoursing since the age of thirteen, and not once have I ever orgasmed. At first I, too, thought it was me, that I was "hung up," "neurotic," etc. But discussion with friends and consciousness-raising sessions with sister feminists opened my eyes to the very widespread reality that *hardly anybody* orgasms from intercourse. I have since tried to communicate this to my lover, but you know how men are. He just wants to stick it in, pump it off, and come. Well, maybe by now he's beginning to get the message. And if he doesn't believe me, maybe he'll believe these reports:

"I've never come with a man inside me, but maybe that has something to do with the fact that I have this hate-hate thing for men in general, and have never met a man I really respect, and think that basically most men are inferior to me anyway, and have never actually had a man inside me, and have really never had sex with anyone, really."

"From clitoral stimulation, yes. From penis inside going in-out, no. Feels good when yes. Feels bad when no."

There are many reasons women give for not being able to orgasm during intercourse. They blame themselves, their family life, and society. They blame their bodies, their lovers, or some mysterious "reason." The fact is, women—most women—do not orgasm from "vaginal stimulation." And yet we have seen that women can orgasm from masturbation. This brings us to the next section of the study, in which we inquire as to what actually "works" for "women."

# CLITORAL STIMULATION

### HOW HAVE MOST MEN HAD SEX WITH YOU?

The following responses reveal that the overwhelming majority of sexual activity for women has been modeled after the reproductive pattern (dominated by the activities of the male) and consisting of "foreplay," "insertion," "thrusting," "orgasm," "finishing," "getting off," and "crawling over to the TV to see if the Yankee game is still on."

This is how women describe their usual sexual activity with men:

"Jabbing me with that thing."

"Shoving the pole in and out until I want to puke."

"Incessant poking with the stiff penile member."

"In the dark, crude fumbling, shoving it in, coming, The End."

"Kiss, brief fondle, suck tit, stroke mons, massage pubis, insert phallus, rhythmic undulations, scream, clutch, clench, come, faint."

"Most of the men I've slept with couldn't care less what I want or need. Or, if they said they did, it was certainly out of guilt, not out of any consideration for my feelings or pleasure. They have been cowboys, who jump on and ride, or hit men, who shoot bang bang (I'm dead!), or simply the usual run of male chauvinist pig creeps. It burns me up. I like sex. I like holding another body and sharing pleasure. I get off on it. So sue me. But men are a washout, a total loss, as far as I'm concerned. I can think of maybe one man who might be able to satisfy me, but he's been dead for two thousand years, physically speaking. At this point, the only partner I can really get it on with is the Mother Superior, and even she is beginning to get a little iffy about cunnilingus. Says the other sisters are beginning to talk."

Obviously, the classic male-dominated form of sex isn't providing what these women need. Then what does?

**"If intercourse does not enable you to orgasm, what does?"**

"Masturbation."

"Masturbation."

"Masturbation."

"Masturbation."

**"If your answer is 'masturbation,' why is this?"**

"Because only I know where it feels good."

"Well, basically, because my sensitive area sort of moves around a bit...usually it centers on my clitoral region, but when I am really stimulated, it moves up my thigh, onto my arm, etc. Once it moved over onto the clock radio, and once it went out the door, caught the F train uptown, and I finally caught up with it standing in front of that new Frank Stella at the Museum of Modern Art. What a turn-on, coming at the MOMA!"

"If you must know, it's because I'm the only one who knows just how and where to stimulate myself. Men have a penis you can usually see, and once you locate it, all they need is for you to stroke it until they come. But my clitoris is a tricky son of a bitch, and only I can handle it, ha-ha."

Evidently, most women feel they really don't need the classic form of "fucking" to attain orgasm. And indeed, these findings seem to be confirmed by "common knowledge." It is not very surprising to discover that most women masturbate, and are able to do so to orgasm. And it is certainly not very shocking to learn that many women (in fact, most) do not orgasm from standard intercourse. But, by putting these two facts together, the conclusion we reach is, I would say, profound:

*Women do not need men for sexual satisfaction.*

### DO WOMEN NEED MEN FOR SEXUAL SATISFACTION?

No, I already said that they do not.

### MY GOD! WHAT DOES THIS MEAN?

I was getting to that. At first glance, it would seem that sexual contact between men and women is in danger of becoming obsolete, except for purposes of reproduction. After all, if women need only themselves to provide adequate clitoral stimulation to

orgasm, then why should they put up with the insensitivity, the chauvinism, the exploitation, and the oppression visited upon them by men? However, if we recall the findings of the Orgasm section, we remember that there are really two kind of orgasms for women: what used to be called *clitoral* and *vaginal* orgasms, and which I have called *clitoral* and *emotional* orgasms.

It is this second that most women find to be of almost equal importance as a basic physical sexual release. (Some women, in fact, prefer it to the clitoral orgasm.) This suggests the next question.

### WHAT DO MEN DO FOR YOU THAT YOU CANNOT DO FOR YOURSELF?

**Some women mentioned cunnilingus (oral stimulation of the clitoris).**

"I appreciate cunnilingus a great deal because my lover shows by his willingness to engage in stimulating activity 'down there' that he is a person first and a phallus-wielding male second. That a man should negate his penis-bearing identity in deference to the consummately intimate activity of eating my cunt demonstrates a respect for my being that transcends mere phallus-vagina identity-roles. However, some men feel that their masculinity is jeopardized by the non-use of their organs in pleasuring me, and often hasten to emplace their hitherto 'obsolete' cocks inside me just at the preorgasmic moment of peak stimulation. The resultant sudden cessation of gobbling my box and consequent rude enthrustment of the reclaimed dick causes me great distress and negative reinforcement, whereupon my immediate tendency is to either weep bitter tears of remorse or smash their skulls with a massive ashtray kept at my bedside for that express purpose."

"Cunnilingus! What can I say! What can I say! What can I say!"

"I love it! My husband, who is quite

a witty fellow, often has hilarious conversations with my genitals when he is 'down there.' Trouble is, I ask them to speak up, and they just start whispering!"

"I enjoy cunnilingus, but the only time I've ever tried it was when my husband was kicked out of the army. We were making love and he began to eat me, and then he stopped and said he couldn't because my vaginal discharge made him gag. So I told him his dishonorable discharge made *me* gag! We got divorced a week later, and today he is a millionaire and I am dying of an incurable and rare disease."

**Another function men can perform is that of simply being there.**

**"What else besides direct clitoral stimulation can men provide?"**

I'd like to answer that one myself. You see, let me tell you about my lover Steve. He's a good-looking guy, has an interesting mind, respects me as a human being, and has a nice body. But we just aren't clicking in the sack. I like long, slow lovemaking that consists of more than the "old in-out in-out," but that seems to be all he has time for. I've told him about this repeatedly, but he just laughs and says, "Sheere, you've got so many reasons and arguments for why you're frustrated, you should write a book." Some understanding! And all I really ask of him—now that I've finally figured out how to masturbate successfully to orgasm—is that he hold me every now and then, and maybe just lie there for ten goddamn minutes being nice. Is that too much to ask?

### IS THAT TOO MUCH TO ASK?

**Most women said that no, that was not too much to ask.**

"My boyfriend gets me so mad. Right after sex, he jumps up and goes to the kitchen to get some cookies or something. All I can do is act hurt and mad and say, 'You don't want to cuddle or be nice or anything!' And it's true, 'cause he doesn't!"

"All I ask for—and God knows I don't ask for much—all I ask for is a little hug. Just a little hug after he's climaxed and thrashed around like a hooked fish. That's all. Please. For the love of God, just a little hug. An embrace. Please."

"To me, the feeling-close with another human being is an Ultimate. The sex thing is fine, as a pleasure-activity. But the warm-embracing is a love-act, a caring-for-the-other that brings a body-sense of well-being."

"The best thing I like about Ronnie is after he would have come, he holds me and we just lie there, and he says warm and tender things like, 'Gee, that would have been fantastic,

JULY, 1972

"Now quick, spell rhinoceros."

wouldn't it?' and 'You know, I think that time would have been the best of them all,' and things like that. It makes me feel so good, makes me feel like a real woman when he tells me how great it would have been. If only he hadn't got his thingie shot off in 'Nam."

"I super get off on snuggling and cuddling and giggling and stuff."

# TOWARD A NEW THEORY OF FEMALE SEXUALITY

### THE FUTURE OF INTERCOURSE

We have seen that women mostly do not orgasm from intercourse. We have also seen that, for many women, the best part of intercourse is the holding-cuddling-being nice phase that follows male orgasm—if it does in fact follow it, and the male does not light up a cigarette and get restless to put on a record or the television or get a snack. Unfortunately, many males do just that, and thus cut short this crucial phase of being-together. (Steve does it a hell of a lot.)

What is needed, therefore, is a new theory and practice of female sexuality—which means, of course, a new theory and practice of male sexuality, for those females who have sex with males. Intercourse seems to have outlived its usefulness as a ritual of oppression. Therefore, from now on, intercourse only for reproduction. Period. Oh dear—I've made a sex joke.

In place of being humped and stabbed and throttled with the erect penis, we must move toward a more generalized acceptance and endorsement of self-stimulation in the clitoral area. This is the most effective and efficient means of orgasming, and now we know it. Let men do the same for themselves, whether manually, or with whatever horrid and revolting vagina-substitutes they use (raw liver, an apple core, a chicken, mud, etc.). But then let us both come together in blissful sharing and warmth, and let us not consider sex "good" unless we have enjoyed that crucial but heretofore underappreciated latter phase.

There will be many women who prefer intercourse, and naturally this is their right and prerogative. Intercourse, for the small minority of women who find it satisfying, may still be performed—as, indeed, may any form of sexual activity. What is needed is a new awareness of women's abilities to orgasm *by doing it for themselves,* and of the importance of holding, snuggling, cuddling, and being nice.

This, as it happens, is exactly what I have been telling my partner for months. I can only hope that all this effort has been worth it, and that he gets the message. It hasn't been easy, writing six hundred pages of different attitudes toward everything from touching your nipple to cunnilingus with a dachshund. You try it sometime.

### WAIT A MINUTE. WHAT IS THAT SUPPOSED TO MEAN?

Nothing. Just a slip of the typewriter. And now I would like to thank all of the five thousand women who helped with this study by returning the questionnaire—

### FIVE THOUSAND? BEFORE YOU SAID IT WAS THREE THOUSAND.

Did I? Three thousand, then. I must have been thinking of something else.

### JUST A SECOND. WHERE EXACTLY ARE THE ANSWER SHEETS FROM THOSE WOMEN?

I don't know. I lost them. I ate them. Mind your own business.

### YOU DON'T HAVE THEM, DO YOU? WHAT ARE YOU HIDING?

Nothing. Leave me alone. Get out of here.

### THEY NEVER EXISTED, DID THEY? YOU'VE MADE ALL THIS UP, HAVEN'T YOU?

Oh, fuck it. Yes, I did. Everything, questions, answers, the works. As long as you've read this far, you might as well know the truth. It was the only way I could think of to get my man to cuddle me more. That's all I ever really wanted. Not national fame, not

sexual notoriety, not a book listed simultaneously on both hardcover and paperback best-seller lists. Just some nice snuggling after sex. Jesus Christ, now I wonder if it's been worth it, frankly.

### WHY WOULDN'T IT BE WORTH IT?

Because it turned out too damn long. Steve's been reading it for three weeks now, nonstop. I haven't been cuddled in a month! What kind of person wants to sit and read six hundred pages of repetitious and redundant answers which repeat themselves over and over?

### YOU'D BE SURPRISED.

I guess so. Anyway, it's my reply to his "you're so frustrated you should write a book" remarks.

### BUT DOESN'T THAT MEAN THAT MORE OF YOUR SO-CALLED RESEARCH IS A FRAUD? AND ALL THIS EXCITEMENT ABOUT YOUR "FINDINGS" IS JUST—

—a lot of public relations baloney, yes. I know. I guess I found out how to masturbate, and got carried away. Look, just think of it as being like the Castaneda books, or like *Roots:* whether or not it's true, it gives you something to talk about in bed.

### "TALK"!? WHAT ABOUT MAKING LOVE?

You call ramming a woman with your rod just so you can come "making love"? Forget it. The honeymoon is over for you guys. We demand equal orgasms—even if we have to do it ourselves.

### AH, FUCK YOU.

Not any more, buster. ☐

JULY, 1973

PEOPLE WHO DON'T BRUSH TEETH

B. Kliban

# Busting out of Suburbia

## How One Family
## Threw It All Away and Got Back to Basics
## on Their Own Island

### by Danny Abelson

At five A.M. it is bitterly cold on the Isle of Rock, especially if you are a pampered North American journalist unused to foraging in icy water for seaweed. I feel a mixture of awe and horror at Gerry Greene's ability to simultaneously withstand this physical discomfort and talk enthusiastically about the changes in his lifestyle that have brought him and his family all the way from an affluent Westchester suburb to a life of bitter hardship in the Orkney Islands.

"It's all a matter of priorities," he begins, shouting to be heard above the thunderous surf. "Back there, my priorities were fairly typical and completely artificial. I was just another successful rodent on an inside track—the hundred grand house, the orthodontia for the kids, the Caribbean vacation every winter, the right Gucci briefcase, Picasso litho, you name it. Know what my priorities are now?" I shake my head. "There are only two. Firstly, seaweed. That's number one. Then comes number two, which is more seaweed. If we stopped collecting it, we'd die. That's real life priorities for you."

Later that morning, Gerry looks up at the pale sun that is beginning to seep through the low gray clouds and gives a short, derisive laugh. "Eight o'clock," he says, shaking his head slowly. "Know what those poor slobs are doing? They're standing on a station platform exercising their ulcers over some bullshit quarterly quota while their wives knock back a morning pick-me-up before heading out to spend their husbands' money buying a decent fuck from an expensive tennis pro. It depresses me to even think about it!"

Listening to the former investment counselor, I am struck by the determination and enthusiasm he continues to bring to an experiment in living that has been anything but easy. By all accounts, there have been few of the family's eighteen months on Rock that have not seen their share of disappointments and setbacks. Supplies

**From Scarsdale:** *"Just another rodent on an inside track."*

failed to arrive. Early attempts at cultivation were disastrously unsuccessful. The island peat proved to be woefully inadequate fuel. Food could not be cooked properly, and within two months, the entire family had severe dysentery. The perpetual cold led to bronchial infections that were compounded by malnutrition.

By now, the children—Mandy, eleven, and Chris, nine—are accustomed to bleeding gums and infections that do not heal. Even more remarkably, they perform their virtually endless round of tasks with listless but uncomplaining obedience.

I discuss this with Gerry's wife, Lisa, who strikes me as the less committed of the two adult Greenes. Among other things we talk about is the vacation the family took some months ago, an episode that has not been mentioned before. Lisa's voice breaks with emotion as she recounts the story of their first holiday from Rock. The experience began well enough with the building of a raft and the trip out to Gryppe, the nearest island in the Orkney chain. The return trip, however, turned into a nightmare when heavy seas broke up the raft. Gerry narrowly escaped drowning trying unsuccessfully to retrieve lost supplies. And the four days that followed before their

rescue by a Norwegian fishing boat were spent without food and almost no water. Mandy still wakes up sobbing from terrifying nightmares about the experience, though Gerry has told the family that he considers it the first "real holiday" the four Greenes have ever taken *together*.

It is clear to me that Lisa feels deeply ambivalent about the move. In response to my gentle prying, she begins to voice some of these feelings, talking about the busy routine of her life in Scarsdale, a routine she remembers as demanding but rewarding, especially the time that she had for herself, for seeing friends, relaxing, and pursuing her interests. "I know that the children were being taught artificial values, but now they're too exhausted to be taught any. And they're terribly lonely, being half the population of the..." Her voice trails off as footsteps approach. Gerry and the children enter with loaded baskets of seaweed. They unharness each other, and the children gratefully flop down on sleeping mats. Gerry joins the discussion.

"My wife telling you about her life of deprivation?" he asks, seeing Lisa's teary eyes. "Don't worry, precious, we're having your tennis pro shipped in real soon." I sense a deep wound be-

neath his flippant teasing, and decide to change the subject by asking them if they remember the moment when they decided to make the move. Gerry remembers it well.

"There we were, my wife and I and the two couples who were our closest friends. We were sitting in the usual well-appointed living room after the usual excellent dinner, and as I was leaning across the usual Danish coffee table to take the usual brandy snifter, I suddenly thought—'Hey, who needs this?' It was that simple."

There is a long silence after Gerry finishes talking. For a few moments, it seems that everything the Greenes have left behind is with us in the small mud-walled shelter. The peat smoke drifts up the walls, the children lie, open-eyed but quite still, on the floor, and the three of us at the table sit silently, each thinking about Scarsdale and Rock and the lonely sound of the waves crashing against the cliffs far below. I know that I will leave soon to return to New York, and I know, also, that it will not be easy to write about this dramatic experiment in lifestyles.

Then, as if on cue, Lisa and I rise from the table, she to tend the cauldron of seaweed that hangs above the smoky fire, me to pack my things for the journey home. ☐

**To Rock:** *"Real life priorities...seaweed, and more seaweed."*

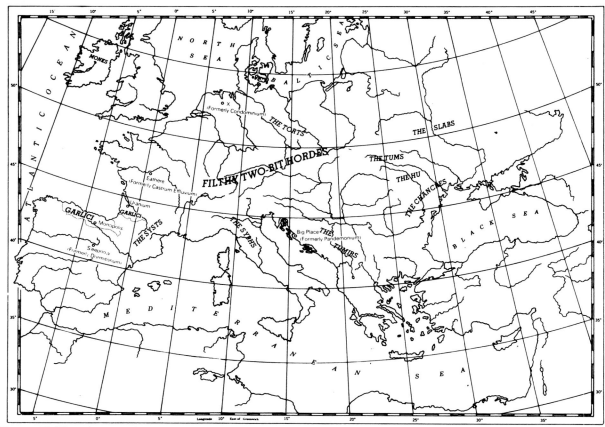

5:30 P.M., Friday, August 2, 587 A.D. A series of sudden and violent migrations change the face of Europe.

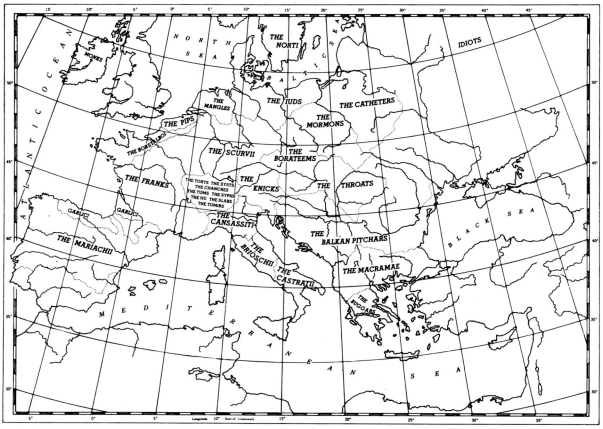

Early afternoon, Saturday, August 3, 587 A.D. Following extended turmoil and upheaval, the invading barbarians fragment into better-defined subunits, leading to a period of settlement and stabilization.

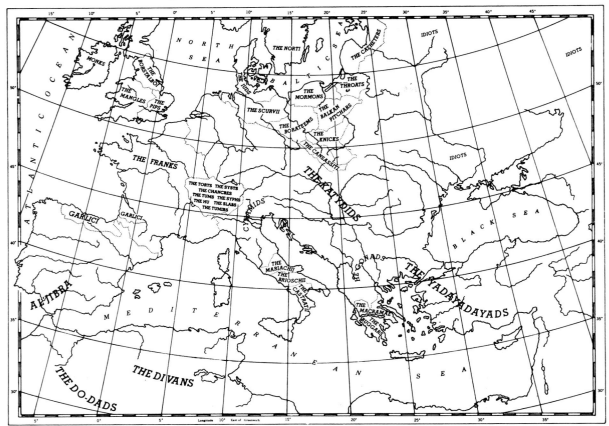

Sunday morning, August 4, 587 A.D. Sweeping northward from their Middle Eastern power base, the ancient peoples of the desert wage ferocious holy wars, or *jihads*, which once again change the face of Europe.

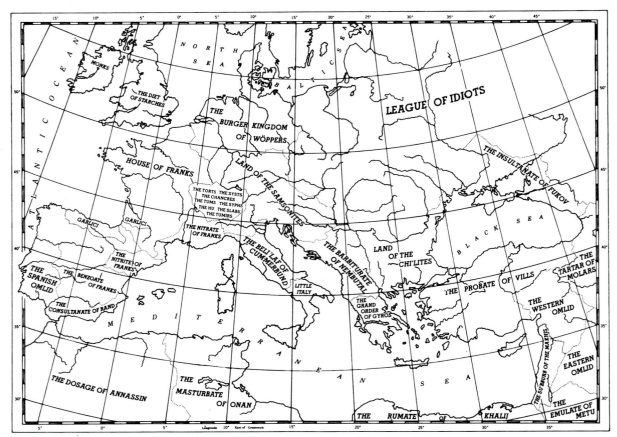

Monday, August 5, 587 A.D. The invaders from the east fall back to secure their territories, while the tribes that had been forced northward do likewise. Shortly after breakfast on Tuesday, the Dark Ages begin.

# How to Drive Fast on D Wing-Wang Squeezed a

**W**hen it comes to taking chances, some people like to play poker or shoot dice; other people prefer to parachute jump, go rhino hunting, or climb ice floes, while still others engage in crime or marriage. But I like to get drunk and drive like a fool. Name me, if you can, a better feeling than the one you get when you're half a bottle of Chivas in the bag with a gram of coke up your nose, and a teenage lovely pulling off her tube top in the next seat over while you're going a hundred miles an hour down a suburban side street. You'd have to watch the entire Mexican air force crash-land in a liquid petroleum gas storage facility to match this kind of thrill. If you ever have much more fun than that, you'll die of pure sensory overload, I'm here to tell you.

But wait. Let's pause and analyze *why* this particular matrix of activities is perceived as so highly enjoyable. I mean, aside from the teenage lovely pulling off her tube top in the next seat

over. Ignoring that for a moment (despite these perfect little cone-shaped breasts that stand right up from her chest and end in a pair of eager hot pink lust-hardened nipples as thick as your thumbs), let's look at the psychological factors conducive to placing positive emotional values on the sensory end product of experientially produced excitation of the central nervous system and smacking into a lamppost. Is that any way to have fun? How would your mother feel if she knew you were doing this? She'd cry. She really would. And that's how you know it's fun. Anything that makes your mother cry is fun. Sigmund Freud wrote all about this. It's a well-known fact.

Of course, it's a shame to risk young lives behaving this way—speeding around all tanked up with your feet hooked in the steering wheel while your date crawls around on the floor mats opening zippers with her teeth

and pounding on the accelerator with an empty liquor bottle. But it wouldn't be taking a chance if you weren't risking *something*. And even if it is a shame to risk young lives behaving this way, it is definitely cooler than risking *old* lives behaving this way. I mean, so what if some fifty-eight-year-old butt-head gets a load on and starts playing Death Race 2000 in the rush-hour traffic jam? What kind of chance is he taking? He's just waiting around to see what kind of cancer he gets anyway. But if young, talented *you*, with all of life's possibilities at your fingertips, you and the future Cheryl Tiegs there, so fresh, so beautiful—if the two of *you* stake your handsome heads on a single roll of the dice in life's game of stop-the-semi—now *that's* taking chances! Which is why old people rarely risk their lives. It's not because they're chicken—they just have too much dignity to play for small stakes.

# ugs While Getting Your
# d Not Spill Your Drink

by P.J. O'Rourke, Technical Consultant: Joe Schenkman

Now a lot of people say to me, "Hey, P.J., you like to drive fast. Why not join a responsible organization, such as the Sports Car Club of America, and enjoy participation in sports car racing? That way you could drive as fast as you wish while still engaging in a well-regulated spectator sport that is becoming more popular each year." No thanks. In the first place, if you ask me, those guys are a bunch of tweedy old barf mats who like to talk about things like what necktie they wore to Alberto Ascari's funeral. And in the second place, they won't let me drive drunk. They expect me to go out there and smash into things and roll over on the roof and catch fire and burn to death when I'm sober. They must think I'm crazy. That stuff scares me. I have to get completely fuck-faced to even think about driving fast. How can you have a lot of exciting thrills when you're so terrified that you wet yourself all the time? That's not fun. It's just *not fun* to have exciting thrills when you're scared. Take the heroes of the *Iliad*, for instance—they really had some exciting thrills, and were they scared? No. They were drunk. Every chance they could get. And so am I, and I'm not going out there and have a horrible car wreck until somebody brings me a cocktail.

Also, it's important to be drunk because being drunk keeps your body all loose, and that way, if you have an accident or anything, you'll sort of roll with the punches and not get banged up so bad. For example, there was this guy I heard about who was really drunk and was driving through the Adirondacks. He got sideswiped by a bus and went head-on into another car, which knocked him off a bridge, and he plummeted 150 feet into a ravine. I mean, it killed him and everything, but if he hadn't been so drunk and loose, his body probably would have been banged up a lot worse—and you can imagine how much more upset his wife would have been when she went down to the morgue to identify him if he'd been twisted up and smashed to pieces and covered in bloody gore.

Even more important than being drunk, however, is having the right car. You have to get a car that handles really well. This is extremely important, and there's a lot of debate on this subject—about what kind of car handles best. Some say a front-engined car; some say a rear-engined car. I say a *rented* car. Nothing handles better than a rented car. You can go faster, turn corners sharper, and put the transmission into reverse while going forward at a higher rate of speed in a rented car than in any other kind. You can also park without looking, and can use the trunk as an ice chest. Another thing about a rented car is that it's an all-terrain vehicle. Mud, snow, water, woods—you can take a rented car anywhere. True, you can't always get it back—but that's not your problem, is it?

Yet there's more to a really good-handling car than just making sure it doesn't belong to you. It has to be big. It's really hard for a girl to get her clothes off inside a small car, and this is one of the most important features of car handling. Also, what kind of drugs does it have in it? Most people like to drive on speed or cocaine with plenty of whiskey mixed in. This gives you the confidence you want and need for plowing through red lights and passing trucks on the right. But don't neglect downs and 'ludes and codeine cough syrup either. It's hard to beat the heavy depressants for high speed spin-outs, backing into trees, and a general feeling of not giving two fucks about man and his universe. Try a little heroin. Sometimes it makes you throw up, but if you haven't used all the ice in the trunk, you can spread some around on the back seat floor and that way when you forget whether you're in England or not and can't remember which side of the car you're on, you can just puke over your shoulder and the ice will keep the smell down, if you still care. Plus, some of the cubes will slide under the front seat and you can grab them and use them on the girl (which is really a kick in case you've never tried it).

Over all, though, it's the bigness of the car that counts the most. Because when something bad happens in a really big car—accidentally speeding through the middle of a gang of unruly young people who have been taunting you in a drive-in restaurant, for instance—it happens very far away—way out at the end of your fenders. It's like a civil war in Africa; you know, it doesn't really concern you too much. On the other hand, when something happens in a little bitty car it happens all over you. You get all involved in it and have to give everything a lot of thought. Driving around in a little bitty car is like being one of those sensitive girls who writes poetry. Life is just too much to bear. You end up staying at home in your bedroom and thinking up sonnets that don't get published till you die, which will be real soon if you keep driving around in little bitty cars like that.

Let's inspect some of the basic maneuvers of drunken driving while you've got crazy girls who are on drugs with you. Look for these signs when picking up crazy girls: pierced ears with five or six earrings in them, unusual shoes, white lipstick, extreme thinness, hair that's less than an inch long, or clothing made of chrome and leather. Stay away from girls who cry a lot or who look like they get pregnant easily or have careers. They may want to do weird stuff in cars, but only in the back seat, and that's already filled with ice and has throw-up all over it and, any-way, it's really hard to steer from back there. Besides, they'll want to get engaged right away afterwards. But the other kind of girls—there's no telling what they'll do. I used to know this girl who weighed about eighty pounds and dressed in skirts that didn't even cover her underwear, when she wore any. I had this beat-up old Mercedes, and we were off someplace about fifty miles from nowhere on Christmas Eve in a horrible sleet storm. The road was really a mess, all curves and big ditches, and I was blotto, and the car kept slipping off the pavement and sliding sideways. And just when I'd hit a big patch of glare ice and was frantically spinning the wheel trying to stay out of the oncoming traffic, she said, "I shaved my pussy today—wanna feel?"

That's really true. And then, about half an hour later the head gasket blew up, and we had to spend I don't know how long in this dirtball motel, although the girl walked all the way to the liquor store through about a mile of slush and got all kinds of wine and did weird stuff with the bottle necks later. So it was sort of O.K., except that the garage where I left the Mercedes burned down and I used the insurance money to buy a motorcycle.

Now, girls who like motorcycles really will do *anything*. I mean, really, *anything you can think of.* But it's just not the same. For one thing, it's hard to drink while you're riding a motorcycle—there's no place to set your glass. And cocaine's out of the question. And personally, I find that grass makes me too sensitive. You smoke some grass and the first thing you know you're pulling over to the side of the road and taking a break to dig the gentle beauty of the sky's vast panorama, the slow, luxurious interplay of sun and clouds, the lulling trill of breezes midst leafy tree branches—and what kind of fun is that? Besides, it's rough to "get it on" with a chick (I mean in the biblical sense) and still make all the fast curves unless you let her take the handlebars with her pants off and come on Greek style or something, which is harder than it sounds; and pantless girls on motorcycles attract the highway patrol, so usually you don't end up doing anything until you're both off the bike, and by then you may be in the hospital. Like I was after this old lady who pulled out in front of me in an Oldsmobile, and the girl I was with still wanted to do anything you can think of, but there was a doctor there and he was squirting pHisoHex all over me and combing little bits of gravel out of my face with a wire brush, and I just couldn't get into it. So, take it from me and don't get a motorcycle. Get a big car.

Usually, most fast driving maneuvers that don't require crazy girls call for use of the steering wheel, so be sure your car is equipped with power steering. Without power steering, turning the wheel is a lot like work, and if you wanted work you'd get a job. All steering should be done with the index finger. Then, when you're done doing all the steering that you want to do, just pull your finger out of there and the wheel will come right back to wherever it wants to. It's that simple. Be sure to do an extra lot of steering when going into a driveway or turning sharp corners. And here's another important tip: Always roll the window down before throwing bottles out, and don't try to throw them through the windshield unless the car is parked.

O.K., now say you've been on a six-day drunk and you've just made a bet that you can back up all the way to Cleveland, plus you've got a buddy who's getting a blowjob on the trunk lid. Well, let's face it—if that's the way you're going to act, sooner or later you'll have an accident. This much is true. But that doesn't mean that you should sit back and just let accidents happen to you. No, you have to go out and cause them yourself. That way you're in control of the situation.

You know, it's a shame, but a lot of people have the wrong idea about accidents. For one thing, they don't hurt nearly as much as you'd think. That's because you're in shock and can't feel pain or, if you aren't in shock, you're dead, and that doesn't hurt at all so far as we know. Another thing is that they make great stories. I've got this friend—a prominent man in the automotive industry—who flipped his MG TF back in the fifties and slid on his head for a couple hundred yards, and had to spend a year with no eyelids and a steel pin through his cheekbones while his face was being rebuilt. Sure, it wasn't much fun at the time, but you should hear him tell about it now—what a fabulous tale, especially at dinner. Besides, it's not all smashing glass and spurting blood, you understand. Why, a good sideswipe can be an almost religious experience. The sheet metal doesn't break or crunch or anything—it flexes and gives way as the two vehicles come together, with a rushing liquid pulse as if two giant sharks of steel were mating in the perpetual night of the sea primordial. I mean, if you're on enough drugs. Also, sometimes you see a lot of really pretty lights in your head.

One sure way to cause an accident is with your basic "moonshiner's" or "bootlegger's" turn. Whiz down the road at about sixty or seventy, throw the gearshift into neutral, cut the wheel to the left, and hit the emergency brake with one good wallop while holding the brake release out with your left hand. This'll send you spinning around in a perfect 180° turn right into a culvert or a fast-moving tractor-trailer rig. (The bootlegger's turn can be done on dry pavement, but it works best on loose gravel or small children.) Or, when you've moved around backwards, you can then spin the wheel to the right and keep on going until you've come around a full 360° and are headed back the same way you were going; though it probably would have been easier to have just kept going that way in the first place and not have done anything at all, unless you were with somebody you really wanted to impress—your probation officer, for instance.

An old friend of mine named Joe Schenkman happens to have just written me a letter about another thing you can do to wreck a car. Joe's on a little vacation up in Vermont and will be until he finds out what the statute of limitations on attempted vehicular homicide is. And he was writing to tell me about a fellow he met up there, saying:

*...This guy has rolled (deliberately) over thirty cars (and not just by his own account—the townfolks back him up on this story), inheriting only a broken nose (three times) and a slightly black-and-blue shoulder for all this. What you do, see, is you go into a moonshiner's turn, but you get on the brakes and stay on them. Depending on how fast you're going, you roll proportionately: four or five rolls is decent. Going into the spin, you have one hand on the seat and the other firmly on the roof so you're sprung in tight. As you feel the roof give on the first roll, you slip your seat hand under the dash (of the passenger side, as you're thrown hard over in that direction to begin with), and pull yourself under it. And here you simply sit it out, springing yourself tight with your whole body, waiting for the thunder to die. Naturally, it helps to be drunk, and if you have a split second's doubt or hesitation through any of this, you die.*

This Schenkman himself is no slouch of a driver, I may say. Unfortunately, his strong suit is driving in New York City, an area that has a great number of unusual special conditions, which we just don't have the time or the space to get into right here (except to note that the good part is how it's real easy to scare old Jewish ladies in new Cadillacs and the bad part is that Negroes actually *do* carry knives, not to mention Puerto Ricans; and everybody else you hit turns out to be a lawyer or married to somebody in the mob). However, Joe is originally from the South, and it was down there that he discovered huffing glue and sniffing industrial solvents and such. These give you a really spectacular hallucinatory type of a high where you think, for instance, that you're driving through an overpass guardrail and landing on a freight train flatcar and being hauled to Shreveport and loaded into a container ship headed for Liberia with a crew full of homosexual Lebanese, only to come to and find out that it's true. Joe is a commercial artist who enjoys jazz music and horse racing. His favorite color is blue.

There's been a lot of discussion about what kind of music to listen to while staring doom square in the eye and not blinking unless you get some grit under your contacts. Watch out for the fellow who tunes his FM to the classical station. He thinks a little Rimsky-Korsakov makes things more dramatic—like in a foreign movie. That's pussy style. This kind of guy's idea of a fast drive is a 75-mph cruise up to the summer cottage after one brandy and soda. The true skidmark artist prefers something cheery and upbeat—"Night on Disco Mountain" or "Boogie Oogie Oogie" or whatever it is that the teenage lovely with nipples as thick as your thumbs wants to shake her buns to. Remember her? So what do *you* care what's on the fucking tape deck? The high, hot whine of the engine, the throaty pitch of the exhaust, the wind in your beer can, the gentle slurping noises from her little bud-red lips—that's all the music your ears need, although side two of the first Velvet Underground album is nice if you absolutely insist. And no short jaunts either. For the maniacal high-speed driver, endurance is everything. Especially if you've used that ever-popular pickup line, "Wanna go to Mexico?" Especially if you've used it somewhere like Boston. Besides teenage girls can go a long, long time without sleep and, believe me, so can the police and their parents. So just keep your foot in it. There's no reason not to. There's no reason not to keep going forever, really. I had this friend who drove a whole shitload of people up from Oaxaca to Cincinnati one time, nonstop. I mean, he stopped for gas but he wouldn't even let anybody get out then. He made them all piss out the windows, and he says that it was worth the entire drive just to *see* a girl try to piss out the window of a moving car.

Get a fat girl friend so you'll have plenty of amphetamines and you'll never have to stop at all. The only problem you'll run into is that after you've been driving for two or three days you start to see things in the road—great big scaly things twenty feet high with nine legs. But there are very few great big scaly things with nine legs in America anymore, so you can just drive right through them because they probably aren't really there, and if they *are* really there you'll be doing the country a favor by running them over.

Yes, but where does it all end? Where does a crazy life like this lead? To death, you say. Look at all the people who've died in car wrecks: Albert Camus, Jayne Mansfield, Jackson Pollack, Tom Paine. Well, Tom Paine didn't *really* die in a car wreck, but he probably would have if he'd lived a little later. He was that kind of guy. Anyway, death is always the first thing that leaps into everybody's mind—sudden violent death at an early age. If only it were that simple. God, we could all go out in a blaze of flaming aluminum alloys formulated specially for the Porsche factory race effort like James Dean did! No ulcers, no hemorrhoids, no bulging waistlines, soft dicks, or false teeth...bash!! kaboom!! *Watch this space for paperback reprint rights, auction, and movie option sale!* But that's not the way it goes. No. What actually happens is you fall for that teenage lovely in the next seat over, fall for her like a ton of condoms, and before you know it you're married and have teenage lovelies of your own—getting gang-fucked on a Pontiac Trans-Am's shaker hood at this very minute, no doubt—plus a six-figure mortgage, a liver the size of the Bronx, and a Country Squire that's never seen the sweet side of sixty.

I guess it's hard to face the truth, but I suppose you yourself realize that if you'd had just a little more courage, just a little more strength of character, you could have been dead by now. No such luck. □

SEPTEMBER, 1976

...UNDREAMED OF LUXURIES. A PILLOW FOR YOUR HEAD, SALAD DRESSING, WEATHER STRIPPING TO STOP THE DRAFTS A PIECE OF CHEWING GUM.

# They deserve their share of the catch.

And they'll get their share of the ocean's bounty with new Senior Vittles Fishin' Snacks™

There is nothing that satisfies a finicky appetite or a picky craving for variety like fish. And new Senior Vittles Fishin' Snacks™ contain a little of almost every fish in the sea.

That's because Fishin' Snacks™ are harvested right from the ocean's

bottom, where most fish, fish parts, and fish byproducts collect.

Don't forget either that Senior Vittles Fishin' Snacks™ are so inexpensive and full of natural variety that you can serve them every day at your home, hospital, or institution.

**Senior Vittles** ©
**Serve them with confidence.**

# A FRIEND IN NEED

WHAT DO YOU THINK ABOUT NOW WHEN YOU COME?

MY PSYCHIATRIST.

ARE YOU COMING TO BED, JANE?

IN A MINUTE, TED.

SO DON'T WORRY... IF YOU TOTALLY FLIP OUT, TED AND I WILL BE HERE TO HELP PUT YOU AWAY.

I'M GOING TO SLEEP NOW, JANE.

I HAVEN'T SLEPT IN DAYS... EVERY TIME I CLOSE MY EYES, I SEE SUSAN AND HIM, ROMPING AROUND IN PLASTIC RELIEF BAGS.

WHY DON'T YOU TAKE OFF YOUR SHIRT AND I'LL GIVE YOU A NICE BACK RUB.

THINK OF YOURSELF AS A BIG ZIT... AND I'LL SQUEEZE OUT ALL THE PAIN.

I'VE NEVER BEEN GOOD AT EXPRESSING MY EMOTIONS.

IT'S EASY... JUST TRY... LIKE...

WHAT ARE YOU FEELING RIGHT NOW?

I... I WANT...

DO YOU WANT ME TO LEAVE THE LIGHT ON, JANE?

AAH...

I FEEL MUCH BETTER NOW.

MMM....

I WAS LYING THERE THINKING ABOUT WORLD HUNGER AND MY OWN PERSONAL ENNUI.... THEN I ASKED MYSELF... "WHAT COULD BE WORSE?"

ZZZ...

I WAS JUST TRYING TO HELP....

WHY DON'T YOU MOVE IN WITH US FOR A WHILE, JANE?

YOUR FIRST MISTAKE WAS GETTING MARRIED.

I WAS REALLY LUCKY TO GET THIS APARTMENT... IT HAD TOO MANY BAD MEMORIES FOR THE COUPLE WHO LIVED HERE BEFORE.

©79 SHARY FLENNIKEN

# my VAGINA

**by Larry Taft
as told to John Hughes**

One morning last winter, um, I woke up and, well, I was asleep and then I woke up, and what I found was, um, well, I woke up and there it was, and my...what should have been there wasn't and what was there was...it was...a vagina. I mean, *I was a sixteen-year-old guy with a box!* I had a damn ugly, hairy woman's privates and it was gross and sickening, and I was so pissed off I wanted to punch it right in the face!

When I went to bed I had a regular guy's cock and nuts and pubic hair. But when I woke up and looked inside my pajamas, all that stuff was gone and instead I had this...vagina and hardly any hair down there and a butt that was pink and bald. It was so disgusting I'm surprised I didn't just march downstairs and go out in the garage and not pull up the door and start my mom's station wagon and die. How could I be a guy when I had a twat? I mean, what was I? Where was my "dick"? Where were my balls? Why did all of this happen?

I thought about it a lot and I think what *maybe* happened was I tried to get high off the gas that's supposed to be inside a can of whipped cream and I was also smoking a lot of Kools, and I eat real shitty and I always sit too close to the TV and I never read with good light and I...well, like a lot of guys my age I...do a lot of..."self-jacking off." It was either that or God did it.

But anyway, there I was with a vagina. Oh, by the way, it isn't polite to say this and I'm not being conceited, but the dick I used to have was a pretty good one. It wasn't so big that it was gross and it wasn't so tiny that it was a joke, and it didn't have moles or spots on it like that of a guy who was in my gym class two years ago (Jim S.), and it didn't bend over to one side when it was in a "hard-on." My balls were O.K., too, and my hair was decent and my rear end was normal, and I was

overall happy with that stuff and I was super-sorry to see it gone, really.

So, like, there I was, you know, on the edge of the bed looking down into my lap, and instead of seeing this thing, I just saw this shitty little wad of hair. I wouldn't exactly say I cried, but I will admit that I felt so bad that my eyes got really runny, and I felt sad because, you know, I was All-Conference in three sports and I wanted to eventually get a football scholarship to Michigan State or USC, and I had just bought a motorcycle (Kawasaki) and a new stereo (with Bose speakers, MAC amp, and Nakamichi deck), and I had started to shave, and all my friends were friends because I was a guy, and who the fuck but a girl would ever want to be a girl except a homo and I am *not* a homo! That's a fact. Even though I had a pussy I was not a queer! I hate that and I hated it then and I will hate it all of my life, and I looked up "homosexuality" in the dictionary and in a bunch of other books, and having a vagina doesn't make you a homosexual. Liking guys makes you a homosexual, but you have to like them so much that they are like girls to you (and that is a requirement), and I didn't so I wasn't a homo, I swear to God.

Well, anyway, there I was. I had this pussy and I was feeling real pissed off because I thought my life was over. Then it occurred to me: like, there was a girl's thing only about a foot and a half from my eyes and only about two inches from my hand, you know. So I figured that it's not every day that a guy my age gets to look at an actual living girl's thing, and as long as I wanted to in the daylight and do to it whatever stuff I wanted to do to it, it was O.K., you know? So I sort of "forgot" about how I was freaking out and I opened the thing up and took a peek.

I never saw one in the light. I only felt them in the dark, and, of course, I saw a few hundred in magazines, you

know, but never one in the light that was a 3-D one. It was quite a shock to see how big it was. I measured it with a sheet of notebook paper, which is eight-and-one-half inches wide, and it was almost as long as the whole sheet of paper was wide from the top of the hair down to the edge of the butt. A vagina is not like a dick, you know. A dick is just a thing, which is just a stick with a knob on the end and two balls, and that's it and it's real simple. But a vagina is a whole bunch of stuff all crammed in there and buried in a whole bunch of skin and called a vagina although, according to my dictionary, the vagina is only the actual hole part.

Starting at the top, which was the closest part to me and which was just a lot of hair: it was a nice V shape and it didn't spread out all over and become leg hair, like on a guy. It was pretty soft hair, sort of like camel's hair sport coat material only longer and curlier, and sort of darkish-brownish blond. You know how guys' hairs are really weirded out, you know, all twisted up and strange? Girls' hairs are perfect and cool.

O.K., so then I moved down to the middle part and I poked around in there and I found the beginning of the inside skin part. Do you know that the Mississippi River is so small up in Minnesota, where it starts, that you can step over it? That's sort of like the same with a vagina. It's very small at the top and then it gets big and complicated. Where I had my thumb was like the "source" and it was just the beginning, and there weren't any holes or flaps or anything. Just a small curve.

Then all the skin started. Boy, is there ever a lot of skin! There is probably enough extra skin down there to make a whole face. It's all tucked in and wrinkled up, and at first, it doesn't make any sense. It just looks like somebody got it drunk and just mushed everything in there. That skin is sort of two-tone. It's fleshish/pinkish outside, and then when you get inside it's redder, like inside-the-mouth skin, and it is very soft and sticky. And it gets stickier the closer you get to the hole, and then it's just "wet." It also can be, like, "molded," and I made a bird shape out of the real long flaps that sort of hang out.

Anyhow, it's all defined into things called, I think, lips, and I think there are about four sets of them, although I'm not sure because they are all attached to each other. Inside all those lips is the actual hole. I'm not sure what all that skin is for except maybe for "show" because, who knows, when we were cavemen maybe guys thought all that stuff looked cool. But anyway, the hole itself isn't even just a hole. Like, it has lots of ridges and bumps and stuff in it, and it's not really a hole like a hole in the ground is a hole—it's more like an opening because it's sort of closed up, and it moves around and opens up and closes; like if you cough, it shuts and if you yawn, it opens up.

It was as deep as a Little League trophy and it stretched, too. So, like, it fit a Magic Marker, and it also stretched big enough to hold a Polaris submarine model. There is a lump up at the end of the hole, and I don't know what it is exactly because it's awful dark in there, even if you take the mirror off your desk and lay it on the floor and squat over it and shine a great big hunter's flashlight up there. But I guess it's just all that reproduction stuff that girls have.

Also, another kind of gross thing about a vagina is that it smells kind of bad. Pardon me for being kind of sickening, but it's true. I smelled one before on my old girl friend and then it smelled O.K., but I think that when you are a guy and you are real hot and with a girl and you are kissing and feeling and all that, I think your nose gets confused, and a vagina doesn't smell bad at all—in fact, it smells pretty cool in a kind of gross way. But when you are just a guy and you are by yourself, your vagina reeks. They must all do that because there seems to be a lot of those antiperspirant deodorant sprays for females over by the Kotexes at the grocery store.

The other important thing about the vagina was that I located that "little thing." It is so small you can hardly see it! Which is ridiculous because, man, there's a lot of room down there for all kinds of stuff that doesn't even have anything to do with sex. This "little thing" was about as big as the pusher-inner thing on a ball-point pen—it's that tiny! So that may be why girls are not all that crazy about sex, not like guys are. But anyway, besides being so tiny, it's also buried in a wad of

skin. I had to uncover it to get to the good part, and it's really good because it's so sensitive that when I touched it I got a huge shiver! It was a sex shiver, but I think it was also a go-to-the-bathroom shiver because I had to whizz like crazy!

"Holding it in" when you are a girl is hard because, where are the hold-it muscles? In a guy they are back near your rear end. So I had to get to the bathroom pretty fast since I didn't know how to use that thing. I was very glad that my mom and my dad and my sisters were gone, because my sister was in a figure skating thing so I didn't have to worry about anybody seeing me, which was one good thing so far.

By having two sisters and a mom, you know, I knew a little bit about how girls go to the bathroom and, I know, thank God, that you better sit down because you don't have anything to point. You just have a little hole, and if you stand up, believe me, it won't work very well; in fact, it will be a huge mess. Sitting down is the stupidest way in the world to take a leak. It's over so fast you don't have time to read or anything, and like, what do you do with your hands? Another thing about sitting down is that you get everything wet and you have to waste a lot of toilet paper.

Also a vagina makes a *rude* sound when you use it to go to the bathroom. It's like this—*fiiiiiiissssssss, fiss, fiss, fiiiiiiissssssss*. It's a typical girl's sound, real high and dainty and gross. Well, after getting the go-to-the-bathroom business out of the way, I decided to have a look at myself in the big mirror on the back of the door and look at my whole body. I took off my pajama bottoms and then my top and then I got more bad news!

*I had two tits!* Shit! What a fucking pain in the ass this whole thing was turning into—next thing I knew I would be down in the basement doing a load of laundry with my mom! Well, at least nobody in my family except my Grandma Jessie, who had torpedo tits but is dead now, has large tits, so I was flat like my mom and my sisters. But . . . I had big brown nipples. I wouldn't have anything to do with the girls who had brown nipples myself. I personally consider that a deformity and if I ever found out that my wife had them I would get a divorce. Plus, they were *huge* and lopsided! So, not only did I get screwed by having tits in the first place, but I also got screwed by having gross ones. Just my luck!

I looked at myself and it was *weird*. I had muscular-type arms

(with the kind of veins that stick out from working out with weights) and hairy pits like normal and good shoulders and neck, and then these smallish tits with big nipples and a belly button and good stomach ripples and no hair on my chest or on my stomach or below my belly button, and then . . . the vagina. My legs were slimmer than they used to be, I think. When I turned around and looked at my butt it was real neat. I kind of liked it. It was real round and, well, it was pink and cute and there wasn't any hair on it and it was just . . . cute. It was a girl's cute little butt.

Anyway, you know, that got boring real fast, just looking in the mirror, so I kind of walked back to my room and I looked around to see if I walked like a girl does and I did, sort of. Then I went into my room. Then what I did was . . . well, I think, but I'm not sure, what I think I did was what would still be considered "jacking off." It felt pretty good and I had an "orgasm," but I wasn't doing it just to jack off. It was more like an experiment that kind of turned into jacking off, only with a girl's vagina it's more like "rubbing off" because there's nothing to jack.

What I did at first was pretend my hand was me and my vagina was this girl friend I used to have so I could sort of see what it was like for her what I did to her when we were on dates and once at her parents' cottage up north. I think it must have felt lousy because what I did seemed like it had been good, but it wasn't at all. It doesn't feel that great to have somebody shoving their finger in and out of you real fast, and it doesn't feel good at all to get your breasts squeezed and pinched. What does feel good is just old-fashioned rubbing down there. You don't have to fool around with the hole at all because it doesn't have hardly any nerves, so don't waste your time. I know, because later on I tried a lot of stuff, like carrots and candles and hot dogs and breakfast links and one of those toilet paper holder things and rolled up Cliff Notes (*Brave New World*) and bananas and a cucumber and a hairbrush handle and even an old GI Joe's head, and none of them made me have an orgasm. The hole is just for "intercourse" with men.

So, I was rubbing away and then, all of a sudden, I hit the jackpot, and my legs started jumping around and my hips started going back and forth automatically and there was this tremendous tickle feeling up my butt and then *zing!* It was over, but then another one started coming. *Zing! Zing! Zing! Zing!* More and more! Not like a guy's at all! Smaller, but tons and tons of them! Guys' are over right away and that's the end of it, and you don't ever want to do it again in your whole life and you feel like a slob and girls are revolting to think about and you want to just burn the magazine you were looking at, you know. But not with a vagina! You can keep going and going and going and there isn't even any mess to clean up. All the messy stuff goes on inside. Also no "hard-on" is required, you know. You're ready to do it any time of the day or the night—it's really pretty cool. And there is no way for anybody to tell that you did it because there's nothing to poke out of your pajamas. Finally, I had to stop because all that feeling good was starting to feel bad, and I was getting sort of afraid that I might have a heart attack or something. When I looked at the clock, I couldn't believe it! I had been masturbating that thing for almost three hours and, boy, was it sore!

Also, it was almost time to go to my swim meet, which was real important, and I would be in a lot of trouble if I missed it, and I'd let down all the guys on the team and they'd be pissed off. So I washed my hands about fifty times until they smelled like hands again, and then I got dressed. But my shirt scratched up my nipples and my underpants didn't fit because there wasn't a guy's "thing" to fill it up right. I figured I better wear a bra or I might make my tits bleed or something, or I could get cancer or who knows. *I* sure didn't!

It was really creepy and weird to be going through my sister's underpants and bras and boyfriends' letters drawer looking for a bra to wear. There were a whole bunch of them, so I picked out the lightest-weight one that wouldn't show the most, and it was one of those real thin ones and it was O.K. except, how do you put it on? They are real easy to fasten and unfasten when you are holding them in your hand, but when you put them on and put your bosoms in the holders you can't reach behind you far enough to fasten them, which I think is stupid unless women have longer arms and narrower backs. I tried and tried and it was no use, so finally I had to just fasten it, then lay it on the floor, and then step into it and pull it up over my legs and my hips and my stomach and then over my chest, and then stick my bosoms in. But that kind of stretched it out and tore it a little in the middle between the holders. Boy, what a pain!

I decided that I may as well take

a pair of underpants as long as I was in her drawer and was feeling creepy anyway. At first, I didn't think I would wear any underpants at all, but if you have a vagina you have to wear underpants because those things leak all the time. I found a nice pair of red ones with a little kitten sewed on the butt. They were real soft and smooth and silky and cool, and they were much better than guys' underpants, and I thought it's too bad that guys don't get a chance to appreciate really nice underwear, except that I guess if guys wore this kind of underwear they'd just spend too much time thinking about how good their underpants felt and they wouldn't get their work done and they'd get fired. By the way, if I had had my regular guy's "thing," I would have gotten a hard-on when I looked at myself in my sister's mirror, because without my arms and my head and my feet I was a pretty cool-looking girl.

So I was all ready to go and I went out to the garage to get my motorcycle. I had a lot of trouble just holding it up, and kicking it over was almost impossible for me because I was just weaker, it seemed, than I was before, and I didn't know if it was because I spent so much time masturbating the vagina, or that I didn't eat breakfast, or that maybe I was losing my muscles as part of the deal of getting a vagina in the first place.

But after I got it going I had another problem. I was sitting right on top of my "little thing" and the motorcycle was vibrating. That made me have more orgasms, and I just sat there and revved the engine for about ten minutes enjoying it until I was afraid that it would blow up. Then I had to ride, and it's pretty dangerous to drive a motorcycle when you are having nonstop orgasms, especially making a left-hand turn when you are moaning and your hips are moving automatically. I almost creamed myself by running into a truck because I didn't want to let up on the gas since the vibra-

tions were just perfect. It is no surprise to me why there aren't any girls motorcycle gangs or motorcycle cops. I made it to school, but almost not, and my bottom was soaking wet.

I had two problems with the swim meet. Actually, I had three, but number three was the problem of changing into my bathing suit in front of the other guys (and that problem went away because I was late because I went around the parking lot a couple of extra times to finish off my last orgasm). The other two problems were hiding my tits and not having a lump to make it look like I had my regular guy's "thing" when I put on my bathing suit. We wear little thin bathing suits and your thing shows a lot, so to not have your thing show would make people suspicious, and the last thing I needed was to have the whole school know about my vagina, so I put a sock in there, took off my bra, and put my shirt back on and wore it into the pool area and didn't take it off—and that covered up my tits.

The coach was pissed, but I was in the next race they were just about to start so he couldn't be pissed for too long. Anyway, I walked over to the edge of the pool and bent over like I was going to dive in with my arms in front of me, and I took off the shirt and I sort of tossed it to the side (but close enough so I could get it when the race was over), and I just stayed in that tucked position so that no one would see my tits or my brown nipples. Except that this dipshit guy from the other school took forever to get ready, and I must have looked like a real jerk being all tucked under and ready to begin the race three or four minutes before we started. Then when we started the race I was so stiff I could hardly keep up, but that was my smallest problem as it turned out.

When I hit that warm water something happened to my stomach and it started to hurt, and when I got to the end of the pool the coach was waving his arms like crazy, and when I finished going into my first turn I saw what he was waving at! It was red and it was a

JUNE, 1976

S.GROSS

big cloud in the water and—guess what—it was coming out of me. I had my period!

Holy shit! I wanted to drown! I was treading water with my period and my tits and my vagina, and about 100 people were all watching me! Somehow I had enough brains at the time to swim over to where my shirt was and I grabbed it and climbed out and covered my tits, and the coach came running over and he was real concerned. I told him I had an infected pimple on my groin and that it was bleeding, and he got kind of mad at me for not telling him about it because of the dangers of spreading infection and all that crap. Then he said to go get dressed and go see my family doctor and not to get blood poisoning.

I was so glad to get out of there! But I wasn't that glad because I still had my period and I had a long way to go to get home. But after just a couple of minutes I knew I would never make it home unless I did something that was so horrible and embarrassing and terrible that I almost didn't do it.

Do you know what it's like to go into a girls bathroom when you are not a girl? It's awful, but where else can a guy get a Kotex? I hurried down the hall as fast as I could with a whole towel stuffed in my pants. I went across the hall and through the cafeteria to the girls' bathroom way over by the music room where there wouldn't be anybody, and there *wasn't* anybody so I was happy about that.

There were two machines in there. One was for Kotexes and the other was for Tampaxes. I didn't know anything about that stuff (my only experience with female hygiene equipment was filling up a sink and soaking them to see how big they get), and I didn't know what to do then, but I bought one of each. They were only ten cents a piece, which was pretty cheap. I am not a moron, it's just that when a guy gets his period he's really out of it because that period stuff isn't taught to guys, and girls don't talk about it. It's one of the "female mysteries." Even the fat, ugly girls don't tell you anything about it. But then, how many guys

ever think they're going to get their period.

Anyway, I know that the object of a Kotex is to soak up stuff, and so it has to go into the hole. And that also is the object of a Tampax, which is much, much smaller than a Kotex and is shaped a little different but is made out of the same stuff and smells like toilet paper, too. So it was obvious that the Kotex must go in the vagina hole because that hole was the biggest of the holes down there, and the Tampax must go in the rear end because it was smaller. The third hole is for taking a leak, but it's so tiny that I don't know what you could shove up there, and I never saw a commercial for anything smaller than a Tampax so I just left it alone.

Now I know why there are couches in girls' bathrooms. You need them to lay down on to get the Kotex in your vagina and the Tampax in your butt. A Kotex, you know, is about as big as half a box of Kleenex, and it doesn't slide too well. But anyway, after shoving for about ten minutes I got most of it up there. Getting the Tampax in my ass was a little easier but it hurt more.

So there I was with this giant wad of stuff in my vagina and another wad in my rear end. I guessed it was all fixed up, but it sure was hard to walk normal with all that crap in my holes. No wonder women get so crabby when they get their periods. I was pretty crabby myself about having to go through all that, and I felt real sorry for all the girls and I also felt pissed off at the female period supply companies for making their products too big and too hard to put in and not slippery enough.

Anyway, I got home and everything, and by about 4:00 my period stopped and I took a bubble bath. My parents came home about 5:00. It was real weird being around my dad when I had a vagina. But it wasn't so weird around my mom and I helped her cook dinner, which was fun. I made the frozen peas and mashed up the potatoes and I did really good, and it wasn't boring or anything, which was neat.

During dinner I got a phone call. It

was my best friend, Dan. He asked about how my groin, which was bleeding at the swim meet, was and I said it was O.K. and it was just nothing and it was all gone away, and he asked if I was still going to go with him and Jeff and Steve and Steve's cousin, who goes to junior college, and I said no, and he got pissed off because before I said I would and I said no again, and he asked why not, but I couldn't tell him the real reason why so I said O.K. and he said, "Great! We're going to get high and look for girls."

I finished dinner, and my sister, Kristen, gave me a whole bunch of shit about hogging the bathroom and leaving hair in the sink, and I started to cry and my mom told Kristen to shut up, and I went upstairs to steal another pair of her underpants, because the other ones were buried in the backyard along with my pants. By the way, don't flush Kotexes down the toilet because they back it up, which is what happened in our downstairs bathroom, and there was a big fight between my dad and my younger sister, Mandy, who is thirteen, for flushing Kotex, and she got embarrassed and screamed, "I don't have my time of month, I don't have my time of month, it's Kristen!" And Kristen screamed back, but louder because she is nineteen and really an asshole, "I don't even use Kotex, you little shit!" That earned her no car for two weeks, and finally my old man got so embarrassed listening to his daughters fight about periods that he left and said he was going to the hardware store to buy some washers for his sailboat. Boy, what would he have done if he knew it was *my* Kotex that caused the trouble?

I was not in love with the idea of going out with all those guys, but at about 8:00 they showed up, and while I took one last look at my face and hair and checked to see if there was anything up my nose, the guys joked around downstairs with my dad. Finally, my dad got sick of them and yelled at me to come down, and I did.

I was the last guy to be picked up so I had to sit in the back seat in the middle, which is not a great place to sit. I had Steve on one side of me and Steve's cousin, who goes to junior college, Jim, on the other side. Up in front Dan was driving and Jeff was shotgunned, and there was a case of Steve's beer in the middle. We smoked some joints and drank and talked and listened to Ace Frehley's solo album (he is the guy who plays lead for KISS), which I used to love but suddenly did not love anymore, and I think I would have rather listened to Fleetwood Mac or Chuck Mangione or the Bee Gees, but even though I didn't like the music, I still sort of sang along with it like my sisters do. Jim told me to shut

JULY, 1971

WOODMAN

274

up. It hurt my feelings real bad and I almost wanted to cry.

I was real quiet (except for singing that time) because my vagina was sort of pulsating and throbbing. I think it was doing that because of the Kotex being up there before, and also my butt was in pain. Everybody wanted to know why I was so quiet and I said I didn't feel too good. If you ever want a bunch of guys my age to leave you alone, don't tell them you don't feel too good, because if they know that something is wrong they will attack you and take advantage of you and try to make you feel worse, which is just what Jeff did when he turned around on the seat and looked right at my face and said, "Ass Patrol on alert!" "Alright!" Dan shouted. And I freaked out inside.

Ass Patrol is the same as mooning, and mooning is hanging your ass out of a car window, and I couldn't hang my ass out of the window because (a) I was wearing my sister's underpants, and (b) the vagina was right in front of my ass. "It's your turn, Larry," Dan said. "Flash flesh."

"I can't," I said. "I have a cold."

"Bullshit!"

"Fuck you!"

No matter how much I said no they said yes, and they would have pulled my pants down and shoved my ass out (they were so drunk and high), and the dangerous part about that is that when you are going sixty-five miles an hour and a bunch of drunk guys are trying to get your butt out the window, you can fall out and die or get into a crash and have to die with your pants down and have people laugh at you for the rest of your life—and even laugh louder if you have a vagina! So I said I would do it then. On top of everything terrible that had just happened, Steve's cousin said, "Why don't we moon the drive-in window at the Burger King?"

Everybody thought that was the coolest thing they ever heard, and we turned around and headed back for the Burger King. One good thing was that it gave me time to figure out how to put my ass out without revealing my sister's underpants or the vagina and also to get my pants ready so that I could do it quickly and get it over with. Except everything got fucked up because Dan was too busy trying to watch and not busy enough driving, and he crashed into the Burger King and I flew forward into the front seat and hit my head on the ashtray. I knew I was in big trouble because I could see four faces staring at the beaver I was flashing.

"It's a cunt!"

"Larry's got a cunt!"

"It's real!"

I didn't do anything except almost shit in my pants, which were down by my knees. And do you know what else?

All the people who worked at the Burger King were crowded in the window looking at my vagina. I think they must have thought I was a girl but still, shit, that's super embarrassing! Dan suddenly got smart and saw that he was going to get into trouble for hitting a Burger King, so he pulled out into the street and swerved to miss a car and we were gone.

"Far out!" Steve said.

"It's incredible, look at it!"

I just laid there, mainly because of the position I was in I couldn't do anything else. My head was down on the floor and my back was on the beer and my legs were hanging over the back seat, and there was a guy on either side of me and two guys in the back about a foot from my vagina, just staring like morons. Then the guy from junior college reached out and touched it.

"*Get out of there!*" I screamed!

"Where's your dork?" Jeff asked me.

"What's happened?" Dan said.

Then the guy from junior college tried to open my legs up, and I kicked him but he just started laughing like an animal and then he made me faint when he said, "Let's fuck Larry!"

Oh, God! I was in deep-shit trouble!

When I woke up, the car was parked at the golf course and my pants were completely off. I tried to get up but no one would help me.

"You can't fuck me!" I said. "I am a guy!"

That sort of slowed them down, and they were all quiet for a minute and then Dan said that I was right. But then Jeff said, "If he's a guy, what's he doing with that!"

"You know what?" Steve said, like he suddenly figured out what was going on but he really didn't, "Larry's a girl who's pretending to be a guy and has always been a girl!"

"I have not," I said. "You guys have seen my…"

Nope, I never had gym with any of those guys and as far as I know they never saw my "thing" out in the open, and it didn't make any difference because they were so drunk and high that I could have been a zebra and they wouldn't have known it.

"I don't want to take any chances on being a homo," Dan said.

"It's a vagina, dumb shit!" Jeff said.

"You can't be a homo if it's a vagina."

"Yeah," Dan said. "I guess so."

"Let's do it," Steve said.

"Is it O.K. with you, Larry?"

"No!" I screamed!

I was scared shit and I was struggling like crazy, and normally I could have whipped those guys in about one and a half minutes, but I just didn't have any muscles left. I have to admit this and it's really gross and disgusting and horrible and a nightmare but…my friends all fucked me.

Everything worked out O.K., I guess. I never talked to those guys again and they never talked to me, either, and then my dad got transferred to California and we moved there in the summer, so I don't know what happened to them, except I heard Steve's cousin joined the navy and got thrown out for setting fire to a guy's bed. The vagina went away after a few months. The "little thing" just got bigger and bigger until one day it was my regular guy's thing again. It doesn't bother me any more that I had the vagina. I mean, it didn't make me insane or anything. I guess the worst thing that happened was that I had to use up most of my money I was saving for new skis and waste my Easter vacation having to get an abortion. ☐

JULY, 1974

GLAD YOU LIKE IT, DOROTHY

BOY, FARMER GREEN, THIS IS REALLY GOOD!

**FOTO FUNNIES**

I'M PETER PAN.

I DON'T SUPPOSE YOU RECOGNIZED ME. BUT, THEN, IT'S BEEN SOME TIME SINCE YOU SAW ME LAST.

SINCE THEN I'VE PROSPERED NICELY, THANK YOU.

WENDY CONVINCED ME TO EMIGRATE FROM NEVERLAND, YOU SEE, AND MR. DARLING, HER FATHER (YOU REMEMBER HIM, SURELY), FOUND ME A POSITION IN A LONDON INVESTMENT HOUSE. VERY KIND OF HIM, I MIGHT ADD.

LET'S SEE, WHAT ELSE HAS HAPPENED? WELL, WENDY MARRIED A BANKER FELLOW FROM SYDNEY. AND SHE'S A GRANDMOTHER NOW. THE LOST BOYS FOUNDED AN ADVERTISING AGENCY: TOOTLES, NIBS, AND LOST BOYS, LTD. I SUPPOSE YOU'VE HEARD OF THEM. THEY HAVE THE P.J. LORILLARD ACCOUNT.

OH, YES, AND TINKER BELL DIED. POOR GIRL, IT'LL BE FIVE YEARS AGO NEXT MONTH.

BUT I CAN STILL FLY, YOU KNOW...

...AND *FIRST CLASS*, TOO!

# DR. JEKYLL AND MR. DRUNK

### BY TOD CARROLL

DR. VERN JEKYLL, D.O., OPERATED AN INSUBSTANTIAL PRACTICE OUT OF HIS HOME IN SOUTHERN ILLINOIS. ONE DAY, HE SUMMONED HIS WIFE FOR THE PURPOSE OF GIVING HER SOME INSTRUCTIONS. THIS APPARENTLY ROUTINE AND SIMPLE ACT WAS REALLY MUCH MORE--IT WAS THE BEGINNING OF ONE OF THE MOST DEPRESSING STORIES YOU HAVE EVER READ.

DARLING, I EXPECT THERE SHALL BE A STRANGE GENTLEMAN VISITING US FROM TIME TO TIME, AND I WOULD LIKE EVERYONE IN THE FAMILY TO TREAT HIM WITH COURTESY AND RESPECT.

WHO IS THIS INDIVIDUAL, VERN?

VERN JEKYLL D.O. OSTEOPATHIC CLINIC PLEASE USE SIDE DOOR

I CAN TELL YOU ONLY THAT HIS NAME IS MR. DRUNK. *THE REST IS MY PERSONAL AFFAIR!*

ALTHOUGH BEA JEKYLL WAS PUZZLED BY THE EXPLANATION, SHE APPRISED HER CHILDREN OF THEIR FATHER'S COMMAND. THEN, ONE EVENING...

TONI, I MUST INSIST THAT YOU GET AWAY FROM THE BARE FLOOR BEFORE YOU CATCH A COLD. VERN, PLEASE TELL HER TO ASSEMBLE HER PROJECT ELSEWHERE.

ASSEMBLE YOUR PROJECT ELSEWHERE!

...WHERE HE BEGAN TO CONCOCT A MYSTERIOUS POTION.

He began to tremble and convulse as insidious chemicals seized control of his entire body.

TAKE NOTICE, DR. JEKYLL...I AM RID OF YOUR PEEVISH, MISERABLE MANNER COMPLETELY. NO LONGER SHALL THE BITTERNESS OF INCOMPETENCY AND MISFORTUNE IMPINGE UPON MY ABSOLUTE RIGHT TO HAPPINESS. BE GONE, DR. JEKYLL--MEET...

...MR. DRUNK!

WHERE'SSH MY FAVORRRITE LI'L MAJOR LEEEAGUER?...

WHA...?

I KNOWWW YOURR OL' DAD DOESN' BELIEVE IN AAAALLOWANCE, BUT I WWWANT YOU TO TAKE THISSH SO YOU'LLLL ALWAYSSH HAVE A BUCK IN YOURRR POCKET.

AND HOWWW'SH MY BESSHT ANGEL?...

ANYYYTHING YOU EVERRR WANT, YOU JUS' COME TO ME.

OH, NO!

MR. DRUNK ISSH SOOO SORRRY, HONEY...COME ON. LE'S HAVE A SPECIALLL TREAT TO MAKE UP FORRR IT.

WL847, THISSH ISSH HB766Y STANDING BY WITH A COOOUPLE A LI'L HAMS WHOOO BI'N BUGGINNN' THEIR DAD FORRR YEARSSH TO TALK ON THE RIG AND--COME ONNN, KIDS, THISSH ISSH YOUR TREAT, YOU'RE ONNA AIR... *GET OVER HERE!*

SUDDENLY, MR DRUNK EXPERIENCED A PRONOUNCED SHIFT IN HIS NATURE.

YOU SQUAWLING BASTARDS WILL SPEAK TO WL847, AND YOU WILL DO SO IMMEDIATELY!

GOOD HEAVENS, THE POTION IS GOING AWRY. I MUST HAVE THE ANTIDOTE.

MR. DRUNK QUICKLY LAID HIMSELF UPON THE ANTIDOTE. BY MORNING, HE HAD REVERTED TO THE PERSON OF DR. JEKYLL, VOWING NEVER AGAIN TO REPEAT HIS FOOLISH EXPERIMENT.

BUT THE DOCTOR FAILED TO HONOR HIS PLEDGE, AND MRS. JEKYLL REMAINED WHOLLY MYSTIFIED BY HER HUSBAND'S ALLEGIANCE TO THE STRANGE INTRUDER WHO TERRIFIED THE CHILDREN, DROVE THE AUTOMOBILE INTO MAILBOXES, DISGORGED MASSIVE VOLUMES OF RED-GREEN BILE ON THE TOILET AND BATH MATS, BATTERED HOLES IN THE DOORS, SOLD DR. JEKYLL'S PRESCRIPTION PADS TO NARCOTICS ADDICTS, IMBUED THEIR HOME WITH THE WRETCHED MORNING STINK OF LIQUOROUS RESPIRATION, CALLED HER A CUNT, AND LEFT BURNING CIGARETTES ON THE DINING ROOM TABLE. THEN, ONE DAY, AS SHE WAS STROLLING WITH A FRIEND...

FROM PREVIOUS EXPERIENCE WITH AN INDIVIDUAL SIMILAR TO YOUR MR. DRUNK, I TELL YOU THERE IS ONLY ONE WAY TO EXPOSE HIM. YOU MUST ORGANIZE THE CHILDREN. YOU MUST DRILL THEM RELIGIOUSLY ON HIS FAULTS.

THEN I PROPOSE THEY EXECUTE A THOROUGH CAMPAIGN OF HUMILIATION.

MRS. JEKYLL STATIONED TONI AND HOWARD NEAR THE DOOR AND WAITED FOR MR. DRUNK TO GO OUTSIDE.

REMEMBER YOUR INSTRUCTIONS.

LOOK, MR. DRUNK--WE'RE FOLLOWING IN YOUR FOOTSTEPS.

AND WE'RE HAVING LIQUOR DRINKS JUST LIKE YOU.

OH, MY GOD!

MR. DRUNK DASHED TO THE LABORATORY, BOLTED THE DOOR, AND INGESTED A LETHAL DOSE OF HIS FORMULA. LATER, WHEN THE FAMILY INVESTIGATED...

MR. DRUNK!...VERN!! DR. JEKYLL AND MR. DRUNK WERE ONE AND THE SAME ALL ALONG!

HE'S DEAD.

NOW WHAT?

LOOK FOR WORK, I SUPPOSE....

THE END

# The Churchill Wit

Churchill was known to drain a glass or two and, after one particularly convivial evening, he chanced to encounter Miss Bessie Braddock, a Socialist member of the House of Commons, who, upon seeing his condition, said, "Winston, you're drunk." Mustering all his dignity, Churchill drew himself up to his full height, cocked an eyebrow and rejoined, "Shove it up your ass, you ugly cunt."

When the noted playwright George Bernard Shaw sent him two tickets to the opening night of his new play with a note that read: "Bring a friend, if you have one," Churchill, not to be outdone, promptly wired back: "You and your play can go fuck yourselves."

At an elegant dinner party, Lady Astor once leaned across the table to remark, "If you were my husband, Winston, I'd poison your coffee."

"And if you were my wife, I'd beat the shit out of you," came Churchill's unhesitating retort.

During the darkest days of World War II, when each night brought waves of Luftwaffe bombers raining death and destruction on a near-defenseless London, Prime Minister Churchill went on the air to address the British people. "I read in this morning's paper that Herr Hitler plans to wring England's neck like that of a chicken," he began, "and I was reminded of what the Irish poacher said as he stood on the gallows. It seems the poor fellow was approached by a well-meaning if somewhat overzealous priest who, in horrific detail, described the unfading torments of Hades which awaited him if he did not repent of his misdeeds. The condemned man listened patiently to all that the priest had to say, and when he was done, grinned broadly and replied, 'Eat it raw, fuzz-nuts.'"

Shortly after Churchill had grown a moustache, he was accosted by a certain young lady whose political views were in direct opposition to his own. Fancying herself something of a wag, she exclaimed, "Mr. Churchill, I care for neither your politics nor your moustache."

Unabashed, the young statesman regarded her quietly for a moment, then wryly commented, "Suck my dick."

While serving as a subaltern in the Boer War, the young Churchill was asked by a superior officer to give his opinion of the Boers as soldiers.

"They're assholes, sir," he ventured, then paused briefly and added, with a whimsical smile, "They're assholes."

Sir Winston carried on a life-long feud with Labour party leader Aneurin Bevan and, on one occasion, while Mr. Bevan was delivering an unusually long speech to the House of Commons, Churchill slumped into his seat and appeared to doze off. When Bevan noticed this, he inquired in his loudest voice, "Must the right honorable gentleman fall asleep during my speech?" Receiving no reply, Mr. Bevan continued until, a few minutes later, the sound of snoring was distinctly audible to all present. This time Mr. Bevan slammed his hand on the rail and fairly shouted, "Until now, the Conservative party had usually managed to conceal the fact that it was asleep." Without even opening his eyes, Churchill quipped, "Flake off, touch-hole" and unconcernedly resumed his nap.

Churchill was given to reading in the bathtub and, while staying at the White House, he once became so engrossed in an account of the Battle of Fonteney that he forgot President Roosevelt was due to drop by to discuss the upcoming conference in Yalta. At the appointed hour, the president was wheeled into Churchill's quarters only to be informed that the prime minister had not finished bathing. Roosevelt was about to apologize for the intrusion and depart when Churchill, puffing his customary cigar, strode into the room stark naked and greeted the nonplussed world leader with a terse, "What are you staring at, homo?"  □

# First Blowjob

*A Young Girl's Senior Prom Can Mean Many Things: A Bouquet of Memories…Or a Pillow Full of Tears…*

### by Doug Kenney

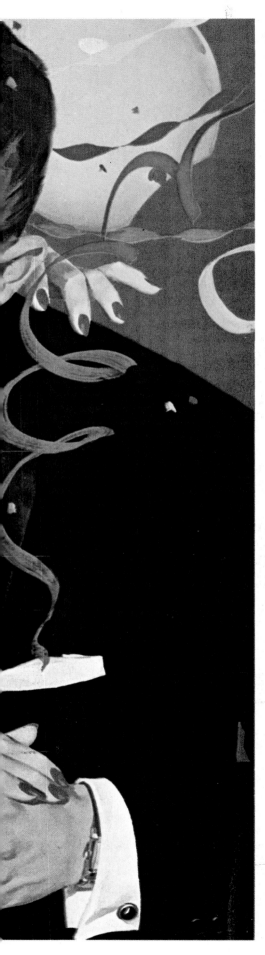

"Connie! Connie Phillips! You'd better hurry, Jeff will be here any minute!"

Mrs. Phillips's call from downstairs found Connie, still in her freshly ironed slip, sitting crosslegged on the bedspread to put the finishing touches on her nails. A startled glance at the clock on the bureau reaffirmed her mother's warning—it was almost half past seven. Fanning the air with her hands to dry the polish, Connie gulped and hurried to dress.

Carefully, she drew the sheer nylons over her tan, athletic legs and slipped on the white organdy gown that hung in its plastic bag on her closet door. (Thank heaven Mrs. Phillips had relented at the store in her preference for the green taffeta—a high-necked confusion of bows, flounces, and spaghetti straps that looked more like a circus tent than a party frock.) Connie fastened the three simple strands of cultured pearls around her neck and took the rhinestone bracelet Mrs. Phillips had lent her especially for tonight from the dressing table. Blotting her cherry-frost lipstick on a tissue and giving her pert, blond curls one last flick with her brush, Connie sighed and stepped back from the mirror for final inspection.

Looking at the unfamiliar figure who peered back from the glass with equally wide-eyed astonishment, Connie suddenly felt a curious sense of elation. What this afternoon was only a gum-snapping, floppy-shirted teen with one ear glued to the telephone and the other permanently cocked toward the hi-fi had been miraculously transformed somewhere between this afternoon's bubble bath and that teetering test-walk in her new yellow satin pumps—into an undeniably attractive, grown-up woman.

*Good looks aren't a passport to a happy and productive life,* Connie reminded herself as she lingered another moment before the mirror, *but is it wrong to know you're pretty and be glad of it…at least for one special night?*

"Hey, nobody told me *Grace Kelly* was in here! I wonder where that dumb old Connie is?"

Connie started from her reverie and quickly flushed with embarrassment as she saw Didi's reflection behind her. Didi Phillips was a pesky, pug-nosed, freckle-faced imp who Connie's parents persisted in maintaining was her own little sister.

"And I suppose no one told you it's impolite to barge into other people's rooms without knocking either?" retorted Connie, whirling around to confront her impudent sibling.

"No-o, but I hear you can get stuck-up from looking at mirrors too long," Didi returned airily. "Anyway, Prince Charming's in the living room getting the third degree from Mom an' Pop, so you'd better trot on down before he shrivels up like a raisin."

Snatching her handbag from the bureau, Connie brushed by Didi and, pausing at the top of the stairs to take a deep breath, descended in a slow, "ladylike" manner to the living room where she found Jeff sitting on the couch chatting amiably with her parents. Everyone turned toward Connie as she appeared and Jeff, rising to stand, stared at her with an appreciative grin.

"Ho-ly Bananas," exclaimed Jeff, making a comical bow, "I didn't know I had a date with a *movie star!*"

"And *I* didn't know I had a date with such a *smoothie!*" laughed Connie, joining in the general amusement.

"Oh yes," chuckled Mr. Phillips as he lit his pipe, "Jeff and I have just been discussing that forty-yard pass he made against Hillcrest last season, and now I see why you think he's such a 'dreamboat'!"

For the second time that evening, Connie blushed, then joined Jeff, whose tan, athletic good looks were set off by merry blue eyes and a bow tie in a smart green plaid.

"Now, Wayne," said Mrs. Phillips, "leave the jokes to Jack Benny and let the children go—they don't want to sit around listening to *us*."

"You're right, Ruth," said Mr. Phillips sheepishly as he knocked the ashes from his pipe and slipped it into the pocket of his cardigan sweater. "You know, it wasn't until you came down those stairs that I realized what a beautiful young woman my little Connie has become."

"Oh Daddy, don't be silly," chided Connie affectionately, as she kissed her father's cheek. "You know I'll *always* be 'your little girl.'"

"I know you will," said Mr. Phillips, "and I also know that Jeff is a fine boy—but there'll be other fine lads around when you go to State in the fall, so I'd like you to promise a prehistoric old dad one thing...."

"Sure Daddy," said Connie, giving a mock conspiratorial wink to Jeff over her father's shoulder, "what is it?"

"Just promise me," said Mr. Phillips, fumbling for his pipe cleaners, "that no matter how wonderful the dance may be tonight, and no matter what Jeff and you may be feeling...promise me that you won't give him a blowjob."

"A w-what?" stammered Connie, backing away slightly.

"A blowjob," Mr. Phillips repeated. "You know, when a fellow forces his dork down your throat and makes you suck on it until he eventually shoots his pecker-snot all over your tonsils."

In the silence that followed, Connie, suddenly quite pale, looked beseechingly from Mrs. Phillips to Jeff, both of whom could only avert their eyes to the carpet.

"Oh my God," gasped Connie, "th-that's ...horrible...*sickening*...."

"You bet it is," replied Mr. Phillips, puffing his pipe alight, "just ask your mother."

* * *

Once in Jeff's convertible, Connie tactfully passed over Mr. Phillips's unusual behavior and admired the single, perfect white gardenia Jeff had brought. "What a gorgeous flower," she said as she admired the blossom in Jeff's rear view mirror, "but you shouldn't have spent so much!"

"Oh, a couple of weekends at hard labor on my pop's lawn mower," Jeff admitted, "but seeing how fabulous you look wearing it makes it a bargain."

"It *is* a grand evening, isn't it?" Connie said, inhaling the fresh late spring greenery as they sped along Lakeshore Drive to the prom.

"And a grand date for me," Jeff returned. "I feel like the luckiest senior in the history of Parkdale High."

"And *I'm* the luckiest girl," Connie smiled. "After all, it isn't *everybody* who goes to the Spring Bounce with Jeff Madison—cocaptain of the Varsity Football Team, chairman of the Student Senate, *and* Hi-Tri-Y activities coordinator!"

"Aw, cut the softsoap," Jeff laughed. "Let's just say that we're *both* lucky before we get swelled heads!"

"Fun ahoy!" Jeff sang as he turned off Glenview Boulevard into the already crowded parking lot. "Last one

on the dance floor is a wallflower!"

"Not me!" cried Connie excitedly, "and you'd better've eaten your Cheerios because I'm not going to sit out a single dance!"

The Senior Bounce was everything Connie hoped it would be, and together with Jeff she floated and swayed to the lilting rhythms of fox trots, sambas, and polkas until Connie thought her heart would burst.

"I have to powder my nose," said Connie, excusing herself at the break as the crowd eagerly gathered at the tempting tables of Hawaiian Punch and gingersnaps. For Connie it was a perfect evening, or almost perfect, for when Connie went to the coat rack to get a handkerchief from her wrap, she overheard Mary Ellen Peterson and Doris Wilkins whispering by the drinking fountain.

"Doesn't Connie Phillips look... *sophisticated* tonight?" said Mary Ellen archly.

"Who wouldn't," Doris sniffed, "with that swanky rhinestone bracelet of her mother's?"

"Well," said Mary Ellen, "she certainly seems to have Jeff Madison on a string. Do you think they'll get engaged?"

"Maybe," said Doris vaguely, "although I can't *imagine* Connie not minding Jeff's personality problems...."

At that point Connie "accidentally" dropped her compact and the two gossips, both red-faced, ended their discussion in mid-meow.

"Hel-lo girls," said Connie. "Did I hear you mention Jeff?"

"W-well, as a matter of fact," began a flustered Mary Ellen, "I was just this minute telling Doris that...with a *personality* like Jeff's he certainly has no *problem* snagging the most popular girl in Parkdale!"

"Oh," said Connie uncertainly.

The band tuned up again, but this time as Connie whirled around the floor in Jeff's appreciative arms, her happiness was clouded by the snatch of conversation she had overheard in the Ladies Room. Even the intoxicating, quicksilver arpeggios of the accordion could not drown out the two false notes in the evening. *Personality problems...blowjob...personality problems...blowjob,* a small, nagging voice kept repeating.

Too soon, the band struck up "Good Night Ladies" and it was time to go. Connie and Jeff were invited to join some of the crowd at the Snak Shoppe for post-prom munchables and, it was darkly hinted, some good-natured hijinx. But Jeff begged off and, as he held Connie's hand, shyly murmured that there was something he wished to ask her alone.

As they drove away under a sky pinpointed with stars, Connie noticed

that he was strangely silent. Finally, she asked Jeff if something was troubling him.

"Yes, Connie, there *is* something," Jeff replied as he turned off Lakeshore Drive onto Clinton Avenue. Without a word, he reached into his breast pocket and offered Connie a tiny, velvet-covered box.

She still was staring at the unopened box in her hand when Jeff pulled off Clinton Avenue into a deserted alley next to the Apex Dry Cleaners.

"Oh Jeff, I don't know what to say," Connie began. "I know we've *talked* about marriage, but I really feel we both should complete our college education at State before I could even *think* of accepting your ring."

Jeff shut off the motor and turned questioningly to Connie. "State... marriage...ring?" Jeff said puzzledly. "*I'm* not going to the State *College*. My folks are sending me to the State *Mental Hospital*—that box I gave you has a couple of Dramamines in it so you don't gag too much when you give me my blowjob."

"Y-your what?" said Connie tonelessly.

"My blowjob," Jeff explained. "You know, when a guy crams his meat into your gullet and you eat on it until he goes spooey all over your uvula."

"Aaah!" Connie screamed, fumbling at the door handle. "No! Jeff, no!" But before she could escape, Connie felt inhumanly powerful hands seize her by the neck and force her head down below the dashboard. There, plainly revealed in the green fluorescent glow of the "Apex" sign, Connie saw Jeff's tan, athletic penis straining toward her.

"Oh, God, please *no!*" Connie pleaded a last time before Jeff pried her clenching jaws apart with his powerful thumbs and began by inches, to introduce his swollen flesh past her cherry-frost lipstick. As Jeff plunged and withdrew with pistonlike insistence, Connie felt her glottis constrict involuntarily, seizing the intrusive column.

"Atta girl, Connie," encouraged Jeff, "shake hands with it!"

At last Jeff rose to his final, shuddering spasm and Connie felt a wad of viscous fluid splatter off her palate and slowly begin to trickle through her vitals.

"Not bad for a beginner," reassured Jeff as he tied Connie's wrists and ankles to the steering wheel with his matching plaid suspenders. "You should learn to breathe through your nose, though," he added thoughtfully.

When Connie was firmly trussed and secured to the wheel, Jeff excused himself and returned a few moments later wearing a makeshift Nazi uniform, a snapped-off car aerial clutched in his hand.

"Gee," exclaimed Jeff as he began to lash out viciously at her unprotected body, "I've been wanting to try this ever since I first heard Negro music!"

\* \* \*

It was many minutes past midnight when a blue convertible screeched to a stop in front of the Phillips's home. A car door could be heard opening, and, under the yellow radiance of the streetlight, a limp weight was kicked from the automobile onto the sidewalk before it roared off with a muffled growl.

Slowly, the girl began to stir. Connie, still only semiconscious, opened her eyes to a brilliant starscape. This puzzled her because she had landed face first. *Sky up, not down*—Connie reminded herself with the characteristic common sense that had made her one of the most popular seniors at Parkdale, *why stars on ground?*—Then, as her eyes began to focus, Connie realized that the twinkling array before her was not stars, but a scattering of precious rhinestones on the pavement.

"Uh-oh, gonna get it now,..." Connie sang to herself sadly as she crawled across the moist green lawn to her door. Hauling herself to her feet with the aid of a pair of lawn flamingos, Connie used them as simple crutches to stagger the last few steps to the front porch. There, she collapsed and began to scratch feebly at the screen.

Answering the door, Mr. Phillips was surprised to find Connie's crumpled form on the steps, her half-naked body crisscrossed with red welts and her tattered nylons seamed with thin rivulets of dried blood.

"Well, it certainly looks like you've had *your* fun," said Mr. Phillips, "do you have any idea what time it is, young lady?"

Connie remained motionless on the steps as Mr. Phillips puffed his pipe angrily. Finally, Mr. Phillips sighed and lifted the dazed girl to her feet and leaned her against the screen door.

"I suppose you think your old Dad's an ancient old stick-in-the-mud," said Mr. Phillips. "But I *can* sympathize with the problems facing young people today...heck, you may not believe it, but I'm even 'hep' to a lot of your kookie teen lingo."

With that, Mr. Phillips's fist struck Connie in the face and sent her somersaulting through the screen door back out onto the lawn, the force of his blow immediately closing her right eye.

"Padiddle, for example," chuckled Mr. Phillips. □

# Greatest Farts Of the Century

## by B. Kliban

No. 9 IN A SERIES

No. 25 IN A SERIES

No. 3 IN A SERIES

DECEMBER, 1972

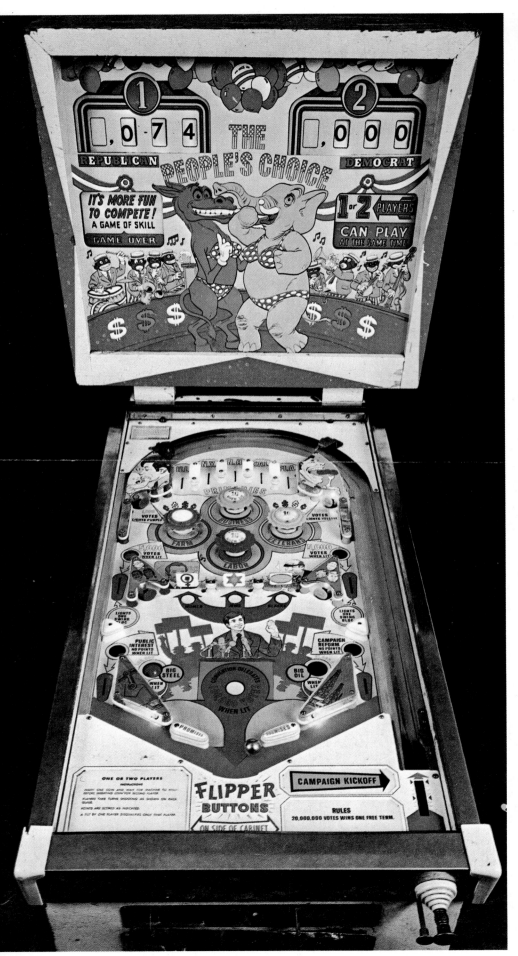

*The following essay by John Weidman ran as an introductory explanation of the "American System" in* National Lampoon's *pre-Bicentennial special,* The 199th Birthday Book (*1975*).

"The American System," President Eisenhower once remarked, "is the greatest system of its kind in the world today. It is the secret envy of non-Americans everywhere, be they communists, socialists, or what have you. My brother Milton tells me it is the greatest system since sliced bread, which it is in fact greater than, since on the one hand it will never go stale, like bread, and on the other hand my advisers tell me sliced bread was invented in America, which means that sliced bread is only one small part of it, it being the System as a whole. The American System is many things, according to my speechwriters. It's the Declaration of Independence, french fries and a milkshake, 'getting out the vote,' and wealthy men in Cadillacs being driven to the office by starving Negroes in little blue suits. It's tickets to the World Series, Adlai Stevenson's concession speech, the Ed Sullivan Show, and something that somebody wrote down here called the military-industrial complex, whatever that is. God bless the American System."

Eisenhower was right, just as he had been on Omaha Beach in 1944, and as he would be again in 1961 when he finally gave America a break and retired to his farm in Gettysburg, Pennsylvania. The American System *is* the greatest system in the world today, and understanding how it works is a duty which too many Americans take lightly, for granted, with a grain of salt, or (depending on the color of their skin), in the ear or up the ass.

Just how *does* the American System work? Well, it's complicated; there's no denying it. It involves checks and balances, three coequal branches of government, a free and independent judiciary, freedom of the press, universal suffrage, public education, collective bargaining, the minimum wage, tax deductions, freedom of worship, giving at the office, reading you your Miranda rights, surreptitious surveil-

# SYSTEM

by John Weidman

lance, freedom of contract, the right to bear arms, home rule, redeeming social value, and alternate side of the street parking.

Indeed, the System is an intricate web of institutional interplays, systemic interactions, organizational interrelationships, static interference, and third-down interceptions. Some would say that ultimately, it is so complex as to defy description.

We disagree. And so does the U.S. Immigration Service, which insists that each of the semiliterate, undereducated aliens who arrogantly aspire to become citizens of this lánd of 99 percent fat-free milk and petroleum-based honey master the complex workings of our System before they raise their right hands (an act which in and of itself often requires the assistance of an immigration official) and take the oath of allegiance. We quote from the Immigration Service pamphlet "America: A Place for Everything and Everyone in His Place":

*Remember how in the Old Country you never knew* who *made the laws against wearing bright-colored bermudas,* what *government agency to call when your toilet backed up,* where *the old president went after he was retired from office,* why *the village telephone was always out of order, and* when *your letter to grandma was going to get there, no matter how many stamps you put on it? Those five crucial* ws, *and a hundred others just like them, are no mystery in the United States of America! No, sir (as you may one day earn the right to be called in this land of equal opportunity). In America, those five crucial* ws, *and a hundred others just like them, are no mystery because in America we have a* System, *a System which works, and which, most importantly, works for you! It tells each and every one of us who we are, what we're doing, where we're going, why we're going there, and when we're going to arrive (although even in America we're sometimes delayed when the car won't start or the 8:32 breaks down on its way out of Stamford).*

Assuming that the American Sys-

tem *does* work (and Joe McCarthy had a name for people who don't accept that assumption), the next crucial question is, "How?" Is there any easy way to understand the inner workings of a socioeconomic, politicoreligionic, cryptodemocratic, texacoplutocratic, hypoallergenic system which Will Rogers once said was as complicated as "the inside of a cancer-riddled chicken"? Probably not, but we think the easiest way to proceed is by analogy. What, we may ask, is the System like?

Well, it's like this. Think for a moment of the way in which your own human body works. Just like the American System, it, too, is complex, but again, like the American System, each of its parts—the lungs, the brains, the knees, and the penis, works in harmony with all the other parts to get the job done, whether that job be standing, eating, kissing, sitting, or running away from angry Negroes. The American System is like that; all the various parts—labor, industry, government, the press, the church, and a small group of wealthy Jewish businessmen in New York, all working together to keep the "body" politic on the go and running smoothly.

Sometimes, of course, the body gets sick, feverish, or out of sorts. One little part "goes bad," stops doing the job, or, in the most serious cases, begins actively working against the other happy, healthy parts. Just so the American System. Suppose, for example, your body has organized itself to watch a little Sunday night television. Down goes the ass, up come the feet, out goes the hand and on comes "Columbo." An hour and a half passes pleasantly. When the show is over everything regroups to go out to the kitchen for a ham and swiss sandwich. You stand up to stretch and fall flat on your face. Your foot's gone to sleep.

Now how about the American System? Suppose, for the sake of argument, that *it's* organized itself to fight a friendly little war in some silly country on the other side of the world. A president's elected, appropriations bills are passed by the Congress, newsmen write patriotic editorials, Negroes

get drafted, the economy gears up, tanks and planes roll off the assembly line, unemployment drops as more Negroes get drafted, the Red Sox win the pennant, the theaters are filled, and everything hums along in harmony and happy unison. And then the foot falls asleep. All across America, overprivileged undergraduates enjoying four years of communistically-inclined edu-vacations turn off their stereos and start whining and crying like a bunch of bleeding heart fairies. And next thing you know, just like your body, the American System falls flat on its face.

And what do we do when one part of the body contracts a crippling disease which threatens the health and harmony of the whole? Well, what do we do when our foot falls asleep? Do we throw up our hands in a gesture of surrender? Not on your life. We form those hands into rock-hard little fists, and with all the energy that the healthy parts of the body can summon up, we beat our sleeping foot savagely until Mr. Circulation is moving again and our slumbering extremity has come to its senses. And that's the way the American System heals itself and holds down its national doctor bills, without any help from socialized medicine, thank you very much.

Yes, indeed, self-help is the American way, unlike social security, unemployment insurance, and welfare benefits, which were invented in Leningrad in 1917 by Leon Trotsky, imported by Woodrow Wilson, patented by Franklin Roosevelt, and shoved down the throats of an unsuspecting and unprotected (Roosevelt saw to that when he provoked the Japs into bombing Pearl Harbor so he could send all our soldiers overseas to fight somebody else's battles for them) American public. And if any of America's college students are reading this, assuming that they still know how to read, which they probably don't, since the only two subjects they seem to teach in school anymore are "Elementary Bus Riding" and "How to Get Along with Negroes," it might be a good idea if they went back and read that last paragraph again. And if after that they still don't get the message, then maybe they ought to seriously consider writing a letter, assuming they still know how to write, to their hero Fidel "Fuck America" Castro and ask him if they can come over to his Caribbean People's Paradise and stay for awhile, like maybe forever.

And you know who they can take with them? Mr. Ivy League, candyass, "Let's change the system by working within it," that's who. I mean who the fuck asked them to change the System, anyway? Who's complaining? I'll tell you who's complaining. Bums and freeloaders, that's who. Piss-colored midgets in pointy shoes whose idea of a real American Thanksgiving dinner is rice and beans and a side order of cranberry sauce. Tap-dancing shvartzes who think Uncle Sam owes them a day's pay for standing on the corner telling women what they think of their tits. Human tortillas who want $15,000 a year, a home of their own, and all the Tito Puente albums they can eat for running around on all fours pulling salad out of the ground. These something-for-nothing-'cause-I'm-too-lazy/dumb-to-work-for-it bastards are everywhere. They're all around us. They're the guys who put fluoride in your water, funny ideas in your wife's head, and midget chinks in the Little League World Series. You remember that one? "Welcome to the All-American finals of the All-American Little League World Series, featuring *Puerto Rico* versus *Nationalist China*." Good Christ! And while we're watching some slant-eyed little slope throw curve balls at some American kid's head in McKeesport, Pennsylvania, who's slipping the little zipper-eyes' big brothers into the United Fucking Nations? Henry Zo Vat If I Vas Not Born in America Kissinger, that's who! When the fuck are we going to wake up to what's going on around here, for Christ's sake? What do we need, an announcement that the country's going to hell, hand delivered by Comrade Cut-Your-Nuts-Off from the Kremlin? You wanna wake up one morning and find out your kids are being bussed all the way to Peking to go to school? You don't? Then do something about it, meathead. And whatever you do, you better do it quick, 'cause I read in the papers where Gene McCarthy is gonna run for president again, and maybe he lost last time but maybe he won't this time (Happy two-hundredth birthday, America), and if that cocksucker gets to be commander in chief, he'll move the capital to Havana and put Salvatore Allende's picture on the ten-cent stamp. And that'll just be the beginning. You like Chinese food? You like it enough to eat it three meals a day for the rest of your life?

You'll be one of the lucky ones.  □

294

## Black and White Prints from the British Museum

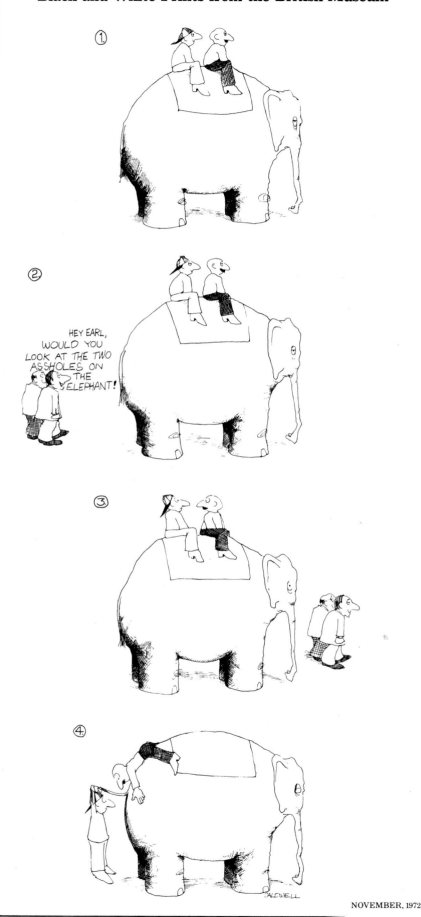

NOVEMBER, 1972

The cultural exchange program that traded Jerry Lewis to France for Marcel Marceau also entailed the swap of Topo Gigio for Clint Eastwood. The spaghetti western became popular. The rest is history—Gibbon, to be exact.

LA SERA, IL VIENE.
CERCANDO LA VENDETTA...

# IL SHOWDOWN A RIO JAWBONE

REALIZZATO DA ALFREDO DENTE

...IL COWHAND PIÙ FURIOSO DEL WEST, UN DUDE CHI FA TREMBLARE I CUORI DI TUTT'ALTRI, GOODGUYS O BADGUYS...

...O'MAC HUGGINS!

CINQUE ANNI CHE SU FRATELLO È HUMILIATO NEL TUMBLEWEED DI OKLAHOMA, HUMILIATO A MORTE. CINQUE ANNI LA SUA VENDETTA. ADESSO ARRIVE... IL SHOWDOWN!

SI, SIGNORE?

GALLIANO!

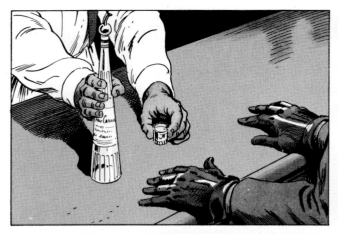

E TU COGNO!

FIGATI FINOCCH' VAI SEDETI SOPRA UNA BANANA!

CABEZA DI VACCA, MANGIA LA MIA POOP!

TUTTA LA SERA IL SHOWDOWN CONTINUA...

...MA VERSO LA NOTTE O'MACHUGGINS APPARE UN UOMO TERMINATO.

TU L'AI FATTO CON UN CANE E IL CANE NON PUÒ VENIRE! TU SEI SUSPENDATO COME UN GERBIL! E UN' ALTRA COSA...

CRETINO...

POI...

LA TUA MAMA È UNA PUTA...

AAARGH!

IL COGNO DELLA TUA MAMA HA L'ACNE TERMINALE! QUESTO COGNO SENTA COME UN KILO DI GORGONZOLA DEL SECOLO QUINCESIMO!

NO! PER PIACERE! NON LA MAMA!

QUESTO PER LA TUA MAMA!

E QUESTO!

E QUESTO!!!

LA SERA, LUI VA VIA. LA VENDETTA È FATTA. E IL SHOWDOWN A RIO JAWBONE PASSA NELLA STORIA.

SALUMERIA

PASTICCERIA

OGGETTI RELIGIOSI

-FIN-

298

*Five years after its inception in 1972 as a half-page collection of true and amusing news stories, the "True Facts" section was expanded by then managing editor P. J. O'Rourke to include "Lives of the Great," "What's Your Sign?" "Spoilers," "Bullshit," "Recent Notable Headlines," "Your Tax Dollars at Work," and a variety of advertisements, photographs, and otherwise sterling incidences of the embarrassing, the ironic, and the macabre.*

*Most material used in this section has been contributed by readers, whose personal files of vinyl slipcover ads and funeral home magazines have made "True Facts" one of the most popular features in the magazine.*

• A Brazilian was fishing on the banks of the Rio Negro when his line became snagged in a tree. As he tried to free it, a swarm of wild bees flew out of the tree and attacked him. The man escaped by running into the river, where he was eaten by a school of piranha. *Edmonton Sun* (contributed by John Burke) MAY, 1979

• Alpha Xi Delta sorority held a rush party at its house near the University of Texas campus in Austin, Texas. As eighteen-year-old Regina Gerling waited to enter the party with other rush candidates, she suffered a massive heart attack and dropped dead. Her corpse was removed, and the party continued. When a sorority member was informed Gerling had died, she replied, "All I know is you're ruining our rush party." *Dallas Times Herald* (William Landrum) MARCH, 1979

• Mark Maybry of Albuquerque, New Mexico, was arrested when he attempted to use his mother's Master Charge card in a California liquor store. The card was listed as stolen because she had been found shot to death in her garage, and Mark became implicated when police reportedly found a list in his room which read: "Things to do: (1) Buy shells. (2) Shoot father. (3) Shoot mother." *Los Angeles Times* (contributed by J.K. Jones) APRIL, 1979

• An eighteen-year-old Iranian youth called Hassan was arrested after he attempted to cure his sister Fatemeh's supposed mental illness with a home-rigged electric shock treatment. The treatment was administered by means of a metal clothes hanger wired to an electrical outlet, which Hassan instructed the girl to hold. Fatemeh received burns on her hands, and began to cry out for help after Hassan demanded money from her for the therapy. *Kayhan International* (contributed by J.V. Poplin) JULY, 1978

• A young actress was auditioning for a play in Highland Park, Michigan, when, at the height of a pitched scene between an arguing couple, the playwright became aggravated with the woman. He approached her from behind with a five-pound sledgehammer and bashed her several times in the head until dead. The actress's small child was also pummeled, but escaped with injuries. The title of the play was *Hammer. New York Post* AUGUST, 1978

• A civil court found Dr. Howard Eddy guilty of medical malpractice and ordered him to pay $175,000 in damages to a patient he had treated for a rectal disorder. Eddy inserted a high-intensity electrical instrument up Richard Schwartz's anal canal when the device came in contact with a pocket of intestinal gas. The gas exploded, blowing out a portion of Schwartz's colon. The court held that Eddy was negligent, in that a prudent physician should have foreseen that Schwartz might fart. *Newsday* (contributed by David Begler) FEBRUARY, 1979

• In an attempt to cut down on airplane hijacking, one enterprising airline recently hired two psychiatrists as special security officers. The two men were instructed to arrest anyone who showed signs of mental instability. Within minutes of their first spell of duty, one of the psychiatrists arrested the other. *The Police Journal* (J. Quiros) DECEMBER, 1977

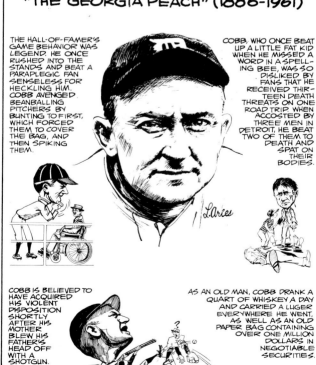

## · LIVES OF THE GREAT·
### THIS MONTH:
### TYRUS RAYMOND "TY" COBB "THE GEORGIA PEACH" (1886-1961)

THE HALL-OF-FAMER'S GAME BEHAVIOR WAS LEGEND. HE ONCE RUSHED INTO THE STANDS AND BEAT A PARAPLEGIC FAN SENSELESS FOR HECKLING HIM. COBB AVENGED BEANBALLING PITCHERS BY BUNTING TO FIRST, WHICH FORCED THEM TO COVER THE BAG, AND THEN SPIKING THEM.

COBB, WHO ONCE BEAT UP A LITTLE FAT KID WHEN HE MISSED A WORD IN A SPELLING BEE, WAS SO DISLIKED BY FANS THAT HE RECEIVED THIRTEEN DEATH THREATS ON ONE ROAD TRIP. WHEN ACCOSTED BY THREE MEN IN DETROIT, HE BEAT TWO OF THEM TO DEATH AND SPAT ON THEIR BODIES.

COBB IS BELIEVED TO HAVE ACQUIRED HIS VIOLENT DISPOSITION SHORTLY AFTER HIS MOTHER BLEW HIS FATHER'S HEAD OFF WITH A SHOTGUN.

AS AN OLD MAN, COBB DRANK A QUART OF WHISKEY A DAY AND CARRIED A LUGER EVERYWHERE HE WENT, AS WELL AS AN OLD PAPER BAG CONTAINING OVER ONE MILLION DOLLARS IN NEGOTIABLE SECURITIES.

MAY, 1979

# T R U E

## Bulgaria

*Below are excerpts from three pamphlets soliciting entries to the Bulgarian House of Humor and Satire's biennial Festival of Humor and Satire.*

ДОМ НА ХУМОРА И САТИРАТА
ГАБРОВО, БЪЛГАРИЯ, ТЕЛ. 2-72-29

HOUSE OF HUMOUR AND SATIRE —
GABROVO, BULGARIA, TEL. 2-72-29

TWELFTH
NATIONAL FESTIVAL
OF HUMOUR AND SATIRE
GABROVO
BULGARIA

THE ORGANIZING COMMITTEE OF THE TWELFTH NATIONAL FESTIVAL OF HUMOUR AND SATIRE - GABROVO, BULGARIA i n v i t e s y o u t o t a k e p a r t i n t h e FOURTH INTERNATIONAL BIENNIAL OF CARTOON AND SATIRICAL SCULPTURE - GABROVO'79

☐ T o p i c o f t h e e x h i b i t i o n

LAUGHTER HAS ENABLED THE WORLD TO SURVIVE

☐ P r i z e s
GRAND PRIX        - "GOLDEN AESOP" /Sculpture/ and 1500 levs
FIRST PRIZE FOR A SCULPTURE- GABROVO NECKLACE (gold) and 750 levs
TWO SECOND PRIZES   - GABROVO NECKLACE (silver) and 500 levs
FOUR THIRD PRIZES - 250 levs    TEN CASH PRIZES  - 100 levs

THE HOUSE OF HUMOUR AND SATIRE IN GABROVO, BULGARIA announce an INTERNATIONAL COMPETITION PHOTO JOKES'79 for amateurs, professionals and editor's offices

☐ T h e h e a d l i n e o f t h e C o m p e t i t i o n

HUMAN SMILES AND FUNNY SITUATIONS IN FRONT OF THE CAMERA

☐ P r i z e s
FIRST PRIZE - GOLDEN PLATE
SECOND PRIZE - SILVER PLATE
THIRD PRIZES - BRONZE PLATES

THE ORGANIZING COMMITTEE OF THE TWELFTH NATIONAL FESTIVAL OF HUMOUR AND SATIRE IN GABROVO, BULGARIA i n v i t e s y o u t o p a r t i c i p a t e i n t h e SECOND INTERNATIONAL EXHIBITION OF HUMOUR AND SATIRE IN PAINTING,

☐ A i m a n d t a s k s
The exhibition is aimed at activating the artists to create works of art in the field of humour and satire, works that express a cheerful and merry atmosphere and satirical rejection of everything that hinders the development of mankind to humanism, social progress and moral perfection.

MAY, 1979

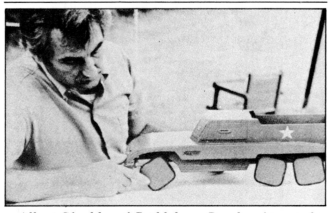

*Albert Sfredda, of Bethlehem, Pa., has invented a square wheel. According to the UPI story which accompanied this photograph, the square wheel produces "impact forces" which "increase relative to increased speed. This allows for a smaller and lighter vehicle than the conventional types." Patent is presumably pending.*

AUGUST, 1977

## From the Slush Pile

*The following excerpts have been culled from unsolicited manuscripts sent to a prominent editor of (serious) fiction who wishes, understandably, to remain anonymous.*

She divined from the sounds emitted from upstairs that Ernie was playing solitaire.

\* \* \*

The owner of the laundrymat was annoyed by the police guard—how could she expect to get customers with all this fuzz underfoot?

\* \* \*

"I can't tell for sure," the medicinal examiner said, "but I don't think she was molested in anyway."

\* \* \*

After letting Gloria off at the shopping area, Jim was able to drop his casual front.

\* \* \*

Mrs. Smith's radio was singing a popular ditty.

\* \* \*

"Butch" was as homely as a "mud fence" and even in his "Sunday best" he was no "heart stopper," yet more often than not he received "VIP treatment" from "the fair sex."

\* \* \*

She laughed and smoked and made rash statements like "The grasshoppers are dying." She was looking out of the window of the car as she said it. She didn't turn around. Her fawn-colored hair was shining in the afternoon sun. It was October.

\* \* \*

From the moment he crushed Cora's skull, he knew it was going to be a rotten Monday.

\* \* \*

Onwards down the street he trod, passing all those that passed him.

\* \* \*

My family was very close, having all grown up together.

\* \* \*

"She's sensational," Mike said enthusiastically. "Wait till you see her thick eyelashes and her jet blonde hair."

\* \* \*

She listened intently, with all her ears.

\* \* \*

A girl like Evelyn would stop at nothing to get her name in the footlights.

\* \* \*

Gerald wondered if throwing up would make much noise.

\* \* \*

The cup of tea further relaxed the atmosphere.

\* \* \*

"Oh, hi, Sarah," he said. "Would you pop a meal into the oven while I shower away the sweat I've worked up canoeing?"

\* \* \*

The effort had bathed her in perspiration even though her dress was of lightweight cotton and polyester.

\* \* \*

In the distance a siren wahwahhed.

\* \* \*

The football game in his stomach had entered the third quarter.

\* \* \*

Her brain shouted "No, no!" but her feet screamed "Yes!"

\* \* \*

"I'll take care of it, Sarah," said the heavy male voice that belonged to Bob.

\* \* \*

She was not only well educated, but well versed in philosophy, history, literature, and languages.

\* \* \*

He snorted mentally.

\* \* \*

Her wince was almost audible.

\* \* \*

The wind, its straitjacket removed, went wild inside the car.

\* \* \*

JULY & DECEMBER, 1978

## Patents Pending

## Media Notes

*These devices, garments, and furnishings have been registered at the U.S. Patent Office by individuals who believe others will buy them.*

### TONGUE CLEANER
Features a scraper blade at the end of a thin handle, intended for use by smokers, cold and hangover sufferers, and others who may accumulate substances on their tongues.

### SOFA DUST GUARDS
Clear vinyl sheets designed to supplant opaque cloth and lace arm guards, which disturb pattern flow of upholstery. Plastic lets fabric show through while protecting it.

### ZIPPER-SLEEVED SHIRT
Sleeves unzip at the elbow to provide both short- and long-sleeve option in same shirt. Offered as an aid to parents wishing to avoid the expense of replacing shirts of youngsters whose arms grow faster than the rest of their bodies.

### COMBINATION FOOT-STOOL AND CHRISTMAS TREE HOLDER
Top of hassock removes to expose center hole, into which a tree trunk may be inserted. Footstool is adjustable so trees can be supported vertically on uneven floors.     APRIL, 1979

*The clippings below are from the* New York Times, *and were gathered by art director and designer Sam Antupit. They represent only a small part of Mr. Antupit's collection of* Times *bus plunges. The collection was originally published in* More *magazine, accompanied by the following comment from More's editors: "Until now, we had serious reservations about the amount of thought and imagination that goes into the* Times *foreign coverage. But the comprehensiveness of the paper's bus plunge reportings has forced us to rethink some of our preconceptions."*

### Cairo Bus Plunge Kills 15
CAIRO, June 27 (Reuters) — Fifteen persons were killed and 17 injured today when a truck plunged into a canal near the Nile River after the driver had swerved to avoid another vehicle.

### Ecuador Bus Plunge Kills 19
QUITO, Ecuador, Aug. 28 (Reuters) — Nineteen people were killed and five seriously injured when a crowded bus plunged down a 150-foot ravine in northern Ecuador last night, the police said today. The dead, they said, included an American couple, identified as Thomas and Elsy O'Kelly.

### Afghan Bus Plunge Kills 21
KABUL, Afghanistan, May 11 (AP)—Twenty-one persons were killed and six injured when a bus plunged into an irrigation canal in Lashkargah, western Afghanistan, the police reported. They attributed the accident to careless driving.

### Chilean Bus Plunge Kills 13
OSORNO, Chile, March 20 (UPI)—Thirteen persons were killed and 34 injured when a bus with an inexperienced driver at the wheel plunged off a mountain road at Puyehue, near the Argentine border 625 miles south of Santiago, the police said today.

### Bus Plunge Kills 14 in India
NEW DELHI, July 27 (UPI) — A bus plunged into a 100-foot gorge near a Himalayan hill station at Simla, 250 miles north of here, yesterday killing 14 persons and injuring 45 others, the Press Trust of India reported today.

### Six Killed in Bus Plunge
SARAGOSSA, Spain, Dec. 19 (Reuters) — A bus carrying about 50 Spanish workers and their families home for Christmas from West Germany and Switzerland plunged off a bridge into the Ebro River here early today. At least six persons were killed and about 40 were injured. Most of the passengers escaped through a rear exit.

### Mexican Bus Plunge Kills 8
PALMAR CHICO, Mexico Oct. 27 (UPI)—Eight persons died of injuries suffered when a bus plunged off a wet road into a 400-foot-deep gully, the police reported. The police said the bus had been overloaded, carrying more than 50 passengers.

### 12 Die in Ceylon Bus Plunge
COLOMBO, Ceylon, Sept. 12 (AP) — A bus plunged down a 100-foot precipice today at Agraptatana, killing 12 persons and injuring 50.     DECEMBER, 1977

## Recent Notable Headlines

*Oklahoma County News 7/7/77*
### Parents have seven weeks to have children shot

*Miami Herald 6/15/77*
**American Neighbors Complain**
*Beware of Eating Your Dogs, Lawmaker Warns Vietnamese*

*New York Times 11/23/75*
Girl to Visit Pair Accused of Killing Her

*Dallas Times Herald*
### Elderly often burn victims
Special to Times Herald ... lighted burners. W... ...u ... Be ...
TER—Elderly p e r- light a burner, he ...

*Dallas Times Herald*
## No violence mars busing in two cities

*Financial Times of Canada 6/20/77*
### Pork bellies back in fashion

*New York Daily News 9/15/77*
### New State Rape Law, in Effect Today, Plugs Escape Route
NOVEMBER, 1977

## Literary Notes

A Doubleday printing error has resulted in a number of copies of *Gone with the Wind* being sold with the cover and dust jacket of Alex Haley's *Roots*.

No objections have as yet been voiced by the readers.

From *Blue Skies No Candy*, by Gael Greene:

"He smells sweet, even his sweat is mildly sweet. His asshole tastes like apple cider."

Ms. Greene is the food editor of *New York* magazine.
AUGUST, 1977

JANUARY, 1978 — *Barbie Wellman, Myrtle Beach, South Carolina*

SEPTEMBER, 1977 — *photo by Pedar Ness*

JUNE, 1978 — *photo by Pedar Ness*

APRIL, 1978 — *Jim White, Ottawa, Ontario*

JULY, 1978 — *Allan Hirsch, W. Hartford, Connecticut*

APRIL, 1978 — *Judy Wilson, Wauconda, Illinois*

SEPTEMBER, 1978 — *Max Alexander, Providence, Rhode Island*

AUGUST, 1977 — *photo by Pedar Ness*

# FUNNY PAGES

*"Funny Pages" is a collection of continuing comic strips that has run as a regular feature in the National Lampoon since January, 1972. It was created by Michael Gross. Some strips only appeared once or twice; others ran continuously for several years. Gahan Wilson's "Nuts" is the only strip that has appeared without interruption since the inception of "Funny Pages."*

NUTS

THOSE OF YOU WHO REMEMBER HOW GREAT IT WAS TO BE A LITTLE KID, GANG, DON'T REMEMBER HOW IT WAS TO BE A LITTLE KID....

THE POOR THING! YOU SUPPOSE HE'S GOT POLIO?

THEY DON'T GET POLIO ANYMORE. HE'S TRYING TO STAY OUT OF SCHOOL.

KA! K!

GUK?

CHOKE!

UUK!

SAY, MAYBE HE IS SICK!

LET'S CALL THE DOCTOR!

OOOOG! UR! GUK, OG!

KAK! KAK! AK! KAK!

YEAH, WELL THE KID DOES HAVE SOMETHING...YOU CALL SMITH'S DRUGSTORE, DON'T CALL ANY OTHER DRUGSTORE, AND BUY WHAT I TELL YOU. DOES IT HURT HERE?

·PROD·

IS HE GOING TO DIE, DOCTOR?

NO, I DON'T THINK SO—BUT THOSE ARE SOME GERMS HE'S GOT—NEED A LOT OF MEDICINE FROM SMITH'S.

HI—I'M ONE OF YOUR GERMS!

HI—I'M ANOTHER!

WE'RE GOING TO KILL YOU, KID!

Gahan Wilson

NEXT MONTH: "DEATH FEAR!"

JANUARY, 1972

303

# MERCURY.
## God's own Messenger

ONE DAY WHILE OUT WALKING GOD'S DOG "RAMONA," YOUNG MERCURY NOTICED A DISTURBANCE AT THE LAKE AND SPOKE ALOUD....

LOOK! LOOK! THE SWANS ARE MATING! IT MUST BE SPRING!

I'M GOING TO TELL GOD IT'S **SPRING!** I'LL BE THE FIRST TO TELL HIM AND HE'LL GIVE ME A SWEET, I KNOW IT.

FOR RELIGIOUS PURPOSES IT WAS GOD'S HABIT TO TRAVEL "INCOGNITO," HIS WHEREABOUTS KNOWN ONLY TO A FEW! AT PRESENT HE IS CLEVERLY DISGUISED AS A BAKERY WINDOW.

WELL GOD, IT IS SPRING.

NO, IT ISN'T.

MK Brown

FOR LONG MOMENTS MERCURY DESCRIBED THE STRANGE MATING RITUAL HE HAD SEEN. UNCONVINCED, GOD AGREED TO DON A NEW DISGUISE AND ACCOMPANY HIS MESSENGER TO THE LAKE....

DISGUISED AS A GIFT SET OF KINGS MEN TOILETRIES, GOD FOLLOWED RAMONA & MERCURY-BUT WHEN THEY GOT TO THE LAKE THE SWANS WERE GONE.

I DON'T SEE ANY SWANS.

JULY, 1972

The adventures of

# FRED KISMIASS,

the man whose name sounds like "KISS MY ASS"!

by E Subitzky

WHEN PARKING BY A FIRE HYDRANT...

HEY, BUDDY, WHAT'S YOUR NAME?

KISMIASS!

I'M GONNA RUN YA'OFF TODA STATION HOUSE!

...LATER THAT NIGHT, ON A SINGLES CRUISE TO THE CARIBBEAN...

HEY, YOU'RE CUTE! WHATSYER NAME?

KISMIASS!

HELP! RAPE!

SHIT

... FINALLY, ON WEST 49TH STREET...

HI THERE BIG BOY! WHAT'S YOUR NAME?

KISMIASS!

THAT'LL BE $5 EXTRA!

FRED DECIDES TO MARRY HIS COMPANION!

WHAT'SYERNAMES YOUTWO?

KISMIASS!

KISMIASS!

AND THEY HAVE SEVENTEEN KIDS!

HI ALL WHAT ARE YOUR NAMES?

KISMIASS! KISMIASS! KISMIASS!

AUGUST, 19

THE END

---

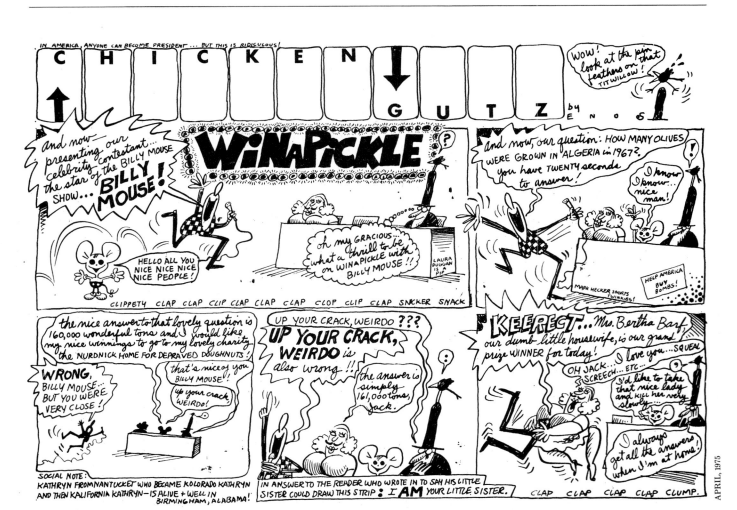

CHICKEN GUTZ by ENOS

IN AMERICA, ANYONE CAN BECOME PRESIDENT... BUT THIS IS RIDICULOUS!

APRIL, 1975

# CHEECH WIZARD

DISCOVERS A
TRAITOR
OR: THE RUTABAGA
TURNS BAD

by VAUGHN BODË ©

EH?

..I'M TELLIN' YA, BABY, IT'S **ME** CHEECH WIZARD'S APPRENTICE, WHO DA **POWER** BEHIND DA HAT, AN DAT'S **NO SHIT.**

DAT HAT IS A **FAKE**...I DA ONE TAUGHT HIM ALL HE KNOWS, AN DAT NOT MUCH. **YES SIR,** I FOUND DA FUKER WHEN HE WAS A LIMPID, HAS BEEN **ORPHAN.**

CHEECH WAS A HANDICAP, OF COURSE, HAIR-LIP AN ALL. I PULLED HIM OUT OF DA GUTTER AN TAUGHT HIM **DIGNITY.**

**WOW,** AN I BEEN BALLIN HIM ALL THIS TIME.

GOOMPH

HE TOLD ME HE WAS GOD...

HE GOT MY BALLS.

...BUT HE NEVER DONE A TRICK.

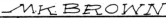

## Russ de la Rocca — Worm Trainer of the Americas

© J·JONES 1972

ME AND THE **DUCK** ARE IN LOVE.

HER AND THE DUCK'S **BILL.**

WHAT I **LOVE** IS MINE.

ARTIFICIAL **EGO** BOUNDARY.

WHAT I LOVE **IS** ME.

INFANTILE SCHIZO.

I'VE FALLEN FOR A **DEVIATE.** WHAT SHE **DOESN'T** LOVE SHE'LL PROJECT ONTO **ME** AND I'LL BE OUTSIDE HER.

MMMPH! MMM. AHH.

I'M THE SNOW.

IT'LL HURT **BAD.**

I GOTTA **GO.**

C'MERE, **DUCK.**

**WHO** THE HELL DOES SHE THINK SHE **IS?**

I'M THE **UNIVERSE.** AND THE **UNIVERSE** IS **MINE.**

. . . MAYBE I'LL STAY.

AUGUST, 1977

# MULE'S DINER

*stan mack*

MULE, YOU LOOK AT ME NOW, YOU WOULDN'T KNOW I ONCE HAD IT MADE.

I HAD MONEY AND SPENT IT — THREW IT AWAY.

THERE WAS THIS RICH OLD GUY—HERMAN—HAD A THING FOR NOSES. I WORKED A DEAL WITH HIM.

EVERY MORNING AT 6:00 A.M. I'D SNEAK INTO HIS PLACE AND SIT QUIET WHILE HE MAKES OUT WITH MY NOSE.

HE GOT REAL EXCITED. IT WAS AWFUL.

AFTER AWHILE HE'D HAVE HAD ENOUGH AND HE'D PAY ME $100.

I'D RACE OUT AND SPEND THE DAY SPENDING AND FORGETTING.

WHAT A GREAT TIME! I NEVER THOUGHT ABOUT TOMORROW.

WELL, SOMEHOW A DUDE NAMED JONES CAUGHT THE ACT AND DECIDED TO MOVE IN.

HE WAS CRAZY CLEVER. FIRST HE BOUGHT RED WINE, PEPPERCORNS, BAY LEAF, CLOVES, ONIONS, AND ROSEMARY.

LATER HE MIXES ALL THIS STUFF TOGETHER, SLICES INTO HIS NOSE, POURS THE MIX INTO THE CUTS, AND CHILLS OVERNIGHT.

NEXT MORNING AT 5:00 HE SNEAKED INTO HERMAN'S KITCHEN AND STUCK HIS NOSE ON A HOT GRILL.

HERMAN SMELLS BURNING FLESH, SPOTS JONES'S NOSE AND IS OVERCOME WITH PASSION.

BY THE TIME I ARRIVE, HERMAN'S MADE A NEW DEAL—EVEN UPPED THE PRICE.

JONES WAS IN AND I WAS OUT. CREDITORS CLOSED IN, FRIENDS LEFT, COULDN'T FIND A JOB. I NEVER GOT ANOTHER BREAK.

HOW CAN YOU FIGURE IT, MULE? A GUY CRAZY ENOUGH TO **MARINATE** HIS OWN NOSE.

THANKS, BUDDY.

JANUARY, 1973

---

# FORTUNE-TELLING COMICS! by ED SUBITZKY

DIRECTIONS: CLOSE EYES, POISE OUTSTRETCHED INDEX FINGER OVER PAGE WHILE YOU MOVE PAGE BACK AND FORTH WITH OTHER HAND. WHEN YOU FEEL "MOMENT IS RIGHT," SUDDENLY DROP FINGER ONTO PAGE. FATE WILL LEAD FINGER TO PANEL WITH CORRECT ANSWER TO THIS MONTH'S QUESTION.

THIS MONTH'S QUESTION: (FOR MEN ONLY) "WILL THAT GIRL I LIKE GO ALL THE WAY WITH ME OR NOT?"

I'M SORRY, BUT I LOVE SOMEONE ELSE!

I FIND YOU PHYSICALLY REPULSIVE AND I WOULDN'T MAKE IT WITH YOU IF YOU WERE THE LAST MAN ON EARTH!

I'LL LET YOU SCREW ME ONCE IF YOU BUY ME A CAR!

I DIG YOUR MIND AND I'LL SLEEP WITH YOU ON OUR FOURTEENTH DATE!

I WOULD RATHER ROT IN HELL TWICE THAN LET YOU EVEN TOUCH ME WITH YOUR PINKY!

I'M MADLY IN LOVE WITH YOU AND I'LL OBLIGE YOUR MOST SECRET DESIRES THE VERY FIRST TIME YOU COME ON!

MARCH, 1975

OCTOBER, 1973

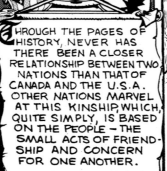

# Bibliography

*During the past ten years,* National Lampoon *has produced over fifty special editions, paperback books, radio and television series, and stage shows. They are listed below.*

## Special Editions

*The Best of National Lampoon No. 1*   Anthology. 1971
*Breast of National Lampoon*   A collection of *National Lampoon* sexual humor. 1972
*The Best of National Lampoon No. 3*   Anthology. 1973
*The National Lampoon Encyclopedia of Humor*   Compendium of original humor. Edited by Michael O'Donoghue. 1973
*The Best of National Lampoon No. 4*   Anthology. 1973
*National Lampoon Comics*   Collection of *National Lampoon* comics from 1970 to 1974. 1974
*The Best of National Lampoon No. 5*   Anthology. 1974
*National Lampoon 1964 High School Yearbook Parody*   Edited by P.J. O'Rourke and Doug Kenney. 1974
*The Very Large Book of Comical Funnies*   A collection of original comics. Edited by Sean Kelly. 1975
*The 199th Birthday Book*   A Bicentennial Tribute. Edited by Tony Hendra. 1975
*The Gentleman's Bathroom Companion*   A collection of *National Lampoon* sexual humor. 1975
*Official National Lampoon Bicentennial Calendar 1976*   Written and compiled by Christopher Cerf and Bill Effros. 1975
*National Lampoon Art Poster Book*   Edited by Sean Kelly. 1975
*The Best of National Lampoon No. 6*   Anthology. 1976
*The Iron On Book*   Original T-shirt designs. Edited by Tony Hendra. 1976
*National Lampoon Songbook*   Songs from *National Lampoon* records, radio shows, and revues. Edited by Sean Kelly. 1976
*The Naked and the Nude*   Satire of Hollywood and the movies. Written by Brian McConnachie. 1976
*The Best of National Lampoon No. 7*   Anthology. 1977
*National Lampoon Presents French Comics*   Edited by Peter Kaminsky. Translated by Sophie Balcoff, Sean Kelly, and Valerie Marchant. 1977
*The Up Yourself Book*   Satire on self-improvement. Edited by Gerald Sussman. 1977
*Gentleman's Bathroom Companion II*   A collection of *National Lampoon* sexual humor. 1977
*The Best of National Lampoon No. 8*   Anthology. 1978
*National Lampoon's Animal House Book*   Written by Chris Miller. 1978
*National Lampoon Sunday Newspaper Parody*   Edited by P.J. O'Rourke. 1978
*National Lampoon Presents Claire Bretécher*   French satirical cartoonist. Edited by Sean Kelly. Translated by Valerie Marchant. 1978
*Slightly Higher in Canada*   Anthology of Canadian humor from the *National Lampoon.* Edited by Sean Kelly and Ted Mann. 1978
*Cartoons Even We Wouldn't Dare Print*   Edited by Sean Kelly and John Weidman. Simon and Schuster. 1979

*Jeff Greenfield's Book of Books*   Parodies of best-sellers. Written by Jeff Greenfield with contributions by Gerald Sussman, Danny Abelson, Sean Kelly, and Ellis Weiner. Edited by Sean Kelly. Simon and Schuster. 1979

## Paperbacks

*Would You Buy a Used War from This Man?*   A collection of political humor from the *National Lampoon.* Edited by Henry Beard. Paperback Library. 1972
*Letters from the Editors of National Lampoon*   Edited by Brian McConnachie. Warner Paperback Library. 1973
*This Side of Parodies*   A collection of literary parodies from the *National Lampoon.* Edited by Brian McConnachie and Sean Kelly. Warner Paperback Library. 1974
*The Paperback Conspiracy*   Anthology of *National Lampoon* stories. Edited by Brian McConnachie. Warner Paperback Library. 1974
*The Job of Sex*   Parody of *The Joy of Sex.* Edited by Brian McConnachie. Warner Paperback Library. 1974
*A Dirty Book!*   Sexual humor from the *National Lampoon.* Edited by P.J. O'Rourke. New American Library. 1976
*Another Dirty Book*   Sexual humor from the *National Lampoon.* Edited by P.J. O'Rourke and Peter Kaminsky. New American Library. 1979

## Records

*Radio Dinner*   Creative Directors: Tony Hendra and Michael O'Donoghue. Principal writers: Tony Hendra and Michael O'Donoghue. Starring: Christopher Guest. Sound Producer: Bob Tischler. Banana/Blue Thumb BTS-38. 1972
*Lemmings*   Produced by Tony Hendra and Tommy Lipuma. Principal writers: Tony Hendra, Sean Kelly, and the cast. Music composed and arranged by Paul Jacobs and Christopher Guest. Starring: John Belushi, Chevy Chase, Garry Goodrow, Christopher Guest, Paul Jacobs, Mary-Jenifer Mitchell, and Alice Playten. Engineer: Bruce Botnick. Banana/Blue Thumb BTS-6006. 1973
*Missing White House Tapes*   Creative Directors: Tony Hendra and Sean Kelly. Principal writers: David Axelrod, Henry Beard, Tony Hendra, and Sean Kelly. Principal performers: John Belushi, Chevy Chase, Rhonda Coullet, Tony Scheuren, and Zal Yanovsky. Engineer: Mark Linett. Tape doctors: Vic Dinnerstein and Irving Kirsch. Banana/Blue Thumb BTS-6008. 1974
*Official National Lampoon Stereo Test and Demonstration Record*   Written by Ed Subitzky. Produced by Windy Craig and Gerald Taylor. Sound Engineer: John Hechtman. Narrated by Stan Sawyer. Voices: John Belushi, Chevy Chase, Emily Prager, and Ed Subitzky. National Lampoon 1001. 1974
*National Lampoon Gold Turkey (Radio Hour/Greatest Hits)*   Creative Director: Brian McConnachie. Principal writers: John Belushi, Christopher Guest, Sean Kelly, Doug Kenney, Brian McConnachie, Brian Doyle-Murray, Bill Murray, and Harold

Ramis. Principal performers: John Belushi, Christopher Guest, Brian Doyle-Murray, Bill Murray, Gilda Radner, and Harold Ramis. Sound Producer: Bob Tischler. Epic PE 33410. 1975

*Good-bye, Pop 1952-1976* Creative Director: Sean Kelly. Principal writers: Christopher Guest, Sean Kelly, Brian Doyle-Murray, and Bill Murray. Principal composers: Christopher Guest, Paul Jacobs, and Paul Shaffer. Principal lyrics: Sean Kelly. Principal performers: Christopher Guest, Paul Jacobs, Bill Murray, Gilda Radner, Paul Shaffer, and Tony Scheuren. Sound Producer: Bob Tischler. Epic PE 33956. 1975

*"That's Not Funny, That's Sick!"* Creative Directors: Brian Doyle-Murray and John Weidman. Principal writers: Christopher Guest, Brian Doyle-Murray, and Bill Murray. Starring: Christopher Guest, Brian Doyle-Murray, and Bill Murray. Produced and engineered by Bob Tischler. Label 21 IMP 2001. 1977

*National Lampoon's Animal House* Original motion picture sound track. Produced by Kenny Vance. Original music composed and performed by Stephen Bishop. Theme music and score by Elmer Bernstein. Arranged by Rob Mounsey with Paul Griffin. Principal engineer: Joe Ferla. Motion picture written by Harold Ramis, Douglas Kenney, and Chris Miller. Starring: John Belushi, Tim Matheson, John Vernon, Verna Bloom, Thomas Hulce, and Donald Sutherland. Produced by Matty Simmons and Ivan Reitman. Directed by John Landis. MCA 3046. 1978

*Greatest Hits of the National Lampoon* Produced by Sean Kelly. Written by John Belushi, Henry Beard, Christopher Cerf, Brian Doyle-Murray, Christopher Guest, Tony Hendra, Paul Jacobs, Sean Kelly, Bill Murray, Michael O'Donoghue, Gilda Radner, Harold Ramis, and Paul Shaffer. Performed by John Belushi, Christopher Guest, Chevy Chase, Rhonda Coullet, Christopher Guest, Tony Hendra, Mark Horowitz, David Hurdon, Brian Doyle-Murray, Bill Murray, Alice Playten, Gilda Radner, Harold Ramis, and Norman Rose. Originally engineered by Bob Tischler. Visa 7008. 1978

## Stage Shows

*Lemmings* Executive Producer: Matty Simmons. Produced by Tony Hendra. Directed by Tony Hendra and Sean Kelly. Written by David Axelrod, Anne Beatts, Henry Beard, John Boni, Tony Hendra, Sean Kelly, and the cast. Starring: John Belushi, Chevy Chase, Garry Goodrow, Christopher Guest, Paul Jacobs, Mary-Jenifer Mitchell, and Alice Playten. Music composed by Paul Jacobs and Christopher Guest. Lyrics by Sean Kelly. 1973-74

*The National Lampoon Show* First company: produced by Matty Simmons, directed by John Belushi. Second company: produced by Ivan Reitman, directed by Martin Charnin. Written by the cast, with the assistance of Sean Kelly. Starring John Belushi, Brian Doyle-Murray, Bill Murray, Gilda Radner, and Harold Ramis. Music composed and performed by Paul Jacobs. 1975

*"That's Not Funny, That's Sick!"* Produced by Matty Simmons. Directed by Jerry Adler. Co-produced and edited by Sean Kelly and

Tony Hendra. Music supervised and produced by Paul Jacobs. Script, lyrics, and music written by Danny Abelson, David Axelrod, John Belushi, Chris Guest, Louise Gikow, Tony Hendra, Nate Herman, Paul Jacobs, Stefan Kanfer, Sean Kelly, Doug Kenney, Jess Korman, Brian McConnachie, Brian Doyle-Murray, Gilda Radner, Paul Shaffer, Tony Scheuren, and Ellis Weiner. Starring: Rodger Bumpass, Sarah Durkee, Lorraine Lazarus, and Andrew Moses. 1978-79

*"If We're Late, Start Without Us!"* Executive Producer: Matty Simmons. Produced by Jonathan Weiss. Directed by Peter Elbling. Head writer: Sean Kelly. Sketches, lyrics, and music by Didi Dobbs, Sarah Durkee, Peter Elbling, Jeff Greenfield, John Hughes, Ted Mann, Tony Scheuren, Gerry Sussman, John Weidman, and Ellis Weiner. Starring: Rodger Bumpass, Didi Dobbs, Sarah Durkee, and Mark King. 1979

## Movies

*National Lampoon's Animal House* Universal Pictures. Produced by Matty Simmons and Ivan Reitman. Directed by John Landis. Written by Harold Ramis, Douglas Kenney, and Chris Miller. Starring: John Belushi, Tim Matheson, John Vernon, Verna Bloom, Thomas Hulce, Stephen Furst, Bruce McGill, Jamie Widdoes, and Donald Sutherland. 1978

## Television

*"Delta House"* Universal Television for ABC-TV Network. Executive Producers: Matty Simmons and Ivan Reitman. Produced by Edward Montagne. Starring: John Vernon, Richard Seer, Bruce McGill, Jamie Widdoes, Peter Fox, Stephen Furst, and Josh Mostel. 1979

*"Disco Beaver from Outer Space"* (Cable TV) Executive Producer: Matty Simmons. Produced by Tony Hendra. Directed by Joshua White. Written by Peter Elbling, Sean Kelly, and Ted Mann. Starring: Jamie Widdoes, Rodger Bumpass, Sarah Durkee, Alice Playten, Michael Simmons, Tony Hendra, and Lee Wickoff. 1979

## Radio

*"National Lampoon Radio Hour"* Produced by Michael O'Donoghue and John Belushi. Principal writers: John Belushi, Chevy Chase, Michael O'Donoghue, Sid Davis, Bruce McCall, Christopher Guest, George Trow, Brian Doyle-Murray, Bill Murray, and Gilda Radner. Principal performers: John Belushi, Chevy Chase, Christopher Guest, Rhonda Coullet, Brian Doyle-Murray, Bill Murray, Emily Prager, and Gilda Radner. Production Coordinator: Polly Bier. Engineer: Bob Tischler. 1973-74

*"True Facts"* Executive Producer: Bob Michelson. Produced by Peter Kaminsky, Ellis Weiner, and Danny Abelson. Written by and starring Peter Kaminsky, Ellis Weiner, Danny Abelson, and Sylvia Grant. 1977-78